THE RAPTURE, THE ANTICHRIST, AND THE TRIBULATION

AN END-TIMES COUNTDOWN AND WHAT HAPPENS NEXT

RICK RENNER

THE RAPTURE, THE ANTICHRIST, AND THE TRIBULATION

AN END-TIMES COUNTDOWN
AND WHAT HAPPENS NEXT

Unless otherwise indicated, all scriptural quotations are from the *King James Version* of the Bible.

Scripture quotations marked (*AMPC*) are taken from the *Amplified® Bible, Classic Edition*. Copyright © 1954, 1958, 1962, 1964, 1965, 1987 by The Lockman Foundation. Used by permission. **www.Lockman.org**

Scripture quotations marked (*ESV*) are from *The Holy Bible, English Standard Version*. ESV® Text Edition: 2016. Copyright © 2001 by Crossway Bibles, a publishing ministry of Good News Publishers.

Scriptures marked as (*GNT*) are taken from the **Good News Translation - Second Edition** © 1992 by American Bible Society. Used by permission.

Scripture quotations taken from the New American Standard Bible® (*NASB*) copyright © 1960, 1962, 1963, 1968, 1971, 1972, 1973, 1975, 1977, 1995 by The Lockman Foundation. Used by permission. **www.Lockman.org.**

Scripture quotations marked (*NIV*) are taken from the *Holy Bible, New International Version®*, NIV®. Copyright © 1973, 1978, 1984, 2011 by Biblica, Inc.™ Used by permission of Zondervan. All rights reserved worldwide. www.zondervan.com The "NIV" and "New International Version" are trademarks registered in the United States Patent and Trademark Office by Biblica, Inc.™

All Scriptures marked (*NKJV*) are taken from the *New King James Version* of the Bible © 1979, 1980, 1982 by Thomas Nelson, Inc. All rights reserved.

Scripture quotations marked (*NLT*) are taken from the *Holy Bible, New Living Translation*, copyright © 1996, 2004, 2015 by Tyndale House Foundation. Used by permission of Tyndale House Publishers, Inc., Carol Stream, Illinois 60188. All rights reserved.

Scripture quotations marked (*RIV*) are taken from the *Renner Interpretive Version*. Copyright © 2021 by Rick Renner.

Illustration and Photo Credit Acknowledgments are listed on pages 401-407.

The Rapture, the Antichrist, and the Tribulation —
An End-Times Countdown and What Happens Next

ISBN: 978-16675-0986-0
eBook: 978-16675-0987-7

1814 W. Tacoma St.
Broken Arrow, OK 74012-1406

Published by Harrison House
Shippensburg, PA 17257-2914
www.harrisonhouse.com

1 2 3 4 5 6 7 / 28 27 26 25
1st printing

Editorial Consultant: Rebecca L. Gilbert
Cover and Text Design: Lisa M. Moore

DEDICATION

I dedicate this book to the many Bible teachers who over the years influenced my life and helped foster a love in my heart for the appearing of Jesus. I also dedicate this book to every person who loves and is watching for Jesus' appearing and who longs to be established in what the Bible says about this soon-coming event.

CONTENTS

FOREWORD

In the world of Christian books, few topics create as much interest, speculation, and sometimes controversy, as end-times theology. The Rapture, the Antichrist, the Tribulation — these subjects both fascinate and concern believers, often leaving them with more questions than answers. That's why Rick Renner's thorough exploration of these important end-times themes arrives at just the right moment.

As I interact with subscribers of **endtimes.com**, I regularly encounter Christians hungry for solid, biblical teaching on these subjects. The questions come with growing urgency: *Are we living in the last days? What should we expect? How do we prepare?* Their desire for clarity isn't just curiosity, but a spiritual need to understand God's prophetic timeline and their place in it. Rick Renner's careful work provides exactly what today's believer needs — a scholarly, yet readable guide through the complex terrain of end-times Bible prophecy.

What sets this book apart from many others on the same subject is Rick's exceptional knowledge of New Testament Greek. For more than 40 years, Rick has devoted himself to studying the original language of the New Testament, discovering insights that often get lost in translation. His understanding of biblical Greek isn't just academic — it's a passionate pursuit that has allowed him to explain Scripture with remarkable precision. When Rick explains what Paul meant by the "restrainer" (Greek: *katecho*) or breaks down the original meaning of "caught up"

(Greek: *harpadzo*), he does so with the authority of someone who has spent decades studying these terms in their original context.

Rick's scholarly approach never sacrifices readability for academic depth. As you read these pages, you'll find a teacher who can translate complex theological concepts into language that connects with everyday believers at every level of spiritual maturity. This gift for clear communication has made Rick a trusted voice for millions through his books, television programs, and ministry around the world.

In this work *The Rapture, the Antichrist, and the Tribulation — An End-Times Countdown and What Happens Next*, Rick methodically examines the key passages about the Rapture, the Antichrist, and the Tribulation with impressive thoroughness. What impressed me most was his commitment to letting Scripture interpret Scripture. Rather than forcing a predetermined view onto the text, Rick allows the biblical evidence to speak for itself. His explanation of First Thessalonians 4, First Corinthians 15, and Second Thessalonians 2 is among the most thorough I've ever encountered, unpacking not just the words themselves but their historical and cultural background.

The section on the identity of the "restrainer" mentioned in Second Thessalonians represents some of Rick's finest scholarly work. By carefully examining the grammar, historical context, and theological implications of various interpretations, Rick provides a compelling case for his conclusions. Even readers who might reach different conclusions will benefit from his methodical analysis of the biblical evidence.

What I particularly value about Rick's approach is his balanced perspective. While firmly holding his own convictions about the timing and nature of end-times events, he presents alternative viewpoints fairly and respectfully. This honesty creates space for readers to examine the evidence and form their own conclusions under the guidance of the Holy Spirit.

The practical applications of end-times theology are never far from Rick's mind. He understands that eschatology isn't just about satisfying our curiosity about future events — it's about living faithfully *now* with our eyes fixed on eternity. Throughout this book, Rick connects prophetic truths to daily Christian living, challenging readers to consider how their understanding of the end should influence their priorities right now.

His discussion of the glorified resurrected body in his second chapter is particularly powerful. By examining what the Bible reveals about our future transformed state, Rick inspires readers to live with an eternal perspective. This isn't just information about what will happen — it's motivation for how we should live in the present.

In both my personal devotional life and my ministry, I have greatly benefited from Rick's teachings. I trust his interpretation of the Word of God completely. His insights into the Greek language have transformed my understanding of the Bible. And because he is a personal friend, I know that the fruit of his marriage, family, and ministry validates that he lives what he teaches.

What makes this book especially valuable today is how timely it is. We live in days marked by growing lawlessness, moral relativism, and spiritual confusion — precisely the conditions Scripture associates with the end times. Rick doesn't engage in sensationalism or "newspaper prophecy," but he does help readers recognize the prophetic significance of cultural trends that align with what the Bible says will happen. His section on the "mystery of iniquity" gives us a sobering but necessary framework for understanding the spiritual forces at work in our world.

I'm particularly grateful for Rick's emphasis on hope throughout this book. While honestly addressing the darkness that the Bible says will accompany the end times, he never loses sight of the glorious hope at the heart of Christian eschatology. The Rapture isn't just about escaping from difficult days — it's a reunion with our Savior. The final judgment isn't just the end of evil — it's the beginning of God's perfect reign of justice and peace.

This balance of seriousness and hope is exactly what the Church needs today. Rick neither downplays the challenges believers may face in the last days, nor gives in to fear and pessimism. Instead, he calls readers to faithful watchfulness, spiritual discernment, and confident expectation of Christ's return.

For pastors and teachers, this book provides rich material for sermons and Bible studies. For new believers seeking to understand these important doctrines, it offers clear explanations rooted in Scripture. For seasoned Christians who have studied prophecy for years, it provides fresh insights and thoughtful analysis that will deepen their understanding.

I believe this book will become a standard reference work on end-times theology — not because it claims to have all the answers, but because it asks the right questions and looks at them with scholarly precision and pastoral care. Rick Renner has given the Church a valuable gift in these pages. I pray it will inspire readers to study the Bible with renewed enthusiasm, watch for Christ's return with eager anticipation, and live each day with eternity in sight.

Jimmy Evans
Founder, Tipping Point Ministries

ACKNOWLEDGMENTS

This book has been percolating in my heart for years, but I waited to write it until I felt a release from the Holy Spirit to do so. To write and produce a book of this kind requires many hearts and hands that are committed to the work, so I want to acknowledge those who helped me craft this important book for my readers.

First, I acknowledge Becky Gilbert, who is the editor-in-chief and Publications director for our ministry. As I've stated in previous books, Becky diligently hovers over and absorbs every word I write to make sure it correctly communicates each point I'm making. She enables me as a writer to present the truth of Scripture more excellently on the printed page. I am so grateful to Becky for performing her role in this huge task with such merit and grace.

I also want to acknowledge Lisa Moore, who not only designed the book's cover, but who text-designed the interior pages to make this work shine for readers. I oversaw Lisa's work as she typeset text and cropped art, enriched it, and skillfully set it in place page by page. As I've said before, it is a joy to work with a designer who exhibits the fruit of the Spirit and seeks to produce works of excellence to the glory of God.

I additionally recognize our other Publications team members, including our senior editor Roni Bagby, whose assistance was invaluable in working out the bugs in the early stages of the manuscript. Editors Kalea Ellison, Kaitlyn Hong, and Pamela Page skillfully proofread the typeset manuscript, along with Roni, and shored up the research on this project as they immersed themselves in the content. I also want to thank our proofreader Beth Parker for her keen eyes on this task and her giftedness in attending to the overall look of each page. Our entire Publications team ensures we maintain a high level of excellence on the printed page, and I am thankful for their hearts of service to Jesus and to this ministry.

Because I wanted to include images in this book to help readers further *"see"* what they're reading, I must acknowledge Ron Young, our Web/Technologies director, and Danyelle Lee, who researched to find just the right art to characterize every point I wanted to illustrate in some way. Danyelle procured most of the photos, artwork, and other representations we needed for the project to symbolically convey the message presented in the text. I am so grateful for her diligence and expertise in performing this task.

I also want to thank several friends whom I greatly respect, who made time to read portions of this manuscript before it was finalized. I trust their spirits, their minds, and their scholarship — and their insights and feedback on this project proved invaluable. Those who pored over large parts of this book include: Tony Cooke, Alan DiDio, Joel Renner, Paul Renner, and Joseph Z. Maxim Myasnikov, my assistant in Russia, who also reads New Testament Greek, looked at everything I wrote to confirm I accurately communicated the meanings and nuances of the Greek words I expounded on in this text. Lastly in this list of friends, I'm grateful to Keith Trump, an American Bible Society scholar who reads both Hebrew and Greek. Keith checked all the places in Chapter Four where I referenced the Hebrew and Aramaic languages of the Old Testament.

Just as the foundation of a fully constructed building is never seen, there are people at the foundation of my life, without whom I could not do what I do for the Kingdom of God. That's why I want to importantly thank my precious wife Denise and our sons Paul, Philip, and Joel and their families. My family is an amazing support to me — not only do they "hold up my arms," they are all ministers, too, and are so vital to the effectiveness of our ministry. Also at the very foundation of our family and ministry — besides the One who called and equipped us all to do what we do — is *our family of ministry partners*, whose financial gifts and prayers are crucial to all the work of the ministry we do worldwide. It would be impossible to overestimate their contribution to the success of every part of RENNER Ministries.

Last, but certainly not least, it is the Lord Jesus Christ who ultimately empowers me to do what He has called me to do with my life. If it were not for His enabling touch, I would not be able to write, broadcast, minister publicly, and produce the volume of ministry materials I've been able to produce on the printed page. That's why I gratefully, humbly acknowledge the One who gives the increase to everything every one of us on this team puts our hands to. He is worthy of all the glory for helping us produce work that is honoring of His name — work that I pray will strengthen the minds and transform the lives of many readers.

INTRODUCTION

WHY A BOOK ON THE RAPTURE?

I want to begin this Introduction by telling a little of my life story, which can be read in greater detail in my autobiography, *Unlikely*. I was saved at the very tender age of five, and I understood exactly what I was doing on the Sunday morning I walked the aisle at Glenwood Baptist Church in Tulsa, Oklahoma, to give my heart to Jesus Christ.

As an even younger child, every night as I lay in bed to fall asleep, my precious mother would read Bible stories to me and speak passionately about my need to give my heart to Christ. As a result, by the time I reached five years of age, she had lovingly prepared me to give my life to Jesus and to *really* understand what I was doing.

I'll forever be thankful to God for the wonderful church where I was reared, for the spiritual foundation that church gave me, and for how my pastor and Sunday school teachers, as well as my parents, taught me to love the Bible and to love Christ's Church, including, of course, the local church.

Although this is not directly related to the subject of this book, I want to say it is a mistake to underestimate the ability of a child to understand spiritual things. In fact, the early formative years in a child's life are the most important time for a parent or responsible adult to speak the Word of God to that child. Regretfully, many parents miss the opportunity, taking the position, *I don't want to overload my children with deep spiritual things while they're young, so I'll wait until they're older.*

The problem is that when children grow older, it is often too late to impart vital spiritual truths to their lives, as their hearts can become closed, or they can become distracted by other things. If you are a parent or grandparent of young children, I urge you to use these early formative years to speak to your young ones with whom you have influence.

As I grew in my own faith and became a teenager in the church, I noticed that visiting evangelists who came every year to preach "revival meetings" would frequently ask, "If Jesus came tonight, are you absolutely certain you're saved and that you would go in the Rapture?"

The question was asked in such a scary way that it terrified me. But, honestly, this is a serious question that is eternally important to ask!

This question and challenge issued by those evangelists always caused me to evaluate my salvation experience and my heart condition: Was I really saved and "in the faith" — or would I regretfully wake up one day to discover my faith was defective and that I had missed the Rapture? But because the message of the Rapture was preached with fear — the whole idea of the Rapture became a frightening thought to my young and inexperienced mind.

Then in 1972, when I was about 14 years old, a low-budget movie was released called *A Thief in the Night.*[1] In that film, a young woman who was not a Christian, awakes one morning to hear a radio broadcast announcing the disappearance of millions of Christians around the world. She turns to the other side of the bed to look for her husband, a born-again believer, only to discover that he is missing among the millions who had disappeared in the night. From that point on in the movie, the various scenes showed her terror as she faced the prospect of living during the time of the Tribulation.

That movie scared the wits out of me!

In fact, for a long time after seeing that film, if I ever came home and found no one in our house, it would throw me into a near state of panic. I feared that like the young woman in the movie, my faith was flawed, the Rapture had occurred, *and I had missed it!* In terror, I would race to the phone on the wall in our kitchen, grab the church directory, and start calling people I knew were really born again. As I dialed number after number, I thought, *Please...please answer!* If no one answered at one number, I'd call the next and the next until, finally, someone answered the phone, and I knew it meant the Rapture had not occurred.

Then about a year and a half later, after I was baptized in the Holy Spirit, all my inner doubts about my faith being flawed dissipated as the Holy Spirit led me into the truth of the Bible concerning my salvation, strengthening and establishing me and helping me fall in love with the Word of God and with Jesus as never before. As I've often said, the Lord doesn't tell us about future events in advance *to scare* us, but, rather, *to prepare* us. And in speaking of end-time occurrences, which may seem scary to some, Paul himself said, "Wherefore *comfort* one another with these words." (*see* 1 Thessalonians 4:18).

But due to all those experiences I had as a young person, the whole idea of the Rapture was unpleasant to me. Although I knew the Rapture was an important Bible doctrine, I tended to avoid the subject. Then in the late 1970s when I attended a university church, a book was released that became popular, which called into question the entire doctrine of the Rapture and suggested that perhaps the idea of a pre-Tribulation rapture was a more recent, manmade doctrine that the Early Church did not teach. It seemed there was so much confusion, division, and fear related to this subject that, as a minister, I didn't tread near it for years.

Later, I came to my own Bible-based conclusions about the Rapture, which I, of course, share in this book. However, earlier in my ministry, because the subject of the Rapture seemed to be such a debatable topic among many, I chose to steer clear of it because I didn't want to lose the opportunity to reach someone who needed the trusted teaching of the Bible that I could bring to them.

I avoided the subject of the Rapture for many years. But as I matured in my walk with God and realized the Holy Spirit had given me a responsibility to bring trusted Bible teaching to people around the world, I finally embraced my need to address publicly what the Bible says about this very important subject.

I also discovered that when someone like me publicly takes a position concerning the Rapture, critics come out of the woodwork to nitpick, and they often accuse those who believe in a pre-Tribulation rapture of being false teachers. I don't understand this behavior, for although I may disagree with the conclusions of others who take a different view than my own, I have always found it beneficial to hear their views and learn from their perspectives. Even if I don't agree with their conclusions, I respect their views and appreciate their convictions.

In this book, I cover the following:

- What Jesus, Paul, and Peter said about the Rapture.
- Eight views about the timing of the Rapture.
- What the Bible tells us about the Tribulation and when it will begin.
- What the Bible says about the Antichrist and the mark of the beast.
- What the Bible says about the Marriage Feast of the Lamb.
- What the Bible says about Christ's Second Coming (or Second Advent) and about the Great White Throne Judgment.
- What we must do to be prepared for the rapture of the Church.

Also, the images depicted in this book are intended as characterizations — not exact representations, necessarily — to help convey the deeper meaning of the truth from Scripture that I wish to communicate in these pages.

Please remember that I have given and *am giving* my life on the frontlines for the life-saving message of the Gospel to be preached — to bring the trusted teaching of the Bible to those in need of spiritual life and strength around the world. There are many powerful men and women of God, even among some of my personal friends, whom I do not see eye-to-eye with on every point. But it does not mitigate, nor interrupt my honor for them or my fellowship with them. I pray that in the spirit of Jesus, readers will maintain a similar generous mindset toward me.

After you read each chapter and see my own final conclusions, it is my prayer that you can come to your own conclusions concerning these end-time events. But if you disagree with my findings, I ask you to treat me like a brother who knows and loves the Word of God, who believes in and stands on the integrity of God's Word, and who is convinced that this is the greatest hour of the Church Age. Although I am rock-solid in what I believe about a pre-Tribulation rapture, if we are all incorrect about the timing of this glorious event, we are all only off by a matter of a few years. In the end, *Jesus will gloriously come!*

Rick Renner
Moscow, Russia

1 Thessalonians 4:15-18

For this we say unto you by the word of the Lord, that we which are alive and remain unto the coming of the Lord shall not prevent them which are asleep. For the Lord himself shall descend from heaven with a shout, with the voice of the archangel, and with the trump of God: and the dead in Christ shall rise first: then we which are alive and remain shall be caught up together with them in the clouds, to meet the Lord in the air: and so shall we ever be with the Lord. Wherefore comfort one another with these words.

CHAPTER ONE

WHAT PAUL SAID ABOUT THE RAPTURE OF THE CHURCH IN FIRST THESSALONIANS 4:15-18

For this we say unto you by the word of the Lord, that we which are alive and remain unto the coming of the Lord shall not prevent them which are asleep. For the Lord himself shall descend from heaven with a shout, with the voice of the archangel, and with the trump of God: and the dead in Christ shall rise first: then we which are alive and remain shall be caught up together with them in the clouds, to meet the Lord in the air: and so shall we ever be with the Lord. Wherefore comfort one another with these words.

— 1 Thessalonians 4:15-18

The times in which we live are bizarre to say the least. Things are rapidly taking place around us that are unprecedented. The *last of the last* days have come, and lawlessness is on the rise, increasing with each passing day. And a day is soon coming when the Lawless One — the Antichrist — will be revealed to the world. Later in this book, I will discuss the timing of the Antichrist's appearance, but before his long-forecast debut occurs, another event will take place that is called *the rapture* of the Church.

The rapture of the Church is the undeniable doctrine of Scripture that affirms there is a soon-coming event, at which time Christ will descend into the lower atmosphere above the earth, and "the dead in Christ" will be supernaturally resurrected. Also at that time, or immediately afterward — so quickly that it will be nearly imperceptible — Christ will supernaturally "catch away," or *rapture*, the authentic Church, those in Christ "which are alive and remain." He will snatch that remnant from harm's way at the very end of this present age. (*See* 1 Thessalonians 4:16-17.)

People want to know at what point in the end-times timeline the rapture of the Church will occur, and we will eventually get to the answer to that question. But the apostle Paul's writing in First Thessalonians about the rapture of the Church itself is paramount, and that is where I will begin this chapter. So before we dive into the subject of *when* — or the moment in time in which this glorious event will occur — we need to see that the rapture of the Church is one of the clearest-stated doctrines in the New Testament. Although people have different views about when it will occur (and I'm talking about *pre-*, *mid-*, or *post-*Tribulation, etc.), the reality of a future rapture of the Church is undeniable in Scripture.

Paul Wrote Three Times About the Rapture of the Church

Paul wrote about this event in three of his epistles — including his first and second letters to believers in Thessalonica and one of his letters to believers in Corinth. Paul's first letter to the Thessalonians was written in approximately 48-51 AD. In it, he addressed the rapture of the Church in depth. Then when he wrote his second epistle to the Thessalonians shortly afterward — many scholars say in approximately 52 AD — Paul again vividly addressed this event we call *the Rapture.*

Paul also addressed the rapture of the Church approximately five years later when he wrote his first epistle to the Corinthians. In First Corinthians 15:51 and 52, Paul stated that although the event known as the rapture of the Church was once unknown, it has now been revealed to the Church by the Holy Spirit. Paul said, "Behold, I shew you a mystery..." (v. 51). We'll look at that word "mystery" in greater detail in the next chapter.

The apostle Paul wrote about this event in three of his epistles — including his first and second letters to believers in Thessalonica and one of his letters to believers in Corinth. He wrote authoritatively about what God revealed to him on the resurrection of the bodies of the righteous and about the rapture of the Church. Paul's first epistle to the Thessalonians was likely his first epistle to write, and this is important, for it tells us that even at that early time in Church history, he was already expounding on the mystery of the Rapture.

In all three of these important texts, Paul wrote authoritatively about what God revealed to him about the resurrection of the bodies of the righteous and the rapture of the Church at the end of the age. But in this chapter, I will primarily focus on what Paul wrote in First Thessalonians about this monumental event. Paul's first epistle to the Thessalonians was likely his first epistle to write, and this is important, for it tells us that even at that early time in Church history, he was already expounding on the mystery of the Rapture.

Some may argue, "The word 'rapture' doesn't even appear in the Bible, so it's not really a New Testament doctrine." But in just a few pages, you will see that the word "rapture" *does* appear very clearly in the pages of the New Testament.

'We Which Are *Alive and Remain* Unto the Coming of the Lord'

In First Thessalonians 4:15, Paul wrote, "For this we say unto you by the word of the Lord, that we which are alive and remain unto the coming of the Lord shall not prevent them which are asleep."

The words "alive and remain" are so important that Paul repeats them *verbatim* in verse 15 and again in verse 17. And in both verses, these words are the exact same, *identical* Greek phrase. Paul was making a statement so profound that he found it necessary to repeat it twice in this passage *verbatim*.

Since Paul repeated this particular sequence of words exactly the same way *twice*, it is necessary that we see precisely what the words "alive and remain" mean and why Paul repeated this exact wording twice within this succession of verses.

Those Who Are *Alive*

Let's begin with the word "alive" that appears in verse 15 and again in verse 17. In both verses, the word "alive" is translated from the words *hoi zoontoi*, a plural form of the Greek word *zao*, which not only means *to be alive*, but here, it conveys the meaning of those who are *fully alive, robust, thriving, vibrant, and vigorous.* It doesn't refer only to those who are merely *physically* living — rather, it pictures those who are *spiritually* living, *spiritually* robust, *spiritually* thriving, *spiritually* vibrant, and *spiritually* vigorous. This description contrasts with those who are *physically* alive, but who are not *spiritually* alive and vibrant.

The use of this particular Greek word tells us that Christ is coming for those who are *spiritually engaged.* He is not coming for those who merely have a form of godliness, but for those who are, as one expositor states, *the living ones* or *the vibrant ones.*

Forgive the redundance, but this particular Greek wording emphatically does not portray people who are simply physically alive, but of those who are so engaged in their faith that they are *spiritually alive, spiritually robust, spiritually thriving, spiritually vibrant*, and *spiritually vigorous.* What does this mean for those who are *not* spiritually engaged? I'll answer that in the pages to come.

The fact that the Greek depicts those who are *spiritually alive, spiritually robust, spiritually thriving, spiritually vibrant*, and *spiritually vigorous* informs us prophetically that there will be a *fully alive* and *vibrant* people of God at the time of the Rapture. These will be those who stand by the Word of God, who know the power of the Holy Spirit, and who radiate the glory of God.

Pictured here is a remnant of a royal garment. The word "remain" that Paul used specifically depicts *the remaining outer remnant of a garment; a fragmented, left over, end piece of a garment*; or *residue*. It denotes a smaller amount that is left over from a larger original piece. It indicated that the greater part had been used, removed, or destroyed — and now only a remnant is left over and remains. The word "remnant" was also used to describe soldiers who had endured or survived a battle, and in this context, it meant the larger majority of soldiers had been lost along the way, but a remnant endured, remained, and survived. This word "remnant" implies that only a remnant of authentic believers may be existing at the time of the rapture of the Church who have endured and remained faithful to the end.

THOSE WHO *REMAIN*

Paul then added that he was specifically referring to those who "remain," using the Greek words *hoi perileipomenoi*, the plural form of *perileipomai*, which is a compound of the words *peri* and *leipo*. The word *peri* means *around*, and it depicts *a circumference* or *an outer edge*, and the word *leipo* pictures what is *left over*. The *King James Version* translates the words *hoi perileipomenoi* as "remain" — but pay attention, for this Greek wording specifically depicts *the remaining outer remnant of a garment; a fragmented, left over, end piece of a garment*; or *a residue*. It denotes *a smaller amount that is left over from a larger original piece*.

Typically, this Greek word was used to picture a remnant piece of material. It indicated that the greater part had been used, removed, or destroyed — and now only a remnant is *left over* and *remains*.

It is also important to note that in early New Testament times when Paul wrote these words, they were also used militarily to describe soldiers who had *endured* or *survived* a battle (hence, those men were the *"residue"* or residual, remaining soldiers).

The use of this word in a military context meant the larger majority of soldiers had been lost along the way, but there was *a remnant who had endured, remained, and survived.*

Paul was a brilliant linguist who knew exactly what these words meant as he penned them. Their use clearly implies that only *a remnant* of authentic believers may be existing at the time of the rapture of the Church. Those who remain will be a faithful remnant who endured, remained faithful to the end, and survived the storms of life — and possibly persecution — yet they kept the faith.

Who this remnant is that Paul is describing is qualified by the word "alive." The remnant who will be raptured are those who are spiritually alive, spiritually robust, spiritually thriving, spiritually vibrant, and spiritually vigorous. The Greek words Paul used in First Thessalonians 4:17 for the word "remain," again, literally mean *the remaining ones, the surviving ones*, or *those who are left*. So this could indicate a remnant of all those who have ever been saved — or possibly a small number of believers who are left on the earth.

The foremost idea expressed in these verses is that at the end of the age, there may be only a surviving remnant of in-faith believers at the time of this grand event we call *the Rapture*. This idea coincides with what Paul wrote in Second Thessalonians 2:3 about a widespread apostasy that will occur at the end of the age. It also agrees with First Timothy 4:1, where the Holy Spirit forecasts through Paul that there will be a defection from the Christian faith in the time frame before Jesus' return for the Church at the end of the age.

Spiritual Mannequins

In my book *Last-Days Survival Guide*, I expound on Second Timothy 3:5, where Paul wrote that at the end of the Church Age, there will be a number of false believers in the Church at large. In that verse, he wrote that they will be present, "having a form of godliness, but denying the power thereof...."

The word "form" in this verse is translated from a form of the Greek word *morphosis*, a word that depicts an *outward shape* or *outward form*. This verse prophetically states that numbers of so-called Christians in the last days may possess the right words and the right forms in their religious practices, but inwardly, they will be *empty*. To explain what this means, I will use the example of a mannequin to make my point.

Today mannequins look so human that to a casual onlooker, they can mistakenly pass for a real human being. I've personally had the experience of turning to speak to someone in a store, only to discover it was a mannequin. The mannequin had such a dimensionally accurate outward "form" that it passed momentarily for a real human being. The outward form was correct, yet it was nothing but an empty form with no life.

Pictured here is a mannequin dressed in religious attire with a gold-chained cross draped across its chest and posed with a Bible in its hands. Imagine a mannequin dressed to bear a striking resemblance to a real Christian. Today mannequins look so lifelike that someone might even actually mistake such a mannequin for a real believer, as it would have all the right outward trappings. Second Timothy 3:5 prophesies a time will come when some in the Church would dress themselves in religious paraphernalia and "look the part" — but, like mannequins, they would be empty shells, inwardly lifeless.

This mannequin example perfectly captures the idea presented by the word "form" in Second Timothy 3:5. The Holy Spirit foretells that some so-called Christians at the end of the age will have a "form" of godliness, but inwardly they will lack the power that makes faith real. They may look right, and they may speak the right words, but because they are devoid of spiritual power, they will be mere "mannequins" of a genuine Christian.

The word "godliness" in Second Timothy 3:5 is from a form of the word *eusebeia*, a word that denotes *piety* or *religiosity*. The "outer form" of these spiritual mannequins may possibly include clerical clothing, religious actions, religious language, religious symbols, and other external trappings that people associate with someone or something that is religious. The outer attire and trappings may seem outwardly correct and impressive, but if that person's inner life is devoid of the life of God, he or she has only a "form of godliness."

In the context of Second Timothy 3:5, we discover that the Holy Spirit prophesied that there will be people at the end of the age who have all the external trappings of godliness — the right symbols and the right words and actions. They may even wear religious clothing or have a cross draped around their neck and hold a Bible in their hands. But many will be like spiritual mannequins who have an outward "form of godliness," yet lack the life-giving power of God.

Imagine a mannequin that is dressed in religious attire with a gold-chained cross draped across its chest and posed with a Bible in its hands. A good mannequin artist could dress it to bear a striking resemblance to a real Christian.

In fact, someone might even mistake such a mannequin for a real believer, as it would have all the right outward markings or indications. Yet it would be nothing more than *a shell* or *a form* dressed in religious clothes. In Second Timothy 3:5, Paul was prophesying by the Spirit that a time would come at the end of the age when some within the Church would dress themselves in religious paraphernalia and "look the part" — but, like mannequins, they would be empty shells, inwardly lifeless.

Paul wrote that these kinds of individuals would "deny" the power of authentic godliness. The word "deny" is translated from a form of the Greek word *arneomai*, which means *to deny, to disown, to reject, to refuse*, or *to renounce*. It was mostly used to refer to *a person who disavowed, forsook, walked away from, or washed his hands of another person or group of people*. The motive for this denial was usually fear of others, fear of suffering ridicule or persecution, or anxiety about what others would think.

By using this word, Paul unmistakably forewarned of a time when a category of so-called believers and even religious leaders, who were confronted with truth and power but were no longer embracing it, would reject and rebuff its operation and those who do embrace it. Regardless of why these deniers walk away, Paul simply states that some believers at the end of the age will abandon and walk away from the faith they once held to be true.

The Holy Spirit therefore warns that at the end of the age, there will be a widespread apostasy that emerges inside the Church, and there will be a large group who may "dress" in the guise of a Christian. But rather than suffer the brunt of a society gone astray, many will defect from truth and become a part of *a mannequin-filled apostate church*.

The word "find" in Luke 18:8 is a translation of *heurisko*, a Greek word that points to *a discovery resulting from an intense investigation or from serious research.* The use of this word categorically means that when Jesus returns to gather those who are truly His own, it may be that real faith is so scant that finding people with a genuine, engaged faith will require *a search.* It implies that when Jesus looks for people who are engaged with the faith at His return for the Church, He may possibly see large numbers who are merely attending church and observing religious rituals, while those who are avidly pursuing the faith may not exist in large numbers.

WILL JESUS FIND FAITH ON THE EARTH WHEN HE COMES?

In Luke 18:8, Jesus asked the question: "...When the Son of man cometh, shall he find faith on the earth?"

Jesus will most definitely find people who are fully engaged in faith when He comes, but in this verse, Jesus questions how easily such faith will be found at the time of His coming. This agrees with Paul's use of a form of *perileipomai* — the Greek word meaning "remain" — that we already saw in connection with First Thessalonians 4:15 and 17. The word "remain" that he used in both of those verses describes a remnant of authentic believers who will have survived a stormy end-time season at the time the rapture of the Church occurs to catch them away.

But Jesus asked the question concerning the time of His coming, "Will I find faith on the earth?" In Luke 18:8, the word "find" is a translation of a form of *heurisko*, a Greek word that points to *a discovery resulting from an intense investigation or serious research.*

The use of this word categorically means that when Jesus returns to gather those who are truly His own, it may be that real faith is so scant that finding people with a genuine, engaged faith will require *a search.* Jesus asked the question about whether He would find real faith, so we know the question is a legitimate one!

In this verse, the word "faith" in the Greek is preceded by a definite article, and thus, it should actually be translated as "*the faith*." This implies that when Jesus looks for people who are engaged with "the faith" at His return for the Church, He may possibly see large numbers who are merely attending church and observing religious rituals, while those who are avidly pursuing "the faith" may not exist in large numbers. Again, this implies a widespread apostasy in the Church at the time of the Rapture — and that *not many* will still be spiritually vibrant and will therefore be "remaining" at that time.

But there will be a remnant whose faith is fully engaged and who know and walk in the power of God at the end of the age. This will be those who are *spiritually alive*, *spiritually robust*, *spiritually thriving*, *spiritually vibrant*, and *spiritually vigorous* — those whom God will use to restrain evil until the very end of the Church Age and the rapture of the Church.

There are those who believe the Church is going to bring the world to perfection during the Church Age and then present it to Christ as a gift at His Second Coming (or Second Advent). They claim the Church is going to take over the economy, education, and governments — virtually every sphere of human existence — and they're going to do it *prior* to the Millennium and Christ's thousand-year reign.

I admire the optimism of those who believe this, as well as their desire to make things right that have gone terribly wrong because of the sinful choices of mankind over eons of time. But for me, it takes more faith to believe this changing of human landscape will occur than it does to believe the clear-stated plan of God to consummate the Church Age with Christ's intervention of a powerful *catching away of the church* — the *Rapture*.

Make no mistake: Where sin abounds, the grace of God will much more abound (*see* Romans 5:20). The Church is going to "arise and shine" by the grace and glory of God amidst an ever-darkening world before Jesus returns (*see* Isaiah 60:1), and Christ's Body of believers are going to do supernatural exploits in the face of growing evil — and they're going to do it for the purpose of eternally rescuing those who are perishing.

The old saying, "This world is not my home — I am just passing through" is a biblically accurate statement. We as the Church are called to fulfill God's plans and purposes, reap the precious fruit of the earth — the eternal souls of men, women, and children — and remain "white hot" with the zeal and the love of Christ as we await His return and the beginning of a new phase on God's prophetic timetable.

First Things First

In First Thessalonians 4:15, Paul wrote, "...We which are alive and remain unto the coming of the Lord shall not prevent them which are asleep."

The word "unto" is a translation of the word *eis*, which pictures the time *leading right up to the very last moment* of the age that Paul was describing. Thus, Paul was prophetically pointing to the *very end* of the Church Age and to those who will be *spiritually living, spiritually robust, spiritually thriving, spiritually vibrant*, and *spiritually vigorous* at that time — those who will *have survived everything* and *remain* engaged in the faith at the time of the rapture of the Church.

Paul also alerted us that those who fall into the category of spiritually engaged, vibrant believers "...shall not prevent them which are asleep." In Greek, the word "not" is a negative particle, and the word "prevent" is translated from a form of the Greek word *phthano*, which means *to precede others*. As a phrase, these words mean that those who are *spiritually living, spiritually robust, spiritually thriving, spiritually vibrant*, and *spiritually vigorous* and *who have survived everything and remain* at the time of this event will not *precede* or *go before* those which are "asleep" in Jesus.

The word "asleep" is translated from a form of the Greek word *koimao*, which pictures *the sleep of death*. Thus, the word "asleep" describes *the physical dead bodies* of those who have previously died in the faith. As a phrase, these words in the Greek text are emphatic, and it indicates *first things first*. In other words, we who are spiritually alive and engaged in the faith at that moment will be second in line to be miraculously transformed and caught up — *after* the dead in Christ are raised *first*.

To Be Absent From the Body Is To Be Present With the Lord

In regard to the death of believers, Paul wrote in Second Corinthians 5:8, "We are confident, I say, and willing rather to be *absent* from the body, and to be *present* with the Lord."

In this verse, Paul used the words "absent" and "present" to describe the experience of a Christian after physical death. The word "absent" is translated from a form of the word *ekdemeo*, which is a compound of *ek* and *demos*. The word *ek* means *out*, and it is where we get the word *exit*. The word *demos* pictures *a place where people feel naturally*

at home. As a compound, the word *ekdemeo* that is translated "absent" in this verse pictures *one who has made an exit from home*. By using this word, Paul communicated that when a real believer dies, he *exits* his body, which had been his temporary, natural human home. But Paul also declared that at that moment of death, a real Christian is instantly *present* with the Lord.

The word "present" is a form of the Greek word *endemeo*, a compound of the word *en* and *demos*. The word *en* means *in*, as in to be *in* a particular place, and *demos*, as we just saw, pictures *a home* or *a place of residency*. By using this particular word, Paul declared that when a person dies in the faith, his human spirit makes *an exit from his natural human home* — his body — and immediately finds himself — his spirit — *at home with the Lord*.

Thus, Scripture unequivocally teaches that the moment an authentic Christian dies, his spirit exits the body that he has lived in during his natural life, and, *instantly*, he is transported into the presence of the Lord. Although his mortal, corruptible body lies as an empty shell, his spirit is instantly at home in the presence of the Lord. There with the Lord, he, along with others who have died in faith before him, awaits the moment when Jesus will return to resurrect his mortal body from the grave — a feat that will occur just before the rapture of the Church. At that time, all the spirits of those who have died in faith will be miraculously reconnected to their transformed, resurrected bodies!

As we've already seen, at the moment of Christ's descent into the lower atmosphere of the earth on the cusp of His rapture of the Church, those on the earth who are spiritually living, spiritually robust, spiritually thriving, spiritually vibrant, and spiritually vigorous at that time will not be the first to experience transformed bodies. *First*, Paul said the dead bodies of those who have died in faith will be raised and changed — and *then*, next in line, those who are *spiritually living, spiritually robust, spiritually thriving* (that is, the *remaining remnant* who have endured) will immediately afterward be caught up into the air with their bodies supernaturally transformed as they join those who were just resurrected before them!

Scripture unequivocally teaches that the moment an authentic Christian dies, his spirit exits the body that he has lived in during his natural life, and, instantly, he is transported into the presence of the Lord. Although his mortal, corruptible body lies as an empty shell, his spirit is instantly at home in the presence of the Lord. Along with others who have died in faith before him, he awaits the moment when Jesus will return to resurrect his mortal body from the grave, a feat that will occur just before the rapture of the Church.

The Greek meanings of these words in First Thessalonians 4:15, and their usages and nuances, are brought out in the *Renner Interpretive Version* (*RIV*) of this verse:

For we declare this to you by the word of the Lord: Those who are spiritually living, spiritually robust, spiritually thriving, spiritually vibrant, and spiritually vigorous — I'm talking about the remaining remnant of spiritually alive and vibrant believers who have endured and will still be left around at the time of the coming of the Lord — will not precede those who have already died.

The Lord Shall Descend From Heaven

But Paul elaborated even further in First Thessalonians 4:16 when he wrote, "For the Lord himself shall descend from heaven...."

The word "descend" is a form of the Greek word *katabaino*, which is a compound of the words *kata* and *baino*. The preposition *kata* means *down*, and it carries a sense of *domination* and *subjugation*. The Greek word *baino* means *to step*, as one who is *stepping forward* or who is making *forward movement*. As a compound, the Greek word *katabaino* — translated "descend" in the *King James Version* — means *to step down, to come down, to move downward from a higher place to a lower place*, or *to descend*, and it pictures *one who makes downward movement with a dominating and subjugating force*. The word "from" is a translation of the Greek word *apo*, which means *directly from*, and the word "heaven" is from the Greek word *ouranos*, a word that speaks of *the highest heaven*.

When Paul wrote in First Thessalonians 4:16 that the Lord shall "descend from heaven," he meant Christ Himself will make a move from the highest heavens to the air above the earth — and when He does so, He will come with a dominating and subjugating force. At that moment, He will rouse the dead in Christ, He will snatch those who are actively engaged in faith, and He will begin the process of dominating and subjugating evil powers as *the worst of the worst* times ensue on the earth for a season — during the Great Tribulation — on God's prophetic timetable.

Jesus Will Make a Move From His Highly Exalted Position in the Highest Heavens

In Ephesians 1:21, Paul wrote that God exalted Jesus "far above all principality, and power, and might, and dominion, and every name that is named, not only in this world, but also in that which is to come."

In Greek, the word "above" is a translation of the Greek word *huperano*, which means *high above* or *far above*, and it refers to both *rank* and *dignity*. In the context of this verse, it means that no one in the universe has a higher rank, name, or position than Jesus Christ!

And to affirm Jesus' highest position above all, Paul then added the word "all." The word "all" is a translation of a form of the Greek word *pas*, which means *anything* and *everything*. By using the words *huperano* and *pas* together, Paul excluded any misunderstanding or doubt regarding his message. Jesus Christ holds *the highest* and *most exalted* position in the entire universe or any known world or sphere. He is literally, supremely "above all."

The word "principality" refers to all human rulers, including kings and politicians and also angelic beings.

But then Paul began to specifically describe the exact categories that Christ is above. First, Paul stated that Christ is "above all principality...."

The word "principality" is from a form of the Greek word *arche*, and it denotes *rulers of the highest level*. This term refers to all *human rulers*, including *kings* and *politicians*, but the word *arche* is also used in Scripture to refer to *angelic beings*. Thus, Paul was declaring that Christ's exalted rank is far above all

The word "powers" refers to those who hold public office and wield authority entrusted to them by way of an election.

The word "might" denotes explosive power and was used to describe the full strength of a military force.

The word "dominions" refers to any world system — political, financial, or any system of any type.

human rulers and all angelic beings. Both the natural and the spiritual realms are under the dominion of Jesus Christ, and there is absolutely no one in any realm more highly exalted than Him.

Paul then mentioned Christ's superiority over "powers." The word "powers" is the Greek word *exousias*, a word that describes those who have received *delegated power*, and it is therefore often translated *authorities*. This word refers to *people who hold public office and wield authority entrusted to them by their superiors or by way of an election*. Paul was hereby declaring that although such individuals yield substantial power and influence in the affairs of the world, their authority pales in comparison to the authority and highly exalted position of Jesus Christ.

Next, Paul wrote that Jesus is exalted above all "might." This word "might" comes from a form of the Greek word *dunamis*, a word that denotes *explosive power* but was regularly used to describe *the full strength of a military force*. By using this word, Paul was emphatically declaring that Jesus is exalted in His authority and power even above all the military forces that exist in the world.

Then, as if this list is not already complete enough, Paul added that Christ is supreme above all "dominions." The word "dominions" is translated from a form of the Greek word *kuriotes*, which means *lordships*. It could refer to *any world system* — political, financial, or any system of any type. Thus, Paul was announcing that there is no system anywhere in the world that is more high-ranking than the Lord Jesus Christ!

But then, to make sure that he had included everyone and everything, Paul added, "...And every name that is named, not only in this world, but also in that which is to come" (Ephesians 1:21). In one sweeping statement, Paul declared that *Jesus is Lord over all.* He is superior to rulers (*arche*), elected leaders (*exousias*), military powers (*dunamis*), and all worldly systems (*kuriotes*). Jesus Christ is literally Lord over all!

The word "under" is a military term meaning to dominate or to subjugate. The use of this word means that Jesus Christ — through His death on the Cross, subsequent resurrection, and ultimate ascension on High — has literally put every foe that ever has existed or ever will exist under His feet.

Paul then victoriously adds in verse 22 that God "...hath put all things *under* his [Jesus'] feet, and gave him to be the head over all things to the church." The word "under" is a translation of the Greek word *hupotasso*, which was a military term meaning *to dominate* or *to subjugate*. It described *forcibly subduing a conquered people and putting them in their place*. The use of this word in this verse means that Jesus Christ — through His death on the Cross, subsequent resurrection, and ultimate ascension on High — has literally put every foe that has ever existed or ever will exist *under His feet*.

But wait! There's more we need to understand about Jesus' highly exalted place.

In Philippians 2:9-11, Paul also wrote, "Wherefore God also hath highly exalted him, and given him a name which is above every name: that at the name of Jesus every knee should bow, of things in heaven, and things in earth, and things under the earth; and that every tongue should confess that Jesus Christ is Lord, to the glory of God the Father."

The word "bow" is translated from a form of *kampto*, a Greek word that means *to bow low*. The same word is found in Romans 11:4, Romans 14:11, and Ephesians 3:14, where the apostle Paul used it to picture *a person who bends his knee* in acknowledgment of God's authority. Thus, Paul was stating that a day is coming when those in Heaven, earth, and hell will bow their knees in honor, respect, humility, and worship of Jesus Christ! All will bow their knees in acknowledgment of Jesus Christ's lordship!

And the bending of mankind's knees in acknowledgment of Jesus' lordship will be no quiet affair, for Philippians 2:11 goes on to tell us that "...every tongue should confess that Jesus Christ is Lord, to the glory of God the Father."

The word "confess" is from the Greek word *exomologeo*, which is a compound of the words *ek* and *homologeo*. The word *ek* means *out*, and the word *homologeo* speaks of *a verbal confession*. When compounded, it means *to audibly and publicly declare a fact*. It means *to blurt it out, to speak it out, to yell it loudly*, or *to declare it*. This means a day is coming when Heaven, earth, and hell will resonate and resound at once, along with the voices of all who have ever lived, as they all thunderously shout and acknowledge, *"JESUS IS LORD!"*

But the point in all these verses is that absolutely nothing and no one in the universe is more highly exalted than Jesus Christ. His throne rules above all — above all human authorities, military authorities, and all worldly systems. There is simply no one who rules higher or more majestically than Jesus.

But in Second Thessalonians 4:15, Paul wrote that a moment is coming when Jesus, in all His exalted rule and authority, will *move directly down from Heaven — swiftly* from His enthroned position — and He will do it with a dominating and subjugating force. With that dominating force, He will release, or *resurrect*, the dead bodies of the righteous and rapture — "catch away" — the Church.

At that moment, Jesus will end one era and set in motion the powerful process of righting all wrongs and putting things in order on the earth.

And in First Thessalonians 4:16, Paul said this event will begin with a shout!

The Lord Will Descend With a Thunderous Shout!

In First Thessalonians 4:16, Paul wrote, "For the Lord himself shall descend from heaven with a shout...."

According to this verse, a "shout" will be heard as Christ descends into the lower atmosphere to resurrect the dead bodies of those who died in Christ and rapture the

The word "shout" was used to describe *an order, a command,* or *a loud shout that was intended to arouse horses, charioteers, hounds, hunters, rowers, and masters of ships to prepare for action and for war.* Jesus will come with a shout that calls His people to break camp and move upward and to move others into combat positions to start battle. Those who break camp and move upward will be the dead in Christ, as well as those who are fully alive and remain at that moment.

Church, transporting this faithful remnant from the earth into Heaven. The Greek text implies this "shout" will be from Christ Himself.

The Greek word "shout" is translated from a form of the Greek word *keleusma*, which does not appear anywhere else in the New Testament. It is a word that was specifically used to describe *an order, a command,* or *a loud shout that was intended to arouse horses, charioteers, hounds, hunters, rowers, and masters of ships to prepare for action and for war.* It means *to muster the troops to action.* It is an imperative call to action that summons troops to break camp and get ready to move, and this thunderous call beckons other forces to action. It is the word used to excite riders to move their horses to greater speed, to huntsmen to pursue their prey, and to sailors to give themselves to rowing vigorously in order to make forward movement.

This Greek word translated "shout" portrays a war shout. The fact that Jesus will come with a shout means it will be time for some to break camp and move upward, while others will be moved into combat positions to start battle. Those who break camp and move upward will be the dead in Christ, as well as those who are fully alive and remain at that moment. In John 5:28, we are told that the dead will arise at the voice of Christ — surely this is the shout that Paul was speaking of in his words to the Thessalonians!

The truth concerning the Rapture has been a mystery in times past — and we will dive into the word "mystery" in detail in the next chapter. But God is not hiding the truth about the events that will unfold on His timeline in the very last days as we look for Christ's appearing (*see* 1 Corinthians 2:9-10). Although we can only imagine what some of these end-time events will look like, we have a general sense concerning them as we look to the Scriptures and allow the Spirit of Truth to reveal them.

For example, we know that at the sound of His shout, Christ will raise up those who died in faith, and He will also "catch away" His saints who are alive and spiritually engaged. And as we will see, soon afterward, there will ensue a time of tribulation on the earth while the Church in Heaven celebrates the Marriage Supper and stands before Christ's Judgment Seat.

But that summons is not the end because still more will transpire after the time of that seven-year tribulation period….

At the time of Christ's return to resurrect the bodies of the righteous dead and to rapture the faithful remnant of the Church, the ultimate Commander-in-Chief will Himself give a "shout" that rouses the dead from their graves and catches away those who are alive and still in faith. And all Heaven's armies and troops will be summoned into combat positions for what is about to unfold. It will be Christ's way of rousing those who died in faith and catching them up into the air — and snatching up His faithful ones similarly — for the battle of the ages.

When this event occurs, it will set off what the Bible calls "The Day of the Lord." The Day of the Lord is an expression used throughout Scripture to describe the time frame immediately following the resurrection of the righteous dead and the rapture of the remnant Church. As soon as this event is complete, a day will occur — a seven-year period — in which God will deal with the wicked and pour judgment upon the earth. When the righteous dead and the remnant Church are raised and transported to Heaven, the trigger will be pulled for The Day of the Lord to commence as God wages war against the enemies of righteousness. We will see more about this seven-year time frame in a later chapter.

The word "archangel" refers to a chief angel, a principal angel, or one who holds special authority among the heavenly hosts. The voice of an archangel will be heard that will galvanize Heaven's troops to action; summon the dead bodies of the righteous from their graves; and alert those who are spiritually alive, robust, thriving, vibrant, and vigorous — the remaining remnant of believers who have endured and are still around at the time of this event.

The Voice of the Archangel

But in First Thessalonians 4:16, Paul went on to say, "For the Lord himself shall descend from heaven with a shout, with the voice of the archangel...."

This verse says that in addition to Christ's commanding shout, there will also be heard the voice of the archangel. The word "voice" is from the Greek word *phone*, which indeed describes *a voice, sound*, or *noise*, but it also means *to whirl* and depicts *the sound of wind, wings, or rushing water*. It pictures *the sound of a massive multitude* or *an overwhelming sound*. Paul does not tell us if every person on Earth will hear this sound, but God's people and all the hosts of Heaven will hear it. The mighty voice of the archangel will also be a part of the process of rousing all God's troops to full attention and calling them to action!

Paul said this massive voice would come from the "archangel." The word "archangel" is a compound of the Greek words *archo* and *angelos*. The word *archo* means *chief* or *first*, and the word *angelos* is the Greek word for *a heavenly angel*. As a compound, this word refers to *a chief angel, a principal angel,* or *one who holds special authority among the heavenly hosts.* In Scripture, such angels make powerful announcements and divine declarations and carry out mighty deeds. Often, archangels are portrayed as *warriors* who are dispatched to carry out God's decrees with great authority and power. Although Paul does not say which archangel this is, it is generally believed by scholars to be the archangel Michael, who is referred to in Jude 9, Revelation 12:7, and Daniel 10:13.

Thus, we find that at the time of this event, the voice of a mighty archangel will also be heard and will galvanize Heaven's troops to action; summon the dead bodies of the righteous from their graves; and alert those who are spiritually *alive, robust, thriving, vibrant, and vigorous* — the remaining remnant of believers who have endured and are still around at the time of this event — that *the long-awaited moment has arrived to meet the Lord in the air!* This angelic voice will also sound the proclamation that a battle of the ages is about to commence.

God commanded His people to blow the trumpet to call His people for the purpose of breaking camp, advancing, assembling, and to fight against an enemy until victory was won — and the sound of such a trumpet blast caused the enemy's heart to shake and tremble, for enemies understood that the blasting of such trumpets meant the onslaught of war was about to commence.

The Trump of God — A Proclamation of War and Victory

In First Thessalonians 4:16, Paul added, "For the Lord himself shall descend from heaven with a shout, with the voice of the archangel, and with the trump of God...."

In the Old Testament, trumpets were used for multiple reasons. *First,* a trumpet blast was used to call God's people to assemble. *Second,* it was used as a command for Israel's troops to march forward into full-scale war. There were other purposes for trumpets as well, and we see several of these purposes listed in Numbers 10:1-10, which says:

> **And the Lord spake unto Moses, saying, Make thee two trumpets of silver; of a whole piece shalt thou make them:** ***that thou mayest use them for the calling of the assembly, and for the journeying of the camps.*** **And when they shall blow with them, all the assembly shall assemble themselves to thee at the door of the tabernacle of the congregation. And if they blow but with one trumpet, then the princes, which are heads of the thousands of Israel, shall gather themselves unto thee. When ye blow an alarm, then the camps that lie on the east parts shall go forward. When ye blow an alarm the second time, then the camps that lie on the south side shall take their journey: they shall blow an alarm for their journeys.**
>
> **But when the congregation is to be gathered together, ye shall blow, but ye shall not sound an alarm. And the sons of Aaron, the priests, shall blow with the trumpets; and they shall be to you for an ordinance for ever throughout your generations.**
>
> ***And if ye go to war in your land against the enemy that oppresseth you, then ye shall blow an alarm with the trumpets; and ye shall be remembered before the Lord your God, and ye shall be saved from your enemies.*** **Also in the day of your gladness, and in your solemn days, and in the beginnings of your months, ye shall blow with the trumpets over your burnt offerings, and over the sacrifices of your peace offerings; that they may be to you for a memorial before your God: I am the Lord your God.**

In this passage, God commanded His people to blow the trumpet to call them for the purpose of breaking camp, advancing, assembling, and fighting against an enemy until victory was won. The overpowering sound of such a trumpet blast caused the enemy's heart to shake and tremble, for enemies understood that the blasting of such trumpets meant the onslaught of war was about to commence.

Paul, therefore, stated that when the trump of God is blasted at the end of the age, it will be God's call for His people to break camp and move onward to gather for a final assembly (which explains Paul's wording about the rapture of the Church in Second Thessalonians 2:1, which we will look at in Chapter Three). It will be the signal that war is commencing that will be consummated in complete victory. No army, no power, and no force — physical or spiritual — will be capable of withstanding the onslaught of invincible power that will be released in that moment.

As we have just seen, there are nuances of this word "trump" in First Thessalonians 4:16 that can be viewed in light of the use of trumpets among Israel in the past. But in this book, we will keep our focus on the historical meaning of the Greek word for "trump" that Paul used in this verse. This word was very well known in the Greek and Roman world, and Paul, a linguist, was familiar with all the connotations and images associated with this word.

In Greek, the word "trump" is a form of *salpingx*. In most commentaries, scholars drop the "g" in the spelling, so I will use this form as *salpinx* in the remainder of this book. The word *salpinx* is a very specific word that depicted *a war trumpet that announced the commencement of battle*. But in addition to summoning troops to battle, the blast of this particular *salpinx* trumpet was intended to be *a declaration from the outset of a military campaign that ultimate victory and the vanquishing of all enemies was about to occur*.

If you combine the "shout" — given at the time of Christ's descent — with the mighty voice of the archangel, intended to galvanize Heaven's troops and muster God's forces for the final battle, along with this fearsome trumpet blast, the message is significant. It categorically means that when the resurrection of the dead and the rapture of the Church occurs, it will trigger the moment when Christ makes a pre-war declaration that He is about to wage WAR on His enemies and that His foes are about to be vanquished.

That trumpet blast will not only declare it is time for us to break camp and move up higher — but also that Heaven's troops are being mustered and the war has begun!

What Do We Know About the *Salpinx*?

As we have seen, the word "trump" is a translation of the Greek word *salpinx*, an important term that is found in the writings of ancient Greek authors, such as *Aristotle*, *Homer*, and *Plutarch*.[1] This particular trumpet was a long and slender instrument that the blower held to his lips and downward toward the ground. Because of

This illustration on a Greek vase depicts a soldier playing a *salpinx* and dates back to the late Sixth or early Fifth Century BC. The *salpinx* — exactly as Paul described in First Thessalonians 4:16 — is the long slender instrument that he holds from his mouth and is directing toward the ground.

the downward-pointed position, writers from antiquity likened it to the trunk of an elephant that hung toward the ground.

The sound of this trumpet was enormous. And because it was pointed downward, its sound reverberated through the ground, so that it was not only *heard*, but also *physically felt* due to its reverberating operation. Imagine an acoustical system so loud that it causes your body to vibrate, and you'll get a sense of the effect of the *salpinx*. This instrument filled the ears with an overpowering sound and literally caused enemies to quake. The sound of the *salpinx* sent a message of dominance, and at the hearing of its terrible blast, enemies knew they would need to surrender or suffer annihilation.

The Salpinx in War and Court

The blasting of the salpinx was used in connection with war and also with legal proceedings in a court of law. But when associated with war, this instrument released a sound of invincible power so aggressive and menacing that enemies shuddered in dismay. The horrific blasting of the salpinx expressed *terror* to enemies, and at the same time, it mustered troops and incited warship fighters to strike the water with their oars as warriors moved ahead speedily to take military action.

The blasting of the salpinx was considered to be the loudest sound produced by the breath of a human without some form of surrounding mechanical reverberation. It could be heard at such great distances that there was no other known sound that compared to the salpinx as it blasted forcefully and clearly even from a distance. Its deafening sound was so great that the ancient writer Aristoxenus documented that a man was once driven mad by it.[2] It sent waves of fear across the bodies and minds of enemies, as the invincible sound sent a message of the *onslaught of battle*, the *plundering of the opposition*, and *imminent destruction* soon to come. That "supernatural" sound was a prophetic declaration that triumph would surely be achieved and all adversaries would be conquered. Their soon-coming demise sent uncontrollable shivers throughout the bodies of enemy forces as the instrument eerily prophesied their doom.

But the blasting of the salpinx was also used in courtroom proceedings, as we just saw. Similar to the way its sound signaled the onslaught of war, in a legal courtroom, its blast heralded the commencement of court and the execution of justice. And just as its blasting imparted terror to the hearts of adversaries on the battlefield, it likewise caused terror for those who were about to be judged in a court of law. When the blasting of the salpinx occurred at court, it was an announcement that serious legal action was about to take place and that inescapable judgment was about to occur.

How Does All This Relate to the Trump of God?

As we've seen, First Thessalonians 4:16 says, "For the Lord himself shall descend from heaven with a shout, with the voice of the archangel, and with the *trump* of God...."

Because Paul used the well-known Greek word *salpinx* in this verse, it means that:

- In the moment this trumpet is blasted, it will not be a mere trumpet; it will be the blasting of a *war* trumpet.
- In the moment this trumpet is blasted, its deafening, invincible sound will send terror to the enemies of God in every realm, spiritual and physical.
- In the moment this trumpet is blasted, God will summon His people to break camp, advance, and move upward, which of course refers to the resurrection of the bodies of the righteous dead and the rapture of the living remnant of authentic Christians who remain at that time.
- In the moment this trumpet is blasted, its sound will be a signal that musters all of Heaven's troops to engage in the war of the ages.
- In the moment this trumpet is blasted, not only will it be a declaration of war against God's enemies, but it will also be a declaration that the battle will be consummated in total victory.
- In the moment this trumpet is blasted, it will mean that the judgments against the ungodly from God's court of law are about to be carried out as righteous judgment prepares to be poured out on the earth.

All these points are the exact, explicit reasons Paul used the word *salpinx* to describe the trump of God that will be blasted as this series of events commences. But I want to add that in Second Corinthians 5:20, Paul wrote that we are all called to be "ambassadors" for Christ. Remember that before a natural war commences, nations begin to recall their ambassadors before the onslaught begins. And before God pours His wrath on the earth during the seven years of the Tribulation, Christ will recall *His* ambassadors — all authentic believers — and initiate a divine rescue operation to supernaturally snatch them to Heaven so they will escape the wrath poured out on Earth during the seven years of the Tribulation.

But you may ask, "While wrath is being poured out in the seven years of the Tribulation, what will the resurrected and raptured saints be doing in Heaven during that time?" That is an important question, and it will be answered in Chapter Nine.

The Resurrection of the Bodies of Those Who Died in Faith

But Paul added in First Thessalonians 4:16, "For the Lord himself shall descend from heaven with a shout, with the voice of the archangel, and with the trump of God: and *the dead in Christ shall rise first.*"

The word "dead" in Greek is the plural form of *nekros*, which describes *lifeless corpses.* It refers to all believers who have died in faith and whose bodies are buried in the earth, in the sea, or in other places. According to this verse, the trump of God will summon the dead bodies of the righteous. Paul stated that they "*shall rise* first." The words "shall rise" are from the Greek word *anastesontai*, a form of *anistemi*, which is a word that means *to rise, to be resurrected*, or *to stand again.* This word was also used at times to denote the rising of *emperors, kings, nobility, and royalty*. Thus, when the bodies of those who died in faith are resurrected, they will not only *rise* and *be resurrected*, but they will rise *to rule as royalty* with Christ in His Kingdom.

But Paul wrote that the dead in Christ "shall rise *first.*" The word "first" in Greek is *proton*, which means *in first place* or *first in order*. On this long-awaited glorious day, the *first event* of the day — the *first* in order — will be the resurrection of the bodies of those who have died in faith. The rapture of the living — those vibrant in the faith of Jesus — will come next, but chronologically, the dead will be raised *first* on that day.

Taking into account the original Greek meanings of all these words, the *Renner Interpretive Version* (*RIV*) of First Thessalonians 4:16 says:

> **For the Lord Himself will descend from Heaven and take charge with a mighty military command to arouse the saints and galvanize God's troops to action. And along with that command, precisely at that time, will also be heard the immense voice of an archangel, along with the blast of God's war trumpet intended to give the signal that the final battle, ultimate victory, and the vanquishing of all God's enemies are about to occur. That war-trumpet blast will be the declaration that God's enemies have lost their longstanding battle with Him and that He reigns victorious and supreme over everyone, over every situation, and over every realm — in total victory! And exactly when that war-trumpet sound goes forth is when the dead in Christ will immediately stand upright on their feet as they are resurrected to a brand-new, resurrected, royal status. This resurrection will take place as a first priority before the next sequence of events takes place.**

FINALLY...THE RAPTURE OF THE CHURCH

In First Thessalonians 4:17, Paul continued, "Then we which are alive and remain shall be caught up together with them in the clouds, to meet the Lord in the air: and so shall we ever be with the Lord."

This verse begins with "then." This is a translation of the Greek word *epeita*, which means *precisely upon that moment*, *exactly at that moment*, *precisely then*, or *exactly then*. Paul therein declared that in the moment when the dead in Christ are raised, *then, exactly and precisely after that*, "we which are alive and remain shall be caught up together with them in the clouds, to meet the Lord in the air: and so shall we ever be with the Lord."

Once again, we see the words "alive and remain" that were used earlier in verse 15. As a matter of fact, this is the same phrase Paul used in verse 15, which means that what he was stating here was so important he repeated it *verbatim* in the Greek. Now, in verse 17, for the second time, Paul described *those who are spiritually living, spiritually robust, spiritually thriving, spiritually vibrant, and spiritually vigorous — the remaining remnant of vibrant believers who will have endured and survived every storm and will be alive and present at that time.*

Forgive the redundancy, but Paul used the Greek words *hoi perileipomenoi* in both verse 15 and verse 17, and he did it for a reason. Here, again, we find that this is the plural form of *perileipomai*, a compound of *peri* and *leipo*. As stated earlier, the word *peri* means *around* and depicts *a circumference* or *an outer edge*.

The word *leipo* pictures what is *left over*. This word categorically pictures *the remaining outer edge of a garment* — *a fragment*, *a leftover*, *a remnant*, or *a residue*. As noted before, this word pictures *the remnant of a piece of material*, and it meant the greater part is gone and only *a remnant* is *left over* and *remains*.

However, as I wrote earlier, this Greek word was also used militarily to describe brave soldiers who *endured* or *survived* a battle. In a military context, it meant the larger majority of soldiers had been lost along the way, but at the end of the battle, there *remained a faithful remnant that endured* and *survived* everything.

Paul thus alluded that there may only be a remnant of spiritually vibrant Christians left at the time Christ returns for the Church. Then Paul elucidated what happens next to this fully alive Church when He wrote that after the dead bodies of the righteous are raised, *precisely in that moment* or *exactly then* is when the remaining remnant "shall be *caught up* together with them in the clouds, to meet the Lord in the air…."

The words "caught up" are translated from a form of the Greek word *harpadzo*, which undeniably means *to catch*, *to seize*, *to take away*, or *to snatch suddenly*. It pictures *snatching someone out of danger just in the nick of time.*

This insinuates that the rapture of the Church will occur in a moment when things look ominously dark — but suddenly, *just in the nick of time*, Christ will come to snatch His Church out of danger. Not only will they who remain be snatched out of a dark spiritual climate, but they will be snatched just in the nick of time before divine wrath is poured out on the evil in the earth (*see* 1 Thessalonians 1:10).

Some argue that the word "rapture" isn't even in the Bible by name. But we're about to see it by *definition* and by *description* — and later we'll see several incidences of *raptures* or rapture-type experiences that have already occurred as recorded in Scripture.

Pictured here is an illustration of Jerome, who created the first-ever translation of the Greek Scriptures into the Latin language in about 390 AD from the original languages of the Old and New Testaments. This translation is called the Vulgate version of the Bible.

Is the Word 'Rapture' in the New Testament?

Some people ask, "If the rapture of the Church is real and such an important doctrine, why doesn't the actual word 'rapture' appear in the New Testament?"

That is a good question, and I invite you to journey with me through linguistic history as I provide an answer! Many critics have argued that the idea of a "rapture" is a man-made concept because they can't find the actual English word "rapture" in the pages of the New Testament. But it really *is* there, so let's solve this riddle.

The first-ever translation of the Greek Scriptures into the Latin language was carried out by Jerome when he translated what became known as the *Vulgate* translation of the Bible.[3] As noted in my Introduction in my first volume of the *RIV* (*Renner Interpretive Version*):

> **One of the earliest** [Bible] **translations was performed by Jerome in about 390 AD when he translated the original languages of the Old and New Testaments into what is called the *Vulgate* version of the Bible. The word 'vulgate' refers to the *common language* of the people at that time. Jerome was a scholar who knew Hebrew, Greek, and Latin. Although Greek was widely known throughout the Roman Empire, significant populations**

knew no Greek at all, and their primary tongue was Latin. For this reason, Jerome produced a Latin translation of the Bible so that the Word of God would become accessible to a wider Latin-speaking audience. To do this monumental work, Jerome moved to Bethlehem, where he lived in a small grotto that was connected to the Church of the Holy Nativity. For 23 years he worked nonstop on his translation and commentary. His *Vulgate* translation became so highly regarded that it was used as the basis for translations in other languages for a thousand years.

We owe much to Jerome for his monumental work in translating the Greek word *harpadzo* — which is the word Paul used from the Greek in First Thessalonians 4:17 to describe the *catching away* of the Church. Jerome translated it using the Latin word *rapiemur*, which is related to the Latin word *raptus*, and this is where we get the word "rapture." The Greek word *harpadzo*, which Paul used, and the Latin word that Jerome used to translate it, both have the same exact meaning. In both cases, the Greek and Latin words mean *to abduct, to carry away, to carry off, to catch, to forcibly grasp, to seize*, or *to snatch*. Both the Greek word *harpadzo* and the Latin word *rapiemur* picture *suddenly snatching someone out of a dangerous situation* or *suddenly snatching someone out of danger just in the nick of time.*

Pictured here is the 1592 title page of the Vulgate that was translated by Jerome.

Because Jerome's translation was the first-ever to be translated from the Greek version of the Scriptures into Latin, his translation became the foundation of all Bible-translation work for nearly 1,000 years. Because he translated the Greek word *harpadzo* as the Latin word *rapiemur* to describe the *catching away* of the Church that Paul vividly wrote about in First Thessalonians 4:17 — from the time of Jerome throughout all the Middle Ages and to the present — this word became well known as the biblical term describing the moment when Christ will supernaturally *abduct, carry away, carry off, catch, forcibly grasp, seize*, or *snatch* the Church out of danger *just in the nick of time.*

The *Vulgate* version calls this event in Latin *a rapture* (*rapiemur*), and the *King James Version* translators translated it from the Greek as *caught up* or *caught away* (*harpadzo*). But this word was used to describe an event so important to this conversation that we will look next at each of its usages in the New Testament.

EVERY USE OF THE WORD *HARPADZO* IN THE NEW TESTAMENT

Because Paul used the word *harpadzo* in First Thessalonians 4:17 to describe the rapture of the Church — translated as *caught away* by *King James* translators — it is important to see every use of the word *harpadzo* in the New Testament so we can grasp its various nuances.

- In **Matthew 11:12**, Jesus said, "And from the days of John the Baptist until now the kingdom of heaven suffereth violence, and the violent *take it by force*." The words "take it by force" are translated from *harpadzo*, and in this verse, it pictures *a sudden seizing* or *an abrupt taking by force*.

- In **Matthew 12:29**, when speaking of taking away demonic power, Jesus said, "Or else how can one enter into a strong man's house, and *spoil* his goods, except he first bind the strong man? and then he will spoil his house." The word "spoil" in this verse is translated from *harpadzo*, and here it means *to suddenly plunder*, *to suddenly seize*, or *to suddenly take away* and carries the idea of *immediacy* and *suddenness*.

- In **Matthew 13:19** in His parable of the sower and the seed, Jesus said, "When any one heareth the word of the kingdom, and understandeth it not, then cometh the wicked one, and *catcheth away* that which was sown in his heart. This is he which received seed by the way side." The words "catcheth away" are translated from the Greek word *harpadzo*, picturing here *a sudden coming to catch* or *to suddenly snatch away* seed that has been sown into a person's heart.

- In **John 6:15**, we are told, "When Jesus therefore perceived that they would come and take him by force, to make him a king, he departed again into a mountain himself alone." In this verse, the words "take...by force" are translated from *harpadzo*, and they describe a moment when Jesus perceived the multitude would attempt *to suddenly abduct* Him or *suddenly and forcibly take* Him.

- In **John 10:12**, speaking of false shepherds, Jesus said, "But he that is an hireling, and not the shepherd, whose own the sheep are not, seeth the wolf coming, and leaveth the sheep, and fleeth: and the wolf *catcheth* them, and scattereth the sheep." The word "catcheth" is translated from *harpadzo* and it pictures *a sudden and clandestine snatching* of sheep from the fold.

- In **John 10:28**, speaking of His followers, Jesus said, "And I give unto them eternal life; and they shall never perish, neither shall any man *pluck* them out of my hand." The word "pluck" is translated from *harpadzo*, and it pictures one who attempts *to forcibly take* or *to forcibly seize* someone from the hand of Jesus.

- In **John 10:29**, again speaking of His followers and His firm grip on them, Jesus said, "My Father, which gave them me, is greater than all; and no man is able to *pluck* them out of my Father's hand." Again, we find that the word "pluck" is translated from *harpadzo* and it likewise pictures one who attempts *to forcibly take* or *to forcibly seize* someone from the hand of the Father.

- In **Acts 8:39** we read that Philip was preaching to the Ethiopian eunuch. The verse says, "And when they were come up out of the water, the Spirit of the Lord *caught away* Philip, that the eunuch saw him no more: and he went on his way rejoicing." The words "caught away" are translated from *harpadzo* and describe Philip being *suddenly and supernaturally snatched away* and *supernaturally transported* from one place to another place.

- In **Acts 23:10** we read about an event in Paul's life. It says, "And when there arose a great dissension, the chief captain, fearing lest Paul should have been pulled in pieces of them, commanded the soldiers to go down, and *to take* him *by force* from among them, and to bring him into the castle." The words "to take...by force" are translated from *harpadzo* and picture Roman soldiers who wished to *suddenly and forcibly seize* and *snatch* Paul away.

- In **Second Corinthians 12:2**, Paul gave testimony of an earlier moment when he was taken into the Third Heaven. He wrote, "I knew a man in Christ above fourteen years ago, (whether in the body, I cannot tell; or whether out of the body, I cannot tell: God knoweth;) such an one *caught up* to the third heaven." The words "caught up" are exactly translated from *harpadzo* and are used by Paul to describe that earlier event in his life in which he was *suddenly and supernaturally transported* into the Third Heaven.

- In **Second Corinthians 12:4**, Paul expounded again on that earlier moment when he said, "How that he was *caught up* into paradise, and heard unspeakable words, which it is not lawful for a man to utter." Again, the words "caught up" are translated from *harpadzo* and were used by Paul to describe that moment when he was *suddenly and supernaturally transported* into Heaven.

- In **First Thessalonians 4:17**, Paul used this word *harpadzo* to picture the rapture of the Church when he wrote, "Then we which are alive and remain shall be *caught up* together with them in the clouds, to meet the Lord in the air: and so shall we ever be with the Lord." The words "caught up" are translated from *harpadzo*. Paul, a linguist, used this word to describe the future moment when the Church will be *suddenly and supernaturally transported* into Heaven.

- In **Jude 23**, Jude used the word *harpadzo* to state how we should respond to believers who are being lured back into the world. Jude wrote, "And others save with fear, *pulling them out* of the fire; hating even the garment spotted by the flesh." The words "pulling them out" are translated from *harpadzo* and depict *a sudden and forcible seizing* or *snatching* of someone from a dangerous predicament. It pictures *intervention* or *a rescue operation that occurs just in the nick of time.*

- In **Revelation 12:5**, speaking of the woman and the dragon, John wrote, "And she brought forth a man child, who was to rule all nations with a rod of iron: and her child was *caught up* unto God, and to his throne." The words "caught up" are translated from *harpadzo* and describe one who is *abruptly, suddenly, and supernaturally transported* to God and His throne.

All these scriptures demonstrate that the word *harpadzo* that was used by Paul in First Thessalonians 4:17 to describe the rapture of the Church portrays someone or something that is *abducted, carried away, carried off, caught up, forcibly grasped,* or *suddenly snatched away*. In this verse, Paul explicitly used this exact word to depict the soon-coming moment when Christ will *abruptly abduct, carry away, carry off, catch, forcibly grasp, or suddenly snatch* the Church out of danger, just in the nick of time.

After the dead are raised first, next those who are *spiritually living, spiritually robust, spiritually thriving, spiritually vibrant, and spiritually vigorous* — the remaining remnant of *spiritually alive believers who have endured and will still be left around* at the time of the coming of the Lord — will be *suddenly and supernaturally snatched out of imminent danger just in the nick of time*! The Lord will instigate a divine rescue operation to transport them into the clouds to join those whose bodies have just been resurrected.

We live in a day when some mock those who believe in this event. But you will see in a later chapter that multiple raptures have already occurred in history; there are multiple rapture-type experiences in Scripture; and the Bible speaks of *the* rapture of all raptures — the rapture of the Church, which is the subject of this book. This event will stand as the grand finale of the Church Age that gloriously ends one epoch in history so that another can begin. Thus, the idea of a "rapture" is well established in Scripture and can be consistently seen from Genesis to the end of the book of Revelation.

A Meeting in the Lower Atmosphere

In First Thessalonians 4:17, Paul added, "Then we which are alive and remain shall be caught up together with them in the *clouds*...."

The word "clouds" simply means *clouds* — thus we find that Christ will not physically touch the earth until He returns in His visible Second Coming (or Second Advent) at the end of the Tribulation. But at the time of the resurrection of those who died in faith and of the rapture of the Church, Christ will descend into the *clouds* — and He will do it to *suddenly and supernaturally seize, snatch, and transport* the Church from imminent danger as God's prophetic timetable continues to unfold.

The Darkness of the Hour at the Time of Our Deliverance Is Undeniable

Before I close this chapter, I need to say that I am a firm believer in a pre-Tribulation rapture. But because the word *harpadzo* means *to snatch out of danger in the nick of time,* it strongly implies that it will be so dark before the rapture of the Church that it might feel as if the Tribulation has started. However, experiencing hardship is emphatically not on the same level as God's wrath being aggressively poured out on the earth during the seven-year period of the Tribulation.

But because *harpadzo* describes *a rescue operation*, it indeed alerts us that the world may become very dark before the Rapture actually occurs. And just when it seems things could not get darker, that is when the Lord will descend to spectacularly snatch the Church out of imminent danger, and He will do it just in the nick of time. It will be *a divine rescue operation to transport us* into His glorious presence!

The word "meet" pictures *a grand encounter* or *a royal or VIP reception*, and it is a word that specially describes *the reception of a newly arrived official or newly arrived royalty*. In history, when such individuals arrived, the red carpet was rolled out and they were given a VIP reception. This word is used to tell us that when we meet Jesus in the air, Christ is going to roll out the red carpet to give us a grand and glorious VIP reception!

We Will 'Meet' the Lord in the Air!

In First Thessalonians 4:17, Paul added something else in connection with our being transported into the air. He stated, "Then we which are alive and remain shall be caught up together with them in the clouds, to *meet* the Lord in the air...."

The word "meet" is interpreted from a form of the Greek word *apantesis*, which pictures *a grand encounter* or *a royal or VIP reception*. It is a word that specially describes *the reception of a newly arrived official or newly arrived royalty*. In history, when such individuals arrived, the red carpet was rolled out and they were given a VIP reception. Paul understood the usage of this word when he used it here to tell us that when we meet Jesus in the air, *Christ is going to roll out the red carpet to give us a grand and glorious VIP reception!*

Then Paul wrote in First Thessalonians 4:17, "...And so shall we ever be with the Lord." The words "ever be" are a translation of the Greek word *pantote*, which means *at all times, all the time, always, continually*, or *perpetually*. In this moment, when we are suddenly and supernaturally snatched into Heaven, we will find ourselves at the Marriage Feast of the Lamb. And over the course of the next seven years, each believer will stand before the Judgment Seat of Christ to be rewarded for his faithfulness to obey God's plan for his life, a very eternally important future event that we will cover in a later chapter.

But putting together all the original Greek meanings of these words in First Thessalonians 4:17, the *Renner Interpretive Version* (*RIV*) reads as follows:

> **Then at that exact synchronized moment, those who are spiritually living, spiritually robust, spiritually thriving, spiritually vibrant, and spiritually vigorous — I'm talking about the remaining remnant of spiritually alive believers who have endured and will still be left around at the time of the coming of the Lord — will be suddenly and supernaturally snatched away out of imminent danger, just in the nick of time, as the Lord initiates a divine rescue operation to transport them into the clouds to join those who have been resurrected. There in the air's lower atmosphere where the Lord has descended to meet them, those who were raised from the dead and the remnant that was supernaturally snatched out of danger will encounter the Lord. And at that encounter, the Lord will roll out the red carpet to give the new arrivals a royal reception to match the VIP status He knows they deserve! After that, we will always — at all times and forevermore — be with the Lord.**

But because all of First Thessalonians 4:15-17 is so crucial to this important core Bible doctrine, let's see the *RIV* (*Renner Interpretive Version*) of all three of these verses together. Combining all the original Greek meanings of these words in all three verses, we read:

> **15 For we declare this to you by the word of the Lord: Those who are spiritually living, spiritually robust, spiritually thriving, spiritually vibrant,**

and spiritually vigorous — I'm talking about the remaining remnant of spiritually alive and vibrant believers who have endured and will still be left around at the time of the coming of the Lord. That living, surviving, and thriving remnant will not precede those who have already died.

16 For the Lord Himself will descend from Heaven and take charge with a mighty military command to arouse the saints and galvanize God's troops to action. And along with that command, precisely at that time, will also be heard the immense voice of an archangel, along with the blast of God's war trumpet intended to give the signal that the final battle, ultimate victory, and the vanquishing of all God's enemies are about to occur. That war-trumpet blast will be the declaration that God's enemies have lost their longstanding battle with Him and that He reigns victorious and supreme over everyone, over every situation, and over every realm — in total victory! And exactly when that war-trumpet sound goes forth is when the dead in Christ will immediately stand upright on their feet as they are resurrected to a brand-new, resurrected, royal status. This resurrection will take place as a first priority before the next sequence of events takes place.

17 Then at that exact synchronized moment, those who are spiritually living, spiritually robust, spiritually thriving, spiritually vibrant, and spiritually vigorous — I'm talking about the remaining remnant of spiritually alive believers who have endured and will still be left around at the time of the coming of the Lord — will be suddenly and supernaturally snatched away out of imminent danger, just in the nick of time, as the Lord initiates a divine rescue operation to transport them into the clouds to join those who have been resurrected. There in the air's lower atmosphere where the Lord has descended to meet them, those who were raised from the dead and the remnant that was supernaturally snatched out of danger will encounter the Lord. And at that encounter, the Lord will roll out the red carpet to give the new arrivals a royal reception to match the VIP status He knows they deserve! After that, we will always — at all times and forevermore — be with the Lord.

Friend, this is *indisputably* the New Testament teaching about the rapture of the Church. In the next chapter, we will look further at First Corinthians 15:51-53 to see what Paul wrote in that passage about the resurrection of the dead bodies of the righteous and the Rapture. We will see what Paul wrote about the supernatural transformation of the physical bodies of true believers that will occur at the time of this amazing event. In "the twinkling of an eye," we who have been faithful in Christ Jesus will be *gloriously changed.*

QUESTIONS TO PONDER

1. Do you remember the first time you heard about the rapture of the Church? Were you ever taught this subject in your local church? When was the first time you realized it meant Christians would be lifted into the air to meet with the Lord?

2. The Greek word for "alive" in First Thessalonians 4:15 and 17 means *to be fully alive, robust, thriving, vibrant, and vigorous.* Do you feel you are spiritually "alive" based on the description in this chapter? If not, what are some ways in which you can become more vibrant and alive to the things of God?

3. Did it surprise you to learn that there are "spiritual mannequins" among us? Have you ever encountered someone who had the outward appearance of being a godly person but did not exhibit the inward fruit of the Spirit as listed in Galatians 5:22 and 23? Read Second Timothy 3:1-5. Do you see evidence of these things in the world around you? Does what you see increase your expectation that we are closer to the Rapture than ever before?

4. Were you intrigued by the Greek definitions of the four types of authority listed in Ephesians 1:21? Do you need victory in any of these areas in your own life? Using Scripture as your guide, in what ways can you invoke the name of Jesus over those areas so that victory can be accomplished?

5. Read the *RIV* of First Thessalonians 4:15-17 again, which is found at the end of this chapter. What stands out to you from this passage that you have never seen before? Does it inspire you to live more fervently for the Lord in these last days?

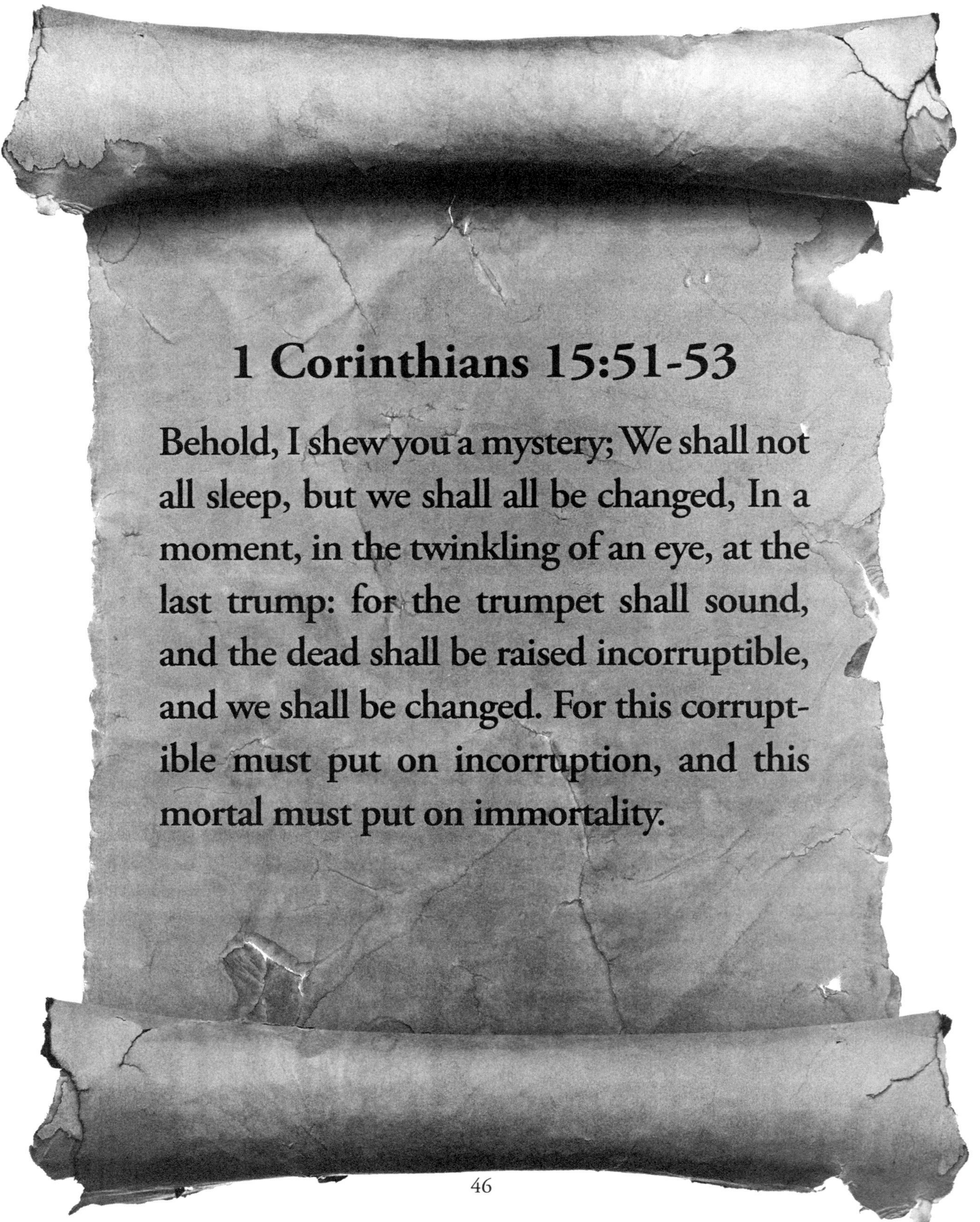

1 Corinthians 15:51-53

Behold, I shew you a mystery; We shall not all sleep, but we shall all be changed, In a moment, in the twinkling of an eye, at the last trump: for the trumpet shall sound, and the dead shall be raised incorruptible, and we shall be changed. For this corruptible must put on incorruption, and this mortal must put on immortality.

CHAPTER TWO

THE RAPTURE...A MYSTERY FINALLY REVEALED!

Behold, I shew you a mystery; We shall not all sleep, but we shall all be changed, in a moment, in the twinkling of an eye, at the last trump: for the trumpet shall sound, and the dead shall be raised incorruptible, and we shall be changed. For this corruptible must put on incorruption, and this mortal must put on immortality.

— 1 Corinthians 15:51-53

In the previous chapter, we saw what Paul wrote about the resurrection of the bodies of the righteous dead and the rapture of the Church in First Thessalonians 4:15-18. In this chapter, we will examine what Paul wrote about these topics in First Corinthians 15:51-53. Paul discussed the rapture of the Church when he wrote his first epistle to the Thessalonians in approximately 50 AD. Then shortly afterward, he addressed this subject again when he wrote his first epistle to the Corinthians. It is important to see both passages, for it shows that Paul was consistent over many years in what he wrote about the rapture of the Church.

In First Corinthians 15:51, Paul wrote that the dual resurrection of the bodies of the righteous dead *and* the righteous living had previously been a *mystery*, but that it was now being "shown" or revealed. Based on the clear teaching of Scripture, we can confidently declare there *will* be a day when the bodies of the righteous dead will rise — *and* there will be a generation of Christians who will never taste physical death but will be *raptured* — *caught up* to meet the Lord in the clouds. On that day, *first* the dead in Christ will be raised, and *then* those who are alive and are still vigorously engaged in the faith will suddenly be *caught up* in the air to meet the Lord.

Again, the words "caught up" in First Thessalonians 4:17 are translated from the Greek word *harpadzo*, which is the Greek word that vividly describes the rapture of the Church. In Chapter One, I explained that in his *Vulgate* translation, Jerome used the Latin word *rapiemur* to translate the Greek word *harpadzo* — and *rapiemur* is where the word "rapture" comes from. And because the *Vulgate* impacted all other translations of the Bible for 1,000 years, the word "rapture" was carried into theological vocabulary even though the actual Greek word is *harpadzo*. As noted, both the Greek word *harpadzo* and the Latin word *rapiemur* picture *snatching someone out of a dangerous situation* or *snatching someone out of danger just in the nick of time*.

Still, many argue that because the word "rapture" does not appear in the English text, it is not a biblical concept. But, as I have shown, the Greek texts use the word *harpadzo*, which, like *rapiemur*, emphatically describes *the catching away*, *sudden snatching*, or *rapture* of the Church.

Paul taught that in the moment when the bodies of the righteous dead are raised, at nearly the same time, those who are spiritually living, spiritually robust, spiritually thriving, spiritually vibrant, and spiritually vigorous will be thusly *caught away*

Pictured here is an ancient copy of the Vulgate translation, in which Jerome used the Latin word *rapiemur* to translate the Greek word *harpadzo* — and *rapiemur* is where the word "rapture" comes from. Because the Vulgate impacted all other translations for one thousand years, the word "rapture" was carried into theological vocabulary even though the actual Greek word is *harpadzo*. Both the Greek word *harpadzo* and the Latin word *rapiemur* pictures snatching someone out of a dangerous situation or snatching out of danger just in the nick of time.

or *snatched* — *raptured* — by the Lord. I'm talking about the remaining remnant of spiritually alive believers who have endured assaults against their faith and are present on the earth at the time of the coming of the Lord. They will be suddenly and supernaturally "caught up" to meet the Lord in the air. In a split second, they will, from their natural, physical bodies, be transformed into immortal, indestructible beings.

We can anticipate from Scripture much of what the last-days countdown will look like for true saints who are alive on the earth when Jesus finally shouts and pierces the sky in the long-awaited event called the Rapture. But as He appears from behind the veil that separates time and eternity, we can only imagine what the saints will experience in that exact moment — what they will think and feel as they are changed in the "twinkling of an eye." Those who are vibrantly filled with this blessed hope are living their lives in purity and holiness, looking earnestly for this time of Christ's appearing (*see* 1 John 3:3).

Although the rapture of the Church was a *mystery* that was unknown in Old Testament times, Paul clearly stated that it was revealed in the time of the New Testament, along with other mysteries that were not previously known. Old Testament believers may have seen faint glimmers of the rapture of the Church, along with other mysteries, but there were a number of mysteries that were simply not known until the Holy Spirit revealed them as New Testament writers wrote under inspiration of the Holy Spirit.

The word "mystery" appears multiple times in the New Testament to describe truths that were not known in Old Testament times. The word "mystery" itself is a translation of the Greek word *musterion*, a word that denotes *a hidden thing*, *a mystery*, or *a secret that is not naturally knowable and that can only be divinely revealed.* Paul used this Greek word *musterion* to inform us that *mysteries* and *secrets* that were previously unknown have now been revealed in Christ.

For the sake of learning, I am providing a list of previously concealed *mysteries* that were finally revealed in the pages of the New Testament. These mysteries are not listed in order of importance, and some of them run parallel to one another in terms of the truth that was being revealed. I simply provide them here so you will see what types of mysteries were revealed in the time of the New Testament.

You will notice in this list that I give the meaning of certain words *repeatedly*, and I do so because Paul used them *repeatedly*. While I do not want to be redundant, that Paul would use these particular words over and over is important, so I want to be sure you understand what these words mean in each of the following instances.

The MYSTERY of the Incarnation

The *mystery of the Incarnation* is at the very core of the Christian message. Paul referred to this *mystery* in First Timothy 3:16 (*NIV*) when he wrote, "Beyond all question, the *mystery* from which true godliness springs is great: He appeared in the flesh, was vindicated by the Spirit, was seen by angels, was preached among the nations, was believed on in the world, was taken up to glory."

As noted, the word "mystery" is translated from the Greek word *musterion*, and it denotes *a hidden thing, a mystery*, or *a secret that is not naturally knowable and that can only be divinely revealed.* Although the *mystery of the Incarnation* was a previously kept *secret*, it was revealed in the Person of Christ, and it is now well known as a theological matter of fact. In Old Testament times and among pagan cultures, it was *unthinkable* that a god would become a man or, even more, that a god would die for others. But Paul wrote about the mystery of the Incarnation in Philippians 2:8, where he vividly described God Himself becoming a man — and *this* is the mystery of the Incarnation.

In this verse, Paul stated that Jesus was "...found in *fashion* as a man...." That word "fashion" is translated from the Greek word *schema*, a word that was used in ancient times to depict *a king who for a brief period of time exchanged his kingly garments for the clothing of a beggar.* The use of this word tells us that when Jesus came to the earth, it was a moment when God Almighty shed His glorious appearance and exchanged it for the clothing of human flesh. For the sake of our redemption, God laid aside all His external, radiant glory and took upon Himself flesh, manifesting Himself as a human being. This is the true story of a King who traded His glorious kingly garments and took upon Himself the clothing of a servant — in the case of the Incarnation, the "clothing" of human flesh.

This *mystery of the Incarnation* is what Paul wrote about in First Timothy 3:16 (*NIV*) when he stated, "Beyond all question, the *mystery* from which true godliness springs is great: he appeared in the flesh, was vindicated by the Spirit, was seen by angels, was preached among the nations, was believed on in the world, was taken up to glory."

The *mystery of the Incarnation* was previously incomprehensible, but in Christ — and in the pages of the New Testament — the wrappings were removed from this *mystery*, and it became divinely revealed. Now the *mystery of the Incarnation* is the very center of Christian dogma and is no longer a secret.

The MYSTERY of the Kingdom of God

The *mystery of the Kingdom of God* was a frequent topic of Jesus' teaching. He referred to this *mystery* in Mark 4:11, when He said to the disciples, "...Unto you it is given to know the *mystery of the kingdom of God:* but unto them that are without, all *these* things are done in parables."

Again, the word "mystery" is translated from the Greek word *musterion*, and it denotes *a hidden thing, a mystery*, or *a secret that is not naturally knowable and that can only be divinely revealed.* Jesus freely spoke of the mystery of the Kingdom of God to His disciples, but when speaking to others about it, He spoke in parables because He was speaking of a secret that He only wished to reveal to His disciples at that time.

Although the *mystery of the Kingdom of God* was previously incomprehensible, in Christ's ministry, and in the pages of the New Testament, many facets of this *mystery* have been divinely revealed. Now Jesus' teachings about the *mystery of the Kingdom of God* are well known and are no longer a secret.

The MYSTERY of Salvation for All Nations

The *mystery of salvation for all nations* was completely unknown in Old Testament times, but Paul spoke about this *mystery* in Romans 16:25 when he wrote, "Now to him that is of power to stablish you according to my gospel, and the preaching of Jesus Christ, according to the *revelation* of the *mystery*, which was kept *secret* since the world began."

In these verses, there are several key words. Paul referred to the "revelation" of the "mystery" that was kept "secret" since the world began. Again, the word "mystery" is the Greek word *musterion*, which denotes *a hidden thing, a mystery*, or *a secret that is not naturally knowable and that can only be divinely revealed.*

Paul wrote that the *mystery of salvation for all nations* was given by "revelation." The word "revelation" is a translation of the Greek word *apokalupsis*, which is a compound of the word *apo* and *kalupto*. The word *apo* means *away*, and the word *kalupto* pictures *a covering* or *a veil* that is intended to *hide* something from view. When the words *apo* and *kalupto* are compounded, the new word refers to *something that has been veiled or hidden for a long time, but suddenly becomes clear and visible to the mind or eye.* It is like pulling the curtains out of the way so you can see what has always been just outside your window. The scene was always there for you to enjoy, but the curtains blocked your ability to see it. However, once the curtains are drawn back or pulled apart, suddenly you can *see* what was there all along but was hidden from view. The moment you see beyond the curtain for the first time to observe what was there all along, *that* is what the Bible calls a "revelation."

Paul furthermore wrote that the mystery of salvation for all nations was a previously kept "secret." The word "secret" is translated from the Greek word *sigao*, which denotes something that is *kept silent* or *under wraps*. However, Paul stated that this previously kept "secret," kept under wraps since the world began, has now been revealed.

The *mystery of salvation for all nations* was previously incomprehensible, but in Christ, and in the pages of the New Testament, this amazing *mystery* has been divinely revealed. Today the belief in the *mystery of salvation for all nations* is no longer a secret.

The MYSTERY of the Church

The *mystery of the Church* was always in the heart of God but was unknown until the time of the New Testament. Paul referred to this mystery in Ephesians 5:25-33, where he wrote, "Husbands, love your wives, even as Christ also loved the church, and gave himself for it; that he might sanctify and cleanse it with the washing of water by the word, that he might present it to himself a glorious church, not having spot, or wrinkle, or any such thing; but that it should be holy and without blemish. So ought men to love their wives as their own bodies. He that loveth his wife loveth himself. For no man ever yet hated his own flesh; but nourisheth and cherisheth it, even as the Lord the church: for we are members of his body, of his flesh, and of his bones. For this cause shall a man leave his father and mother, and shall be joined unto his wife, and they two shall be one flesh. This is *a great mystery:* but I speak concerning Christ and the church."

Although in this passage, Paul was addressing the marital relationship between husbands and wives, he likened this husband-wife relationship to Christ and the Church, which Paul said is a "great mystery." The word "great" is from the Greek word *mega*, and it speaks of that which is *enormous, giant, huge*, or *massive.* The word "mystery" is again translated from the word *musterion*, which denotes *a hidden thing, a mystery*, or *a secret that is not naturally knowable and that can only be divinely revealed.* As a phrase, the words "great mystery" tell us that the unveiling of the Church was *an enormous, great, huge, massive mystery* that previous generations did not see or understand.

In Ephesians 3:9 and 10, Paul wrote that part of his own ministry was "...to make all men see what is the fellowship of the *mystery*, which from the beginning of the world hath been *hid* in God, who created all things by Jesus Christ: to the intent that now unto the principalities and powers in heavenly places might be known *by the church* the manifold wisdom of God."

Paul herein stated that the Church was a "mystery" that was "hid" in God since the world began. The word "mystery" is again translated from the word *musterion*, which denotes *a hidden thing, a mystery*, or *a secret that is not naturally knowable and that can only be divinely revealed.* The word "hid" is an interpretation of a form of *apokrupto*, a compound of the words *apo* and *krupto*. The word *apo* means *away*, and the word *krupto* means *to conceal* or *to hide.* As a compound, it means *to hide away from sight, to put out of sight*, or *to tuck away from visibility*. It pictures *concealing something so no one can see it* or *to ensconce something so deeply that no one will come across it.*

Thus, the *mystery of the Church* was previously incomprehensible, but in Christ, and in the pages of the New Testament, *the mystery of the Church* was divinely revealed. What was kept hidden since the world began is now completely understood and accepted. Previously the idea of the Church was God's big mystery, but now it is no longer a secret.

The MYSTERY
of the Riches of God's Glory Among the Gentiles

The *mystery of the riches of God's glory among the Gentiles* was absolutely unthinkable in Old Testament times, but it was revealed in Christ. Paul spoke of this mystery in Colossians 1:26-27 where he wrote that "even the *mystery* which hath been *hid* from ages and from generations, but now is made *manifest* to his saints: to whom God would make known what is the riches of the glory of this *mystery* among the Gentiles; which is Christ in you, the hope of glory."

Notice the italicized words above. In these verses, Paul repeated the word "mystery" twice, and each time, it is again a translation of the word *musterion*, which denotes *a hidden thing, a mystery*, or *a secret that is not naturally knowable and that can only be divinely revealed.*

Paul stated this mystery of the riches of God's glory among the Gentiles was a mystery that was "hid" from ages and generations. The word "hid" is translated from the Greek word *apokrupto*, which we saw in the previous point. It is a compound of the words *apo* and *krupto*. The word *apo* means *away*, and the word *krupto* means *to conceal* or *to hide.* As a compound, the word *apokrupto* means *to hide away from sight, to put out of sight*, or *to tuck away from visibility.* It pictures *concealing something so no one can see it* or *to ensconce something so deeply that no one will come across it.*

However, Paul ardently stated that although this mystery was once deeply ensconced and hidden from view, in Christ it has been made "manifest." The word "manifest" is translated from the word *phaneroo*, which means *to bring that which is invisible into the light.* It means *to enlighten, to illuminate*, or *to make plain in order to see and understand.* Paul then added that God's intention was always to make "known" the "riches" of God's glory among the saints. The word "known" is interpreted from the word *gnoridzo,* which means *to broadcast, to declare,* or *to make known.* The word "riches" is translated from the Greek word *ploutos,* which pictures *abundance, riches,* or *nearly unimaginable wealth.* Paul used the word *ploutos* to picture the *vast riches of God's glory* that now reside among the Gentiles.

Although the reality of God's riches among the Gentiles was a secret kept under wraps for ages, God's intention was to make it known. Although this secret was wrapped tightly until the time came for it to be unwrapped and to become manifest, today no one questions God's glory among the Gentiles.

The *mystery of the riches of God's glory among the Gentiles* was previously completely incomprehensible, but in Christ and in the pages of the New Testament, this *mystery* has been divinely revealed.

The MYSTERY That Jews and Gentiles Could Be Members of One Body

The *mystery of Jews and Gentiles being members of one Body* was a completely unthinkable thought in Old Testament times, but in Christ this *mystery* has been revealed and it has become a reality.

Paul referred to this *mystery* in Ephesians 3:2-6, where he wrote, "If ye have heard of the dispensation of the grace of God which is given me to you-ward: how that by revelation he made known unto me the *mystery*; (as I wrote afore in few words, whereby, when ye read, ye may understand my knowledge in the *mystery* of Christ) which in other ages was not made known unto the sons of men, as it is now revealed unto his holy apostles and prophets by the Spirit; that the Gentiles should be fellowheirs, and of the same body, and partakers of his promise in Christ by the gospel."

Notice that the word "mystery" appears *twice* in these verses where Paul wrote of Jews and Gentiles becoming members of one Body in Christ. Again the word "mystery" is translated from the word *musterion* and denotes *a hidden thing, a mystery,* or *a secret that is not naturally knowable and that can only be divinely revealed.* However, Paul stated that "...by *revelation* he [God] made known unto me the *mystery*...."

The word "revelation" appears again in connection with mysteries. This is once again an interpretation of the Greek word *apokalupsis,* which refers to *something that has been veiled or hidden for a long time and then suddenly becomes clear and visible to the mind or eye.* As previously noted, when such a revelation occurs, it is like pulling the curtains out of the way so you can see what has always been just outside your window. Although the scene was always there for you to enjoy, the curtains blocked your ability to see the real picture, but when the curtains are drawn apart, you can suddenly *see* the scene outside your window that had been hidden from view. The moment you see beyond the curtain for the first time and observe what has been there all along, *that* is what the Bible calls a "revelation."

But the mystery that Jews and Gentiles could be members of one Body was such an amazing mystery that Paul said, "...In other ages [this mystery] was not made known unto the sons of men...," but now it has been "revealed" first to apostles and prophets by the Spirit. Paul used the word "revealed" in this sequence of verses to state that Jews and Gentiles becoming members of one Body in Christ was always God's plan, but it was incomprehensible until the Holy Spirit pulled back the veil and revealed it first to holy apostles and prophets.

Against all odds and societal norms, a single, united Body emerged and became supernaturally, mysteriously, blended — joined, fused, intermingled, amalgamated, and divinely melded — into one, single Body of believers! Think of the magnificent, supernatural unifying work God performed by His Spirit at the moment of the new birth, in which, *in one instant,* all classes and distinctions — Jew, Greek, etc. (*see* Galatians 3:28) — vanished inside this one, new Body, the Church.

The *mystery that Jews and Gentiles could be members of one Body* was previously incomprehensible, but in Christ, this *mystery* was divinely revealed. Now the *mystery that Jews and Gentiles can be members of one Body* in Christ is a well-established New Testament fact and no longer a secret.

The MYSTERY That Israel Will One Day Be Saved

The *mystery that Israel will one day be saved* is revealed in Romans 11:25 and 26, where Paul wrote, "For I would not, brethren, that ye should be ignorant of this *mystery*, lest ye should be wise in your own conceits; that blindness in part is happened to Israel, until the fulness of the Gentiles be come in. And so all Israel shall be saved...."

Again, the word "mystery" is translated from the word *musterion*, which denotes *a hidden thing, a mystery*, or *a secret that is not naturally knowable and that can only be divinely revealed.* In context, Paul was writing about Gentiles being grafted into the Vine and about a future day when the fullness of the Gentiles will be reached and Israel will recognize Jesus the Messiah and be saved.

Although the *mystery that Israel will one day be saved* in Christ the Messiah was previously incomprehensible, in the pages of the New Testament, this *mystery* has been divinely revealed. Now we confidently anticipate that future moment, and it is no longer a secret.

The MYSTERY of Iniquity

In Second Thessalonians 2:7, Paul wrote, "For the *mystery of iniquity* doth already work...."

Again, we find that the word "mystery" is translated from the Greek word *musterion*, and it denotes *a hidden thing, a mystery*, or *a secret that is not naturally knowable and that can only be divinely revealed.* Although the mystery of iniquity was a previously kept secret, it has been revealed in Scripture.

Paul states that the *mystery of iniquity* has been working a long time. It is a covert, secret plan that the devil has been slowly executing right under people's noses, as he methodically and tediously walks the world away from the law of God to become a society that eventually throws off moral restraints. When Paul wrote about the "mystery of iniquity," he was speaking of a clandestine plan that will be culminated in *the last of the last days* to lead society worldwide into a state of rebellion, or mutiny, against God.

The *mystery of iniquity* was hidden, but in the pages of the New Testament — the wrappings were also removed from this mystery, it was divinely revealed, and the mystery of iniquity is no longer a secret.

The MYSTERY of the Rapture of the Church

All the previous points covered were mysteries that were unknown before they were finally revealed in New Testament times. Likewise, the *mystery of the rapture of the Church* was a secret that was completely hidden from view until the Holy Spirit pulled back the curtains and revealed it in the pages of the New Testament.

This *mystery* was especially revealed in the writings of the apostle Paul, who referred to the rapture as a *mystery* in First Corinthians 15:51. He wrote, "Behold, I shew you a mystery; We shall not all sleep, but we shall all be changed."

Again, we see that Paul used the word "mystery," again, translated from the word *musterion,* which denotes *a hidden thing, a mystery*, or *a secret that is not naturally knowable and that can only be divinely revealed.* Thus, we find that the mystery of the rapture of the Church was previously incomprehensible, but in the pages of the New Testament, this amazing *mystery* has been divinely revealed.

To better understand this mystery, in this chapter we will deeply study what Paul wrote about the rapture of the Church in First Corinthians 15:51-53. Although the Rapture was an unknown mystery in the time of the Old Testament, it is no longer a secret.

To review, this word "mystery" appears multiple times in the New Testament, mostly in connection with:

1. The Mystery of the Incarnation

2. The Mystery of the Kingdom of God

3. **The Mystery of Salvation for All Nations**
4. **The Mystery of the Church**
5. **The Mystery of the Riches of God's Glory Among the Gentiles**
6. **The Mystery That Jews and Gentiles Could Be Members of One Body**
7. **The Mystery That Israel Will One Day Be Saved**
8. **The Mystery of Iniquity**
9. **The Mystery of the Rapture of the Church**

All these were mysteries that were revealed in Christ and in the pages of the New Testament. The rapture of the Church — which is the subject of this book — was among these mysteries and one of God's biggest secrets until it was revealed in the New Testament as the writers wrote under the inspiration of the Holy Spirit.

A Review of What Paul Wrote About the Rapture of the Church in First Thessalonians 4:15-17

In Chapter One, we unpacked what Paul wrote about the rapture of the Church in First Thessalonians 4:15-17. Let's review again the *Renner Interpretive Version* (*RIV*) of First Thessalonians 4:15 to see all the nuances of the original Greek words in the text.

RIV of First Thessalonians 4:15

For we declare this to you by the word of the Lord: Those who are spiritually living, spiritually robust, spiritually thriving, spiritually vibrant, and spiritually vigorous — I'm talking about the remaining remnant of spiritually alive and vibrant believers who have endured and will still be left around at the time of the coming of the Lord. That living, surviving, and thriving remnant will not precede those who have already died.

Paul then elaborates more about this remarkable event in First Thessalonians 4:16. In the *Renner Interpretive Version* (*RIV*) of this verse, we again find nuances of the original Greek meanings in this verse.

RIV of First Thessalonians 4:16

For the Lord Himself will descend from Heaven and take charge with a mighty military command to arouse the saints and galvanize God's troops to action. And along with that command, precisely at that time, will also be heard the immense voice of an archangel, along with the blast of God's war trumpet intended to give the signal that the final battle, ultimate victory, and the vanquishing of all God's enemies are about to occur. That war-trumpet blast will be the declaration that God's enemies have lost their longstanding battle with Him and that He reigns victorious and supreme over everyone, over every situation, and over every realm — in total victory! And exactly when that war-trumpet sound goes forth is when the dead in Christ will immediately stand upright on their feet as they are resurrected to a brand-new, resurrected, royal status. This resurrection will take place as a first priority before the next sequence of events takes place.

But Paul added more about this event in First Thessalonians 4:17. To get the full flavor of the original Greek text, let's look again at the *Renner Interpretive Version* (*RIV*) of this verse.

RIV of First Thessalonians 4:17

Then at that exact synchronized moment, those who are spiritually living, spiritually robust, spiritually thriving, spiritually vibrant, and spiritually vigorous — I'm talking about the remaining remnant of spiritually alive believers who have endured and will still be left around at the time of the coming of the Lord — will be suddenly and supernaturally snatched away out of imminent danger. Just in the nick of time, the Lord will initiate a divine rescue operation to transport them into the clouds to join those who have been resurrected. There in the air's lower atmosphere where the Lord has descended to meet them, those who were raised from the dead and the remnant that was supernaturally snatched out of danger will encounter the Lord. And at that encounter, He will roll out the red carpet to give the new arrivals a royal reception to match the VIP status He knows they deserve! After that, we will always — at all times and forevermore — be with the Lord.

Paul wrote about a restraining force (*see* 2 Thessalonians 2:6) that God will use to hold back evil at the end of the age. When this mighty hand of resistance is removed, it will trigger the moment for the curtains to be pulled back for the Antichrist to appear on the stage before the world.

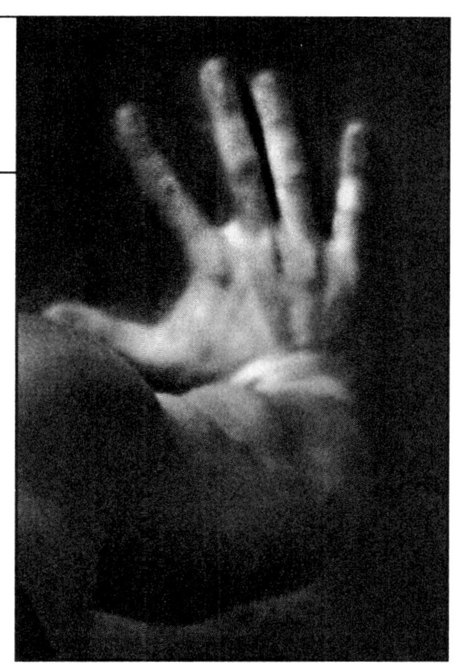

The words "a divine rescue operation to transport them...supernaturally snatched out of danger" in the *RIV* are interpreted from the Greek word *harpadzo*. We have affirmed that this word means *to seize* or *to snatch out of danger just in the nick of time.* Again, it is indicated that those included in this rescue operation will be the Christians who are alive at the moment of this event and who may feel surrounded by extreme difficulties. But suddenly, Christ will descend from Heaven to supernaturally snatch them from danger and transport them to meet Him in the air.

Although difficulties — and perhaps even harsh difficulties — will surround a last-days remnant of vibrant, faithful believers, that remnant will nevertheless be actively engaged in the Great Commission and the plans and purposes of God on the earth. The enemy will be actively waging war on God, His Word, His Church, and all humankind, which was created in God's likeness and image. But in the midst of this spiritual confrontation, that glorious remnant will shine the brightest.

Paul wrote about that colliding of kingdoms in his second epistle to the Thessalonians, where he mentioned a *restraining force* (*see* 2 Thessalonians 2:6). God will use this restraining force to hold back much of this evil at the end of the age. Whoever or whatever this restraining force is, it is so strong that the Antichrist will be unable to make his appearance to the world until this "restrainer" has been removed. But when the restraining force is removed, it will trigger the moment for the curtains to be pulled back, and that is when the Antichrist will appear on the stage before the world.

Exactly who this great restrainer is has been widely debated. In the chapter entitled, "Who Is the Great Restrainer?," we will discover the identity of this restrainer and see other important details Paul wrote concerning the end of the age and the rapture of the Church.

But for now, let's turn our attention to see what Paul wrote to believers in Corinth about the Rapture.

What Paul Wrote About the Rapture of the Church in First Corinthians 15:51-53

In addition to what Paul wrote about the Rapture in First Thessalonians 4:15-18, he wrote about this event in his first letter to the Corinthians. Paul introduced this topic, saying, "Behold, I shew you a mystery; We shall not all sleep, but we shall all be changed" (1 Corinthians 15:51).

Notice that Paul began with the word "behold." This is an interpretation of the Greek word *idou*, which conveys a sense of *amazement, bewilderment, shock, and wonder.* The use of the word "behold" is the equivalent of Paul saying, *"Wow! Wow! Wow! Hold on and listen to what I'm about to tell you because it's going to blow you away!"* It conveys Paul's own sense of *amazement, bewilderment, shock, and wonder* at what he was about to describe.

Then Paul added the words, "...I shew you a mystery...." As we have seen, the New Testament contains multiple mysteries, but here, Paul was unwrapping what was one of the greatest *mysteries* of the ages. The word "mystery" is again translated from the word *musterion*, which denotes *a hidden thing, a mystery*, or *a secret that is not naturally knowable and that can only be divinely revealed.* Although Paul knew this mystery, it is so amazing that he was overtaken by it even as he wrote — and that is why the Greek text conveys a sense of *amazement* and *wonder* as he communicated it.

Paul emphatically stated that the dead bodies of the righteous whom Christ resurrects — and the remaining remnant of spiritually alive believers who will be left at the time of the coming of the Lord — will be "changed." At this moment, both the dead bodies of the righteous and the living bodies of vibrant believers will be miraculously *altered, changed, exchanged, and transformed* by divine power, and they will be transported miraculously into the air.

'We Shall Not All Sleep, But We Shall All Be Changed'

In First Corinthians 15:51, Paul continued to say, "Behold, I shew you a mystery; We shall not all sleep, but we shall all be changed."

Paul said we will not "all sleep." These words are translated from the Greek word *koimethesometha*, a plural form of *koimao,* a word that describes *the sleep of death.* Paul used exactly the same word in First Thessalonians 4:15 to describe the "dead" in Christ — those who died in the faith of Jesus. But in this verse in First Corinthians, he stated explicitly that not everyone will *sleep* or *die* — that there will be a generation of authentic believers who will escape death.

As we well know by now, when Jesus comes for the resurrection of the bodies of those who died in Christ and for the rapture of the Church, He will *first* resurrect the "righteous dead" and immediately afterward, He will raise up the "righteous living" — those who are *spiritually living, spiritually robust, spiritually thriving, spiritually vibrant, and spiritually vigorous.* These raptured saints will be the remaining remnant of spiritually alive believers who have endured the tests of the age and will be present at the time of the coming of the Lord. They will be suddenly and supernaturally snatched away, out of imminent danger, just in the nick of time as the Lord initiates a divine rescue operation to transport them into the clouds to join those who have been resurrected.

These are the saints who will not "sleep," or die (*see* 1 Corinthians 15:51).

In this verse, Paul emphatically stated that the dead bodies of the righteous whom Christ resurrects — and the remaining remnant of spiritually alive believers who will be left at the time of the coming of the Lord — will be "changed." The word "changed" is a translation of the Greek word *allagesometha*, which is a plural form of the word *allasso*, a word that means *to alter, to change, to exchange one thing for another*, or *to completely transform.* This means that at this moment, both the dead bodies of the righteous and the living bodies of vibrant believers will be *miraculously altered, changed, exchanged, and transformed* into a new type of body. In each case, it will be an instantaneous, miraculous, and supernatural transformation.

All the nuances of the words Paul used in the original Greek text are important, so let's look at the *Renner Interpretive Version* (*RIV*) of First Corinthians 15:51 to see all these nuances.

RIV of First Corinthians 15:51

What I am about to tell you is so amazing that it nearly leaves me speechless, and I'm sure it will totally flabbergast you. Listen carefully, for I am going to tell you something that was previously an unknown mystery, but it has been revealed to us. Here it is: All of us will not die, but in this particular moment, all of us, both the dead and the living — those who are spiritually living, spiritually robust, spiritually thriving, spiritually vibrant, and spiritually vigorous — will be altered or changed, miraculously modified, and supernaturally transformed.

What these transformed bodies will be like will be discussed toward the end of this chapter, but right now, let's see how *fast* Paul said this divine transformation will happen!

This Transformation Will Occur in a Microscopic Moment — in the 'Twinkling of an Eye'

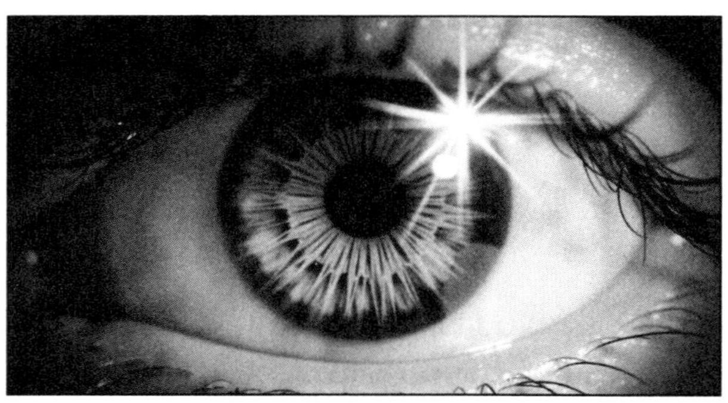

In First Corinthians 15:52, Paul wrote that all these events will occur "in a *moment*, in the twinkling of an eye, at the last trump...."

The word "moment" is interpreted from the Greek word *atomos*, which is a word that describes *an indivisible moment*, *a split second*, or *an instant*. It is where we get the word "atom." It denotes something *tiny* or *microscopic*. In this case, it pictures *a microscopic, indivisible moment of time*.

Paul then defined this tiny moment of time as the "twinkling of an eye." The word "twinkling" is translated from the Greek word *rhipe*, which is a word that describes *a twinkling, a twitch, a blink*, or *something that happens so fast it is undetectable*. One scholar notes that the speed of an *eye twitch* or *the blink of an eye* is *a tenth of a second* or 100 milliseconds.

To try to understand how fast this event will be, simply look into a mirror, and *blink*, and see how much time it takes for you to blink your own eyes. Paul used this word in First Corinthians 15:52 to reveal how *fast* these miraculous events will take place. In *a microscopic, indivisible moment of time* — like the *twinkling, twitch*, or *blink of an eye* — the bodies of the righteous dead will be raised, and those who are alive, living vibrantly in the faith, will be transformed in their bodies, and they will be caught up to meet the Lord.

Many scholars agree that the words "the twinkling of an eye" are used to signify how speedily and suddenly these events will transpire. The transformation of the bodies of the resurrected and living saints will be so quick that it will be done before one can shut his eyes and open them again. It will be, as it were, imperceptible, without the least sensation of pain — and quickly and amazingly carried out in a microscopic, nearly indivisible moment of time.

Once Again, We See 'the Trump of God' in Scripture

Exactly as he did in First Thessalonians 4:16, Paul again, in his first epistle to the Corinthian church, reiterated that this grand event will be triggered by the sound of the last "trump." In Chapter One, we looked very thoroughly at the Greek word *salpinx* — and now we find that Paul used it again in this verse. As before, it depicts *a war trumpet that boldly announces victory and the vanquishing of God's enemies at the outset of a military campaign.*

When the *salpinx* is portrayed on ancient Greek vases, it usually is pictured in the hands of a soldier who blows it to announce the commencement of war. Because this war trumpet was so famous, many writers wrote of it, including *Aristotle*, who wrote that the *salpinx* was not an instrument known for its musical qualities but as an instrument used to declare war.[1] The ancient writer *Aristides Quintilianus* wrote that the *salpinx* was blasted by a special player who blasted distinct rhythmic sounds to signal armies to move to action.[2]

As we saw in the last chapter, these menacing sounds struck terror in the hearts of the enemy as the signal of their soon demise reverberated through the atmosphere with wave after wave of the acoustic war cry. But at times, these rhythmic sounds could be understood only by some, making it impossible for an enemy to know the exact message that was being signaled. Although, again, the *salpinx* was primarily used before battle to call troops to move into military formation, ready for action.

Also as noted in the previous chapter, the *salpinx* was also used to call people to break camp and to advance onward and upward. It additionally was used at certain times to call people to gather for an assembly. As I note later on page 96, this explains why Paul told the Thessalonians, "Now we beseech you, brethren, by the coming of our Lord Jesus Christ, and by our gathering together unto him" (2 Thessalonians 2:1).

The words "gathering together" are a translation of the Greek word *episunagoge*, which means *to assemble* or *to gather together*. In Second Thessalonians 2, Paul was addressing end-time events, including the rapture of the Church. The majority of biblical scholars agree that the words "gathering together" are a rewording of what Paul wrote in First Thessalonians 4:17 about the Rapture, when all authentic Christians alive on the earth will be "caught up together" to meet the Lord in the air.

Meyer's commentary says that the words "gathering together" describe the instant in "which all believers are caught up to Christ, or gathered together to Him, to be then eternally united to Him, following the resurrection and change."[3] The Pulpit commentary states that these words refer to "those who are alive" at the time of these eschatological events.[4]

Understanding that this particular trumpet — the *salpinx* — was also used *to call for people to break camp, to assemble, and to move forward and upward*, it means that when this last trump is blasted, it will summon the bodies of the dead in Christ to be raised and those who are still alive at that time to break camp — and to gather for upward and forward movement.

When this trumpet is blasted, the bodies of the righteous dead will be raised out of their graves with newly transformed bodies that are no longer subject to the effects of wear, tear, and age. And authentic living Christians at that time will be likewise miraculously transformed as they join those who have been resurrected.

Both the dead in Christ and vibrant, authentic Christians who are alive in that moment will be transformed and freed from frailty, mortality, and corruption.

As noted in Chapter One, the blasting of the *salpinx* was additionally used in connection with a court of law. Its sound caused the guilty to shake with fear because its blast was the declaration that those charged with evil would experience judgment at the hands of the court.

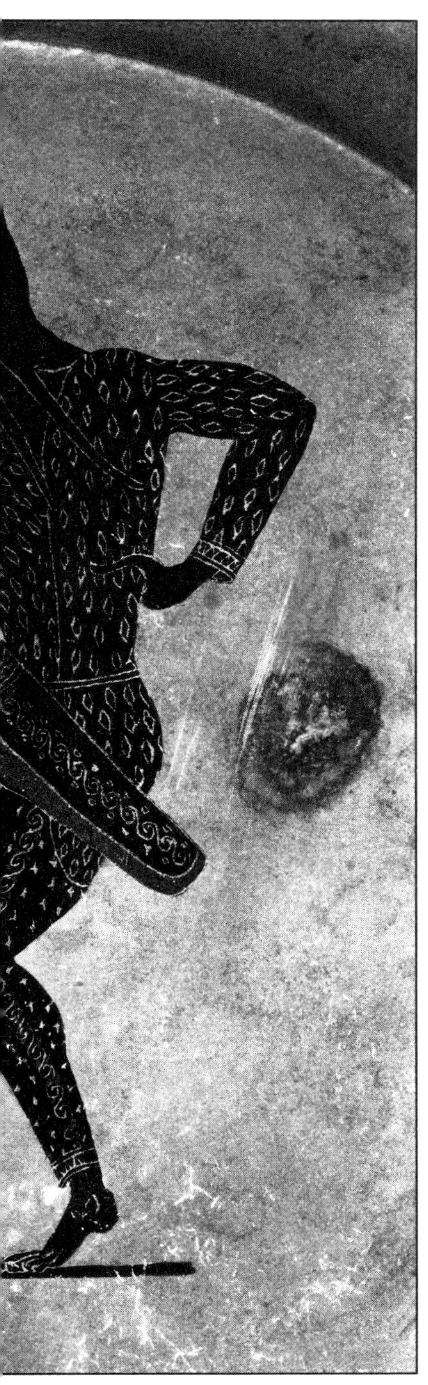

This is an illustration from an ancient plate dating to approximately 550 BC that shows a warrior blowing a *salpinx*, which is the word used in the Greek text to describe the "trump" of God in First Corinthians 15:52.

Likewise, when this last trump is blasted, it will sound the message that Heaven's court has viewed all the evidence, a verdict of guilt has been issued, and judgment will be carried out against the ungodly at the hands of Heaven's court. That judgment will be poured out on the earth as soon as the bodies of the righteous dead are resurrected and remnant believers are snatched out of the way and raptured into the air to meet the Lord.

There is debate about the word "last" in regard to this trumpet blast (*see* 1 Corinthians 15:52). But it is not needful to extrapolate meanings from this word that the verse does not clearly state. Simply, the word "last" denotes the *consummation* or the *close* of things. Indeed, when the resurrection of the dead and the rapture of the Church occurs, there will be a final blast of the trump to announce the official closure of the present age.

In that moment, what has been the Church Age will officially close. The trumpet blast will announce this closure, and the next epoch — the seven-year period known as the Tribulation — will have begun. Thus, the "last trumpet" will signal the consummation, or end, of this present age and the beginning of the Tribulation when great wrath will be poured out upon the earth.

Forgive the redundancy, but because Paul used this word "trump" in First Thessalonians 4:16 and First Corinthians 15:52, it is essential to see that in both passages, it has the same exact meaning.

I remind you again that Paul was a linguist, and he was very aware of the meaning of the word *salpinx*. If we look at this Greek word from the standpoint of how it was used in the ancient world, we can know that:

- In the moment this trumpet is blasted, it will be the blasting of a war trumpet.
- In the moment this trumpet is blasted, its deafening and invincible sound will send shivers of terror to the enemies of God in every realm, spiritual and physical.
- In the moment this trumpet is blasted, God will summon His people to break camp, advance, and move upward, which refers to the resurrection of the bodies of the righteous dead and the rapture of the living remnant of authentic Christians at that time.
- In the moment this trumpet is blasted, it will muster all of Heaven's troops to engage in the fight of the ages.
- In the moment this trumpet is blasted, it will be a declaration that this battle will be consummated in total victory.
- In the moment this trumpet is blasted, it will be a declaration that the judgments against the ungodly issued from God's court of law are about to be carried out as righteous judgment is poured out on the earth.

Paul twice used this word to tell us that when this trump blasts at the time of the resurrection of the righteous dead and the rapture of the Church, it will be a divine summoning of both the righteous dead and the living.

Isn't the faithfulness of God amazing? Not only do we possess a living hope in a living God and a risen Savior — God reveals in His Word what we can expect as the Church Age ends. And He informs us that all these events will be signaled by a trumpet blast.

And that blast will be a living proclamation that:

- the Church Age is closed.
- the Tribulation is starting.
- Heaven's court is ready to execute judgment against the ungodly.
- a grand battle with evil is about to take place.
- God's foes will be vanquished!

'The Dead Shall Be Raised Incorruptible, and We Shall Be Changed'

We studied the first part of First Corinthians 15:52, which says, "In a moment, in the twinkling of an eye, at the last trump...." Paul then added that in that moment, "...the trumpet shall sound, and the *dead* shall be raised incorruptible, and we shall be changed."

The word "dead" is the plural form of the Greek word *nekros*, which describes *a lifeless corpse* or *a cadaver* with no life left in it. In this case, Paul used this word to picture the dead bodies of those who previously died in faith. Here, he stated that believers who had gone the way of the grave will suddenly and miraculously be "raised." The word "raised" is from a form of the Greek word *egeiro,* which means *to awaken, to arise*, or *to be resurrected*, and it depicts the bodies of those who died in faith *rising up* or *being resurrected.*

Paul then jubilantly stated that they will be raised "incorruptible." This word "incorruptible" is from a form of the Greek word *aphthartos*, which refers to that which is *incapable of decay* or *incapable of suffering the effects of wear, tear, and age.* Then Paul added that the dead bodies of the righteous, in addition to those who are alive and in faith at that moment, will be "changed."

The word "changed" is interpreted from the Greek word *allagesometha*, which pictures the dead and the living being *miraculously changed.* This word means *to change, to exchange one thing for another*, or *to transform*. This teaches us that in a microscopic, indivisible moment — like the twinkling, twitch, or blink of an eye — the dead bodies of the righteous, plus those who are alive and in faith at that moment will undergo a supernatural exchange. Their mortal bodies will be *exchanged* and *transformed* into timeless, immortal, and indestructible bodies and beings!

Because all the nuances Paul used in the original Greek text are so very significant, let's see how the *Renner Interpretive Version* (*RIV*) of First Corinthians 15:52 interprets this verse.

In a moment — a split-second, indivisible atom of time, as fast as the twitch of an eye — the last trump, a war trumpet, will loudly sound to signal the closure of the age. It will also signal that the final battle, ultimate victory, and vanquishing of all God's enemies are finally about to happen. That blast will be God's way of letting everyone know that His enemies have

been judged by Heaven's court of law; that they have lost their footing and longstanding battle with Him; that judgment is about to be executed; and that He will reign victorious and supreme in total victory. And in that flash of a moment, the dead will be resurrected and will stand upright on their feet. At that exact moment, they will miraculously receive new bodies that are incapable of decay and that will never again show the effects of wear, tear, and age — timeless, immortal, indestructible bodies. And we who are still alive when all this happens will be supernaturally transformed as our old bodies are exchanged for new ones that also are incapable of decay and that will never again show the effects of wear, tear, and age. Our bodies will literally be altered, changed, miraculously modified, and transformed into timeless, immortal, indestructible bodies.

It is clear Paul taught that the dead in Christ will be resurrected — and that those who are alive and in faith at the time of the Rapture will also be miraculously transformed. In a microscopic moment — about as long as an eye twitch or the blink of an eye — the bodies of the righteous dead and the "righteous living" will be *miraculously modified*, never again to suffer the effects of wear, tear, and age.

The Corruptible Will Put On Incorruptibility

In First Corinthians 15:53, Paul furthermore stated, "For this corruptible must put on incorruption, and this mortal must put on immortality."

The word "corruptible" is a translation of the Greek word *phthartos*, the same word that Paul used in First Corinthians 15:52, which depicts *what is naturally subject to decay* or *suffering the effects of wear, tear, and age.* It portrays *that which is perishable and eventually grows old and disintegrates.*

Aging is a reality most people in our day try to circumvent. There is nothing wrong with doing all within one's power to look good as he or she ages. But the fact is that even with all the chemical and surgical treatments available to curb the effects of age, as one grows older, wrinkles eventually appear; hair may become sparse; hair color often changes; and bones and muscles can weaken and require extra attention to maintain their proper function.

There are many other age-related realities that eventually show up with age. Today cosmetic surgery is a thriving business, as people pay to surgically alter the effects of aging and even change what they don't like about their physical appearance.

In James 1:11, we are told that every person's life is like a blossoming flower that eventually shrivels and wastes away. Likewise, every person's life eventually wilts, and its lovely appearance comes to an end.

But where aging is concerned, no matter what precautions one takes with his or her eating habits or exercise routines, eventually gravity does its work, and things that once stood sturdily in place begin to sag. Although one may try to circumvent the effects of growing older, it is an inevitable fact that every person is eventually confronted with the effects of aging.

In his epistle, James likened every person's life to a blossoming flower that eventually wilts. He wrote, "For the sun is no sooner risen with a burning heat, but it withereth the grass, and the flower thereof falleth, and the grace of the fashion of it perisheth..." (James 1:11). The *RIV* of this verse reads: "For just as the scorching heat of the sun eventually shrivels and wastes away the grass of the field, a time eventually comes when every blossoming flower wilts, and its lovely appearance comes to an end."

Incorruptibility in Aging and Death

Death is another reality that people try to avoid — to the point that the words "died" and "death" have almost disappeared from many people's vernacular. Instead of referring to someone who *died*, people now generally speak of those who *passed* or *passed away*. The word "death" is so final that people try to avoid it, and it is easier to stomach using the words "passed away" than the word "dead" or "death." While it is true that every person *passes* from this life into the next — into some future eternal home — like it or not, unless Jesus comes in our lifetime to initiate the rapture of His Church, we will all physically die.

People don't like to think about aging or dying, but aging and death is something each of us ultimately face. While we hope that Jesus will return for the Church in our lifetime, if He does not, we will each get older, and a day will come when each of us will be laid in a coffin. Unless Jesus comes for the Church in our lifetime, the reality is that there will be a funeral in all our futures.

Let me tell you a story about an event in my young life that impacted me at an early age and helped me to form a serious approach to life. When I was just old enough to get a job, I'd heard about an opening at the cemetery just down the street from where my family lived. The old caretaker needed someone to mow the cemetery lawn, so I walked down to the cemetery and knocked on the door at the caretaker's residence. When he came to the door, I said, "Sir, I understand there's a job opening here. I've come to apply for that position."

The old man, who had been the caretaker for more than 40 years, looked me over and asked me a few questions. Then he told me to report to work on the following Monday. On that Monday afternoon, I started my short career at the local graveyard — my first real job. Every day after school, I quickly dashed down the hallway to put my books in my locker and then rushed across town to the cemetery to pull out the lawnmower. Then I'd push that mower over section after section of the cemetery that needed to be mowed for the day. *Five days a week, I lived and worked among the dead!*

Each day, I mowed and edged the weeds around new graves, old graves, mausoleums, and one section of the cemetery that was so old, no one could decipher any longer the inscriptions on the limestone markers. Not only did those graves hold the disintegrated remains of the dead, I noticed that over time, even the tombstones started disintegrating to the point that it was difficult to read the inscriptions.

When it was time to bury someone new in that cemetery, I helped put up the tent that loved ones stood under during gravesite rites and then later I helped take it down. I was on-site to help dig the grave, lower the casket, and fill the grave with dirt. When the flowers wilted that loved ones had placed on the graves, I was the one who gathered up the dead flowers and threw them away.

My job was to keep up the neat appearance of that cemetery, working among the dead day after day. But working there had a positive effect on my life in those formative years, as God used that time in the cemetery to make me think about the seriousness and temporal nature of life in general, as well as what kind of a difference would be made with my own life.

People generally don't like to think about aging or dying, but aging and death are something each of us ultimately faces. While we hope Jesus will return for the Church in our lifetime, if He does not, we will each continue to grow older, and a day will come when each of us, if buried, will be laid to rest in a coffin. Family and friends will come to our funeral services, the casket lid will be closed for the last time, and we will be lowered into a grave that will then get packed with dirt. Later our graves will have grass growing on top of them — and perhaps a young boy will push a lawnmower over them as a part of his job, just as I did years ago. Unless Jesus comes for the Church in our lifetimes, the reality is that there will be a funeral or some type of memorial gathering in our future.

But when Jesus descends into the lower atmosphere with a shout — and with the voice of the archangel and the trump of God — it will summon forth the dead and decaying bodies of those who died in Christ. They will be raised "incorruptible," and at the same time, those who are alive and in faith in that moment will be caught up to meet the Lord in the air. And in that transformative moment, the dead and the living will "put on *incorruption*." This is what Paul taught in First Corinthians 15:53 when he wrote, "For this corruptible must put on incorruption, and this mortal must put on immortality."

The words "put on" are an interpretation of the Greek word *enduo*, which is a word that portrays *putting on a new set of clothes* — and, specifically, clothes that are *so comfortable that one just sinks into them and feels at home*. Paul used this Greek word *enduo* to describe a divine translation that will occur in a microscopic, nearly indivisible moment — a moment so fast that it will be like the twinkling, twitch, or blink of an eye — when the bodies of the righteous dead and the righteous living will be supernaturally re-clothed with "incorruption." And not only will we be re-clothed, we will be so comfortable in our newly transformed bodies that we will comfortably sink into them as if they were tailor-made just for each of us.

In verse 53, we see the word "incorruption" is again from the Greek word *aphthartos*, which describes *that which is incapable of decay* or *that which is incapable of suffering the effects of wear, tear, and age.* Thus, whereas before we lived in mortal bodies that suffered the effects of wear, tear, age, and death, we will suddenly find ourselves reclothed with new, transformed bodies that are completely incapable of decay or of any effects of wear, tear, age, or death.

The Fleeting Nature of Mortal Life

No wonder Paul triumphantly added that this "mortal must put on immortality." The word "mortal" is a translation of the Greek word *thnetos*, which pictures human beings who are *subject to death* or who will *inevitably die*. This word depicts the fragile and temporary nature of the human body and the fleeting nature of mortal life.

James wrote about the fleeting nature of life in James 4:14 when he asked, "...For what is your life? It is even a vapour, that appeareth for a little time, and then vanisheth away."

The words "what is your life" are a translation of the Greek words *he zoe humon*. It is a definite article combined with the Greek words *zoe* and *humon*. The word *zoe* refers to *life*, but the definite article makes it *specific*. The exact life James was describing is determined in this verse by the word *humon*, which means *of yours*. So in this phrase, James was asking his readers to remember the short-term nature of *their physical life*.

In fact, James further elaborated by stating that one's physical life is but a "vapor." The word "vapour" in the *King James Version* is an interpretation of the Greek word *atmis*, which was used by Aristotle, Herodotus, and Plato, to describe *a mere breath, a short-lived mist, a puff of steam*, or *a passing vapor.*[5]

James used this word to remind his readers — and that includes each of us — that our physical lives are a mere "blip" on the screen of time. Then James added that our physical lives "appeareth" for a little time, and then vanish away. The word "appeareth" is interpreted from a form of the word *phaino*, a Greek word that means *to appear, to shine*, or *to become visible.*

It is God's intention that each of our lives brilliantly shine and make a difference in the world around us. But James stated that the time comes when each person's life passes "like a vapor," or mist. Even a long-lived life filled with fruitfulness and impact on the earth is a short glimmer in the grand context of time immemorial. And that is why James went on to say that our lives appear "for a little time." In Greek, this is interpreted from the word *oligon,* which describes whatever is *small in number.* It refers here to *a small amount of time, a small number of years,* or *something that is brief in terms of time.* Similarly, it depicts *a short period or duration of time* or simply *a little time.*

Then James further stated in James 4:14 that eventually a time comes when each of our lives "vanish away." He wrote, "...It is even a vapour, that appeareth for a little time, and *then* vanisheth away." The word "then" is interpreted from the Greek word *epeita,* which means *after that* or *thereafter.* The words "vanish away" are an interpretation of a form of the Greek word *aphanidzo,* which depicts *what once appeared, but then suddenly disappears.* This section of James 4:14 in the *RIV* says:

> **...Let me ask you...this life of yours...what is it, really? Isn't it in reality a mere breath, mist, or passing vapor that becomes visible only for a relatively brief time? And then — *poof* — it evaporates, passes from the scene, and is gone?**

But as fleeting as mortal life is, in First Corinthians 15:53 Paul declared that for those who either die in faith or are caught into the Lord's presence at the time of the Rapture, "...this corruptible must put on incorruption, and this mortal must put on immortality."

As noted previously, the word "mortal" presents the picture that human beings are *subject to death* and will *inevitably die.* It depicts the *fragile* and *temporary nature* of the human body and physical life. Thus, we find that the reason human beings are called "mortals" is that all humankind is subject to death. Like it or not, this is reality.

James stated that one's physical life is a mere breath, a short-lived mist, a puff of steam, or a passing vapor. God desires for each person to brilliantly shine and to make a difference in the world, but even a long-lived, impacting life is a short glimmer in the grand context of time immemorial.

A Glorious Immortality Will Be Our New Status

But Paul unquestionably declared there will be one generation that will never taste death! Rather than die as other generations before them died, that singular generation who is alive at the time of the resurrection of the bodies of the righteous dead and the rapture of the Church will suddenly and miraculously "put on immortality." When Paul used the words "put on," he repeated the word *enduo*, which again points to *putting on a new set of clothes*. Not only does it mean *to be clothed*, it pictures *one who is so comfortable in new clothes that he settles comfortably into them*. The use of the word *enduo* — "put on" — means that Paul twice affirms that not only will we put on immortality, but *we will settle into this new status with comfort!*

The word "immortality" describes that new status! This word is interpreted from the Greek word *athanasia*, a word that means *not subject to death* and *imperishable*. Thus, when Christ comes to resurrect the dead bodies of the righteous and rapture, or *catch away*, the Church, those Christians who are alive and living in a vibrant faith at that moment will find themselves miraculously and instantly re-clothed in transformed bodies that are no longer subject to death. *Mortality will have put on immortality!*

What Will Your Transformed Body Be Like?

I want you to understand that a core New Testament doctrine is that in this moment when Christ comes for the resurrection of the dead bodies of the righteous and for the rapture of the Church, all the perishable bodies of those who died in faith and those Christians who are alive and in faith, will be re-clothed with bodies that are incorruptible, imperishable, and eternal.

15 Points About the Resurrection When Christ Comes in the Clouds for His People

In First Corinthians 15:42-44, Paul wrote descriptively about what these transformed bodies will be like. In this text, Paul made *15 important points* about the death and resurrection of authentic believers. He wrote, "So also is the resurrection of the dead. It is sown in corruption; it is raised in incorruption: it is sown in dishonour; it is raised

The Bible teaches that the bodies of believers who die in faith are "sown" in corruption. The word "sown" pictures the sowing of seed for a future harvest. Just as a farmer plants seed with the full expectation that one day it will yield a harvest, Paul used this same imagery to say that death is not final — but when we die, one day our body will come forth again.

in glory: it is sown in weakness; it is raised in power: it is sown a natural body; it is raised a spiritual body. There is a natural body, and there is a spiritual body."

First, Paul stated in verse 42 that the bodies of believers who die in faith are "sown in corruption." The word "sown" is translated from the Greek word *speiro*, which pictures the sowing of *seed* for a future harvest. When a farmer plants seed, he does so with the full expectation that one day, it will yield a harvest. Paul used this very imagery to say that death is not final — but when we die, we are sown into the earth like seed, and one day our body will come forth again.

Second, Paul stated in that same verse that when our human bodies are planted in the grave, they are sown in "corruption." The word "corruption" is translated from the Greek word *phthora*, the same word we've seen multiple times that depicts that which is *decaying*, *death-permeated*, or *rotting*. Although we are planted as decaying and mortal bodies, Paul declared that a time is coming when the physical body of each authentic believer will be "raised in incorruption."

Third, Paul said in First Corinthians 15:42 that we will be "raised." The word "raised" is translated from the Greek word *egeiro*, which means *to awaken*, *to arise*, or *to be resurrected*, and it is a word that was used in New Testament times to depict *the arising of royalty.* Thus, Paul emphatically declared that a time is coming when each true believer who dies in faith will be resurrected — and that in the resurrection, they will come forth as the royalty God sees them to be!

Fourth, Paul stated in First Corinthians 15:42 that when the bodies of those who died in faith arise in the resurrection, they will come forth in "incorruption." The word "incorruption" is interpreted from the Greek word *aphtharsia*, which describes that which is *incapable of decay* or *incapable of suffering the effects of wear, tear, age, or death.* Herein, Scripture teaches that although a believer is sown in a decayable condition, when his or her body is raised, it will be raised in a new form that is incapable of decay or the effects of wear, tear, or age — never to experience death again.

Fifth, Paul wrote in First Corinthians 15:43 that those who die in faith are "sown in dishonor," as are all corpses of the living who die and pass from this life. Again, Paul used the word "sown" referring to the *righteous dead* to denote the planting of *seed* for a future harvest. The use of the word *speiro* again and again in this passage is intended to remind us that we will not remain in the condition in which we were buried — but as a seed sown into the ground eventually emerges in a different form, each authentic believer will emerge from the grave gloriously transformed in the resurrection.

Sixth, Paul also stated in First Corinthians 15:43 that when the human body is buried, or sown, it is done so in "dishonor." The word "dishonor" is interpreted from the Greek word *atimia*, a word that pictures that which is *dishonorable.* The fact is, as marvelously as we are made in the image of God, the human body in death becomes a heap of human decay.

Seventh, Paul declared again in First Corinthians 15:43 that the decayed human bodies of true believers will be "raised." The word "raised" is translated from the Greek word *egeiro*, which means *to awaken*, *to arise*, or *to be resurrected*, and it is a word that was used in New Testament times to also depict *the arising of royalty.* Herein, Paul repeated that authentic believers will emerge to a new royal status in the resurrection. That is why he went on to say we will be raised in "glory." The word "glory" is translated from *doxa*, a word that pictures that which is *glorious, luminous, and resplendent,* and it is the same word used in Scripture to describe *the glory of God.* Thus, according to Paul, in our newly resurrected, royal status, our bodies will be raised in and by God's glory as *glorious, luminous*, and *resplendent!*

Eighth, Paul then added that the bodies of those who died in faith are also "sown in weakness." Again, he used the word "sown" to picture the planting of *seed* that is placed into the ground with the hope of a future harvest. It is clear that Paul's repeated use of this word "sown" was intended to instill in us the truth that the grave is not the final home of a believer's body. At the time of Paul's writing, this message would have been powerful for so many believers to hear who were facing persecution and death on account of their faith. Over and over, Paul was telling them that in death, they were planted like seed — but a time is coming when they will emerge as glorious!

Ninth, after Paul again emphasized the body of a believer who dies as being sown, he stated that each person who dies is sown "in *weakness*." Paul used the Greek word *astheneia* to picture *fragility* or *weakness* of every kind. Paul's words remind us all that even at his best, man is *fragile, temporal, and weak.*

Tenth, after Paul stated that the bodies of those who die in faith will be *sown*, he then declared they will be "raised." Again, Paul used the Greek word *egeiro* for this word. It means *to awaken, to arise*, or *to be resurrected.* This was also a word used in early New Testament times to depict *the arising of royalty.* On the day of the resurrection, the dead bodies of the righteous will supernaturally emerge from their burial places as the royalty God knows them to be!

Eleventh, Paul said that although the bodies of believers were sown or buried as fragile, temporal, and weak human beings, they will be raised in "power." The word "power" is interpreted from the Greek word *dunamis*, a word that always denotes *explosive, superhuman power that comes with enormous energy and produces phenomenal, extraordinary, and unparalleled results.* It depicts *mighty deeds* that are *impressive, incomparable, and beyond human ability to perform.* It is also the New Testament word most often associated with *miraculous power* or *miraculous manifestations.* By using this word *dunamis*, Paul made it clear that God's *miraculous power* will be the source of our resurrection, transformation, and glorious, luminous, and resplendent royal status and state!

In fact, the word *dunamis* is the very word used in Ephesians 1:19 and 20 to describe the *explosive power* that raised Christ Himself from the dead. In that passage, Paul wrote, "And what is the exceeding greatness of his *power* to us-ward who believe...which he wrought in Christ, when he raised him from the dead…." Thus, just as the explosive power of God was detonated to raise Christ from death as incorruptible, that same *dunamis* power will be unleashed in our dead bodies so that we, too, rise from the dead incorruptible!

Twelfth, Paul added in First Corinthians 15:44 that those who died in faith are "*sown* a natural body." A final time in this passage, Paul used the word "sown" to remind us that we who die before the time of the Rapture will not remain in the condition in which we were buried.

Thirteenth, Paul stated that at the time of death, we are "sown a *natural* body." The word "natural" is translated from the Greek word *psuchikos*, which pictures what is *natural* as opposed to what is *spiritual.* Even the best among men are natural, physical, mortal beings — thus the reason every person's physical life eventually comes to an end.

Fourteenth, however, Paul stated that in the resurrection we will be "*raised* a spiritual body." Again, "raised" is interpreted from the Greek word *egeiro*, which means *to awaken, to arise*, or *to be resurrected*, and it was also used in early New Testament times to depict *the arising of royalty.* Over and over, Paul repeated the Greek word *egeiro* to awaken us to the fact that even if we die, death in our body is a temporal status or condition, for a time is coming when each authentic believer's body will be summoned forth from the grave and will arise as royalty in the eyes of God.

Fifteenth, Paul said in First Corinthians 15:44 that although we were sown in death as a natural body, we will come forth with a *spiritual* body. The word "spiritual" is interpreted from the Greek word *pneumatikos*, a word that describes what is *spiritual* as opposed to what is *natural*. Just as the natural body was buried with all the characteristics of a dead human body, we will rise in the resurrection with all the characteristics that accompany a *spiritual* body that will never experience death again!

God's power will be released to transform the bodies of all authentic believers. In one moment, the dead bodies of the righteous and those who are alive and are raptured will permanently change their outward appearance as dead bodies and living bodies will be re-clothed with new glorious bodies.

What Are the Characteristics of a Spiritual Body?

To understand the characteristics of the resurrected spiritual body of a believer, we must turn to Philippians 3:20 and 21, where Paul wrote, "For our conversation is in heaven; from whence also we look for the Saviour, the Lord Jesus Christ: who shall *change* our *vile* body, that it may be *fashioned like* unto his glorious body, according to the working whereby he is able even to *subdue* all things unto himself."

Notice the four italicized words or phrases in the passage: *change*, *vile*, *fashioned like*, and *subdue*.

The word "change" in this passage is interpreted from the Greek word *metaschematidzo*, a word that means *to completely alter*, *to change*, or *to be physically transfigured*. This word is used once in First Corinthians 4:6, *three times* in Second Corinthians 11:13-15, and here in Philippians 2:21. In each instance, it depicts an outward form that is *adapted from its original condition* and is so *transformed* that it takes on an entirely new appearance.

In the Greek and Roman world, this word was used to picture the changing of costumes for the theatrical stage. In one moment, an actor on the stage appeared in one form, but with a costume change, he would reappear in a completely different costume. Although this was used theatrically to describe *the superficial changing of an actor's costume*, Paul used this word to describe *a permanent transformation* that will occur as the power of God transforms the bodies of all authentic believers. In one moment, the dead bodies of the righteous and those who are alive and are raptured will permanently change their outward costumes. Dead bodies and living bodies will be exchanged as God re-clothes them with new glorious bodies.

Looking again at the passage in Philippians 3:20 and 21, we read, "...Our conversation is in heaven; from whence also we look for the Saviour, the Lord Jesus Christ: who shall *change* our *vile* body, that it may be *fashioned like* unto his glorious body, according to the working whereby he is able even to *subdue* all things unto himself."

After "change," the next word I want to emphasize is the word "vile." It is interpreted from a form of the Greek word *tapeinosis*, a word that pictures that which is *base, humble, humiliated*, or *lowly*. Although the human body is marvelously made in the image of God, in its present state, its temporal nature is *base* and *lowly*.

This Greek word *tapeinosis* is not generally a positive word. In the Greek and Roman world where people honored greatness, this word was not viewed as a virtue, and it was associated with *weakness* and *shame*. Examples of this word can be found in Luke 1:48, Acts 8:33, James 1:10, and here in Philippians 3:21 — and in each instance, it portrays that which is *base, humble*, or *lowly* in the eyes of man. And in this context, this is the picture of the human body that in death, Jesus will *change*. Not only will we be raised, or resurrected, but our status will be changed from merely human and *base* to one that reflects His glory.

Next, the words "fashioned like" are interpreted from a form of the Greek word *summorphos*, a word that means *being conformed to* or *precisely sharing the same form*. Paul used this word to declare that in the resurrection of the righteous dead and the rapture of the Church, those who were raised and raptured will *share exactly the same type of body* that Jesus possessed after He was raised from the dead. This word is also used in Romans 8:29 where Paul likewise declared that we are predestinated to be "conformed" to the image of Jesus.

Last, the word "subdue" is interpreted from a form of the Greek word *hupotasso*, which is a compound of the word *hupo* and *tasso.* The word *hupo* means *under*, and the word *tasso* was originally a military term meaning *to fall in line.* In the Greek and Roman world, the word *tasso* was commonly used to denote *the arrangement of troops.* But when these two words are compounded to form the word *hupotasso*, it conveys here the powerful image of *one becoming submissive to a higher authority*, and, hence, *one who falls in line.* By using this word, Paul triumphantly stated that at the time of the resurrection of the righteous dead and the rapture of the Church, the dead bodies of the righteous and those vibrantly alive in Christ at that moment will be subjected to a divine power that causes their bodies to *submit to* and *fall in line* with God's transformative power.

When the words "change," "vile," "fashioned like," and "subdue" are taken together in this whole text, it tells us that in the moment the dead in Christ are resurrected and the alive in Christ are raptured, their *base, lowly, mortal* bodies will be *changed.* Like an actor who changes costumes, God will re-clothe us with supernaturally transformed bodies that are exactly fashioned like Jesus' resurrected body. In a nearly indivisible moment of time — like the twinkling, twitch, or blink of an eye — God's *dunamis* power will be released and the bodies of the dead and the living will *fall in line* and *submit* to that glorious power that will *instantaneously transform* them to be like Jesus in His glorious, resurrected state.

What Is Jesus' Resurrected, Glorified Body Like?

In the gospels, we discover explicit examples of what Jesus' resurrected, glorified body was like after He was raised from the dead and ascended to the Father.

In His resurrected body, Jesus' physical appearance was so changed that the disciples did not quickly recognize Him.

On the day of the resurrection, Luke 24:13-30 tells us that two of the apostles were walking to Emmaeus and Jesus joined them. On that long walk, He spent time fellowshipping and sharing scriptures with them. But they did not recognize it was the Lord *until* He broke bread and prayed. Luke 24:31 tells us that in that exact moment, their eyes were *opened*, and that is when they realized it was *Jesus.* After knowing Jesus so well, it is nearly unthinkable that they did not immediately recognize Him, but this shows how transformed His appearance was after His resurrection.

On the road to Emmaus, Jesus spent time fellowshipping and sharing with two disciples, but they did not recognize it was the Lord until He broke bread and prayed. This shows how transformed His appearance was after His resurrection.

John 21:1 also tells us, "After these things Jesus shewed himself again to the disciples at the sea of Tiberias." But, again, Jesus was not quickly recognized. Verses 4-11 read:

> **But when the morning was now come, Jesus stood on the shore: but the disciples knew not that it was Jesus. Then Jesus saith unto them, Children, have ye any meat? They answered him, No. And he said unto them, Cast the net on the right side of the ship, and ye shall find. They cast therefore, and now they were not able to draw it for the multitude of fishes.**
>
> **Therefore that disciple whom Jesus loved saith unto Peter, It is the Lord. Now when Simon Peter heard that it was the Lord, he girt *his* fisher's coat *unto him*, (for he was naked,) and did cast himself into the sea. And the other disciples came in a little ship; (for they were not far from land, but as it were two hundred cubits,) dragging the net with fishes.**
>
> **As soon then as they were come to land, they saw a fire of coals there, and fish laid thereon, and bread. Jesus saith unto them, Bring of the fish which ye have now caught. Simon Peter went up, and drew the net to land full of great fishes, an hundred and fifty and three: and for all there were so many, yet was not the net broken.**

According to John 21:12, Jesus invited the disciples to come and dine with Him, and by this time, they realized it was the Lord. But in His resurrected, glorified outward form, Jesus was so transformed that He did not look the same as He had previously looked to them.

After His resurrection, the disciples gave Jesus a piece of a broiled fish, and He took it and ate it in front of them. Thus, we see that Jesus, in His resurrected and glorified body, was able to eat.

In His resurrected body, Jesus was able to eat.

We saw earlier that Jesus joined the disciples at the shore on the Sea of Tiberias, which is another name for the Sea of Galilee. After a miraculous catch of fish, Jesus said to them, "...Come and dine" (John 21:12). This means that in His resurrected, glorified body, Jesus was able to eat. In Luke 22:15 and 16, Jesus had previously told them, "...With desire I have desired to eat this passover with you before I suffer: for I say unto you, I will not any more eat thereof, until it be fulfilled in the kingdom of God."

The mere fact that Jesus offered to dine with them means the Kingdom of God at this time had already come. But the point here is that in His resurrected, glorious body, Jesus was able to eat with His disciples. Luke 24:42-43 also tells us that after Jesus told His disciples to handle His resurrected and glorified body, they "...gave him a piece of a broiled fish, and of an honeycomb...." The rest of that passage says, "...And he took it, and did eat before them." In Luke 22 and 24, we see that Jesus, in His resurrected and glorified body, was able to eat.

But we must not forget the Bible teaches that the resurrected and those who are raptured will be transported to Heaven to be seated at Christ's table for the "Marriage Supper of the Lamb" (*see* Revelation 19:9). The word "supper" is interpreted from *deipnon,* a Greek word that pictures *a lavish banquet.* This is a time during which the saints will share *food.* Those who participate in this banquet will be in their resurrected or glorified bodies — so we see again that even in a resurrected and glorified body, one can and will eat.

In His resurrected body, Jesus passed through solid matter into the room where the disciples were gathered. Thus, in His resurrected and glorified body, Jesus was able to supernaturally pass through solid matter into another room that was sealed tight.

In His resurrected body, Jesus was able to pass through solid matter.

In John 20:19, we read, "Then the same day at evening, being the first day of the week, when the doors were shut where the disciples were assembled for fear of the Jews...." The words "doors" and "shut" are important in this text. Notice, first, the word "doors" is plural. In Greek and Roman times, homes had *outer doors* and *inner doors* to ensure safety, and in keeping with houses at that time, this particular place had both an *outer door* and an *inner door.* In addition, the word "shut" is interpreted from a form of the Greek word *kleio*, a word that means *to lock tightly*.

But even though both doors were solidly locked, John 20:19 goes on to say that Jesus "...stood in the midst...." The word "midst" is from the Greek word *mesos*, which means *right in the very middle.* Without ever opening a door, in His resurrected and glorified body, Jesus was able to pass through the walls and doors of that room to appear in the very midst of the disciples.

According to Luke 24:36, several days later, when the disciples were behind closed doors, "...Jesus himself stood in the midst of them...." The word "midst" is again a translation of the word *mesos*, which means He suddenly appeared right in the *very middle* of them. Thus, in His resurrected and glorified body, Jesus was able to supernaturally pass through solid matter into another room that was sealed tight.

After His resurrection, Jesus allowed His disciples to handle and touch His hands and feet. Thus, in His resurrected, glorified body, Jesus could be handled and touched.

In His resurrected body, Jesus was capable of being handled and touched.

Luke 24:36 tells us that Jesus again passed through solid matter and appeared in the room where the disciples were gathered behind locked doors. The door was locked, so at first, the apostles were terrified by His presence and thought perhaps they were seeing a spirit (*see* Luke 24:37). But to prove to them that it was really Him in His resurrected form, Jesus pleaded with them to reach out and handle him. In Luke 24:39, we read that Jesus said, "Behold my hands and my feet, that it is I myself: handle me, and see; for a spirit hath not flesh and bones, as ye see me have."

The word "handle" is interpreted from the Greek word *pselaphao*, which means *to handle, to squeeze*, or *to touch*. One scholar notes that in the ancient world, *touching* was a means of verifying the authenticity of objects or persons. In this passage, Jesus asked them to touch His body to verify it was really Him and not a spirit.

Luke 24:40 then goes on to say, "And when he had thus spoken, he *shewed* them his hands and his feet." The word "shewed" is an interpretation of a form of the word *deiknuo*, a word that means *to demonstrate*, *to exhibit*, or *to put on full display*. This word means that Jesus literally raised His hands toward them so the disciples could touch them. Then He showed them His feet so they could be touched. Jesus allowed His disciples to handle and touch Him in this event. Thus, Jesus, in His resurrected, glorified body, could be handled and touched.

In His resurrected body, Jesus could appear and vanish. Thus, we know that in His resurrected, glorified body, Jesus was able to appear and disappear as needed.

In His resurrected body, Jesus was able to appear and disappear.

Luke 24:30-31 tells us, "And it came to pass, as he sat at meat with them, he took bread, and blessed it, and brake, and gave to them. And their eyes were opened, and they knew him; and he *vanished* out of their sight."

The word "vanished" is an interpretation of the Greek word *aphantos*, which means *to disappear* or *to vanish*. Jesus appeared to them near the sea but then *disappeared* or *vanished* right before their eyes. Thus, we know that in His resurrected, glorified body, Jesus was able to appear and disappear as needed.

In His resurrected body, Jesus appeared to the two disciples as they walked to Emmaus and then reappeared a great distance away in an upper room where the disciples were gathered. Thus, Jesus was able to supernaturally travel great distances very quickly.

In His resurrected body, Jesus could supernaturally travel vast distances.

Luke 24:13-36 tells us that in a single day Jesus appeared in multiple locations. Those verses begin by telling us, "And, behold, two of them went that same day to a village called Emmaus, which was from Jerusalem about threescore furlongs. And they talked together of all these things which had happened.

"And it came to pass, that, while they communed together and reasoned, Jesus himself drew near, and went with them. But their eyes were holden that they should not know him...and their eyes were opened, and they knew him; and he vanished out of their sight.... And they rose up the same hour, and returned to Jerusalem, and found the eleven gathered together, and them that were with them, saying, The Lord is risen indeed...and as they thus spake, Jesus himself stood in the midst of them...."

In this one day, Jesus appeared to two disciples as they walked to Emmaus and then reappeared a great distance away in an upper room where the eleven disciples were gathered. This clearly demonstrates that in His resurrected and glorified body, Jesus was able to supernaturally travel great distances very quickly.

In His resurrected body, Jesus ascended and descended back to the earth. Thus, we know that in His resurrected, glorified body, Jesus could ascend and descend from Heaven to Earth as needed.

In His resurrected body, Jesus could ascend to Heaven and descend back to Earth.

When Jesus spoke to Mary Magdalene in the Garden on the morning of the resurrection, she reached out to touch Him, and Jesus told her, "Touch me not; for I am not yet *ascended* to my Father: but go to my brethren, and say unto them, I ascend unto my Father, and your Father; and to my God, and your God" (John 20:17).

However, it was later that same evening that Jesus passed through solid matter into the room where the disciples were hiding, and Jesus told them, "Behold my hands and my feet, that it is I myself: handle me..." (Luke 24:39).

Scholars conclude from this that between the morning when He told Mary Magdalene not to touch Him, and the evening when Jesus urged the disciples to handle Him, He *ascended* to the Father and *descended* back to the earth. This shows that in His resurrected, glorified body, Jesus could ascend and descend from Heaven to Earth as needed.

In Acts 1:9, the Bible says, "While they [the disciples] beheld, he was taken up; and a cloud received him out of their sight." This is another instance that shows Jesus, in His resurrected and glorified body, was able to ascend to Heaven. The limited restraints of a natural body were removed, and in His resurrected, glorified body, Jesus could freely ascend and descend between Heaven and Earth.

Keep in mind that in Philippians 3:21, Paul said Christ will "change our vile body, that it may be fashioned like unto his glorious body, according to the working whereby he is able even to subdue all things unto himself." Based on what we have gleaned from Scripture about Jesus' resurrected and glorified body, this means when the bodies of the dead in Christ are raised and those who are alive and in faith are raptured, their transformed and glorified bodies will:

- Be completely different, just as Christ's resurrected, glorified body had been changed.
- Be able to eat, just as Christ ate in His resurrected, glorified body.
- Be able to pass through solid matter, just as Christ did in His resurrected, glorified body.
- Be able to appear and disappear, just as Christ's did in His resurrected, glorified body.
- Be able to travel vast distances, just as Christ traveled in His resurrected, glorified body.
- Be able to travel through different realms (i.e, Heaven to Earth), as needed, just as Christ did in His resurrected, glorified body.

In the resurrection and the rapture of the Church, those whose bodies are raised from the dead and those who are supernaturally snatched away in the Rapture will forever be freed from corruption and thusly liberated from previous physical limitations. This implies we will be so transformed that we will be able to travel to and fro in our new glorified bodies — even at great distances and speed — precisely as Jesus did after His resurrection.

Friend, if you consider Paul's teaching in First Thessalonians 4:15-17 and in First Corinthians 15:51-53, where he described the resurrection of the dead in Christ and the rapture of the Church, we find that these are core Bible doctrines that are undeniable.

So after studying this topic from First Corinthians 15:51-53 of the resurrection of the "righteous dead" and the rapture of the Church, *are YOU listening for the shout, the voice of the archangel, and the blast of the trumpet?*

QUESTIONS TO PONDER

1. This chapter explains many hidden things of the Kingdom of God that were not revealed until the time of the New Testament. Of the eight "mysteries" that were not known in the Old Testament, which one was most surprising to you to discover?

2. One of the mysteries that has been revealed is the rapture of the Church. And when the Church is raptured, every believer will be given a transformed, resurrected body in the "twinkling of an eye" (*see* 1 Corinthians 15:52). In a moment, the corruptible will be made *incorruptible*, and every believer will be united with Jesus in the air. It's possible that the Rapture is a familiar topic to you, but to the early believers who heard Paul say these words, this was brand new information. What impact do you think this knowledge would have had on the Early Church?

3. Have you ever been in a situation where a trumpet was used as a "call to action" or to signal something important was happening? If so, how were you stirred or affected upon hearing that sound?

4. In this chapter, Rick mentions again that the salpinx will be used to declare the Church Age is closed, the Tribulation is starting, Heaven's court is ready to execute judgment against the ungodly, and a grand battle with evil is about to commence, in which God's foes will finally be vanquished. What kind of response do you think the powers of darkness will have when they hear this trumpet's blast?

5. People generally don't like to think about death, but it's something each of us will ultimately face. While we hope Jesus will return for the Church in our lifetime, if He does not, a day will come when each of us, if buried, will be laid to rest in a coffin. Have you ever pondered what your funeral might be like or considered how you would want to be remembered? If so, how has this awareness shaped the choices you make or the way you live your life today?

6. We live in a world that is obsessed with staying young and keeping a youthful appearance. Although many people may try to slow down the physical effects of

growing older, it is inevitable that all of us will have to confront the realities of aging in some way. Does the thought of your outward appearance changing as you age trouble you? Read First Corinthians 15:51-54 and First Peter 1:23-25. As a born-again believer, how do these passages bring comfort to you regarding the topic of aging?

7. Death serves as a powerful reminder of our fleeting time on the earth. James stated that a time comes when each person's life passes "like a vapor," or mist. With this in mind, take a moment to reflect on your current path. Are there areas of your life that you feel called to change or refine? How can you embrace the urgency of life in a way that aligns with your values?

8. Which characteristic of our future, resurrected bodies is most interesting to you? Does the thought of being able to bypass some natural laws in your new body bring more clarity to the truth that you are a spirit being (*see* Hebrews 4:12; 1 Thessalonians 5:23)?

9. As we read and study the Bible, the Holy Spirit will give us insight into what the Word of God says. Read the 15 points about the resurrection found in this chapter again. Do any of these descriptions help you better understand other spiritual truths found in the Word of God? If so, what are they?

10. God calls each of us to shine brilliantly and make a lasting impact in the world around us. In what small or significant ways can you intentionally brighten someone's day or offer support? How can you help others experience God's love and embrace His grace today?

Second Thessalonians 2:1-8

Now we beseech you, brethren, by the coming of our Lord Jesus Christ, and by our gathering together unto him, that ye be not soon shaken in mind, or be troubled, neither by spirit, nor by word, nor by letter as from us, as that the day of Christ is at hand. Let no man deceive you by any means: for that day shall not come, except there come a falling away first, and that man of sin be revealed, the son of perdition; who opposeth and exalteth himself above all that is called God, or that is worshipped; so that he as God sitteth in the temple of God, shewing himself that he is God. Remember ye not, that, when I was yet with you, I told you these things? And now ye know what withholdeth that he might be revealed in his time. For the mystery of iniquity doth already work: only he who now letteth will let, until he be taken out of the way. And then shall that Wicked be revealed, whom the Lord shall consume with the spirit of his mouth, and shall destroy with the brightness of his coming.

CHAPTER THREE

WHEN WILL THE ANTICHRIST MAKE HIS APPEARANCE AND WHO IS THE GREAT RESTRAINER HOLDING HIM BACK?

For the mystery of iniquity doth already work: only he who now letteth will let, until he be taken out of the way.

— 2 Thessalonians 2:7

In Second Thessalonians 2:5, the apostle Paul addressed end-time events and included the rapture of the Church in his writing. In an interrogative manner, he began his discourse to the Thessalonians, saying, "Remember ye not, that, when I was yet with you, I told you these things?"

It is amazing to me that Paul addressed end-time events — including the rapture of the Church — with the Thessalonians because he was with them for only a short period of time. But even with that very short time frame, he clearly believed understanding these events was important enough that he needed to include it in the foundational teachings he shared with those new believers. Today some think this subject is not really so important, but if Paul found end-time events and the Rapture so important that he used part of his short time with the Thessalonian believers to establish them in these truths, surely we should treat these topics with importance as well.

In Second Thessalonians 2:1, Paul began his passage on end-time events and the rapture of the Church, "Now we beseech you, brethren, by the coming of our Lord Jesus Christ, and by our *gathering* together unto him...."

Notice that I have italicized the word "gathering" in this verse. The reason I draw attention to it is, I want to re-emphasize that this word "gathering" is a reference to God's trumpet call for His people to break camp, advance, and move forward and upward. I'm talking about the righteous who have died and will be raised and "gathered" — and the vibrant saints who are living and will be raptured and "gathered." And all this will take place at the sounding of the *salpinx* — the *war trumpet* — that Paul wrote will be blasted when Christ comes to resurrect the "righteous dead" and rapture, or catch away, the "righteous living" (*see* First Thessalonians 4:15-18).

I'll write more about the word "gathering" in the following paragraphs. But that Paul would begin this text in Second Thessalonians 2 in this way is important because it lays a foundation for the rest of this chapter, which discusses in greater detail the *catching away* of the Church that will occur at the very end of this age.

When the *salpinx* was blasted, it signaled the moment for troops to break camp and prepare to move upward and onward, and it was used regularly for the public calling of assemblies and gatherings.

Pictured here is an illustration of the apostle Paul writing one of his epistles. Paul wrote Second Thessalonians to bring correction to an upsetting false teaching being circulated that the Rapture had already occurred, that believers had missed it, and that the day of the Lord — or the Tribulation — had begun.

The Backstory That Prompted Paul To Write About the Rapture in This Epistle

From the context of Paul's writings in Second Thessalonians, we know that someone in the church there had been falsely stating that the rapture of the Church had already occurred. As you can imagine, the reaction to this error that had begun to circulate was disquieting and upsetting to that local congregation.

In response to this wrong teaching that had caused quite a stir in the church, Paul began addressing this error, saying, "Now we *beseech* you, brethren, *by the coming of our Lord* Jesus Christ, and by our *gathering* together unto him" (Second Thessalonians 2:1). In this verse, Paul set the tone for what he was about to say about end-time events and the rapture of the Church. So we need to start here and understand the importance of who you *should* and *should not* listen to in regard to end-time teaching.

The word "beseech" is interpreted from the Greek word *erotao*, a word that portrays *asking with urgency* and *making the strongest request possible*. By using this word, Paul, at least figuratively, was pleading with the Thessalonian believers to hear what he was saying to them. He was coming right alongside them, as close as he could get, to plead with them to hear him and to respond accordingly to what he was about to communicate. As a senior leader in the church, he was making a heartfelt, urgent appeal.

Again, Second Thessalonians 2:1 says, "Now we *beseech* you, brethren, *by the coming of our Lord* Jesus Christ, and by our *gathering* together unto him." The next phrase I want you to notice contains the words "by the coming of the Lord." The word "coming" is interpreted from the Greek word *parousia*, which is a technical expression for *the royal visit of a king or emperor* or *the arrival of one who alone has the authority and power to deal with a situation and put things in correct order.*

Some state that the word *parousia* only describes the Second Coming (or Second Advent) of Christ at the end of the Great Tribulation — another separate, profound event on God's prophetic timeline that we read about in Scripture (*see* Daniel 7:13-14; Jude 14-15). But a survey of this word's use in the New Testament shows it was used both to describe the coming of Christ at the time of the Rapture *and* His Second Coming *after* the Rapture and the Great Tribulation.

Here in Second Thessalonians 2:1, Paul used the word *parousia* to describe the moment when Christ will descend into the lower atmosphere to resurrect the dead bodies of the righteous and to *catch away*, or rapture, the Church — the event that will trigger the Tribulation that immediately follows.

Because the word *parousia* was also a technical term used to describe the royal visit or arrival of a king or emperor or of one who alone had the authority and power to deal with a situation and put things in order, it also lets us know that when Jesus comes in this particular prophetic moment, He will begin to put forth His power to deal with the wrongs in the world and to put things in order.

Part of the righting of wrongs and setting things straight will occur as judgment is poured out on the ungodly and wicked during the seven-year Tribulation period. But here in Second Thessalonians, Paul returned to what he had written earlier about the rapture of the Church in First Thessalonians 4:17.

The word "gathering" in Second Thessalonians 2:1 is a translation of the Greek word *episunagoge*, and it means *a gathering together*. It is also interestingly found in the second volume of the *Book of Maccabees*, in which it refers to the moment in the future when

When Christ comes for the resurrection of the dead bodies of the righteous and to rapture the Church, He will begin to put forth His power to deal with the wrongs in the world and to put things in order, and a trumpet blast will call upon God's people to break camp and prepare to move forward and upward.

God will *finally gather* His people for Himself. (The *Book of Maccabees* is a series of historical accounts of Jewish persecution in the First Century BC. It is contained in some versions of the *Septuagint* as well as Jerome's *Vulgate*, but it is not canonical Scripture.)

What about this "gathering"? As we have seen in the two previous chapters of this book, at the end of this present age when Christ comes for the resurrection of the dead bodies of the righteous and to rapture the Church, there will be a blasting sound of a war trump to announce Christ is initiating war with evil, but that war trumpet will also be a signal for God's people to break camp and prepare to move forward and upward. In this verse, Paul used the word "gathering" (*episunagoge*) to describe the moment when the Lord will *quickly gather* or *collect* His people together for Himself at the end of the age or to describe the rapture of the Church.

All these words — "beseech," "by the coming of the Lord," and "gathering" — are very important, so let's look at how the *Renner Interpretive Version* (*RIV*) interprets this foundational verse.

RIV OF SECOND THESSALONIANS 2:1

Brothers, I make this urgent, heartfelt request to you today, earnestly and sincerely pleading with you from the bottom of my heart to hear what I'm telling you and to do exactly as I say. The coming of the Lord Jesus Christ is very near. I'm talking about that moment when Jesus will finally gather us together for Himself. And in that moment, He will release power to begin to deal with the situation at hand in the world and to put all things in order.

Then in verse 2, Paul added, "That ye be not *soon shaken* in *mind*, or be *troubled*, neither by *spirit*, nor by *word*, nor by letter as from us, as that the day of Christ is at hand." This verse is filled with important insight, so we will unpack it to understand every nuance of the words therein.

The words "soon shaken" are interpreted from the Greek words *tacheos* and *saleuo*. The word *tacheos* means *quickly*, as something that happens *very fast*, and the word *saleuo* means *to shake*, *to waver*, *to totter*, or *to be moved*. The tense of these words points to events that cause *shock* or *alarm*. It refers to an occurrence (or repeated occurrences) so unexpected that it results in shock or distress that has the potential to throw people into a state of dismay.

But Paul urged his readers not to be soon shaken in "mind." The word "mind" is from a form of *nous*, which is a Greek word that describes everything in the realm of the *intellect*, including one's *will, emotions, and ability to think, reason, and decide*. Whoever or whatever controls a person's mind ultimately has the power to dictate the affairs and outcome of that person's life.

Paul additionally told his readers not to be "troubled, neither by spirit, nor by word, nor by letter…as that the day of Christ is at hand." The word "troubled" is an interpretation of the Greek word *throeo*, which indicates an *inward fright* that causes a person to be filled with *anxiety*, *fear*, or *worry*. Even more, the Greek tense importantly points to *an ongoing state of anxiety, fear, and worry* that results from outward events that keep occurring again and again. The Greek tense suggests events that are occurring one on top of the next, with no pause between them, with the cumulative effect of causing one to be shocked, debilitated, and nerve-racked. The Greek word *throeo* even conveys the idea of one who is *jumpy* or *nervous*, and it pictures people who are in *a state of panic*.

The words "neither by spirit, nor by word, nor by letter as from us" are also very important in Second Thessalonians 2:2. The word "spirit" is a translation of the Greek word *pneumatos*, which literally means *spirit*. However, Paul used it here to refer to *spiritual experiences* or *spiritual utterances* that are out of sync with the revealed Word of God. It pictures *ecstatic utterances*, and Paul used it here to refer to ***strange utterances, weird revelations***, or *euphoric proclamations* that have no root in sound doctrine and that produce the negative effect of spiritually upsetting the church.

Paul added the instruction that his readers are not to be troubled by "word," which is from a form of *logos* simply meaning *word*. But here it describes *a message* that is being communicated. Besides warning against people who make weird spiritual proclamations and off-the-wall utterances, Paul additionally warned the Thessalonians about those who teach unbalanced messages about the end-times that throw people off-balance and into confusion spiritually. This serves as a strong reminder to believers in every generation that we must be careful about what we hear and who we are listening to — and to be sure we are receiving from sound spiritual sources.

The Christian world is exposed to all kinds of Christian celebrities and personalities in a wide variety of platforms. But never forget that we have to stay alert about anything wrong that tries to enter into our personal spaces. We must keep our heads on straight, use our minds, and not give place to strange utterances, weird revelations, euphoric proclamations, or off-base teachings that cause people to be fearful.

Know Who's Speaking Into Your Life

Because of advances made in technology, the Christian world today is exposed to all kinds of Christian personalities and a wide array of teaching. As a Christian broadcaster myself, I seek to extend my voice through various media platforms. I am thankful for the vast range of Christian television programs that are available today. However, I must tell you that I personally guard my home very cautiously and am careful about which Christian TV programs are allowed into our personal space.

In First Thessalonians 5:12, Paul wrote, "And we beseech you, brethren, to know them which labour among you…." The word "know" in this verse is a translation of the Greek word *eido*, which means *to inspect, to know*, or *to perceive.* Paul used this word to inform believers they have a responsibility to know something about those who are ministering to them. In fact, the word "beseech" is emphatic and informs us that God *commands* you to know those who minister to you.

I ask you, what do you really know about those voices you've allowed to speak into your life through your TV, computer, or other devices? Who are they? Do you know where they stand on matters that are non-negotiable in the Word of God and should therefore be non-negotiable to you? Are you allowing someone who is safe to speak into your spiritual life, or are you permitting someone who is spiritually corrupted to influence you? God has made you the guardian of your eyes, ears, and brain. This is a sacred trust. Your mind is the control-center of your life, so whoever influences your mind will ultimately affect your entire life.

If you are confident that you are receiving teaching from safe voices with whom God has connected you, stick with them and support them. They need your help and financial support, and you need what they have to give you. But always do your due diligence in these matters, ensuring that you really know who is speaking to you. Remember, you are the "watchman on the wall" of your mind and heart, from which flows the very issues of life (*see* Isaiah 62:6; Proverbs 4:23).

Never forget that we are navigating end-times territory in which mass deception will more and more become the rule of the day (*see* Matthew 24:4-6). That means that we have to stay alert about anything wrong that tries to enter into our personal spaces. It's our responsibility to determine to keep a sound mind, hold fast to the Scriptures, and refuse to budge from God's truth. As Paul admonished the Thessalonian believers, his words are also telling us that we must keep our heads on straight, use our minds, and not give place to *strange utterances*, *weird revelations*, *euphoric proclamations*, or *any* off-base teaching that causes people to be fearful.

But in his second epistle to the Thessalonians, Paul additionally said they should not be troubled by "letter" (*see* 2 Thessalonians 2:2). The word "letter" is from the Greek word *epistole*, from which we get the word "epistle." Paul knew at the time of his writing that people with fraudulent motives were trying to write their own epistles and circulate them as authoritative. He was aware that they would perhaps try to duplicate his style of writing and claim that their epistle was one Paul wrote himself. He also perceived that some would write in their own name but claim Paul was endorsing their message.

But let me explain to you why Paul wrote these words to the Thessalonian believers. You see, some so-called spiritual leaders were communicating very authoritatively to believers that "the day of Christ is at hand" (*see* 2 Thessalonians 2:2). The words "at hand" are interpreted from the Greek word *enistemi*, which means *to be at hand* or *to be present*.

If this were true, it would have meant *the Rapture had already occurred*, they missed it, and now they were living in the time of the Tribulation — which is scripturally called "the day of the Lord" — the seven years of wrath that are triggered with the rapture of the Church. Such a teaching would indeed stir alarm in the hearts of believers who were waiting for the rapture of the Church, as Paul had promised in Second Thessalonians 2:1. He wrote this letter to comfort them with the fact that this advent was still yet to come.

So in this verse, Paul reaffirmed that the rapture of the Church, or the time when the Church is "collected" and "gathered" to Him, as we saw in verse 1, will indeed occur before the "day of the Lord," when God's wrath will be poured out on the earth. But bogus prophets were prophesying that Jesus had already returned and that they were living in the period of the Tribulation. As you can imagine, these believers were distressed by the inaccuracy of these prophecies.

Have you ever felt unsettled and distraught about information you heard that ended up not being true? God is the God of peace, not confusion (*see* 1 Corinthians 14:33). You can always turn to Him, even in the worst of times, for comfort, hope, and peace, which Colossians 3:15 (*AMPC*) says will settle matters in your heart with finality, much in the same way an umpire makes a call from behind the plate, and the base runner is decisively declared *"SAFE!"*

But how many times have we heard accounts of those who talked *swaths* of undiscerning people into notions that were completely false? We know from history that in many of these cases, the outcomes can become dangerous. Those who don't know the timeless, trusted words of Scripture aren't able to discern or rightly divide the Word of truth (*see* 2 Timothy 2:15) and could act inappropriately on erroneous information without even realizing they're being deceived. That is not Christ's will for His Church!

Pictured here are two Roman coins: one authentic, one fake. The Greek word meaning "prove" was significantly used to describe the process of testing coins to see if they were real or counterfeit. Counterfeit coins look very authentic — and there were so many counterfeit coins in circulation in ancient times that it became an accepted practice to test coins to determine if they were real or counterfeit. Only once coins were tested and proven authentic were they approved for public circulation and accepted for payment. By using the word "prove" in First Thessalonians 5:21, Paul instructed God's people to test both written and spoken spiritual utterances before fully embracing their substance.

'Prove All Things; Hold Fast That Which Is Good'

Paul had reminded these believers in First Thessalonians 5:21 of their need to "prove all things...." The word "prove" is translated from the Greek word *dokimadzo*, which means *to approve after testing*.

This word was used in various ways, but it was significantly used to describe the process of testing coins to see if they were real or counterfeit. Counterfeit coins look very authentic — and there were so many counterfeit coins in circulation in ancient times that it became an accepted practice to test coins to determine if they were real or counterfeit. If tested and proven as fake or counterfeit, they were rejected. Only if the coins were tested and proven authentic were they approved for public circulation and accepted for payment.

That is where the word "prove" comes from that Paul used in First Thessalonians 5:21. Paul didn't tell the Thessalonian believers to simply reject all prophetic utterances; he instructed them to test or *prove* them before embracing and circulating them. God's people are instructed to test both written and spoken spiritual utterances before fully embracing their substance.

But after saying, "Prove all things...," Paul continued and said, "...Hold fast that which is good." The words "hold fast" are a translation of the Greek word *katecho*, a compound of the words *kata* and *echo*. The word *kata* means *down*, and the word *echo* means *to hold* or *to embrace*. When these two words are compounded to create *katecho*, the new word means *to hold firmly* or *to hold down* lest the desired object slip away from you. It is the picture of figuratively wrapping one's arms around an object and refusing to let it go.

Although they had become upset due to inaccurate prophetic teachers, Paul told the Thessalonians they needed to embrace and hold on tight to that which was "good." The word "good" denotes something that is *sound* and *in order*. It has been *tested*, *proven*, and *shown to be authentic*.

Like a coin that has been tested and proven worthy to be put into circulation, what Paul was commanding them, and *us*, to hold fast to is that which has been attested to be *dependable, genuine, reliable, and true*. The Spirit of God is exhorting us to wrap our arms around and hold fast to those spiritual truths that are tested and proven to be authentic and legitimate.

Your Personal Responsibility

Years ago in my travels, I ate in a cafeteria in central Siberia that was visibly unclean, and I knew it was risky to eat there. But because I was hungry, I put aside my hesitation and dove into the food. I knew by looking at the cafeteria — the dirty floors, the dirty interior, the sour smell in the place, and even the dirty plates — that it was likely the food was not safe to eat. Common sense said, "Do not eat here!" If I had listened to my "gut instinct" instead of my appetite, I would have left that cafeteria without eating the food and averted the miserable sickness I contracted shortly afterward as a result of eating unclean food.

In the same way, if you will listen to your spiritual "gut instinct," you'll know not to consume teachings that are detrimental to your life. If you are listening and staying sensitive to the Holy Spirit who's in your spirit, He will warn you. And you can help yourself, too, if you'll just pay attention to the spiritual environment! Watch for spiritually dirty

It's your God-given responsibility to guard your spiritual well-being and to always consider the long-term ramifications of where you are being fed spiritually. God expects you to think and not to mindlessly "eat by faith" whatever is placed before you. God expects you to use your brain, and He has given each believer a responsibility to guard his spiritual health and to discern the quality of spiritual food he is consuming.

floors and plates — and keep alert for a spiritual stench. As you do, you will recognize when you are not in a safe place.

If you find yourself in a dubious spiritual environment and you inwardly sense that it is risky to eat the spiritual food and drink there — a place where you know the spiritual fare you're being served is suspect — don't ignore your gut instinct. Just move elsewhere where you are sure the food that's served there is safe.

What would you do if you found yourself in a dirty restaurant with your family and you sensed your loved ones were on the verge of consuming food that was going to sicken them? Would you stay there and "eat by faith"? Of course not. So just use the same common sense with your spiritual welfare as you would with your physical well-being in that kind of situation. Don't stick around and consume what could potentially make you spiritually sick!

When questionable spiritual food is being put on your plate, God expects you to respect yourself — and the work He is doing in your life — enough to refrain from eating it and go elsewhere. It's your God-given responsibility to guard your spiritual well-being and to always consider the long-term ramifications of what you're taking into your heart and mind.

God wants you to be aware of what you're consuming — and He has given each believer a responsibility to guard his or her spiritual health and discern the quality of spiritual food that is being consumed. But especially in these last days when the Holy Spirit prophesied that strange doctrines will emerge inside the Church, Christians must learn to be "thinking people" who are also spiritually in tune with the Holy Spirit dwelling within them.

As I said previously, I practice this principle on a daily basis in my personal life. Even though we have an array of Christian TV channels available in our home, I do not allow every program on Christian television to be broadcast into the privacy of our living room. I am very selective about what is allowed entrance into our lives under the label of "Christian" because I understand that a little poison ingested over a long period of time, even if it is mixed with good food, can produce ill effects.

It's your God-given responsibility to guard your spiritual well-being and to always consider the long-term ramifications of who is ministering to you as well as what you are consuming — a responsibility that He expects you to take seriously.

I urge you to remove from your table any plate tainted with error and learn to identify and receive only good spiritual food that will make you strong in faith and godly character. Especially in these last days when so many various concoctions of spiritual food are accessible, God expects you to think and not to mindlessly "eat by faith" whatever is placed before you. Use your brain and trust the Holy Spirit within to help you exercise sound judgment, and you'll do well. Because you desire to partake of that which is healthy, He will lead you to sound and trustworthy teaching.

If the Thessalonian believers had been more discerning about who they were listening to — and more discerning about what was being fed to them — it is probable they would have avoided being thrown into a state of panic. This was the issue that Paul was addressing in Second Thessalonians 2:2. They were needlessly brought into confusion, distracted in their spiritual walk, and nearly hopelessly disheartened because they hadn't learned at that point to "rightly divide the word of truth" (*see* 2 Timothy 2:15).

Although I personally love the *King James Version*, it does not convey many important nuances in the Greek text. So let's look at some of the word pictures that are brought out in the *Renner Interpretive Version* (*RIV*) of Second Thessalonians 2:2 that help us better see how Paul's teaching set the record straight.

RIV of Second Thessalonians 2:2

Some things will be happening right before His coming that could shake you up quite a bit. I'm referring to events that will be so dramatic that they could really leave your head spinning — occurrences of such a serious nature that many people will feel alarmed, panicked, intimidated, and unnerved! Naturally speaking, these events could nearly drive you over the brink emotionally, putting your nerves on edge and making you feel apprehensive and insecure.

And I wish I could tell you these incidents were going to be just a one-shot deal — but when they finally get rolling, they're going to keep coming and coming, one after another. That's why you have to determine not to be shaken or moved by anything you see or hear. You need to get a grip on your mind and refuse to allow yourselves to be traumatized by these events. If you let these things get to you, it won't be too long until you're a nervous wreck! That's why you have to decide beforehand that you are not going to give in and allow "fright" to worm its way into your mind and emotions and run your whole life.

I also want to tell you not to be too surprised if people start making weird spiritual proclamations and off-the-wall utterances during the time just before the Lord comes. All kinds of strange things are going to happen during those days! It's going to get so bizarre that you might even receive a letter from some who claim that the day of the Lord has already come! Who knows — they might even attach our name to it, alleging to have our endorsement. Or they might even send it as if it were written and sent from us!

A Last-Days Apostasy and the Manifestation of the Antichrist

Then in the next verse, Second Thessalonians 2:3, Paul began setting the record straight as he continued, "Let no man deceive you by any means: for that day shall not come, except there come a falling away first, and that man of sin be revealed, the son of perdition."

The words "let no man" are important at this juncture. In Greek, Paul used the negative particle *me* to denote *a strong prohibition*, and he was sternly and strongly ordering his readers to reject some type of activity. The word "man" is a translation of *tis*, which means anyone at all, and it means that he expected the Thessalonians to use their minds and discernment and to not allow *anyone at all* to deceive them.

The word "deceive" is a translation of the Greek word *exapatao*, a compound of *ek* and *apatao*. The preposition *ek* means *out*, and is used as an *intensifier*, and the word *apatao* means *to craftily take advantage, to cheat, to beguile, to deceive*, or *to lead into error*. As a compound, the word *exapatao* means *to intentionally take advantage of, craftily beguile, fully cheat, fully deceive*, or *to wholly lead into error*. This word conveys a deep deception and highlights the depth of the deception involved. Among other places, Paul used this word in Romans 16:18 to speak of *flattering speech that is intended to deceive*, and also in Second Corinthians 11:3 to denote how Satan *beguiled* Eve with seducing words.

The next phrase "any means" in this verse is translated from the Greek words *medena tropon*. But it is preceded by the word "by," which is a translation of the word *kata* and means *according to*, but it also carries a sense of that which is *dominating* or *subjugating*.

The word *medena* means *no one, none, not one, none at all*, or *nothing*. The word *tropon*, a form of *tropos*, means *fashion, manner*, or *way*. As a phrase, it is an emphatic statement that means *refuse to allow anyone to wrongly dominate or take advantage of you in any way*.

The words "for that day" are also very important. The word "for" is a translation of *hoti*, a Greek word that means *explicitly because*. Thus, it lets us know that Paul was being very *explicit* about the following point. The words "that day" are not in the original Greek text, but they are implied from the previous verse, as Paul was continuing his conversation from the previous verse.

Paul went on to say, "...For that day shall not come, *except* there come a falling away first, and that man of sin be revealed, the son of perdition...." The word "except" is an interpretation of the Greek word *ean*, which can be interpreted here as the words *except* or *unless*. By using this word, Paul was stating that the Day of the Lord, or the seven-year Tribulation period, will not come *except* or *unless* — or some newer translations say *until* — a falling away comes first. The use of this word "except" at this juncture soundly warns that before the Day of the Lord, or before the seven-year Tribulation period begins, there will first be a "falling away." Not only does this falling away occur

ἀποστασία
Pictured above is the Greek word *apostasia*, which is a compound of *apo* and *histemi*. The word *apo* means away and pictures intentional distance, and the word *histemi* means to step. But when these two words are compounded, it means *to stand apart from, to distance oneself from, to step away from, to withdraw from*, or *to shrink away from*. It is from this very Greek word that we derive the word *apostate* or *apostasy*.

before the Tribulation — it occurs before the resurrection of the righteous dead and the catching away of the saints who are still on the earth vibrantly living for Christ.

This falling away will be a worldwide apostasy — not only in the Church, but also throughout society at large — and this apostasy, or worldwide spiritual mutiny, will pave the way for the Antichrist to eventually be revealed.

The words "falling away" are interpreted from the Greek word *apostasia*, which is a compound of *apo* and *histemi*. The word *apo* means *away* and pictures *intentional distance*, and the word *histemi* means *to step*. But when these two words are compounded, it means *to stand apart from, to distance oneself from, to step away from, to withdraw from*, or *to shrink away from*. It is from this very Greek word that we derive the word *apostate* or *apostasy*.

Some have tried to extrapolate this word *apostasia* to describe the rapture of the Church — a "stepping away," of sorts, as the Church is removed from the earth. But this interpretation is incorrect. This word *apostasia* is used consistently throughout history to emphatically describe *a falling away* or *a revolt*. In fact, the writer Plutarch used the word *apostasia* to describe *political revolt*. And in the *Book of Maccabees*, the word *apostasia* describes *a turning away* from the Lord. This word *apostasia* also occurs in the *Septuagint* version of Joshua 22:22, where it describes *rebellion* against God.

In the Greek and Roman world, this word was used to denote *political rebellion* or *military defection*. Paul, a linguist, used this word correctly to state that a worldwide mutinous attitude will develop toward God and His Word at the very end of the age — in the time frame that precedes the manifestation of the Antichrist. Thus, Paul correctly used the word *apostasia* to predict that a *rebellion* or *mutiny* against God will occur in society at large in the last days.

A Worldwide Modification Process Is Required Before These Biblical Events Ensue

Paul said that this *apostasia* will happen "first" and only then will it be possible for the Man of Sin to be revealed. The word "first" in Greek is *proton*, and it means *first*, as in chronology or sequence of time. Thus, before the Antichrist will make his appearance on the world stage, *first* the world will *stand apart from, distance itself from, step away from, withdraw from*, and *shrink away from* the law of God that it once held to be true.

You see, in order for a "man of lawlessness" to come to power, society must *first* cast aside the law of God and distance itself from it. Eventually, the climate will be so changed that it will be prepared to accommodate and even embrace a man of lawlessness who seems perfect for the times.

The fact is a worldwide modification is already underway as the world is being prepared for the appearance of the Antichrist. An amoral philosophy is being proliferated in media, education, and nearly every sphere of society. Evidence abounds revealing how far delusion and a widespread mutiny against God and His Word have already advanced in the world today. And this way of thinking is being perpetuated in the education of children and young people in schools and universities.

In addition, through the media and every other avenue possible, this worldview is being aggressively pushed by "progressives" who believe they have the right to subject everyone else — including Christians — to their new moral code. But there is a larger satanic plan at work that even these progressives are unaware of. It is a plan to lead society along the prophetic route to a day when the Antichrist will be revealed to the world. The world is being primed and prepared for the ultimate manifestation of the Antichrist at the end of the age.

In the book of Daniel, we find multiple references to the Antichrist making his appearance at the end of the age. Daniel 8:23 says, "And in the latter time of their kingdom, when the transgressors are come to the full, a king of fierce countenance, and understanding dark sentences, shall stand up."

Notice this prophecy refers to the "latter time" and to a moment "when the transgressors are come to the full." This is speaking of a time at the end of the age when society will be led so far off track that it will completely set aside the law of God. This is precisely what we are witnessing in our own times and exactly what Paul prophesied would occur in Second Thessalonians 2:3.

But Daniel 8:23 is so important to this conversation that I want you to see how it is rendered in other versions.

- The *New King James Version* says, "And in the *latter time* of their kingdom, *when the transgressors have reached their fullness*, a king shall arise, having fierce features, who understands sinister schemes."
- The *New American Standard Bible* says, "And in the *latter period* of their dominion, *when the wrongdoers have run their course*, a king will arise, insolent and skilled in intrigue."
- The *New Living Translation* says, "At *the end* of their rule, *when their sin is at its height*, a fierce king, a master of intrigue, will rise to power."

Notice all of these translations speak of latter times when sin has reached its zenith and society runs amuck and goes completely astray.

Exactly at that moment:

- "A king of fierce countenance, and understanding dark sentences, shall stand up" (*King James Version*).
- "A king shall arise, having fierce features, who understands sinister schemes" (*New King James Version*).
- "A king will arise, insolent and skilled in intrigue" (*New American Standard Bible*).
- "A fierce king, a master of intrigue, will rise to power" (*New Living Translation*).

The Antichrist will appear as a progressive world leader, but these versions of Daniel 8:23 tell us that he will in reality be fierce, have fierce features, and be insolent. He will be skilled in darkness, sinister schemes, intrigues, and will be marked with supernatural powers. This goes well with Revelation 13:3-4 where the Antichrist is described as a "beast." We will return to Revelation 13:3-4 in just a few pages so you can more fully understand why the Bible refers to him that way.

But in Second Thessalonians 2:7, Paul stated that the mystery of iniquity has been working for a long time. It is a covert, secret plan that the devil has been slowly executing right under people's noses, as he has methodically and tediously walked the world away from the law of God to become a society that has thrown off moral restraints. This is precisely what Paul had in mind when he wrote of an apostate world that has stepped away from the law of God. So Paul, in agreement with Daniel 8:23, predicted a worldwide society in a state of *rebellion* or *mutiny* against God would emerge in the last days.

There is a reason this worldwide mutiny must happen first — for if the world had remained rooted in Judeo-Christian principles, as it has for many centuries, it would be difficult, if not impossible, for a man of lawlessness (such as the Antichrist) to rise to power. So before the Antichrist will make his grand appearance, *first* the world will go through a worldwide modification process to prepare for his arrival.

This is precisely what we have been observing as society has more and more thrown off the voice of Scripture to create a new world with a new moral code that is both messy and chaotic. I'm sure you would agree that we are living in a mind-boggling period of deceived thinking that most of us wouldn't have imagined possible a generation ago.

And once the "restrainer" (*see* 2 Thessalonians 2:7) is removed from the scene, all guardrails for morality and godliness will be completely cast aside, and Paul said that is when the Antichrist, or the Man of Sin, will make his appearance to the world as a progressive and great new world leader.

In Second Thessalonians 2:3, Paul referred to the Antichrist as the "man of sin." The word "sin" in this case is the Greek word *anomia*, which is actually a form of the word *nomos*, which is the Greek word for *law*, and it is regularly used to depict *the standard of what is legally or morally correct*. But when an "a" is attached to the front of this word, it becomes *anomia*. That "a" has a cancelling effect, so rather than depict the law or a correct moral standard, the word *anomia* holds the opposite meaning — that is, *without law* or *lawless* — and it pictures either a person or a people who possess *no fixed moral standards*. It depicts those who live *void of standards*, *without law*, or *in a state of lawlessness*. It is used prophetically to depict a last-days society that will throw out all previously agreed-upon moral standards and will depart from God's well-established laws at the very end of the age.

The Bible foretells a last-days scheme when society will construct a new world order that has few, if any, hard and fast rules of what is morally right and wrong. In essence, this will be a lawless world — that is, a world that attempts to eliminate what they consider to be the "outdated" voice of the Bible.

Thus, we find that the Bible tells us that as part of a last-days scheme, society will construct a new world order that has few, if any, hard and fast rules of what is morally right and wrong. In essence, this will be a lawless world — that is, a world detached from the "outdated" voice of the Bible.

Society will attempt to disconnect from most moral standards that were once held to be the common rule and view of society. Because Paul used the word "sin" — the Greek word *anomia* — in connection with the Antichrist, we know that this individual will be *void of standards* and *without law.*

This means the Antichrist will throw out all previously agreed-upon moral standards and will rise as an aggressive proponent of departing from God's well-established laws. He will not be just a person with a lawless attitude; he will be *the Man of Lawlessness* — the epitome of one who has fully discarded God's well-established laws to become Satan's perfect candidate to lead a mutinous world that has likewise rejected the voice of God and Scripture as its internal compass. This word *anomia* depicts the Antichrist as one who is free of past moral constraints and, hence, free and unshackled from the law of God that once governed society. Because Paul used a definite article in Greek, it tells us this individual is not just a person with a lawless attitude, but, rather, this is *the Man of Lawlessness*, or *the Antichrist.*

Again, the current trend toward lawlessness — that is, the construction of a new world order with morals contrary to those stated in God's Word — will eventually produce a collective mindset in society that no longer feels the pain or conviction of sin and is numb to its consequences. And according to Paul, that mutinous society will be primed and prepared for the Antichrist to be "revealed" at that time.

Paul added that once the world has generally "chucked" the law of God, and it has been modified to become a world freed of past constraints, that is precisely when this lawless individual — *the Antichrist* — will be "revealed." The word "revealed" is the Greek word *apokalupto*, which is a compound of *apo* and *kalupto*. The word *apo* means *away*, and the word *kalupto* refers to something that is *veiled, covered, concealed*, or *hidden*. But when these words are compounded into *apokalupto*, the new word depicts *a veil that has been removed, thus exposing what was behind the veil, concealed, or hidden from view*.

Paul used this word to inform us that the "man of sin" — the Antichrist — until the time of his revealing, will have been concealed and hidden from public view. But a day is coming when, at just the right time, he will suddenly appear and step onto the world stage for all to see. Although the Antichrist will be center stage and ready for his appearance to the world, the curtains that conceal his identity will remain shut until the worldwide mutiny against God — the *apostasia*, or falling away — occurs and until the "restrainer" is taken out of the way. He will *not* be revealed until the world is lawless enough to welcome and receive him and his new agenda.

In Second Thessalonians 2:3, Paul also called the Antichrist the "son of perdition." The word "perdition" is a translation of the Greek word *apoleia*, and it speaks of something *doomed, rotten, ruinous*, or *decaying*. Although the Antichrist's claim is that he will lead the world into a more progressive future, what he will bring to the world is doom, destruction, rot, ruin, and decay. There will ultimately be absolutely no redeeming values in anything produced by his rule.

As noted previously, in Second Thessalonians 2:7, "...the mystery of iniquity doth already work...." This verse plainly means Satan has been working a secret plan to get the world ready for the Man of Lawlessness to make his grand appearance. But we read in First John 4:3 that the "...spirit of antichrist, whereof ye have heard that it should come; and even now already is it in the world." It's not difficult to look around and observe that the antichrist spirit — that which is antithetical, or *opposite and opposed*, to Christ — is very present in our world system.

Over the centuries, Satan has experimented with various world leaders as "prototypes" of the Antichrist. There have been many visible leaders whom people have "suspected" to be the Antichrist. Among them were Nero, Trajan, Hadrian, Domitian, various Popes, Napoleon, Mussolini, Hitler, Anwar Sadat, Gorbachev, Kissinger, even King Charles — and the list goes on and on. And, certainly, during the leadership of some of these figures, those they governed and the world around them experienced "perditious" times rife with *doom, rottenness, and ruin*. But over the ages — sometimes

Nero Trajan Hadrian Domitian Popes Napoleon

Mussolini Hitler Anwar Sadat Gorbachev Kissinger King Charles

simply based on people's likes and dislikes — many have attempted to guess, *Who is the Antichrist?*

But Paul categorically taught that no one will know the Antichrist's identity until the "restrainer" has been removed from the earth, and we will look at this in the following pages. Furthermore, when Paul described the Antichrist in Second Thessalonians 2:3, he importantly used a definite article before the name or title "Antichrist." This signals that the Antichrist will be in a category like none other before him. He will not simply be an evil person; he will be incarnated evil because this will be *the* son of doom and destruction.

RIV of Second Thessalonians 2:3

In light of these things, I urge you to refuse to allow anyone to take advantage of you in any way. For example, you won't need a letter to tell you when the day of the Lord has come. You ought to know by now that this day can't come until first a worldwide insurgency, rebellion, riot, and mutiny against God has come about in society. Once that occurs, the world will then be primed, prepared, and ready to embrace the Man of Lawlessness, the one who hates law and has rebellion running in his blood. This is the long-awaited and predicted Son of Doom and Destruction, the one who brings rot and ruin to everything he touches. When the time is just right, he will finally come out of hiding and go public!

The Antichrist Will Exalt Himself Above All That Is Called God

In the next verse, Second Thessalonians 2:4, Paul further described the Antichrist as one "who opposeth and exalteth himself above all that is called God, or that is worshipped...." The rest of the verse explains, "...So that he as God sitteth in the temple of God, shewing [declaring] himself that he is God."

The word "opposeth" is translated from the Greek word *antikeimai*, which is a compound of *anti* and *keimai*. The word *anti* means *against*, and *keimai* means *to set* or *to lay in place*. When the two words are compounded, the new word depicts *an entrenched position against everything established.* The tense paints the picture of *a continual, unending, and perpetual resistance*, and it reveals that rebellion is ingrained in this individual.

Even more, he is called the "Antichrist," which is a compound of the word *anti* and the word *Christos*. The word *anti* means *against* or *in the place of*, while the word *Christos* means *Christ*. This alerts us that this evil person will have *a deeply rooted rebellion ingrained in his disposition* that sets him *against* Christ and *against* everything that Christ represents — and in many respects, he will attempt to take the place of Christ in the eyes of society. This means people will see him as a Messiah-type individual who has come to save the world and transform it into his new reality.

But Paul said the Antichrist is one who "opposeth and exalteth himself above all that is called God, or that is worshipped." We already saw the meaning of this word from the Greek, but this fierce opposition categorically tells us that the Antichrist will be *brazenly against* every previous godly way of thinking. He will attempt to lead a lawless world in an effort to "bulldoze" former dogmas and established codes of morality and move them out of the way. His goal will be to construct a new world order — one that is utterly free of God's influence.

After Paul said this Man of Lawlessness would "oppose" God, he furthermore stated the Antichrist will be one who "exalteth" himself. The word "exalteth" is translated from the Greek word *huperairo*, and it means *highly exalted*. Thus, when the Antichrist finally appears on the world stage, he will quickly begin to exalt himself in the eyes of the world — to such an extent that verse 4 says he will even sit in the "temple."

Pictured here are emblems of various world religions. The Antichrist will chiefly exalt himself above Christ, but also over "all that is called God, or that is worshipped." In other words, in addition to exalting himself higher than Jesus Christ, he will also exalt himself higher than all other religious leaders and forms of religion that are known in the world.

The word "temple" is from the Greek word *naos*, the word used to depict *the innermost part of the temple* — and in this case, the Temple in Jerusalem. It refers to the Holy of Holies in a future, rebuilt Temple. Based on this verse, many scholars assert that a day will come when the Antichrist will enter a rebuilt Temple in Jerusalem, go into the Holy of Holies, and actually decree himself to be God.

But Paul specifically said the Antichrist "…exalteth himself above *all that is called God, or that is worshipped….*" This phrase is important, for it tells us that the Antichrist will not only exalt himself above Christianity, but above "all that is called God or worshipped." This clearly means he will exalt himself higher than Jesus Christ, as well as higher than all other religious leaders and forms of religion that are known in the world.

Even more, Paul wrote that the Antichrist will "shew" himself as God. The word "shew" is the Greek word *apodeiknumi*, which means *to vividly portray*, *to point out*, *to illustrate*, *to show off*, or *to make a vivid presentation*. In some way, the Antichrist will declare himself as God and will use all possible means to demonstrate his power to "shew" himself as God — including lying signs and wonders.

Paul's description of the Antichrist's attitudes and actions in this verse becomes even more clear in the *RIV*.

RIV of Second Thessalonians 2:4

Do you understand who I'm talking about? I am describing that person who will be so against God and everything connected with the worship of God that, if you can imagine it, he will even try to put himself on a pedestal above God Himself — sitting in God's rightful place in the Temple and publicly proclaiming himself to be God!

In Chapter Four, we will observe the many details that the Bible specifically tells us about the Antichrist, and you will discover that much of what Paul wrote about the characteristics of Antichrist in Second Thessalonians 2 is drawn directly from the prophetic writings of Daniel.

Paul Had Previously Warned the Thessalonians About All These Things

In Second Thessalonians 2:5, Paul asked the Thessalonians, "Remember ye not, that, when I was yet with you, I told you these things?"

The word "remember" is interpreted from a form of the Greek word *mnemoneuo,* which indeed means *remember.* But this exact word is often translated as *a statue, monument,* or *memorial.* And by using this word, Paul made it clear that the words he had previously told them about these end-time events should *stand tall in their memories.*

Paul pointed out that the Thessalonian believers should already know all these facts because he had communicated these same truths when he had been face to face with them. In fact, he taught them so strongly about these end-time truths that those truths should have sunk deep into their spiritual ears and stood as *a statue, monument,* or *memorial* in their thinking. I say again that if Paul felt it was important to instruct them in these truths to such an extent that what he communicated should forever stand in their memories, this should signal the importance and value we must place on teaching these truths to *our* generation.

RIV of Second Thessalonians 2:5

Don't you remember that when I was there with you, I used to regularly tell you these things?

The Bible says there is a restraining and withholding force at work that is delaying, holding back, postponing, restraining, suppressing, or stalling the manifestation of the Antichrist. One day this powerful restrainer will be suddenly removed — and when it is removed, the Antichrist and his accompanying evil will be unleashed with full force into the world.

Who Is the One That 'Withholds' or *Restrains?*

Then in Second Thessalonians 2:6, Paul said, "And now ye know what withholdeth [or restrains] that he might be revealed in his time." According to this verse, *something* has been holding back Satan from introducing the Antichrist to the world — so the question is, what, or *who*, is it?

In the Greek text, the sentence begins by saying, "And now...." The word "now" is the Greek word *nun*, which means *now* or *at this very moment in time*. Essentially, it means Paul said, "In this very moment, you should already know what *withholdeth* the Antichrist."

According to Paul, the only reason Satan had not already brought this end-time evil leader on to the world stage is because there was a restraining force that had hitherto stopped this diabolical move. This word "withholdeth" is a translation of the Greek word *katecho*, which is a compound of *kata* and *echo*. The word *kata* carries the notion of *domination* or *suppression*, and the word *echo* means *to have*, *to hold*, or *to embrace*. When these words are compounded into *katecho* — which is translated "withholdeth" in this verse — it means *to hold down or suppress something*. It depicts *a restraining force* that is putting forth its energy *to hold down* evil and *to suppress it* from rising to a place of prominence.

Thus, Paul said there was *and is* some force — a restraining and withholding force — at work, and this force is the sole reason the Antichrist and his accompanying evil has not already been unleashed into the world. It is this restraining force that is holding back the manifestation of this satanic agenda.

The word "withholdeth" — translated from the Greek word *katecho* — implies *to delay*, *to hold back*, *to postpone*, *to restrain*, *to suppress*, or *to stall*. But Paul continued to state that one day this powerful restrainer will be suddenly removed — and when it is removed, *that* is precisely the time when evil will be unleashed with full force into the world.

That 'Man of Sin' Will Be Revealed at an Appointed Time

The word "revealed" in verse 6, referring to the Antichrist, comes from the Greek word *apokalupto*, and it pictures *a veil that has been suddenly removed to expose what was behind the veil that had been concealed or hidden from view*. Paul's use of this word means that a day is coming at the conclusion of the age when the restraining force that has been stalling, delaying, and postponing the floodgates of evil from being unleashed will be taken out of the way. When that removal occurs, this evil leader and the wickedness that accompanies him will make an entrance onto the world stage.

Second Thessalonians 2:6 says the revealing of the Antichrist will happen in his "time," a word translated from the Greek word *kairos*. This emphatically tells us that there is a prophetic, appointed moment when the restraining force will be removed, and the manifestation of the Antichrist will quickly occur. At that time, the veil that has concealed his identity will be removed, and he will step out from behind the curtain to reveal himself to the world.

The Antichrist will exalt himself above Christianity and above *all* that is worshipped." This clearly means he will invite worship unto himself as he declares a one-world order with himself singularly as the supreme head and, therefore, ruler of the world.

There is *an appointed time* when the Antichrist will make his appearance center stage before the world. And, as you will see, this "time" will come when the restraining force that has been *stalling, delaying, and postponing* the advent of the Antichrist and all the evil that will accompany him has been removed.

In the moment the restrainer is removed, the curtains will be pulled back, and the Antichrist's identity will be made known to the world. The world will not necessarily perceive him as the Antichrist, but as a man suited for the age and in sync with a world that has tossed aside all moral restraints and the law of God. But the removal of the restrainer will trigger the moment when this evil person finally steps onto the world stage to obtain global attention.

Taking into account all the nuances in each Greek word in Second Thessalonians 2:6, the *Renner Interpretive Version* (*RIV*) of this verse says:

Now in light of everything I've told you before, you ought to be well aware by now that there is a supernatural force at work, preventing the materialization of this person and the disclosure of his identity. This restraining force I'm referring to is so strong that it is currently putting on the brakes and holding back the unveiling of this wicked person, stalling and postponing his manifestation. But when the right moment comes, this evil one will no longer be withheld, and he will emerge on the world scene. The screen that has been hiding his true identity and guarding him from world view will suddenly be pulled back and will evaporate — and he will step out on center stage to let everyone know who he is.

A Secret Plan Is Being Executed Right Now

A secret plan was set in motion long ago to modify the world to prepare for the Antichrist. Current society did not accidentally arrive at its present sad state of affairs. Its downward trend has been strategically orchestrated step by step, year by year, and century by century by a devious satanic plan designed to prepare the way for the Man of Lawlessness.

But in Second Thessalonians 2:7, Paul tells us, "For the mystery of iniquity doth already work: only he who now letteth will let, until he be taken out of the way."

What is the "mystery of iniquity?" The word "mystery," as we've already seen, is the Greek word *musterion*, a word that communicates the idea of *a higher knowledge*. Specifically, it can refer to that which is known only by a limited number of individuals — or it can picture a knowledge that is not available to the general public, but only to those who have been specially initiated and invested with insight. It is a plan, thought, or arrangement that is held in the hands of a few. In this case, the word implies a secret plan, or some type of secret arrangement known to spiritual powers, but held so confidentially or surreptitiously that they are able to execute the plan without anyone catching on to what they are doing.

And once again, the word "iniquity" comes from the Greek word *anomia*, which depicts a people or a world that is *without law* or *lawless*. It pictures people who possess no fixed moral standards living in a lawless world, free from the "outdated" voice of the Bible. The use of "iniquity" (*anomia*) in the same phrase as "mystery" (*musterion*) tells us that the current state of affairs in our time is the result of a secret plan set in motion long ago. Current society did not accidentally arrive at its present sad state of affairs. Its downward trend has been strategically orchestrated step by step, year by year, and century by century by a devious satanic plan designed to prepare the way for the Man of Lawlessness.

The word "already" in this verse confirms this is a plan that has been working for a long time. The word "work" is translated from the Greek word *energeo*, which describes something *energized*. It pictures *a force propelling something forward* or *an energy that ignites a process and facilitates it all the way to its conclusion*. As used here, it describes a secret plan that has been supernaturally energized to keep things moving toward the fulfillment of its demonic agenda over the ages, like a dark force propelling something toward its pre-planned conclusion.

Certainly, it's true that believers of every generation have had to deal with issues of moral degradation and societal ills in the world around them. But in the last of the last days, it will seem that all restraints will be thrown off and society will *gallop* on a collision course with disaster. And the closer we get to the end, the deeper this lost world will sink into deception and depravity.

But rather than fear or run looking for a place to hide, we must press into Christ and clothe ourselves with the power of the Holy Spirit so we can make a mark for eternity in as many lives as possible before this current age ends. The opportunity before us is remarkable and unprecedented. But we must also stay alert to the fact that we are living in the last minutes of the age, relatively speaking, when the devil is attempting to groom and modify society as a whole so that it will receive the Man of Lawlessness.

The world is largely unaware that a satanic agenda is being executed right under their noses. Regardless, a massive undertaking is being executed to lead the world into a state of epic lawlessness so it will more readily embrace this Satan-inspired individual. At this very moment, everything is being primed and prepared for that time. And in the midst of this profound worldwide shift, we will witness things changing around us more and more. Evil spiritual forces will seek to set an entire spectrum of destructive fires, designed to consume as many lives as possible. But as Paul stated, until it is time for the Antichrist to be revealed, a restraining force will be present in the earth to stall the manifestation of this evil one.

The Mystery of Iniquity Is a Precursor to the Revealing of the Antichrist — There's Just One Obstacle to His Appearing...

Looking again at Second Thessalonians 2:7, Paul said, "...Only he who now letteth will let, until he be taken out of the way." The word "only" is the Greek word *monon*, which means *alone*, *only*, or *no one else*. And the word "now" is the Greek word *arti*, which means *now*, *just now*, *at this moment*, or *in the immediate present*. The meaning of these two words explicitly tells us that there is *only one restraining force at this very moment* that is holding back the mystery of iniquity from being fully activated on the earth — or only one thing is stopping the Antichrist from being revealed and taking control of everything.

Paul used the word "let" in Second Thessalonians 2:7 to describe this restraining force. He said, "...only he who now letteth will let, until he be taken out of the way." This old English word "let," or "letteth," is translated from the Greek word *katecho* — the same Greek word translated "withholdeth" in verse 6 to picture the *restraining force* that is stalling and postponing this end-time evil leader and the unprecedented wickedness that will accompany him.

In each instance, the words "letteth" and "let" are a translation of the word *katecho*, which means *to hold down*, *to hold back*, *to prevent*, *to suppress*, *to restrain*, or *to hinder*. Herein, Paul stated that not only has the restrainer been restraining in the past, but this restrainer also "will let" — in other words, will continue to be a restraining force — in the future. This means whoever this restraining force is, was active at the time Paul was writing, and it will continue to be active all the way to the end of the age. Paul declared that there has been and will be a supernatural restrainer holding back and preventing the forces of evil from fully taking control.

Paul stated that the Antichrist will not be revealed "...until he [the restrainer] be taken out of the way" (2 Thessalonians 2:7). The word "until" is the Greek word *heos*, and it means *until that precise moment*. The words "be taken" are an interpretation of the Greek word *genetai*, which is a form of *ginomai*, a word that describes *a surprising event* or *something that happens suddenly or unexpectedly and totally takes one off guard*.

In this phrase, Paul declared that the restrainer will suddenly disappear, suddenly be removed, or suddenly be "taken out of the way." The words "taken out of the way" are an interpretation of the Greek words *ek mesou*. The word *ek* means *out*, and the word *mesou*, which is a form of the Greek word *mesos*, depicts *the middle of things*. As a phrase, it means the restrainer will:

- suddenly and surprisingly disappear.
- be removed.
- suddenly and surprisingly be taken out of the midst of everything.

When this day comes, this hindering force that has continuously delayed the worldwide domination of evil and lawlessness will be removed from the earth. It will be as though this force is suddenly lifted out of the middle of everything — and at that moment, the evil forces that have long been suppressed will no longer be held back, but will be freed, and their wicked plans, purposes, and desires will be abruptly energized. These events will come quickly and with no hesitation once the restrainer is out of the picture.

But from his use of the word *mesou*, Paul indicated that whoever or whatever this restrainer is, its presence can currently be found in the midst of everything, or in every facet of society. And only when this restrainer is removed, "...*then* shall that Wicked be revealed..." (2 Thessalonians 2:8).

The word "then" is a translation of the Greek word *tote*, which means *then* or *at that precise moment*, and it describes what will *immediately take place* once the restrainer has disappeared from the midst of everything. Paul said that once this great restraining force has suddenly disappeared, that is precisely the synchronized moment when the curtain that has concealed the Antichrist will be pulled back, and he will be revealed to the world.

Combining the meaning of all these original Greek words in Second Thessalonians 2:7, the *Renner Interpretive Version* (*RIV*) of this passage reads as follows:

These secretive, surreptitious dark events have been covertly in the making for a long time, yet the world at large doesn't realize that a secret plan is being executed right under their own noses. The only thing that has kept this plan from being already consummated is the restraining force that has been holding it all back until now. But one day this force will be removed from the picture — and when that happens, these iniquitous events will quickly transpire. The removal of this restraining force will signal the moment when the Lawless One will finally make his grand appearance to the world.

Thus, the manifestation of the Antichrist and every dark thing that he will bring to the world, will only become known *after* the restrainer has disappeared and has been removed from the scene. As long as this restraining force is still present in the earth, it will be used by God to "withholdeth" (2 Thessalonians 2:6), or hold back, the appearance of the Antichrist and the full onslaught of evil that will accompany him at the end of the age.

Who, or What, Is the Restraining Force That Is Currently Holding Back the Manifestation of the Antichrist and Evil?

Throughout history, there have been five notorious opinions about who, or what, the great restrainer is that's *holding down*, *holding back*, *preventing*, *suppressing*, *restraining*, or *hindering* the manifestation of the Antichrist and evil that accompanies him at the end of the age. I must point out that the Greek words to describe this restrainer in verses 6 and 7 are both neuter and masculine in the original text. This implies that the identity of the restrainer may be *a thing*, *a person (or persons)*, or *both*.

Although many have their ideas about who or what this restraining force is, I think you will at least have a clearer picture of the identity of this force as you read the following pages.

The following sections briefly outline the five primary beliefs that have been held by various scholars concerning the identity of the restrainer that Paul wrote about in Second Thessalonians 2:6 and 7.

Some believed in earliest centuries that the restrainer Paul wrote about was the Roman Senate. It was believed at that time that if it were not for the Roman Senate, the full evil of various Roman emperors would have been unleashed, and the Roman Senate alone had the civil power to hinder the evil that could have been proliferated.

1. The Roman Senate?

It was staunchly believed in the earliest centuries of the Church that the restrainer Paul wrote about in this epistle was *the Roman Senate*. It was believed at that time that if it were not for the Roman Senate, the full evil of the emperor would have been unleashed without reserve or restraint. This view was carried forward for centuries. Many believed the Roman Senate alone had the civil power to hinder the evil that could have been potentially unleashed by various Roman emperors at different times.

The historian and theologian Tertullian suggested in about 200 AD that the restrainer was the Roman Empire, particularly in its role of maintaining law and order.[1] So he, too, believed the ruling body of the Roman Senate was the restrainer mentioned in Paul's epistle, and certainly government has this responsibility of maintaining and preserving order and "restraining" evil.

It was believed in those days, as it is believed today, that it was a role of human government to exercise restraint on aberrant human behavior, and many believed the

Some suggest the restrainer Paul describes is the archangel Michael, who is noted in Scripture for taking a stand to prevent the activities of evil principalities.

Roman Senate, as corrupt as it was, operated as a check-and-balance on the growing corruptions of the Roman emperor in power at the time — that the senate was a force that hindered an emperor from doing whatever he wished. It was believed that this was the restraint Paul spoke of, but that a day would come when the government would fall, and its collapse would make way for the Antichrist to step forward onto the world stage.

However, human government has often failed in restraining evil acts, and at times has even encouraged them by its own lack of moral restraints. And the obvious problem with this view is that the Roman Senate did eventually cease to exist, yet the Antichrist wasn't revealed once it was "taken away." Hence, the Roman Senate, or even civil authority, is clearly not what Paul had in mind when he wrote about the restrainer.

2. The Archangel Michael?

It has also been suggested that the restrainer Paul described is the archangel Michael, who is noted in Scripture for taking a stand to prevent the activities of evil principalities.

In Daniel 10, we read of a moment when the archangel Michael battled with principalities and powers. When the angel came to Daniel, he told him, "...I am come for [in response to] thy words. But the prince of the kingdom of Persia withstood me one and twenty days: but, lo, Michael, one of the chief princes, came to help me; and I remained there with the kings of Persia." This verse vividly depicts an intense conflict in which the archangel Michael was involved to fight on Daniel's behalf.

About the archangel Michael, Daniel 10:21 also says, "But I will shew thee that which is noted in the scripture of truth: and there is none that *holdeth* with me in these things, but Michael your prince." The Hebrew word translated "holdeth" in this verse means *to restrain*, *to bind*, or *to withstand*. Thus, we see again that the archangel Michael is an agent trusted with restraining evil.

In Daniel 12:1, we also see that the archangel Michael will be the defender of Israel at the end of the age. That verse says, "And at that time shall Michael stand up, the great prince which *standeth* for the children of thy people: and there shall be a time of trouble, such as never was since there was a nation even to that same time: and at that time thy people shall be delivered, every one that shall be found written in the book." Here, we see the archangel Michael *standing to defend* Israel from evil at the end of the age.

Then in Jude 9, we read that the archangel Michael debated back and forth in a fierce disputation with Satan over the body of Moses. That verse says, "...Michael the archangel, when contending with the devil he disputed about the body of Moses...." The Greek words used to describe this disputation are so strong that the *RIV* interprets it, "I tell you that, amazingly, even Michael, the tremendously powerful archangel, at the moment when he was wrangling and going back and forth with the devil in a fierce argument and really hot debate concerning the body of Moses...."

Finally, in Revelation 12:7, we read of a battle between the archangel Michael with his angels against the devil and other fallen angels. That verse says, "And there was war in heaven: Michael and his angels fought against the dragon; and the dragon fought and his angels...." Again, we see the archangel Michael involved in battling and holding back the forces of darkness.

On the basis of these scriptures, some have believed, and some still believe, that the archangel Michael could possibly be the restrainer Paul wrote about in Second Thessalonians 2:6 and 7. According to this view, it is the archangel Michael who is currently putting on the brakes and stalling the eventual manifestation of the Antichrist at the end of the age.

However, there is a major glitch with this view. From expounding the words Paul used in the Greek text, we see that he stated very clearly that the restrainer at the present moment can be found in the midst of every facet of society. The archangel Michael does not fit this description as he, as a singular force, is not in the midst of everything in the world at this time.

When the Word of God is heeded, embraced, and believed, it shines its brilliant light into the dark, murky places of our lives. Whenever any person reads and gives heed to God's Word, allowing its powerful light to shine into his or her life, that light will dispel spiritual darkness.

3. The Preaching of the Gospel?

In Romans 1:16, Paul said, "For I am not ashamed of the gospel of Christ, for it is the *power* of God unto salvation to everyone who believeth...."

In this verse, Paul stated that the Gospel is the power of God. The word "power" comes from the Greek word *dunamis*, an old word that described *power*. This is where we get the word "dynamite." This means the Gospel is the "dynamite" of God. However, the word *dunamis* could also be used to depict *the full force and might of an advancing army*. This means that when a concentrated effort is made to preach the Gospel to the lost, that act is the very trigger that releases the power of God to advance on the scene like a mighty army to drive away darkness, to bring the light of God, and to deliver His saving and delivering power to those who are bound and lost.

Indeed, when the Word of God is heeded, embraced, and believed, it continuously shines its brilliant light into the dark, murky places of our lives. Whenever any person reads and gives heed to God's Word, allowing its powerful light to shine into his or her life, that light will dispel spiritual darkness. In fact, history has proven this to be true, not only in the past, but even in this present time. Entire nations where darkness once ruled are being changed because of the penetrating light of God's Word. When the Bible is proclaimed, believed, and applied, it eradicates spiritual darkness, ignorance, disease, inequality, poverty, and racism. The Bible is a life-enhancer for all who benefit from its shining light. Those who reject the Word remain in darkness, but those who embrace it are delivered from spiritual darkness and ignorance.

It is true that shining the light of God's Word into a dark world drives back darkness and brings illumination. But there is a glitch in the view that this is the restraining force that Paul referred to in Second Thessalonians 2:6 and 7. You see, the preaching of the Word of God will never be removed, not even in the seven years of the Tribulation, for during that time frame, Revelation 7:4-8 tells us that there will be 144,000 Jewish preachers who will preach the truths of God's Word even in that dark season. So even with all the powerful effects that preaching the Word of God has upon society, it specifically is *not* the restraining force that Paul was referring to in Second Thessalonians 2:6 and 7.

4. The Holy Spirit?

Another view is that the one who "withholdeth" — or restrains — is the Holy Spirit. But the Holy Spirit will *never* be removed, suddenly caught away and taken, from the earth. Even during the time of the Great Tribulation, there will be many people who respond to the Gospel and repent in response to the preaching of 144,000 Jewish evangelists (*see* Revelation 7:4). Scores of people will be saved during that time (*see* Revelation 7:9-17).

And as is always the case, for anyone to be saved, it requires the work of the Holy Spirit. He is the consummate "Change Agent" who, in the new birth, removes one's "heart of stone" — or the old, unregenerate nature of sinful man — and plants within him or

Another view is that the one who "withholdeth" is the Holy Spirit, but the Holy Spirit will never be removed from the earth. Even during the time of the Great Tribulation there will be many people who respond to the Gospel and repent, and this requires the work of the Holy Spirit, as it is impossible for anyone to be saved without the work of the Spirit.

her a new, born-again spirit. It is impossible for anyone to be saved without the work of the Spirit.

In Ephesians 2:1, Paul stated that unsaved people are "...dead in trespasses and sins." The words "dead in trespasses and sins" means they are *spiritually dead*. For any spiritually dead person to be roused to life, it requires a special, supernatural work of the Holy Spirit to, first, awaken the human consciousness to the reality of its sinful condition. Thanks to the Holy Spirit's work, one who is spiritually dead *can* be awakened to his sinfulness. But it is the Spirit alone who has the ability to open the eyes of a sinner and bring him to a place where he recognizes that he is a sinner. And in that moment, in effect, the human soul hears the Spirit say to him, "Awake thou that sleepest, and arise from the dead, and Christ shall give thee light" (Ephesians 5:14).

It is a miracle when God's Spirit rouses a human spirit from spiritual death to spiritual life, and it *requires* the ministry of the Holy Spirit. Jesus referred to the convicting work of the Spirit in John 16:8 when He said, "And when he [the Holy Spirit] is come, he will reprove the world of sin...." Only the Holy Spirit can open the eyes of one dead in trespasses and sins to understand his plight, and this is why Jesus said in John 6:44, "No man can come to me, except the Father which hath sent me draw him." You see, it is the Holy Spirit whom the Father has sent to draw sinners to Jesus, and no one can come to the Father without the work of the Holy Spirit.

Thus, if people are going to be saved during the Tribulation — and they *will* be saved in large numbers according to Revelation 7:9-17 — it will necessitate the presence of the Holy Spirit in the earth. This means the specific restrainer Paul wrote about in Second Thessalonians *cannot* be the Holy Spirit. Even in the darkest times of the Great Tribulation, the Holy Spirit will be in the earth so that people may repent and be eternally saved.

Whoever the restraining force is, it is currently in the midst of every facet of society — a description that well describes the Church, which is presently intermingled in every sphere of life throughout the earth. Of all the above suggestions about who is the restraining force, only the Church can be found in every facet of society as described by Paul in Second Thessalonians 2:8.

5. The Church?

There are others who believe *the Church* is the restraining force that Paul wrote about in Second Thessalonians 2:6 and 7. In Matthew 16:18, Jesus spoke of the prevailing power of the Church even against the gates of hell. He said, "…I will build my church; and the gates of hell shall not prevail against it"!

Please remember that whoever, or whatever, the restraining force is, it is currently in the midst of every facet of society. This well describes the Church, for it is presently intermingled in every sphere of life throughout the earth. There are believers in the business world, in the athletic world, in arts, in education, in government, in the medical field, and in every sphere of life. In fact, of all the previously mentioned beliefs about the restraining force, only the Church can be found in every facet of society throughout the world.

Since the rapture of the Church is a core New Testament doctrine that Paul says will occur one day, it categorically means a time is coming when the Church is going to be "taken out of the way." Or, as the Greek text says, it will *suddenly disappear*, it will be *suddenly removed*, and it will be *suddenly taken out of the way* — exactly as Paul states in Second Thessalonians 2:7. And according to Paul, when the restrainer is removed, in that exact synchronized moment, the Lawless One, or the Antichrist, will no longer be restrained, and he will thusly be revealed to the world.

So Who *Is* the Great Restrainer?

Of these possibilities, only one logically fits the identity of the great restrainer that is currently holding back the advent of the Antichrist and the evil that will accompany him. Although there will be an apostasy even in certain segments of the Church at the end of the age, there will be those who are spiritually living, spiritually robust, spiritually thriving, spiritually vibrant, and spiritually vigorous. And that remaining remnant of spiritually alive believers who have endured and are around at the time of the coming of the Lord — *their* very presence will be a restraining force in the earth to hold back the onslaught of evil that will finally be released once the Church is raptured.

Even with all the defects that we may be aware of in the Church, it is nevertheless the Body of Christ in the earth. The Church holds the power of God, and as long as it is on the earth, it will be a force that *holds down*, *holds back*, *prevents*, *suppresses*, *restrains*, and *hinders* the onslaught of evil.

Imagine for a moment what the world would be like if the Church was abruptly moved into Heaven in the twinkling of an eye. Suddenly, the evil forces that are presently being held at bay would *surge* forward, as there would be no force remaining to restrain it. This is what will happen immediately following the rapture of the Church.

But to be fair on all points, the government, angels, the preaching of the Gospel, the Holy Spirit — as well as the Church — can all have a restraining influence in the affairs of man. Only one of these, however, was — *and currently is* — the restrainer Paul wrote about in his epistle to the Thessalonians. The Church is the Restrainer, and from this point forward in this book, I will refer to the "Restrainer" as a proper noun, as it is, *one and the same*, the Church — the Body of Christ!

What Happens to the Antichrist at Christ's Second Coming (or Second Advent)

In Second Thessalonians 2:8, Paul stated that when the Restrainer is removed "...then shall that Wicked be revealed...." As noted before, the word "then" in Greek is *tote*, and it means *exactly then* or *precisely then*. Thus, immediately after the restrainer has been taken out of the way is the exact time when the Antichrist will make his grand appearance, and he will rule for seven years.

But in that same verse, suddenly, Paul jumped in his writings even further into the future and to the end of the seven-year Tribulation when Christ returns in His Second Coming (or Second Advent) with the saints who will accompany Him. He declared that when Christ comes in His Second Coming "...the Lord shall consume [the Antichrist] with the spirit of his mouth, and shall destroy with the brightness of his coming."

The word "consume" is translated from *anelei*, a form of the Greek word *anaireo*, which in this case means *to abolish*, *destroy*, *kill*, *nullify*, *slay*, or *to take away* the life of another. It is often translated as the word "murder." Thus, when Christ comes in His Second Coming, He will obliterate the Antichrist — and He will do it "...with the spirit of his mouth, and shall destroy [him] with the brightness of his coming."

'With the Spirit of His Mouth and the Brightness of His Coming'

The words "spirit of his mouth" refer to *the breath of Christ*. The word "spirit" is interpreted from the Greek word *pneuma,* which is usually translated *spirit.* But here it means *breath*. The Greek word "mouth" is from the Greek word *stomos*, which is simply the Greek word for *the mouth*. Paul thusly declared that on that day of Christ's Second

The Antichrist will be destroyed "with the brightness of his coming." Paul told us that Jesus' coming will take the Antichrist by surprise and that this evil world leader will be disabled by His coming with splendor and glory. Just as a bolt of lightning destroys, Christ's glorious presence will consume the Antichrist.

Coming (or Second Advent) at the end of the seven-year Tribulation period, the Lord will open His mouth and speak — and when He does, so much power will be released that it will permanently remove the Antichrist from the world scene. Although Satan will energize the Antichrist with demonic powers, this evil person won't have enough strength to withstand one puff from the mouth of the Lord!

But Paul also said the Antichrist will be destroyed "...with the brightness of his coming." The word "destroyed" is interpreted from a form of the Greek word *katargeo*, a word that Paul used 25 times in his epistles. And Paul consistently used it to mean *to abolish*, *to bring to nothing*, *to put out of commission*, *to reduce to waste*, or *to render inactive*.

Paul added that the Antichrist will be brought to nothing and put out of commission "with the brightness of His coming," referring to Christ. The word "brightness" is actually the Greek word *epiphaneia*, and it is wrongly translated in the *King James Version*. The word *epiphaneia* was used in classical Greece to describe *the sudden and surprise appearance* of the Greek gods.

Paul, a linguist, knew the usage of this word in Greek society and literature — and in those ancient writings, the word referred to the moment when a so-called god *suddenly appeared* and was so glorious and mighty in appearance that witnesses of this event were nearly disabled by their sudden appearance. Paul was adeptly reaching into classical literature to borrow this word to tell us that Jesus' Second Coming will take the Antichrist by surprise and that this evil world leader will be utterly disabled by His coming with splendor and glory.

Demonically Energized Signs and Wonders

But Paul stated in Second Thessalonians 2:9 that the coming of the Antichrist on the world scene will be "...after the working of Satan with all power and signs and lying wonders."

The word "after" is translated from the word *kata,* a word that carries a sense of *domination.* The word "working" is interpreted from a form of the word *energeia,* which would be better interpreted as *activity* or *operation.* The name "Satan" in Greek is *Satana,* which means adversary, but it is the name ascribed to *the devil,* and it pictures him as one who is *the arch-enemy of God.* This immediately alerts us to the fact that the Antichrist's activities and operations will be energized and dominated by Satan, who is the arch-enemy of God.

But Paul added that the Antichrist will come "...with all power and signs and lying wonders." The word "all" in Greek is actually the words *en pase.* The word *en* means *in,* as in the sphere of something, and the word *pase* means *absolutely everything with nothing excluded.* The Greek words *en pase* used together emphatically declare that the Antichrist will come with *all* power — implying that he will make his grand appearance with *all kinds* of power and supernatural displays. The word "power" is translated from a form of *dunamis,* which carries the idea of *explosive, superhuman power that comes with enormous energy and produces phenomenal, extraordinary, and unparalleled results.*

In the New Testament, the word *dunamis* often depicts *mighty deeds that are impressive, incomparable, and beyond human ability to perform.* It denotes *miraculous power* or *miraculous manifestations.* Thus, if we stopped here, we find that Paul has already informed us that when the Antichrist comes, his activities and operations will be dominated and energized by Satan — the arch-enemy of God — and when the Antichrist makes his appearance to the world, he will come operating in all types of supernatural activities that are way beyond the ability of mere man to perform.

δύναμις

Pictured above is the Greek word *dunamis,* which denotes *mighty deeds that are impressive, incomparable, and beyond human ability to perform.* When the Antichrist comes, his activities and operations will be energized by Satan, and he will come operating in all types of supernatural activities that are way beyond the ability of mere man to perform.

σημεῖον

Pictured above is the Greek word *semeion*, which denotes *the official written notice that announced a court's final verdict*, or *a signature or seal applied to a document to guarantee its authenticity*. Paul used this word to declare that the Antichrist's supernatural signs will be taken by the world as proof of the Antichrist's power.

Paul then stated that the world will stand in awe of these "signs and lying wonders." The word "signs" is a translation of the Greek word *semeion*, a word that describes *the official written notice that announced a court's final verdict*; *a signature or seal applied to a document to guarantee its authenticity*; or *a sign that marked key locations in a city*. By using the word *semeion*, Paul declared that these supernatural signs will prove to the world the Antichrist's power. These supernatural activities will be "signs" to alert the world to the fact that the Antichrist is no mere human being.

τέρασιν ψεύδους

Pictured above are the Greek words *terasin pseudous*, which denote *lying wonders*. They picture *acts or events that leave one baffled, bewildered, astonished, and at a loss of words*. Such miraculous events left spectators awestruck, baffled, bewildered, speechless, shocked, stunned, taken aback, and in a state of wonder. This tells us that the Antichrist will come with every imaginable kind of shocking wonder that will cause the world to be awestruck and baffled at his powers that are designed to deceive.

But Paul declared these activities will actually be "lying wonders." The original text says *terasin pseudous*. The word *terasin* is from a form of *teras*, a word that pictures *an act or event that leaves one baffled, bewildered, astonished, and at a loss of words*. It was used to depict the *astonishment, shock, or surprise felt by bystanders as they observed events that were contrary to the normal course of nature*. Occurrences such as these were viewed as *miracles*, and people believed they could only take place through the intervention of *divine power*.

Such miraculous events left spectators *awestruck, baffled, bewildered, speechless, shocked, stunned, taken aback, and in a state of wonder*. The word *pseudous* is the plural form of *pseudos*, a word that pictures that which is *deceitful*, *dishonest*, *false*, or *done with impure and wrong intentions*. This tells us that the Antichrist will come with every imaginable kind of shocking wonder that will cause the world to be awestruck and baffled at his powers that are designed to deceive.

The response of the world to the Antichrist's power in the seven-year Tribulation period is revealed in Revelation 13:3: "...And all the world wondered after the beast." The words "all the world" in Greek are *hole he ge*, a phrase that literally means *the entire earth* or *the whole earth*, and it lets us know that these devil-energized signs and lying wonders will baffle all the inhabitants of the known world.

The word "wondered" is interpreted from a form of *thaumadzo*, which — similar to the word *terasin* for "lying wonders" in Second Thessalonians 2:9 — means *to be amazed, to be bewildered, to be at a loss of words*, or *to be in a state of shock and wonder.*

In fact, the world will be in such a state of awe and wonder at the supernatural deeds they see the Antichrist perform that they will show great reverence for these wondrous displays of supernatural power. Revelation 13:4 says, "...They [*the entire world* or *the whole world*] worshipped the dragon which gave power unto the beast...." In the next paragraph, we'll see who the "dragon" represents.

The word "worshipped" is translated from the word *proskuneo*, which depicts *one who is collapsed or fallen to the ground or who bows prostrate before a superior*. It means *to adore on one's knees*, or *to worship with all the appropriate physical gestures of worship*. Although the world may not realize it, Revelation 13:4 says people will, in reality, be worshipping the "dragon." The word "dragon" in Greek is *drakon*, and it is the word for *a serpent* or *huge snake* — it is a word used in the Bible to denote *Satan* and *satanic forces*.

The word "power" in Revelation 13:4 is translated from *exousia*, which implies *delegated authority* and *great influence*. Thus, the devil will delegate authority to the Antichrist and give him a position of great influence before the world. Furthermore, Revelation 13:4 refers to the Antichrist as a "beast."

This word "beast" is from a form of *therion*, a word that pictures *a brute beast* or *a savage animal*. The Holy Spirit used this exact term to picture the real nature of the Antichrist. Although he will project himself as a great progressive leader of a new world, at his very core he will be *beastly*, *brute*, and *savage*.

ἀπάτη

Pictured above is the Greek word *apate*, which denotes *deliberate seduction or deception*. This word conveys deep deception. This is a meticulously planned *deception* intended to lead a person or group of people into error. It is intentional *trickery* designed to *deceive*, *seduce*, and *mislead*.

The Antichrist Will Come 'With All Deceivableness'

Furthermore, Paul stated in Second Thessalonians 2:10 that the Antichrist will come "...with all deceivableness of unrighteousness in them that perish; because they received not the love of the truth, that they might be saved."

The words "all deceivableness of unrighteousness" are very significant. The word "all" in Greek is *en pase*. The word *en* means *in*, as *inside the sphere of something*, and the word *pase* means *absolutely all with nothing excluded*. As a phrase, the words *en pase* tell us that the Antichrist will come with *any* and *all* methods needed to successfully seduce and deceive.

The word "deceivableness" is translated from the Greek word *apate*, which denotes a *deliberate seduction* or *deception*. This word conveys *a deep deception* and highlights the depth of the deception involved. This meticulously planned *deception* is intended to lead a person or group of people into error. It is intentional *trickery* designed to *deceive, seduce, and mislead*.

The word "unrighteousness" in Second Thessalonians 2:10 is interpreted from a form of *adikia*, a word that means *unrighteousness, injustice, falsehood, deceitfulness*, or *wrongdoing*. This reveals the true source of the Antichrist's signs, wonders, miracles, and deeds. He operates from a base of deceit, falsehood, and injustice. In Matthew 7:17, Jesus said that "a corrupt tree bringeth forth evil fruit," which tells us the activities performed, methods used, and fruit produced by the Antichrist will reveal his true rotten nature.

Paul added that the Antichrist will come work his schemes of unrighteousness "in them that perish." The word "perish" is translated from the Greek word *apollumi*, a word that denotes *destruction and waste*. The word *apollumi* is used in other places to describe the devil as a destroyer who comes to waste human lives and whatever God intended to be beautiful. But when men and women refuse to accept the truth, they end up *perishing* and *wasting away*, and they are *destroyed*. Paul used this word to remind us that when a person rejects truth that has the power to save him, he places himself into the hands of the *destroyer*, who then *destroys* and *wastes* the person's life on Earth, as well as his eternal destiny.

Paul continued his warning that those whom the Antichrist leads astray will be led astray "...because they received not the love of the truth, that they might be saved." The word "received" is from a form of the Greek word *dechomai*, which means *to take into one's hands, to receive, to welcome, to gladly welcome*, or *to receive with gladness*.

The word "not" is from the word *ouk*, which is the most emphatic form of *not*. The language implies that Paul was describing those who had an opportunity to receive the love of the truth, but instead of welcoming its saving and transforming power, they chose to reject it. According to Paul, had they received the truth, they could have been "saved." The word "saved" is from a form of *sodzo*, which implies eternal life, but it also includes *deliverance* from evil in this life. It encompasses the meaning of *being kept from evil* or of *being saved, rescued from harm, or delivered from danger*. Embracing the truth would have assured them eternal salvation and temporal safety, but because they choose to reject it, they were wasted and destroyed.

In fact, in Second Thessalonians 2:11, Paul said, "And for this cause God shall send them strong delusion, that they should believe a lie."

The words "for this cause" in Greek are *dia touto*, which would be better interpreted *on account of this*, and here it means *on account of the fact* that they chose to reject the truth, "...God shall send them strong delusion...." The words "shall send" are from a form of *pempo*, which literally means *to send*. It is the same word that would be used for the *sending* of mail, the *sending* of a messenger, the *sending* of a message, or the *dispatching* of a messenger. But here we find that when people during the Tribulation — who are living in the epoch of the Antichrist — choose not to receive the truth, but to believe a lie, God will release to them "strong delusion."

The word "strong" is a poor translation of a form of the Greek word *energeia*, which actually pictures *activity, energy*, or *an operation of some type*. This word was used in the Greek and Roman world to depict an energy that brought about changes and results. But rather than produce *good* results, this verse speaks of an activity, energy, or operation that will produce "delusion."

The word "delusion" describes *a deception, a moral wandering,* or *a person or nation that has veered morally from a solid path and is now adrift.* It pictures one who wanders off course or a whole nation or even vast numbers of nations that have veered off course. Although those who are deceived once walked on a solid path, they are now adrift, questioning, teetering on the edge of a treacherous route, and going cross-grain against all that was once a part of a core belief system.

The word "delusion" in verse 11 is from the Greek word *plane* and it describes *a deception, a moral wandering,* or *a person or nation that has veered morally from a solid path and is now adrift.* However, it is also very important to understand that this word can also be translated as the word "delusion," and that is probably the best translation in this context.

This word *plane* or "delusion" depicts the behavior of one who once walked on a solid path, but is now drifting and teetering on the edge of a treacherous route. This person has either already departed from his once-solid path and has lost his bearings as a result, or he is in the process of departing from it. The word "delusion" means he is going cross-grain against all that was once a part of his core belief system, and he is deviating from his former solid moral position to a course that is unreliable, unpredictable, and even dangerous.

We are already watching moral confusion rage as never before among the civilized nations of the world. This confusion is perhaps no clearer anywhere than in the debate over gender identity — a manifestation of confusion so severe that it stuns most thinking minds.

The culture most of us knew as we were growing up was established on Judeo-Christian values. But now, as the winds of change are blowing, we are watching a near abandonment of truth and a throwing away of moral foundations. As a result, confusion abounds, and society is teetering on a treacherous path. The spirit of this world is working furiously to eliminate all remnants of a godly foundation from society and replace it with a last-days deception that will ultimately usher in an era in which the Antichrist will rule a lost world for a temporary period of time. And imagine that when the Church is removed and there is no force to restrain such activity, this process will radically speed up.

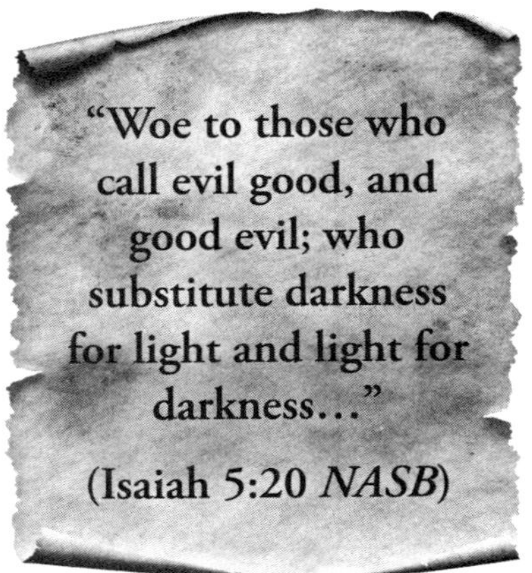

We are already living in the day the prophet Isaiah warned about when he said, "Woe to those who call evil good, and good evil; who substitute darkness for light and light for darkness..." (Isaiah 5:20 *NASB*).

It already seems as if a tsunami is sweeping over our culture, attempting to eradicate all evidence of a godly and moral framework. But what is being experienced now is only a foretaste of the disappearing of all barriers and restraints that will occur when the Church has been removed at the end of this age.

The Holy Spirit prophesied that a time will come — especially when the Restrainer is removed and during the time of the Tribulation — that spirits of delusion will stealthily, methodically, and seductively entice people into doctrines and concepts that are advanced by demon spirits. The devil has been looking for a way to unseat God's authority in the earth. Satan has been conspiring to enact a master plan — a hidden and long-laid agenda, plot, and conspiracy — intended to clandestinely lead the entire world into the lap of the Antichrist. This operation is so stealthy that the population of the world will bite the bait without comprehending it is being led astray.

Paul further said in Second Thessalonians 2:11 that during the time of the Tribulation, when the Antichrist is in power and is operating with all kinds of supernatural signs and lying wonders, "...that they [the people at that time] should believe a lie...." The word "believe" is from a form of *pistis*, which is the Greek word for *transforming faith*.

One must remember that one's faith empowers what he believes to become a reality. If we believe the truth, the truth will become a manifested reality in our lives. If, however, we believe a lie, that lie will become a manifested reality. Our faith empowers whatever we believe. And Paul said that the generation which will be led astray by the Antichrist will believe a "lie."

The word "lie" is translated from a form of *pseudos*, and it pictures that which is *bogus, false, phony,* or *an outright lie.* The generation at that time will be fed a lie — and because people will choose to believe it instead of the truth, the lie will become their reality.

The word "damned" in Greek refers to *a verdict* or *a final sentence* in a court of law. This describes a moment in which, after all the evidence has been presented, the judge and jury who have examined all the facts issue a final verdict. After all the evidence has been presented and the judge has examined all the facts, a final verdict will be issued by the court. This word carries the idea that because people will give themselves so entirely to the enjoyment of wrongdoing, there will be plenty of evidence to use against them in God's court of law on the day they stand before Him to be judged.

From Destruction and Decay to Damnation

Paul told us the result of all this in Second Thessalonians 2:12 where he wrote, "That they all might be damned who believed not the truth, but had pleasure in unrighteousness."

The word "damned" in Greek is actually from a form of the word *krino*, which is a word that refers to a jury who has handed down *a final sentence* in a court of law. It pictures *a verdict* or *a final sentence* that was pronounced as the result of a court trial. This describes a moment in which, after all the evidence has been presented, the judge and jury who have examined all the facts issue a final verdict.

After all the evidence has been presented and the judge has examined all the facts, a final verdict will be issued by the court. For this reason, "damned" carries the idea here that because people will give themselves so entirely to the enjoyment of wrongdoing, there will be *plenty of evidence to use against them in God's court of law on the day they stand before Him to be judged.*

Paul said they will be judged because they "believed not the truth, but had pleasure in unrighteousness." The word "pleasure" is from a form of *eudokeo*, which actually means *to show approval, delight, or pleasure*. In context, Paul was speaking about those who give their approval and who delight and take pleasure "in unrighteousness." The word "unrighteousness" is from the Greek word *adikia*, which means *unrighteousness, injustice, falsehood, deceitfulness*, or *wrongdoing*.

This brings to mind Romans 1:32, where Paul wrote about those who knew what was right and wrong and "who knowing the judgment of God, that they which commit such things are worthy of death, not only do the same, but have pleasure in them that do them."

The word "knowing" is from a form of *epignosis*, which is a compound of the word *epi* and *gnosis*. The word *epi* means *on* and the word *gnosis* means *knowledge*. As a compound, it pictures *one who is on top of his subject* or *one who has a thorough understanding of a matter*.

But Paul wrote that even though this person, or category of people, fully understands the judgment of God, they nevertheless continue to "commit" such things that make them worthy of death. The word "commit" is translated from *prassontes*, a continuous form of *prasso*, meaning *to practice*, but the tense here means *to be continuously practicing* such things that make them worthy of death.

Paul added that not only do they personally practice these things that they are fully aware are damnable, but they also "have pleasure in them that do them." The word "pleasure" is translated from a form of *suneudokeo*, which means *to jointly approve*. It pictures those who *simultaneously give their approval to each other* even though they are well aware that the actions and deeds they approve of are damnable and forbidden by God.

The truth is that we are already living in a time at the end of the age when spirits of delusion have been released into society, and people are approving of and celebrating what is abominable in the sight of God. But during the seven-year period of the Tribulation — when the Church is gone and the Restrainer has been removed — even though people will recall the truths of what is right and wrong in biblical terms, they will freely practice what is morally vile and will approve of those who celebrate and practice it along with them.

But in Second Thessalonians 2, Paul laid out these end-time events and vividly foretold that society at-large will go completely awry once the Restrainer has been removed from the earth. Even though the world knows what is right and wrong, it will be a time of mass delusion. And because people will reject the truth, the delusion they embrace will be activated and empowered to radically take the world in a wrong direction. And all of it will take place under the rule of the Antichrist — that is, the long-awaited and predicted Son of Doom and Destruction, who brings rot and ruin to everything he touches.

Because the entire passage of Second Thessalonians 2 is so paramount to this discussion, here is the *Renner Interpretive Version* (*RIV*) of all these verses:

RIV OF SECOND THESSALONIANS 2:1-12

1 Brothers, I make this urgent, heartfelt request to you today, earnestly and sincerely pleading with you from the bottom of my heart to hear what I'm telling you and to do exactly as I say. The coming of the Lord Jesus Christ is very near. I'm talking about that moment when Jesus will finally gather us together for Himself. And in that moment, He will release power to begin to deal with the situation at hand in the world and to put all things in order.

2 Some things will be happening right before His coming that could shake you up quite a bit. I'm referring to events that will be so dramatic that they could really leave your head spinning — occurrences of such a serious nature that many people will feel alarmed, panicked, intimidated, and unnerved! Naturally speaking, these events could nearly drive you over the brink emotionally, putting your nerves on edge and making you feel apprehensive and insecure.

And I wish I could tell you these incidents were going to be just a one-shot deal — but when they finally get rolling, they're going to keep coming and coming, one after another. That's why you have to determine not to be shaken

or moved by anything you see or hear. You need to get a grip on your mind and refuse to allow yourselves to be traumatized by these events. If you let these things get to you, it won't be too long until you're a nervous wreck! That's why you have to decide beforehand that you are not going to give in and allow "fright" to worm its way into your mind and emotions and run your whole life.

I also want to tell you not to be too surprised if people start making weird spiritual proclamations and off-the-wall utterances during the time just before the Lord comes. All kinds of strange things are going to happen during those days! It's going to get so bizarre that you might even receive a letter from some who claim that the day of the Lord has already come! Who knows — they might even attach our name to it, alleging to have our endorsement. Or they might even send it as if it were written and sent from us!

3 In light of these things, I urge you to refuse to allow anyone to take advantage of you in any way. For example, you won't need a letter to tell you when the day of the Lord has come. You ought to know by now that this day can't come until first a worldwide insurgency, rebellion, riot, and mutiny against God has come about in society. Once that occurs, the world will then be primed, prepared, and ready to embrace the Man of Lawlessness, the one who hates law and has rebellion running in his blood. This is the long-awaited and predicted Son of Doom and Destruction, the one who brings rot and ruin to everything he touches. When the time is just right, he will finally come out of hiding and go public!

4 Do you understand who I'm talking about? I am describing that person who will be so against God and everything connected with the worship of God that, if you can imagine it, he will even try to put himself on a pedestal above God Himself — sitting in God's rightful place in the Temple and publicly proclaiming himself to be God!

5 Don't you remember that when I was there with you, I used to regularly tell you these things?

6 Now in light of everything I've told you before, you ought to be well aware by now that there is a supernatural force at work, preventing the materialization

of this person and the disclosure of his identity. This restraining force I'm referring to is so strong that it is currently putting on the brakes and holding back the unveiling of this wicked person, stalling and postponing his manifestation. But when the right moment comes, this evil one will no longer be withheld, and he will emerge on the world scene. The screen that has been hiding his true identity and guarding him from world view will suddenly be pulled back and will evaporate — and he will step out on center stage to let everyone know who he is.

7 These secretive, surreptitious dark events have been covertly in the making for a long time, yet the world at large doesn't realize that a secret plan is being executed right under their own noses. The only thing that has kept this plan from being already consummated is the restraining force that has been holding it all back until now. But one day this force will be removed from the picture — and when that happens, these iniquitous events will quickly transpire.

8 The removal of this restraining force will signal the moment when the Lawless One will finally make his grand appearance to the world — and not too long after that, when the Lord will come with His saints, His coming will be so grand, so glorious, so overwhelming that He will totally obliterate the Lawless One by the mere breath of His mouth. Just one "puff" from the Lord, and this evil person will be incinerated! The very presence of the Lord will cripple and immobilize him, permanently putting him out of commission.

9 This evil one will be energized by Satan himself as he makes his arrival known to the world with all kinds of dynamic supernatural powers — powers that are truly extraordinary. These lying signs and wonders and supernatural feats have only one purpose: They are designed to draw attention to the Lawless One and to make the world stand in awe of him.

10 He'll do anything to seduce people, exploiting them with illusions, tricks, and all types of unrighteousness designed to deceive and seduce the masses. But these supernatural tricks will primarily be targeted toward those who are perishing — those who had the chance to embrace the love of the truth, but didn't take the opportunity when it was presented to them. They refused

the truth and have therefore forfeited their chance to be rescued, saved, and delivered.

11 Because they chose to reject the truth, God will send delusion and error into their midst, compelling them to believe the lie that is being offered to them [by the Antichrist].

12 God will send a delusion among these truth-rejecters. Oh, they could have accepted the truth and believed, but instead they made the willful decision to participate in and fully enjoy their unrighteous deeds. In the end, they will be thoroughly judged and condemned by their own actions. Because they gave themselves so entirely to the enjoyment of wrongdoing, there will be plenty of evidence to use against them in God's court of law on the day they stand before Him to be judged.

In this chapter, we have looked at what the Antichrist is like, what the world will be like under his reign, and who the Restrainer is who is keeping his wicked agenda at bay. The following chapter will take an even closer look at what the Bible tells us about the Antichrist.

QUESTIONS TO PONDER

1. Just like we can sometimes have a "gut instinct" about something in our daily lives, we can also have a "gut instinct" about things in our spiritual lives. In fact, as we saw in this chapter, First Thessalonians 5:21 says, "Prove all things; hold fast that which is good." In this verse, Paul didn't tell the Thessalonian believers to simply reject all prophetic utterances; he instructed them to test or *prove* them. God's people are called to evaluate both written and spoken spiritual utterances before fully embracing them. Have you been paying attention to your spiritual environment? How can you be more intentional about testing and holding on to what is spiritually good?

2. Romans 1:32 speaks of those who are fully aware of right and wrong yet still choose to participate in sin: "...Who knowing the judgment of God, that they which commit such things are worthy of death, not only do the same, but have

pleasure in them that do them." This verse warns of the dangers of complacency and willful ignorance. In what areas of your life have you turned a blind eye to wrongdoing? How can you address these issues moving forward?

3. The great restrainer is someone or something that holds down, holds back, prevents, suppresses, restrains, or hinders the manifestation of the Antichrist and the evil accompanying him. This chapter states that the Church *is* that restraining force. As long as it remains on the earth, it will hold the power of God and prevent the full onslaught of evil that is being held at bay from being released. In what ways do you see the Church acting as a restrainer against evil today? As a believer and part of the Church, what responsibilities do you think come with being part of a community that acts as a force against evil?

4. In Second Thessalonians 2:2, Paul urged believers not to be "soon shaken in mind, or be troubled," reminding them (and us) not to give in to fear or confusion, even when it seems the world is in turmoil. Throughout Scripture, we're also repeatedly told not to live in fear. One of the most powerful truths about fear is found in First John 4:18, which says, "There is no fear in love; but perfect love casteth out fear…." When we truly rest in God's perfect love for us, fear loses its grip. What fears have you been holding on to? How might anchoring yourself in God's love help you respond differently to those fears?

5. In his letter to the Thessalonian believers, Paul revealed that the Antichrist will be unveiled only after the Restrainer is removed, marking a specific and precise moment in prophetic history (*see* 2 Thessalonians 2:8). He then leapt forward to describe the triumphant return of Christ at the end of the seven-year Tribulation, declaring that Jesus will utterly destroy the Antichrist with "the spirit of His mouth" and the overwhelming brightness of His coming. How does knowing that Christ will ultimately abolish all evil and bring final judgment against the enemy shape the way you view current events, spiritual warfare, or even your own personal struggles? Does this assurance strengthen your faith or shift the way you think about the future?

Daniel 7:24-27

And the ten horns out of this kingdom are ten kings that shall arise: and another shall rise after them; and he shall be diverse from the first, and he shall subdue three kings. And he shall speak great words against the most High, and shall wear out the saints of the most High, and think to change times and laws: and they shall be given into his hand until a time and times and the dividing of time. But the judgment shall sit, and they shall take away his dominion, to consume and to destroy it unto the end. And the kingdom and dominion, and the greatness of the kingdom under the whole heaven, shall be given to the people of the saints of the most High, whose kingdom is an everlasting kingdom, and all dominions shall serve and obey him.

CHAPTER FOUR

WHAT ELSE DOES THE BIBLE TELL US ABOUT THE ANTICHRIST?

And he shall speak great words against the most High, and shall wear out the saints of the most High, and think to change times and laws: and they shall be given into his hand until a time and times and the dividing of time.

— Daniel 7:25

In the next chapter, we will continue our study on the subject of the Rapture and look at what Jesus Himself said about the catching away of the Church. But because I covered so much in the last chapter about what Paul wrote in his second epistle to the Thessalonians concerning the Antichrist, I want to cover what else the Bible tells us about this "man of sin" before we proceed to what Jesus said about the catching away, or the rapture, of the Church at the end of this age.

The scriptures I cover in this chapter from the books of Daniel and Zechariah in the Old Testament and Second Thessalonians and Revelation in the New Testament contain vivid references to the Antichrist, his behavior, and his nature. The Bible shows us that when the Antichrist finally steps onto the world stage to take the leading position, he will falsely lead the world to believe that the long-awaited, one-of-a-kind, unique, marvelous leader has finally emerged to lead society universally into a new age. But 42 months later — or about three and a half years into the Tribulation — is when he will begin to show his true colors.

People are enamored with the subject of the Antichrist and his identity. But for those who are authentic Christians, at least in a certain sense, it is a moot point because, as we have seen, the Church will be supernaturally removed from the earth before the Antichrist's identity is revealed. However, because the Bible does tell us much about him, it is good for us to know what the Bible says about this evil world leader.

Many speculate about whether or not the Antichrist is alive right now. The answer is that he may well be, but as noted, no one will know who he is until the Church has been raptured, or evacuated from the world scene. But in this chapter, I will provide scriptures that give various names, titles, and descriptions of the Antichrist and his activities. We will begin in the Old Testament and then move to the New Testament. But when we come to the writings of the apostle Paul, it will be clear that much of what Paul wrote about the Antichrist is drawn directly from the book of Daniel, and in some instances, Paul quoted Daniel nearly verbatim.

With each of the following subheads, I will show how various translations interpret these verses. We will begin in each instance with the *King James Version* and then follow with up to nine Bible translations so you can see how these verses have been translated or interpreted by others. In addition to the *King James Version*, I have chosen to use the *New King James Version, New American Standard Bible, New Living Translation, New International Version, English Standard Version, Renner Interpretive Version*, and the *Amplified Bible.*

Daniel 7:24-27
The Rising of the Antichrist

In Daniel 7:24-27, we read about a vision in which the prophet Daniel saw the rising up of the Antichrist at the end of the age. Much of this text is similar to what is found in the book of Revelation. This passage prominently speaks of the Antichrist as one who will subdue other kings and kingdoms and speak blasphemous and atrocious words against the Most High at the end of the age. These verses say:

And the ten horns out of this kingdom are ten kings that shall arise: and another shall rise after them; and he shall be diverse from the first, and he shall subdue three kings.

And he shall speak great words against the most High, and shall wear out the saints of the most High, and think to change times and laws: and they shall be given into his hand until a time and times and the dividing of time.

But the judgment shall sit, and they shall take away his dominion, to consume and to destroy it unto the end.

And the kingdom and dominion, and the greatness of the kingdom under the whole heaven, shall be given to the people of the saints of the most High, whose kingdom is an everlasting kingdom, and all dominions shall serve and obey him.

But especially in the book of Daniel, we find many important references to the Antichrist and his attributes, including the following in Daniel 7:24.

DANIEL 7:24
THE ANTICHRIST WILL BE DIVERSE

We first learn from this passage that the Antichrist will be "diverse." In this verse, the word "diverse" pictures *that which is altered or changed.* In the original text, this word brings to mind what Paul said in Second Corinthians 11:14: "And no marvel; for Satan himself is *transformed* into an angel of light."

In Daniel 7:24, Daniel employed the verb form of "diverse" in the masculine, signifying *changing outward forms.* Interestingly, writers also often used this word in some form to describe *a changing of garments.* It is also comparable to the Greek word *metamorphosis,* the word used in Matthew 17:2 to describe the glorious transfiguration of Jesus. But while Jesus' power can produce transformative change from the *inside out* — not in exterior façades but in the core of one's being — the "diversity" Daniel wrote about concerning the Antichrist describes a game of "bait-and-switch." In this frustrating game, the character's appearance, from the *outside in,* conceals a devastatingly corrupt core.[1]

Attempting to keep up with the Antichrist's relentlessly deceptive *changing of outward forms* will lead to a wearying irritation — or the "wearing out of the saints" (*see* v. 25). His "diversity," or ability to change outward forms and appearances, will wear down his subjects and thereby make the peddling of his agenda to circumvent truth much easier. It will be gaslighting — *deception* — of the highest order!

In some way, the Antichrist will be different, or he will seem to be miraculously transfigured and transformed into a kind of leader that's different than all the others. Since Satan is able to transform himself into an angel of light — and Satan is the one empowering and energizing the Antichrist — perhaps this suggests the Antichrist will in some way appear especially bright and shining to the masses.

The following bullet points are how various Bible translations have interpreted this phrase in Daniel 7:24.

- The *King James Version* says he will be "diverse."
- The *New King James Version* says he will be "different."
- The *New American Standard Bible* says he will be "different from the previous ones."
- The *New Living Translation* says he will be "different from the other[s]."
- The *New International Version* says he will be "different from the earlier ones."
- The *English Standard Version* says he will be "different from the former ones."
- The *Amplified Bible* says he will be "different from the former ones."

Daniel 7:24
The Antichrist Will Subdue Kings

Daniel 7:24 also says that the Antichrist will "subdue kings." In the original text, the word "subdue" means, in effect, *to abase*, *to bring low*, *to humiliate*, or *to sink*. In context, the Antichrist will *abase*, *bring low*, *humiliate*, and *sink* three other kings. This word carries the concept of *a person rising higher by means of callously stepping on someone else*. Hence, we find that the Antichrist will spitefully abase and bring to naught other kings or world leaders and then use that occasion to push himself forward and more greatly magnify his own position.

The following points are how various Bible translations have interpreted this phrase in Daniel 7:24.

- The *King James Version* says he will "subdue" kings.
- The *New King James Version* says he will "subdue" kings.
- The *New American Standard Bible* says he will "humble" kings.
- The *New Living Translation* says he will "subdue" kings.
- The *New International Version* says he will "subdue" kings.
- The *English Standard Version* says he will "put down" kings.
- The *Amplified Bible* says he will "subdue" kings.

Daniel 7:25
The Antichrist Will Speak Great Words Against the Most High

Daniel 7:25 tells us that the Antichrist will "speak great words against the most High." In the original text, the words "shall speak" mean *to speak* or *to utter*, and they are the equivalent of the Greek word *laleo*, which pictures *fluent conversation*. Thus, when Daniel 7:25 says he "shall speak," it actually means he will *freely speak* "great words against the most High."

The phrase "great words" is interpreted from a word that depicts *words that are pompous*. The word "against" actually means *beside* or *near* and indicates *proximity*. Here, Daniel brilliantly used a word to describe the Antichrist's tactic to dastardly mislead the world via speech. This word often works adverbially to spotlight something positioned "directly next to something else." Indeed, the Antichrist will cunningly frame his words as standing "directly beside" or "*on the same level with*" God's.

From this, we know the Antichrist will unleash this scheme, presenting his own words as having equal weight to God's words. Furthermore, the Antichrist will be prompt to say that God is seemingly offering no answers to the destruction that is overwhelming the entire world. On the contrary, the Antichrist has the "solution" — therefore, he eventually argues that *his* words have far more relevance than those of a distant, disinterested, and aloof God.

One thing is certain: In some way, the Antichrist will try to position himself near to God in rank or proximity, or claim he is on par with God, in order to freely assault Him with pompous words. The words "most High" in the original text are used in the Old Testament to describe God as *the notably and undisputedly most supreme authority* above all others.

It should be noted that this audacious verbal characteristic of the Antichrist is also mentioned in Daniel 11:36. Freely assaulting the dignity, honor, and integrity of God's authority will be a regular feature of this wicked individual.

The following points are how various Bible translations have interpreted this phrase in Daniel 7:25.

- The *King James Version* says he will "speak great words against the most High."
- The *New King James Version* says he will "speak pompous words against the Most High."
- The *New American Standard Bible* says he will "speak against the Most High."
- The *New Living Translation* says he will "defy the Most High."
- The *New International Version* says he will "speak against the Most High."
- The *English Standard Version* says he will "speak words against the Most High."
- The *Amplified Bible* says he will "speak words against the Most High [God]."

Daniel 7:25
The Antichrist Will Wear Out the Saints

Daniel 7:25 tells us that the Antichrist will "wear out the saints of the most High." In Hebrew, the words "wear out" mean *to afflict*, *destroy*, *devour*, *engulf*, *persecute*, *ruin*, or *swallow up*. This word is used in the Old Testament to picture devastating calamity that leads to utter consumption or obliteration. The word "saints" means *sacred*, and it refers to both the people of Israel, whom the Antichrist will wage war against in the second half of the Tribulation, and to those who come to Christ during the Tribulation and who refuse to worship the Antichrist.

The following points are how various Bible translations have interpreted this phrase in Daniel 7:25.

- The *King James Version* says he will "wear out the saints of the most High."
- The *New King James Version* says he will "persecute the saints of the Most High."
- The *New American Standard Bible* says he will "wear down the saints of the Highest one."
- The *New Living Translation* says he will "oppress the holy people of the Most High."
- The *New International Version* says he will "oppress his holy people."
- The *English Standard Version* says he will "wear out the saints of the Most High."
- The *Amplified Bible* says he will "wear down the saints of the Most High."

DANIEL 7:25
THE ANTICHRIST WILL THINK TO CHANGE TIMES AND LAWS

Daniel 7:25 tells us that the Antichrist will "think to change times and laws." In Hebrew, the words "to think" mean *to intend* or *to purpose.* Thus, during his rule, the Antichrist will intentionally and purposefully do all that is within his power to "change times and laws." The word "change" means *to completely alter.* This tells us that he will seductively work a scheme to completely alter "times and laws." The word "times" refers to *the specific, appointed time or season* during which the Antichrist rules, and the word "laws" refers to *religions, codes, and laws.*

In Chapter Three on page 114, it was noted:

...The Antichrist will throw out all previously agreed-upon moral standards and will rise as an aggressive proponent of departing from God's well-established laws. He will not be just a person with a lawless attitude; he will be *the Man of Lawlessness* — the epitome of one who has fully discarded God's well-established laws to become Satan's perfect candidate to lead a mutinous world that has likewise rejected the voice of God and Scripture as its internal compass. This word *anomia* depicts the Antichrist as one who is free of past moral constraints and, hence, free and unshackled from the law of God that once governed society. Because Paul used a definite article in Greek, it tells us this

individual is not just a person with a lawless attitude, but, rather, this is *the Man of Lawlessness*, or *the Antichrist.*

Thus, we find Daniel prophesied that the Antichrist will aggressively and intentionally try to free the world of all remnants of the law of God and past moral codes as he attempts to change the season to become a world free of God's Word.

The following points are how various Bible translations have interpreted this phrase in Daniel 7:25.

- The *King James Version* says he will "think to change times and laws."
- The *New King James Version* says he will "intend to change times and law."
- The *New American Standard Bible* says that he will "intend to make alterations in times and in law."
- The *New Living Translation* says he will "try to change their sacred festivals and laws."
- The *New International Version* says he will "try to change the set times and the laws."
- The *English Standard Version* says he will "think to change the times and the law."
- The *Amplified Bible* says he will "intend to change the times and the law."

Daniel 7:25
The Antichrist Will Have Times and Laws in His Hand 'Until a Time and Times and the Dividing of Time'

Daniel 7:25 tells us that the Antichrist will have "times and laws...given into his hand until a time and times and the dividing of time." Here, Daniel strangely stated that the Antichrist will take advantage of his season, attempt to alter all known existing moral codes, and abuse God's people until "a time and times and the dividing of time."

In the original text, the words "shall be given" not only mean *to be given*, or *given over to*, but also *to be burdened*. Most scholars believe that the word "they" in verse 25 refers both to the people of God and to the times and laws the

Antichrist will dominate over during his rule. The phrase "a time and times and the dividing of times" refers to the last three and a half years of the Tribulation when the Antichrist will rule the most ruthlessly. Thus, for a limited period of three and a half years, it will seem that this exact season, along with all law and God's people, will be delivered into his hands.

The following points are how various Bible translations have interpreted this phrase in Daniel 7:25.

- The *King James Version* says "they shall be given into his hand until a time and times and the dividing of time."
- The *New King James Version* says "the saints shall be given into his hand for a time and times and half a time."
- The *New American Standard Bible* says "they will be handed over to him for a time, times, and half a time."
- The *New Living Translation* says "they will be placed under his control for a time, times, and half a time."
- The *New International Version* says "the holy people will be delivered into his hands for a time, times and half a time."
- The *English Standard Version* says "they shall be given into his hand for a time, times, and half a time."
- The *Amplified Bible* says "they will be given into his hand for a time, [two] times, and half a time [three and one-half years]."

Daniel 7:26
The Antichrist Will Be Judged, His Dominion Will Be Taken Away, and He will Be Consumed and Destroyed

Daniel 7:26 tells us that the Antichrist's "judgment shall sit, and they shall take away his dominion, to consume and to destroy it unto the end." In the original text, the word "judgment" depicts *a judicial court*, and it is the equivalent of the Greek word *krisis*, which pictures *a legal court, a decision made by a legal court, a court decree, a legal procedure at the court*, or *a verdict delivered that results in judgment.* Here, Daniel stated that the court of Heaven has rendered a final judicial judgment against the Antichrist. It is important to note that the Greek word *krisis* is where we derive the English word *crisis*, and it is certain that when the court of Heaven finally carries out its verdict against the Antichrist, it will be a great moment of *crisis* for this evil individual.

In this verse, Daniel marshalled a word for "judgment" to display *a strikingly vigorous irony of justice.* The Antichrist will seek, above all else and at all costs, to be seated on a throne on par with God. But in the course of this infinitely vain pursuit, he will regularly seek to place his words, titles, and grandeur in juxtaposition with God's. In response, God who sits on the true throne of righteousness will cause His judgment against the Antichrist to "sit in an immovable position," as further indicated in the rest of this verse.[2]

The word "sit" describes what is *set* and *settled*, as the verdict of a court that is already decided and no longer open for discussion. Thus, there will be no negotiating on the day this vengeance is carried out against the Antichrist. In fact, his judgment will be so profound that Daniel said the court of Heaven will "take away his dominion." The words "take away" mean *to remove* or *to strip*, as one would strip a royal robe from a dignitary. The word "dominion" refers to *authority, power*, or *sovereignty*. Thus, when the edict of Heaven's court is fully carried out, it will leave the Antichrist stripped bare of all the authority, power, and sovereignty that he previously exercised.

Even more, Daniel 7:26 states the court of Heaven will take away his dominion "to consume and to destroy it unto the end." The word "consume" means *to annihilate, decimate, destroy, exterminate, obliterate, perish, or to completely wipe out until not a shred of it remains.* On top of that, Daniel added the word "destroy," which means *to destroy, to be completely lost*, or *to utterly waste.* This verb carries the concept of *being irrevocably cut off from pre-designed purpose.* This Old Testament word is also similar to the Greek word for "destroy" in John 10:10, where destruction is the conclusion in the "thief's" pernicious progression to "steal, kill, and *destroy*." All of Heaven surely delighted in Daniel seeing and proclaiming the glorious day when the destroyer will finally face destruction![3]

The following points are how various Bible translations have interpreted this phrase in Daniel 7:26.

- The *King James Version* says the court of Heaven will take away his dominion "to consume and to destroy *it* unto the end."
- The *New King James Version* says the court shall be seated and take away his dominion "to consume and destroy it forever."
- The *New American Standard Bible* says the court will convene for judgment, and his dominion will be taken away, "annihilated and destroyed forever."
- The *New Living Translation* says the court will pass judgment, and all his power will be taken away and "completely destroyed."
- The *New International Version* says the court will sit, and his power will be taken away and "completely destroyed forever."
- The *English Standard Version* says the court shall sit in judgment, and his dominion shall be taken away, "to be consumed and destroyed to the end."
- The *Amplified Bible* says the court of the Most High will sit in judgment, and his dominion will be taken away, "[first to be] consumed [gradually] and [then] to be destroyed forever."

Daniel 8:23
The Antichrist Will Be a King With a 'Fierce Countenance'

Daniel 8:23 tells us that the Antichrist will be "a king of fierce countenance."

In the original Hebrew, the word "fierce" carries the idea of something *defiant, fierce, harsh, impudent, inhuman, mighty, strong,* or *vehement.* Although the word can be used to positively characterize a strong and prevailing leader, it also is regularly used in a negative sense to picture *a fierce disposition* and one who is nearly *inhuman* in his treatment of others.

The following points are how various Bible translations have interpreted this phrase in Daniel 8:23.

- The *King James Version* says he will be "a king of fierce countenance."
- The *New King James Version* says he "shall arise, having fierce features."
- The *New American Standard Bible* says he will arise "insolent."
- The *New Living Translation* says he will be "a fierce king."
- The *New International Version* says he will be "a fierce-looking king."
- The *English Standard Version* says he will be "a king of bold face."
- The *Amplified Bible* says he "will arise insolent."

DANIEL 8:23
THE ANTICHRIST WILL UNDERSTAND DARK SENTENCES

Daniel 8:23 also tells us that the Antichrist will be a man "understanding dark sentences."

In the original Hebrew, the words "dark sentences" carry the idea of *one who deals in secrets*. The word "occult" also has to do with *dark and hidden things*. Since the Antichrist will be empowered by Satan himself, the words "dark sentences" could be a reference to *dark spiritual activity*.

The Antichrist will introduce *dark things* to the world during the seven-year Tribulation period. He will so deal in darkness that a time will come when he will even enter the Holy of Holies in a rebuilt Temple in Jerusalem to exalt himself above all that is called God or that is worshipped (*see* 2 Thessalonians 2:4), and this will be the very apex of his dealing in darkness.

The following points are how various Bible translations have interpreted this phrase in Daniel 8:23.

- The *King James Version* says he will be a man "understanding dark sentences."
- The *New King James Version* says he will be one "who understands sinister schemes."
- The *New American Standard Bible* says he will be "skilled in intrigue."
- The *New Living Translation* says he will be "a master of intrigue."

- The *New International Version* says he will be "a master of intrigue."
- The *English Standard Version* says he will be "one who understands riddles."
- The *Amplified Bible* says he will be "skilled in intrigue and cunning."

Daniel 9:26
The Antichrist Is the Prince That Is To Come

Daniel 9:26 tells us that the Antichrist will be "the prince that shall come." In Hebrew, the word "prince" means one who makes himself known as *a commander, governor*, or *leader*. This word is translated generically to signify *coming into a high level of rulership* or *being clearly identified or publicly announced as a chosen leader*.[4] However, in this case, he will be *a Satan-empowered leader*. Because the Hebrew word can be used to denote one who rules by divine authority, it infers that the Antichrist will claim divine right to rule, which certainly would play into the moment when he will declare himself to be God.

The following points are how various Bible translations have interpreted this phrase in Daniel 9:26.

- The *King James Version* calls him "the prince that shall come."
- The *New King James Version* calls him "the prince who is to come."
- The *New American Standard Bible* calls him "the prince who is to come."
- The *New Living Translation* calls him "a ruler [that] will arise."
- The *New International Version* calls him "the ruler who will come."
- The *English Standard Version* calls him "the prince who is to come."
- The *Amplified Bible* calls him the "prince who is to come."

Daniel 11:21
The Antichrist Will Be a Vile Person

Daniel 11:21 tells us that the Antichrist will be "a vile person." In Hebrew, the word "vile" means *contemptible, despised, disdained*, or *to be scorned*. Although the Antichrist will project himself as the progressive leader of a new world order — and the world will laud his appearing — the Hebrew word used here means God deems him as one who is *contemptible*, *disdained*, and *insignificant*.

It is also important to notice that the original Hebrew word is frequently used to picture individuals who reject God's commands, which also fits into the narrative of the Antichrist being the "lawless one" — or one who has completely rejected the law of God.

The following points are how various Bible translations have interpreted this phrase in Daniel 11:21.

- The *King James Version* says he will be "a vile person."
- The *New King James Version* says he will be "a vile person."
- The *New American Standard Bible* says he will be "a despicable person."
- The *New Living Translation* says he will be "a despicable man."
- The *New International Version* says he will be "a contemptible person."
- The *English Standard Version* says he will be "a contemptible person."
- The *Amplified Bible* says he will be "a despicable and despised person."

Daniel 11:36
The Antichrist Will Do According to His Own Will

Daniel 11:36 tells us that the Antichrist "shall do according to his will." In Hebrew, the words "shall do" mean *to carry out an act*. The words "according to his own will" depict one who acts *in accordance with his own delight or pleasure*. This lets us know that the Antichrist will focus on *doing whatever he wants* or on *carrying out that which brings him the maximum pleasure or the goal that he wishes to obtain*. In context, we find he will be one who is chiefly concerned with himself and *executing his own wishes*.

The following points are how various Bible translations have interpreted this phrase in Daniel 11:36.

- The *King James Version* says he "shall do according to his will."

- The *New King James Version* says he "shall do according to his own will."
- The *New American Standard Bible* says he "will do as he pleases."
- The *New Living Translation* says he "will do as he pleases."
- The *New International Version* says he "will do as he pleases."
- The *English Standard Version* says he "shall do as he wills."
- The *Amplified Bible* says he "will do exactly as he pleases."

Daniel 11:36
The Antichrist Will Exalt and Magnify Himself Above Every God

Daniel 11:36 tells us that the Antichrist "shall exalt himself and magnify himself above every god." In Hebrew, the word "exalt" means *to be highly lifted up*. This brings to mind the original sin of Lucifer, who was lifted up with pride because he shined so brightly.

Recalling that the Antichrist will be empowered and energized by Satan, it should not surprise us that, like Satan, he will highly elevate himself in the eyes of the world. The word "exalt" is frequently used in both the Old and New Testaments to depict *the highly elevated status* of God, but here it pictures how the Antichrist will highly exalt *himself*.

But the verse additionally states that he will "magnify" himself. The Hebrew word for "magnify" means *to become great, to promote*, or *to magnify*. The word "magnify" is usually used to denote magnifying God, but in this verse we discover that as time passes, the Antichrist will promote and magnify himself even "above every god." The word "above" means *against, above, beyond*, and *over*.

Remember that this Man of Lawlessness is called the "Antichrist," translated from the word *antichristos*, which is a compound of the Greek words *anti* and *christos*. The word *anti* means *against* or *in the place of*, and the word *christos* means *Christ*. When compounded, it tells us that the Antichrist will be *against Christ*, and he will in many respects attempt *to take the place* or try *to replicate the place* of Christ. This agrees with the word "above" in Daniel 11:36 that says he will attempt to exalt and magnify himself "above every god," including Christ, the King of all kings and God of all gods.

The word "every" is from a Hebrew word that is all-inclusive and means *all*, *every*, or *the whole*. While Christians see the Antichrist as one who will try to exalt himself above Christ, this prophetic verse from Daniel 11:36 actually means he will eventually exalt and magnify himself above, beyond, and over every god and every religion in the world. Indeed, his greatest assault will be against Christ and His people, but in the process he will also laud himself as being "above every god." You will soon see that these truths in Daniel 11:36 are nearly quoted verbatim by the apostle Paul in Second Thessalonians 2:4.

The following points are how various Bible translations have interpreted this phrase in Daniel 11:36.

- The *King James Version* says he "shall exalt himself and magnify himself above every god."
- The *New King James Version* says he "shall exalt and magnify himself above every god."
- The *New American Standard Bible* says he "will exalt himself and boast against every god."
- The *New Living Translation* says he will be "exalting himself and claiming to be greater than every god."
- The *New International Version* says he "will exalt and magnify himself above every god."
- The *English Standard Version* says he "shall exalt himself and magnify himself above every god."
- The *Amplified Bible* says he "will exalt himself and magnify himself above every god."

Daniel 11:36
The Antichrist Will Speak Blasphemies Against the God of Gods

Daniel 11:36 tells us that the Antichrist "shall speak marvellous things against the God of gods." In the original text, the words "shall speak" carry a range of meanings, including *one who speaks authoritatively* or *one who converses, declares, promises, subdues, or threatens.* This tells us that the Antichrist will *authoritatively speak* and *make declarations* that are blasphemous with the intention of *subduing* and *threatening* God himself.

The original word translated "marvellous things" interestingly means *to speak extraordinarily marvelous and wonderful things that distinguish one thing from another.* In this context, as the Antichrist exalts and magnifies himself above every god, he will be one who speaks extraordinarily marvelous and wonderful things about himself in order to distinguish himself as being more highly exalted and greater than God Himself with the purpose of causing the world to stand in *awe* and *wonder* of him as the new Savior.

But Daniel 11:36 specifically says he will speak blasphemies "against" the God of gods. The word "against" again means *above*, *beyond*, and *over*, and, thus, it implies that he will marvelously exalt himself way *above*, *beyond*, and *over* God himself. It is clear that when Paul stated in Second Thessalonians 2:4 the Antichrist will exalt himself "...above all that is called God, or that is worshipped...," he was drawing his prophetic insight from Daniel 11:36.

The following points are how various Bible translations have interpreted this phrase in Daniel 11:36.

- The *King James Version* says he "shall speak marvellous things against the God of gods."
- The *New King James Version* says he "shall speak blasphemies against the God of gods."
- The *New American Standard Bible* says he "will speak dreadful things against the God of gods."
- The *New Living Translation* says he will be "even blaspheming the God of gods."
- The *New International Version* says he "will say unheard-of things against the God of gods."
- The *English Standard Version* says he "shall speak astonishing things against the God of gods."

- The *Amplified Bible* says he "will speak astounding and disgusting things against the God of gods."

Daniel 11:36
The Antichrist Will Prosper Until the Time of Wrath Is Fulfilled

Daniel 11:36 tells us that the Antichrist "shall prosper till the indignation be accomplished." In the original Hebrew, the word "prosper" means *to advance, to push forward, to succeed,* or *to thrive*. The word primarily carries the idea of *advancement, prosperity,* and *success*. This Hebrew word connotes *the forward advancement of what one zealously purposed to do* and *the moving ahead of plans.*[5] Thus, this prophetic verse tells us that the Antichrist will *make great forward advancement*, that he will *prosper*, and that he will *have tremendous success* — that is, "*till* the indignation [wrath] be accomplished."

In Hebrew, the word "till" means *as far as, during, up to,* or *until*, and that means a time limit will be set to the Antichrist's prospering. Daniel 11:36 says the Antichrist will prosper *up until* "the indignation" has been accomplished. The word "indignation," or "wrath" in Hebrew speaks of *anger, fury, indignation,* or *wrath*, and it is used in the Old Testament to denote *the wrath of God.*

This word corresponds to the Greek word *thumos*, which is the New Testament word for the wrath of God and pictures *the intense outburst of divine wrath*. But it is used in Daniel 11:36 to underscore that an intense outburst of divine wrath will occur during the Tribulation when bowls of wrath will literally be poured out upon the ungodly.

Daniel 11:36 says that the Antichrist will be successful only up until the moment when the outpouring of God's wrath "has been accomplished." The word "accomplished" means *to carry out, to perform,* or *to execute*, as a judicial sentence of a court is carried out, performed, and fully executed.

During the seven-year Tribulation period, the divine sentence of Heaven will be executed as wrath is poured out. Paul drew from Daniel 11:36 when he stated that the rule of the Antichrist will be obliterated by the "spirit of his [Christ's] mouth and by the brightness of his [Christ's] coming" at Christ's Second Coming, or Second Advent (*see* 2 Thessalonians 2:8).

The following points are how various Bible translations have interpreted this phrase in Daniel 11:36.

- The *King James Version* says he "shall prosper till the indignation be accomplished."
- The *New King James Version* says he "shall prosper till the wrath has been accomplished."
- The *New American Standard Bible* says he "will be successful until the indignation is finished."
- The *New Living Translation* says he "will succeed, but only until the time of wrath is completed."
- The *New International Version* says he "will be successful until the time of wrath is completed."
- The *English Standard Version* says he "shall prosper till the indignation is accomplished."
- The *Amplified Bible* says he "will prosper until the indignation is finished."

Daniel 11:37
The Antichrist Will Not Regard the God of His Fathers

Daniel 11:37 tells us "neither shall he [the Antichrist] regard the God of his fathers." In Hebrew, the word "regard" means *to consider*, *to grasp*, or *to understand.* The word "fathers" is from a word that refers to forefathers, and it was used in the Old Testament to denote not only paternal forefathers, but also those who passed their faith to succeeding generations. The Hebrew word, often translated as "regard," signifies *properly discerning the value of something.* In the spirit of his father the devil, the Antichrist will fiercely refuse to acknowledge the value of God.[6]

Some postulate that this means the Antichrist may come from a Jewish heritage, but that he will not *consider*, *grasp*, or *regard* as significant the faith of his predecessors. But others argue that the Antichrist will be a Gentile, and this means he will reject whatever was the faith of his forefathers. Regardless, he will reject that faith, of whatever sort it is, for we have seen that he will blaspheme other religions and will ridiculously exalt and magnify himself above every god and religion that is known.

The following points are how various Bible translations have interpreted this phrase in Daniel 11:37.

- The *King James Version* says "neither shall he regard the God of his fathers."
- The *New King James Version* says he "shall regard neither the God of his fathers."
- The *New American Standard Bible* says he "will show no regard for the gods of his fathers."
- The *New Living Translation* says he "will have no respect for the gods of his ancestors."
- The *New International Version* says he "will show no regard for the gods of his ancestors."
- The *English Standard Version* says he "shall pay no attention to the gods of his fathers."
- The *Amplified Bible* says he "will have no regard for the gods of his fathers."

DANIEL 11:37
THE ANTICHRIST WILL HAVE NO DESIRE FOR WOMEN

Daniel 11:37 tells us that the Antichrist will not have the "desire of women." In the original Hebrew, the word "desire" means *to desire*, *to find delight in*, *to enjoy*, or *to have pleasure in*. It is a word associated with *lust*, as in *sexual lust*. Some scholars take the fact that he has no "desire of women" to mean that the Antichrist will be a *homosexual*. While this verse does not emphatically state that, we can concur that this verse means he will not have a natural, sexual desire for women.

The Antichrist could have an untold number of women throwing themselves at him, but this verse could imply that he, nevertheless, unlike so many leaders before him, will not be brought down via sexual entanglement with either a lover or spouse. Thus, while it is possible that his lack of desire may refer to homosexuality, it could also speak of a notable devaluing of all sexual activity. Rather than communicate a complete disinterest in sexual relations, this phrase may point instead to an astonishing obsession for control, agenda fulfillment, and receiving of worship to the exclusion of all else. Thus, the words of this verse display a darkened heart wherein *self* rules above all.[7]

However, some also speculate this phrase "nor the desire of women" may actually mean that he will not be one that is desired by women. Some speculate that perhaps he will be an individual who has no proper appraisal of women, and therefore women will not be attracted to him. However, it is difficult to imagine the Antichrist taking the world by storm without the approval — at least, in general — of women.

A large number of commentators indeed believe that Daniel 11:37 means the Antichrist will be an individual who is homosexual. This would certainly fall in line with Second Thessalonians 2:3-10, where Paul vividly stated that the Antichrist will be *the Man of Lawlessness* — "man of sin," "son of perdition," and "Wicked" — who has shucked away all past moral codes.

The following points are how various Bible translations have interpreted this phrase in Daniel 11:37.

- The *King James Version* says he will not have "the desire of women."
- The *New King James Version* says he will not have "the desire of women."
- The *New American Standard Bible* says he will not have "the desire of women."
- The *New Living Translation* says he will not be "loved by women."
- The *New International Version* says he will not be "one desired by women."
- The *English Standard Version* says he will not be "beloved by women."
- The *Amplified Bible* says he will not have "the desire of women."

Daniel 11:37
The Antichrist Will Not Regard Any God

Daniel 11:37 tells us again that the Antichrist will not "regard any god." The word "any" is all-inclusive and means *all, every*, or *the whole*. Clearly this point is important, for Daniel — and Paul — repeated over and over again that the Antichrist will disregard every god, the God of gods, and any and every god.

In agreement with what Paul wrote in Second Thessalonians 2:4, the Man of Lawlessness will enter the Holy of Holies in a rebuilt Temple in Jerusalem where he will take his seat and will do all within his means to show that he is god. Once again we see that Daniel's prophetic writings were used by Paul when he also described the Antichrist.

The following points are how various Bible translations have interpreted this phrase in Daniel 11:37.

- The *King James Version* says nor will he "regard any god."
- The *New King James Version* says nor will he "regard any god."
- The *New American Standard Bible* says nor will he "show regard for any other god."
- The *New Living Translation* says he will "have no respect for any other god."
- The *New International Version* says nor will he "regard any god."
- The *English Standard Version* says he shall not "pay attention to any other god."
- The *Amplified Bible* says he will not have "regard for any other god."

Daniel 11:37
The Antichrist Will Magnify Himself Above All

Daniel 11:37 tells us again that the Antichrist "shall magnify himself above all." As we saw in our study of Daniel 11:36, the Hebrew word for "magnify" means *to become great, to promote*, or *to magnify*, and it was most commonly used to denote *magnifying God*. But in this verse, Daniel reiterated again that the Antichrist will promote and magnify himself "above all."

The word "above" again means *against, above, beyond*, and *over*. There will be no god, no religion, no governmental authority — literally nothing or no one — that he will not audaciously exalt himself above.

Writers have used this Hebrew word to speak of *making something rapidly spreading and far-reaching*. The term also signifies *promotion*. The most diabolically powerful leaders in history have all utilized tremendously effective propaganda machines. The Antichrist's promotional campaign will, in both its scope and results, incalculably outdo any who have come before him.[8]

Paul also drew from this prophetic insight about the Antichrist when he wrote Second Thessalonians 2:4, "Who opposeth and exalteth himself above all that is called God, or that is worshipped; so that he as God sitteth in the temple of God, shewing himself that he is God."

The following points are how various Bible translations have interpreted this phrase in Daniel 11:37.

- The *King James Version* says he "shall magnify himself above all."
- The *New King James Version* says he "shall exalt himself above them all."
- The *New American Standard Bible* says he "will boast against them all."
- The *New Living Translation* says he "will boast that he is greater than them all."
- The *New International Version* says he "will exalt himself above them all."
- The *English Standard Version* says he "shall magnify himself above all."
- The *Amplified Bible* says he "shall magnify himself above them all."

Zechariah 11:16
The Antichrist Will Be a Ruthless Leader

Zechariah 11:16 tells us that the Antichrist will be "a shepherd in the land, which shall not visit those that be cut off, neither shall seek the young one, nor heal that that is broken, nor feed that that standeth still: but he shall eat the flesh of the fat, and tear their claws in pieces."

This verse tells us that although the Antichrist may style himself as a benevolent and kind leader, when he actually comes to power, he will not care for the welfare of the world as a true shepherd would care for his sheep or as a leader would represent the best interests of his or her constituents. We have already seen in Daniel 11:36 that he will be *one who is chiefly concerned with himself and with executing his own wishes and interests.*

In fact, Zechariah 11:16 says he will provide no care for those who are cut off, he will not seek the well being of the young, he will not heal those who are broken, and he will not feed or nurture the masses. Instead, it states he will "eat and devour" them. Thus, regardless of how the Antichrist styles himself in order to be marketed to the masses, he will nevertheless be harsh and inhumane to humanity. This inhumane treatment is clearly seen in Revelation 13:10, where we read that anyone who does not fall in line to worship him will be massacred with the sword.

The following points are how various Bible translations have interpreted this phrase in Zechariah 11:16.

- The *King James Version* says he will be "a shepherd in the land, which shall not visit those that be cut off, neither shall seek the young one, nor heal that that is broken, nor feed that that standeth still: but he shall eat the flesh of the fat, and tear their claws in pieces."
- The *New King James Version* says that he will be "a shepherd in the land *who* will not care for those who are cut off, nor seek the young, nor heal those that are broken, nor feed those that still stand. But he will eat the flesh of the fat and tear their hooves in pieces."
- The *New American Standard Bible* says that he will be "a shepherd in the land who will not care for the perishing, seek the scattered, heal the broken, or provide for the one who is exhausted, but will devour the flesh of the fat sheep and tear off their hoofs."
- The *New Living Translation* says that he will be "a shepherd who will not care for those who are dying, nor look after the young, nor heal the injured,

nor feed the healthy. Instead, this shepherd will eat the meat of the fattest sheep and tear off their hooves."

- The *New International Version* says that he will be "a shepherd over the land who will not care for the lost, or seek the young, or heal the injured, or feed the healthy, but will eat the meat of the choice sheep, tearing off their hooves."
- The *English Standard Version* says that he will be "a shepherd who does not care for those being destroyed, or seek the young or heal the maimed or nourish the healthy, but devours the flesh of the fat ones, tearing off even their hoofs."
- The *Amplified Bible* says that he will be "a [false] shepherd in the land who will not care for the perishing, seek the scattered, heal the broken, or feed the healthy; but will eat the flesh of the fat ones and tear off their hoofs [to consume everything]."

SECOND THESSALONIANS 2:3
THE ANTICHRIST WILL BE A MAN OF SIN

In Second Thessalonians 2:3, Paul said the Antichrist will be a "man of sin." As noted in Chapter Three on pages 113-114:

The word 'sin' in this case is the Greek word *anomia*, which is actually a form of the word *nomos*, which is the Greek word for *law*, and it is regularly used to depict *the standard of what is legally or morally correct*. But when an 'a' is attached to the front of this word, it becomes *anomia*. That 'a' has a cancelling effect, so rather than depict the law or a correct moral standard, the word *anomia* holds the opposite meaning — that is, *without law* or *lawless* — and it pictures either a person or a people who possess *no fixed moral standards*. It depicts those who live *void of standards*, *without law*, or *in a state of lawlessness*. It is used prophetically to depict a last-days society that will throw out all previously agreed-upon moral standards and will depart from God's well-established laws at the very end of the age.

Thus, we find that the Bible tells us that as part of a last-days scheme, society will construct a new world order that has few, if any, hard and fast rules of what is morally right and wrong. In essence, this will be a lawless world — that is, a world detached from the 'outdated' voice of the Bible. Society will attempt to disconnect from most moral standards that were once held to be the common rule and view of society. Because Paul used the word 'sin' — the Greek word *anomia* — in connection with the Antichrist, we know that this individual will be *void of standards* and *without law*.

This means the Antichrist will throw out all previously agreed-upon moral standards and will rise as a hostile, aggressive proponent of departing from God's well-established laws. He will not be just a person with a lawless attitude; he will be *the Man of Lawlessness* — the epitome of one who has fully discarded God's well-established laws to become Satan's perfect candidate to lead a mutinous world that has likewise rejected the voice of God and Scripture as its internal compass. This word *anomia* depicts the Antichrist as one who is free of past moral constraints and, hence, free and unshackled from the law of God that once governed society. Because Paul used a definite article in Greek, it tells us this individual is not just a person with a lawless attitude, but, rather, this is *the Man of Lawlessness*, or *the Antichrist*.

All this unmistakably means when the Antichrist rises to his powerful position, he will throw out all previous moral codes, and he will be known as an impressive new kind of progressive leader who leads the world in a direction that is free of all past moral restraints.

The following are nine different translations that communicate how the phrase "the man of sin" in Second Thessalonians 2:3 is interpreted in different versions of the Bible.

- The *King James Version* calls him "that man of sin."
- The *New King James Version* calls him "the man of sin."
- The *New American Standard Bible* calls him "the man of lawlessness."

- The *New Living Translation* calls him "the man of lawlessness."
- The *New International Version* calls him "the man of lawlessness."
- The *English Standard Version* calls him "the man of lawlessness."
- The *Amplified Bible* calls him "the man of lawlessness."
- The *Renner Interpretive Version* calls him "the Man of Lawlessness."

Second Thessalonians 2:3
The Antichrist Will Be *Suddenly* Revealed

In Second Thessalonians 2:3, Paul said the Antichrist will be "revealed." As noted in Chapter Three on pages 114-115:

> **...The current trend toward lawlessness — that is, the construction of a new world order with morals contrary to those stated in God's Word — will eventually produce a collective mindset in society that no longer feels the pain or conviction of sin and is numb to its consequences. And according to Paul, that mutinous society will be primed and prepared for the Antichrist to be 'revealed' at that time.**
>
> **Paul added that once the world has generally 'chucked' the law of God, and it has been modified to become a world freed of past constraints, that is precisely when this lawless individual — *the Antichrist* — will be 'revealed.' The word 'revealed' is the Greek word *apokalupto*, which is a compound of *apo* and *kalupto*. The word *apo* means *away*, and the word *kalupto* refers to something that is *veiled*, *covered*, *concealed*, or *hidden*. But when these words are compounded into *apokalupto*, the new word depicts *a veil that has been removed, thus exposing what was behind the veil, concealed, or hidden from view.***
>
> **Paul used this word to inform us that a day is coming when the 'man of sin' — the Antichrist — who, until the time of his revealing, will have been concealed and hidden from public view. But at just the right time, he will suddenly appear and step onto the world stage for all to see.**

Although the Antichrist will be center stage and ready for his appearance to the world, the curtains that conceal his identity will remain shut until the worldwide mutiny against God — the *apostasia*, or falling away — occurs and until the 'restrainer' is taken out of the way. He will *not* be revealed until the world is lawless enough to welcome and receive him and his new agenda.

Paul said that the Antichrist will be revealed "in his time." That time will not take place until the Restrainer has first been removed, and Paul stated in Second Thessalonians 2:3 and 8 that precisely in that moment the curtains will be pulled back for the world to see the Antichrist standing center stage.

The following points are how various Bible translations have interpreted this phrase in Second Thessalonians 2:3.

- The *King James Version* says he will be "revealed."
- The *New King James Version* says he will be "revealed."
- The *New American Standard Bible* says he will be "revealed."
- The *New Living Translation* says that he will be "revealed."
- The *New International Version* says he will be "revealed."
- The *English Standard Version* says he will be "revealed."
- The *Amplified Bible* says he will be "revealed."
- The *Renner Interpretive Version* says "he will finally come out of hiding and go public."

SECOND THESSALONIANS 2:3
THE ANTICHRIST WILL BE THE SON OF PERDITION

In Second Thessalonians 2:3, Paul called the Antichrist the "son of perdition." As noted in Chapter Three on page 115:

The word 'perdition' is a translation of the Greek word *apoleia*, and it speaks of something *doomed*, *rotten*, *ruinous*, or *decaying*. Although

the Antichrist's claim is that he will lead the world into a more progressive future, what he will bring to the world is doom, destruction, rot, ruin, and decay. There will ultimately be absolutely no redeeming values in anything produced by his rule.

Thus, there will be no redeeming value of any sort in anything that the Antichrist does during his short seven-year rule on the earth. Everything he touches will lead to doom, destruction, rot, ruin, and decay.

The following points are how various Bible translations have interpreted this phrase in Second Thessalonians 2:3.

- The *King James Version* calls him "the son of perdition."
- The *New King James Version* calls him "the son of perdition."
- The *New American Standard Bible* calls him "the son of destruction."
- The *New Living Translation* calls him "the one who brings destruction."
- The *New International Version* calls him "the man doomed to destruction."
- The *English Standard Version* calls him "the son of destruction."
- The *Amplified Bible* calls him "the son of destruction [the Antichrist, the one who is destined to be destroyed]."
- The *Renner Interpretive Version* calls him "the long-awaited and predicted Son of Doom and Destruction, the one who brings rot and ruin to everything he touches."

Second Thessalonians 2:4
The Antichrist Will Oppose and Magnify Himself Above God

In Second Thessalonians 2:4, Paul wrote that the Antichrist will be one "who opposeth and exalteth himself above all that is called God, or that is worshipped; so that he as God sitteth in the temple of God, shewing himself that he is God."

In this chapter, I am providing a list of points that the Bible tells us about the Antichrist, some of which have been covered in Chapter Three. The following text concerning this Man of Lawlessness is noted in that chapter on pages 117-118:

The word 'opposeth' is translated from the Greek word *antikeimai*, which is a compound of *anti* and *keimai*. The word *anti* means *against*, and *keimai* means *to set* or *to lay in place*. When the two words are compounded, the new word depicts *an entrenched position against everything established*. The tense paints the picture of *a continual, unending, and perpetual resistance*, and it reveals that rebellion is ingrained in this individual.

Even more, he is called the 'Antichrist,' which is a compound of the word *anti* and the word *Christos*. The word *anti* means *against* or *in the place of*, while the word *Christos* means *Christ*. This alerts us that this evil person will have *a deeply rooted rebellion ingrained in his disposition* that sets him *against* Christ and *against* everything that Christ represents — and in many respects, he will attempt to take the place of Christ in the eyes of society. This means people will see him as a Messiah-type individual who has come to save the world and transform it into his new reality.

But Paul said the Antichrist is one that 'opposeth and exalteth himself above all that is called God, or that is worshipped.' We already saw the meaning of this word from the Greek, but this fierce opposition categorically tells us that the Antichrist will be *brazenly against* every previous godly way of thinking. He will attempt to lead a lawless world in an effort to 'bulldoze' former dogmas and established codes of morality and move them out of the way. His goal will be to construct a new world order — one that is utterly free of God's influence.

After Paul said this Man of Lawlessness would 'oppose' God, Paul furthermore stated the Antichrist will be one who 'exalteth' himself. The word 'exalteth' is translated from the Greek word *huperairo*, and it means *highly exalted*. Thus, when the Antichrist finally appears on the world stage, he will quickly begin to exalt himself in the eyes of the world — to such an extent that verse 4 says he will even sit in the 'temple.' The word 'temple' is from the Greek word *naos*, the word used to depict *the innermost part of the temple* — and in this case, the Temple

in Jerusalem. It refers to the Holy of Holies in a future, rebuilt Temple. Based on this verse, many scholars assert that a day will come when the Antichrist will enter a rebuilt Temple in Jerusalem, go into the Holy of Holies, and actually decree himself to be God.

But Paul specifically said the Antichrist '...exalteth himself above all that is called God, or that is worshipped....' This phrase is important, for it tells us that the Antichrist will not only exalt himself above Christianity, but above 'all that is called God or worshipped.' This clearly means he will exalt himself higher than Jesus Christ, as well as higher than all other religious leaders and forms of religion that are known in the world.

Again, we find that Paul drew much of his insight from the book of Daniel, where Daniel exactly, precisely communicated what Paul wrote in this verse.

The following points are how various Bible translations have interpreted this phrase in Second Thessalonians 2:4.

- The *King James Version* says he is one "who opposeth and exalteth himself above all that is called God, or that is worshipped."
- The *New King James Version* says he is one "who opposes and exalts himself above all that is called God or that is worshiped."
- The *New American Standard Bible* says he is one "who opposes and exalts himself above every so-called god or object of worship."
- The *New Living Translation* says he "will exalt himself and defy everything that people call god and every object of worship."
- The *New International Version* says he "will oppose and will exalt himself over everything that is called God or is worshiped."
- The *English Standard Version* says he is one "who opposes and exalts himself against every so-called god or object of worship."
- The *Amplified Bible* says he is one "who opposes and exalts himself [so proudly and so insolently] above every so-called god or object of worship."

- The *Renner Interpretive Version* calls him the one "who will be so against God and everything connected with the worship of God."

SECOND THESSALONIANS 2:4
THE ANTICHRIST WILL SEAT HIMSELF IN THE HOLY OF HOLIES

In Second Thessalonians 2:4, Paul wrote that the Antichrist would present himself "as God [that] sitteth in the temple of God, shewing himself that he is God."

This means a moment will come when the Antichrist will exalt himself in the eyes of the world to such an extent that he will even sit in the Temple in Jerusalem. The word "temple" in this verse is from the Greek word *naos*, and it is used to describe *the innermost part of the temple* in Jerusalem. As we saw in Chapter Three, it is used here to refer to the Holy of Holies in a future, rebuilt Temple. And based on this verse, many scholars assert that a day will come when the Antichrist will actually enter a rebuilt temple in Jerusalem, go into the Holy of Holies, and decree himself to be God. This is a connection to Daniel 11:37, where it is stated that the Antichrist will exalt and magnify himself "above all that is called god."

The following points are how various Bible translations have interpreted this phrase in Second Thessalonians 2:4.

- The *King James Version* says he "as God sitteth in the temple of God."
- The *New King James Version* says he "sits as God in the temple of God."
- The *New American Standard Bible* says he "takes his seat in the temple of God."
- The *New Living Translation* says he "will even sit in the temple of God."
- The *New International Version* says he "sets himself up in God's temple."
- The *English Standard Version* says he "takes his seat in the temple of God."
- The *Amplified Bible* says he "[actually enters and] takes his seat in the temple of God."

- The *Renner Interpretive Version* says he "will even try to put himself on a pedestal above God Himself — sitting in God's rightful place in the Temple."

SECOND THESSALONIANS 2:4
THE ANTICHRIST WILL PROCLAIM THAT HE IS GOD

In Second Thessalonians 2:4, Paul wrote that the Antichrist will be "shewing himself that he is God."

We have seen that the word "shew" is interpreted from a form of the Greek word *apodeiknumi*, which means *to vividly portray, to point out, to illustrate, to show off*, or *to make a vivid presentation.* In some way, the Antichrist will declare himself as God and will use all possible means to demonstrate his power to "shew" himself as God — including signs and lying wonders.

Just as Lucifer longed for God's throne in Heaven, the Antichrist — who we know will be demonically empowered and energized by Satan (Lucifer's name in his fallen state) — will do everything in his power to denounce, subdue, and trounce the name of God and Christ and to prove to the world that he is the only "god" worthy of adoration and worship.

The following points are how various Bible translations have interpreted this phrase in Second Thessalonians 2:4.

- The *King James Version* says he will be "shewing himself that he is God."
- The *New King James Version* says he will be "showing himself that he is God."
- The *New American Standard Bible* says he will be "displaying himself as being God."
- The *New Living Translation* says he will be "claiming that he himself is God."
- The *New International Version* says he will be "proclaiming himself to be God."
- The *English Standard Version* says he will be "proclaiming himself to be God."
- The *Amplified Bible* says he will be "publicly proclaiming that he himself is God."

- The *Renner Interpretive Version* says he will be "publicly proclaiming himself to be God."

SECOND THESSALONIANS 2:6
THE ANTICHRIST WILL BE REVEALED IN HIS OWN TIME

In Second Thessalonians 2:6, Paul wrote that the Antichrist will "be revealed in his time." We have already seen in Chapter Three that the time of the Antichrist's revealing will occur at the precise moment when the Restrainer has been taken out of the way. Only then will this evil person step into the spotlight.

As noted in Chapter Three on pages 121-122:

Second Thessalonians 2:6 says the revealing of the Antichrist will happen in his 'time,' a word translated from the Greek word *kairos*. This emphatically tells us that there is a prophetic, appointed moment when the restraining force will be removed, and the manifestation of the Antichrist will quickly occur. At that time, the veil that has concealed his identity will be removed, and he will step out from behind the curtain to reveal himself to the world.

There is *an appointed time* when the Antichrist will make his appearance center stage before the world. And, as you will see, this 'time' will come when the restraining force that has been *stalling*, *delaying*, and *postponing* the advent of the Antichrist and all the evil that will accompany him has been removed. In the moment the restrainer is removed, the curtains will be pulled back, and the Antichrist's identity will be made known to the world. The world will not necessarily perceive him as the Antichrist, but as a man suited for the age and in sync with a world that has tossed aside all moral restraints and the law of God. But the removal of the restrainer will trigger the moment when this evil person finally steps onto the world stage to obtain global attention.

Those who do not know the Scripture fret needlessly that the Antichrist could appear at any moment. But as stated at the first of this chapter, for those who are authentic Christians, much of this information concerning the timing of his appearing is a moot point (but important information to know). Those who are spiritually living, spiritually robust, spiritually thriving, spiritually vibrant, and spiritually vigorous will not be present on the earth when the Antichrist steps forward. I'm talking about the remaining remnant of spiritually alive believers who have endured and will still be around at the time of the Lord's coming.

Many have speculated over the centuries who the Antichrist might be in their respective generations — we looked at several of those names in Chapter Three. And many ask today if it's possible that the Antichrist is alive on the earth right now, although he is not revealed to the masses, as Paul explained, because of the presence of the Church, the Restrainer. We are very near to the catching away of the Church right now, so it is certainly possible that the Antichrist is alive right now, but standing "behind the curtain," awaiting the golden moment to make his grand appearance.

The following points are how various Bible translations have interpreted this phrase in Second Thessalonians 2:6.

- The *King James Version* says he will be "revealed in his time."
- The *New King James Version* says he will be "revealed in his own time."
- The *New American Standard Bible* says he will be "revealed in his time."
- The *New Living Translation* says he "can be revealed only when his time comes."
- The *New International Version* says he will be "revealed at the proper time."
- The *English Standard Version* says he will be "revealed in his time."
- The *Amplified Bible* says he will be "revealed at his own [appointed] time."
- The *Renner Interpretive Version* says "but when the right moment comes, this evil one will no longer be withheld, and he will emerge on the world scene. The screen that has been hiding his true identity and guarding him from world view will suddenly be pulled back and "evaporate" — and he will step out on center stage to let everyone know who he is."

Second Thessalonians 2:8
The Antichrist Will Be the Wicked One

In Second Thessalonians 2:8, Paul called the Antichrist "that Wicked." In the original Greek text, the words "that Wicked (one)" is a translation of *ho anomos*, which is the definite article *ho* with the word *anomos*. The definite article is important, for it lets us know that Paul was not speaking about any ol' wicked person, but, rather, about *the* wicked one.

The Greek word *anomos* is the Greek word *nomos* with an *a* affixed to the front of it. The word *nomos* by itself is the Greek word for *law*, and it is regularly used to depict the standard of what is *legally* or *morally correct*. But when an *a* is attached as a prefix, it has a cancelling effect — so rather than depict *law* or *a correct moral standard*, the word *anomos* holds the opposite meaning: that which is *without law* or *lawless*.

This new word *anomos* pictures one who possesses *no fixed moral standards*. Thus, the Antichrist will be an individual who has completely departed from past moral norms and from God's Word, who sees himself as being unshackled from past codes of conduct and forms of morality.

The following points are how various Bible translations have interpreted this phrase in Second Thessalonians 2:8.

- The *King James Version* calls him "that Wicked."
- The *New King James Version* calls him "the lawless one."
- The *New American Standard Bible* calls him "that lawless one."
- The *New Living Translation* calls him "the man of lawlessness."
- The *New International Version* calls him "the lawless one."
- The *English Standard Version* calls him "the lawless one."
- The *Amplified Bible* calls him "the lawless one [the Antichrist]."
- The *Renner Interpretive Version* calls him "the Lawless One."

Second Thessalonians 2:9
The Antichrist Will Be Empowered and Energized by Satan

In Second Thessalonians 2:9, Paul said the Antichrist will come "after the working of Satan with all power and signs and lying wonders." On pages 138-140, I deal extensively with these words from the Greek, and we will see in this section that when the Antichrist comes, his activities and operations will be energized by Satan himself. Indeed, when this Man of Lawlessness makes his grand appearance to the world, he will operate with all types of supernatural activities that are beyond the ability of a mere man to perform.

The following points are how various Bible translations have interpreted this phrase in Second Thessalonians 2:9.

- The *King James Version* says he will come "after the working of Satan with all power and signs and lying wonders."
- The *New King James Version* says he will come "according to the working of Satan, with all power, signs, and lying wonders."
- The *New American Standard Bible* says he will come "in accord with the activity of Satan, with all power and false signs and wonders."
- The *New Living Translation* says he will come "to do the work of Satan with counterfeit power and signs and miracles."
- The *New International Version* says he will come "in accordance with how Satan works. He will use all sorts of displays of power through signs and wonders that serve the lie."
- The *English Standard Version* says he will come "by the activity of Satan with all power and false signs and wonders."
- The *Amplified Bible* says he will come "through the activity of Satan, [attended] with great power [all kinds of counterfeit miracles] and [deceptive] signs and false wonders [all of them lies]."
- The *Weymouth New Testament* says his appearing "will be attended by various miracles and tokens and delusive marvels."

- The *Renner Interpretive Version* says his coming "will be energized by Satan himself as he makes his arrival known to the world with all kinds of dynamic supernatural powers — powers that are truly extraordinary."

REVELATION 13:1
THE ANTICHRIST WILL BE A BEAST

In Revelation 13:1, we see that the Antichrist is called "a beast." In the original Greek text, the word "beast" is a translation of the word *therion*, a word that describes *a brute, dangerous, savage, wild beast*. The word *therion* could be used to denote any force that was *chaotic, dangerous, evil, hostile*, or *wild*. This was the very word that described *ferocious, ravaging beasts* that were dispatched into ancient coliseums and theaters to attack and devour victims, and it was also used in the time of the New Testament to describe *callous, cold-blooded, cruel, vicious rulers*. Although the Antichrist may feign benevolence and kindness as a leader — at least at first — he will eventually no longer be able to hide that he is a *callous, cold-blooded, cruel, vicious ruler*.

The following points are how various Bible translations have interpreted this phrase in Revelation 13:1.

- The *King James Version* calls him "a beast."
- The *New King James Version* calls him "a beast."
- The *New American Standard Bible* calls him "a beast."
- The *New Living Translation* calls him "a beast."
- The *New International Version* calls him "a beast."
- The *English Standard Version* calls him "a beast."
- The *Amplified Bible* calls him "a [vicious] beast."
- The *Renner Interpretive Version* calls him "a brute, savage beast."

A Summary of All These Verses

To summarize all the previous points in this chapter, there are 30 descriptions and characteristics that the Scriptures in Daniel, Zechariah, Second Thessalonians, and Revelation — as we have seen — foretell about the Antichrist.

1. The Antichrist will be diverse (Daniel 7:24).
2. The Antichrist will subdue kings (Daniel 7:24).
3. The Antichrist will speak great words against the Most High (Daniel 7:25).
4. The Antichrist will wear out the saints (Daniel 7:25).
5. The Antichrist will think to change times and laws (Daniel 7:25).
6. The Antichrist will have times and laws in his hand until "a time and times and the dividing of time" (Daniel 7:25).
7. The Antichrist will be judged, his dominion will be taken away, and he will be consumed and destroyed (Daniel 7:26).
8. The Antichrist will be a king with a fierce countenance (Daniel 8:23).
9. The Antichrist will understand dark sentences (Daniel 8:23).
10. The Antichrist is "the prince that shall come" (Daniel 9:26).
11. The Antichrist will be a vile person (Daniel 11:21).
12. The Antichrist will do according to his own will (Daniel 11:36).
13. The Antichrist will exalt and magnify himself above every god (Daniel 11:36).
14. The Antichrist will speak blasphemies against the God of gods (Daniel 11:36).
15. The Antichrist will prosper until the time of wrath is fulfilled (Daniel 11:36).
16. The Antichrist will not regard the God of his fathers (Daniel 11:37).
17. The Antichrist will have no desire for women (Daniel 11:37).
18. The Antichrist will not regard any god (Daniel 11:37).

19. The Antichrist will magnify himself above all (Daniel 11:37).
20. The Antichrist will be a ruthless leader (Zechariah 11:16).
21. The Antichrist will be a man of sin (2 Thessalonians 2:3).
22. The Antichrist will be suddenly revealed (2 Thessalonians 2:3).
23. The Antichrist will be the "son of perdition" (2 Thessalonians 2:3).
24. The Antichrist will oppose and magnify himself above God (2 Thessalonians 2:4).
25. The Antichrist will seat himself in the Holy of Holies (2 Thessalonians 2:4).
26. The Antichrist will proclaim that he is God (2 Thessalonians 2:4).
27. The Antichrist will be revealed in his own time (2 Thessalonians 2:6).
28. The Antichrist will be the Wicked one (2 Thessalonians 2:8).
29. The Antichrist will be empowered and energized by Satan (2 Thessalonians 2:9).
30. The Antichrist will be a beast (Revelation 13:1).

Where Will the Antichrist Come From?

Many people ask, "Where will the Antichrist come from?" While I do not see a solid answer to this question, I will attempt to provide what some scholars believe are clues to the answer. Entire books have been written on this subject, but here, I will only briefly summarize *four primary thoughts* about where the Antichrist will come from.

The person called "the Antichrist" — who will be *one who is against Christ, who is against the true anointing of God, and who wants to usurp the authority of Christ* — will be a real individual who will make his appearance on the world scene after the Restrainer has been removed. Scripture reveals some of the details surrounding this event that we need to know. But it is important where Scripture is unclear on a particular subject, that we do not try to dogmatically insert our opinions about what something means or about what will occur.

This person we're studying, called the Antichrist, is described in Revelation 13:1-10, where we read:

Revelation 13:1-10

And I stood upon the sand of the sea, and saw a beast rise up out of the sea, having seven heads and ten horns, and upon his horns ten crowns, and upon his heads the name of blasphemy. And the beast which I saw was like unto a leopard, and his feet were as the feet of a bear, and his mouth as the mouth of a lion: and the dragon gave him his power, and his seat, and great authority. And I saw one of his heads as it were wounded to death; and his deadly wound was healed: and all the world wondered after the beast. And they worshipped the dragon which gave power unto the beast: and they worshipped the beast, saying, Who is like unto the beast? who is able to make war with him? And there was given unto him a mouth speaking great things and blasphemies; and power was given unto him to continue forty and two months. And he opened his mouth in blasphemy against God, to blaspheme his name, and his tabernacle, and them that dwell in heaven. And it was given unto him to make war with the saints, and to overcome them: and power was given him over all kindreds, and tongues, and nations. And all that dwell upon the earth shall worship him, whose names are not written in the book of life of the Lamb slain from the foundation of the world. If any man have an ear, let him hear. He that leadeth into captivity shall go into captivity: he that killeth with the sword must be killed with the sword. Here is the patience and the faith of the saints.

Notice that in verse 1, the apostle John described the Antichrist — whom he calls a "beast" — as one that will "rise up out of the sea." The sea, as used in this fashion, depicts *the nations of the world* and frequently depicts *Gentile nations*. For this reason, some postulate the Antichrist will be a *Gentile*. Some more specifically state that he will likely emerge from the territory of the former Roman Empire.

Primary Thought Number One: The Antichrist Will Arise From the Former Roman Empire

Especially during the 1970s to the late 1990s, it was popular to believe the Antichrist would emerge and reign from a revived form of the ancient Roman Empire.

The dream Daniel interpreted for King Nebuchadnezzar in Daniel chapter 2 seems to provide some prophetic clues concerning nations and empires.

Daniel 2:1 tells us that Nebuchadnezzar dreamed dreams, and he was so troubled that he could not sleep. Eventually Nebuchadnezzar called for Daniel to interpret the dream. In Daniel 2:31-33, we read a part of the dream. Daniel told Nebuchadnezzar:

> **Thou, O king, sawest, and behold a great image. This great image, whose brightness was excellent, stood before thee; and the form thereof was terrible. This image's head was of fine gold, his breast and his arms of silver, his belly and his thighs of brass, his legs of iron, his feet part of iron and part of clay.**

Notice Nebuchadnezzar saw that the image had:

- A head of fine gold.
- Breast and arms made of silver.
- A belly and thighs of brass.
- Legs that were made of iron.
- Feet fashioned partly of iron and clay.

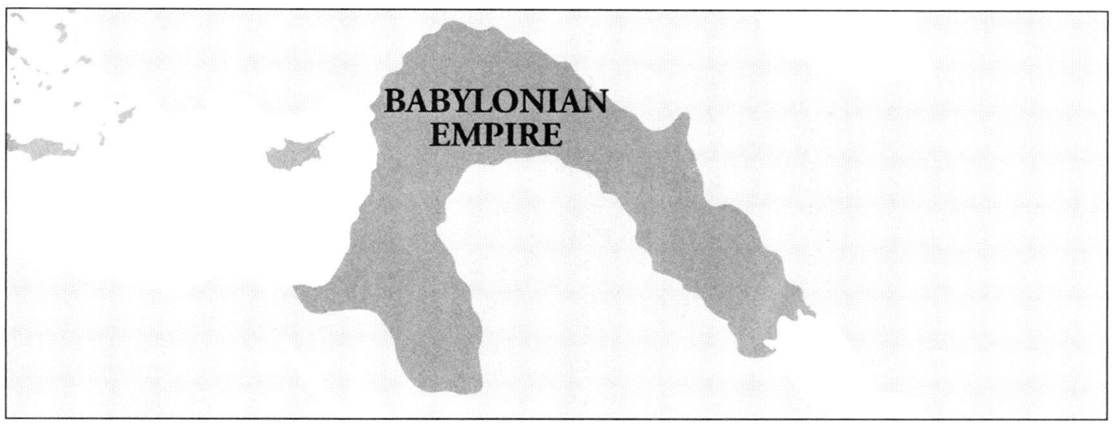

As Daniel interpreted this dream, he explained that these various parts represented different empires. It is generally believed that:

- The head of fine gold is known to have represented *the Babylonian Empire.*
- The arms made of silver are known to have represented *the Mede* or *Persian Empire.*
- The belly and his thighs of brass are known to have represented *the Greek Empire.*
- The legs of iron are known to have represented *the Roman Empire* (with two legs representing both the west and eastern parts of it).
- The feet made partly of iron and of clay, according to some, are representative of a revived *Roman Empire* in the last days — but today, there are serious scholars who believe it instead represents ten Arab nations that will form an alliance at the end of the age.

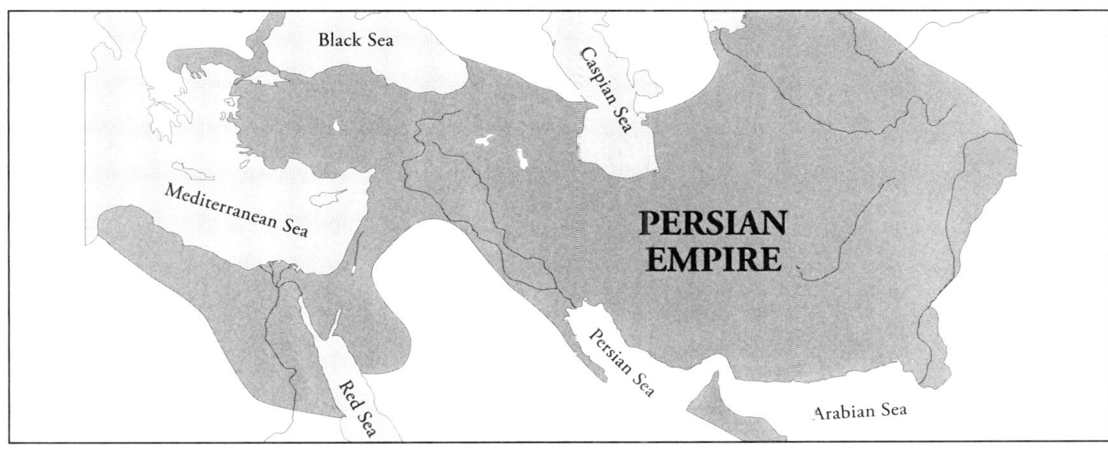

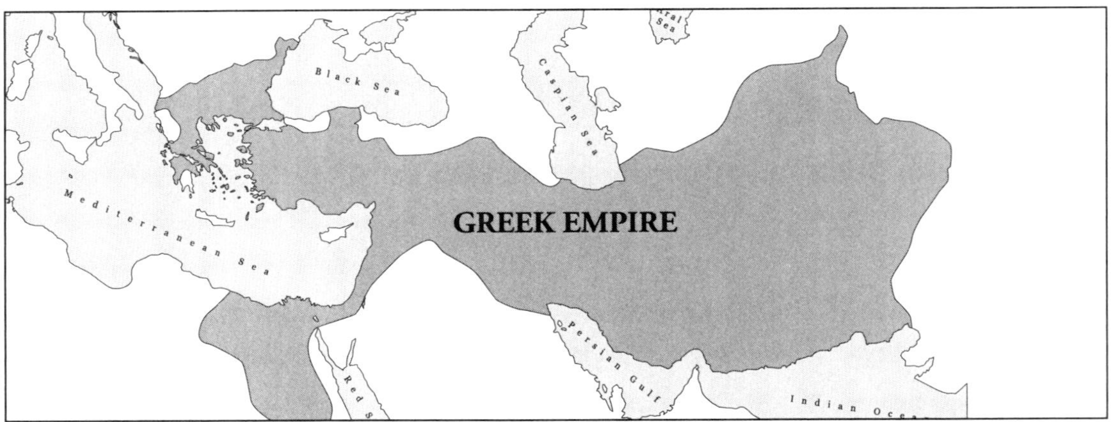

There are those who teach that the "feet part of iron and part of clay" is important because two feet also means ten toes. And some infer that the "ten toes" represent ten future nations — or ten global territories — that will unite at the end of the age, from which the Antichrist will emerge, basing his headquarters among them.

When the European Union began to take shape and was officially created in 1993, a vast number of prophecy teachers proclaimed that this was the "ten toes" or ten nations that would unite and eventually be led by the Antichrist.

However, the European Union kept adding more and more nations and, in recent years, has become comprised of 27 nations, which far surpasses the "ten toes," or ten nations, that prophecy teachers previously projected. This has greatly complicated matters for those who hold this view.

But it is important to note that prophecy teachers have also interpreted Revelation 13:3 to mean the Antichrist will personally suffer a mortal wound and later be "resurrected" and experience a miraculous recovery (vv. 3-4). As noted previously, the word "Antichrist" speaks of *one who is against Christ, who is against the true anointing of God, and who wants to usurp the authority of Christ.*

Hence, some stick to the idea that the Antichrist will be mortally wounded to the point of death and that it will appear he is resurrected, as Jesus was resurrected — and the world will view this simulated resurrection as proof that the Antichrist is divine.

Primary Thought Number Two: The Antichrist Will Arise From an Islamic Nation

Today there are those who believe the Antichrist will arise from an Islamic nation and that the mortal wound may possibly even allegorically refer to the once great Ottoman Empire, which was so badly wounded that it fell and crumbled into pieces. Those who adhere to the belief that the Ottoman Empire will be resurrected — and that the Antichrist will rise from an Arab or Islamic nation — suggest that this may possibly be a revival of the Ottoman Empire.

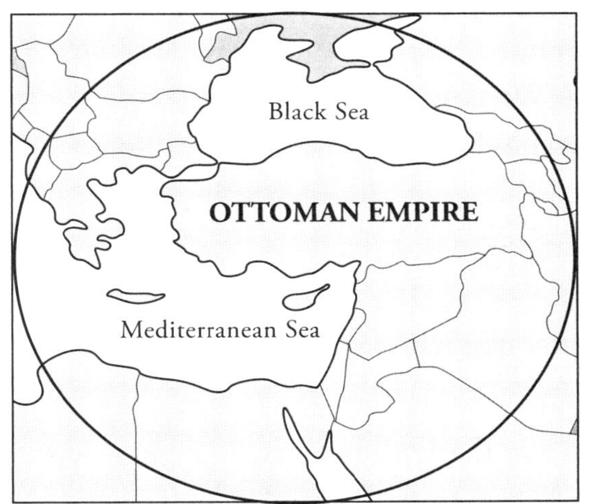

Turkiye was the heart of the Ottoman Empire, and as that nation has emerged in a more leading role in the Middle East in our day, it has further fueled this idea that the Antichrist may arise from the resurrected Ottoman Empire.

Let's briefly explore the thought about the Antichrist emerging from an Islamic nation. In Revelation 13:5, we are told the most brutal and ruthless period of the Antichrist's rule will last 42 months, or three and a half years, which marks the second half of the Tribulation. During those 42 months, we are told in Daniel 7:25 that the Antichrist will "wear down the saints." In like manner, Revelation 13:7 says that the Antichrist will "make war with the saints." Again, the "saints" that the Antichrist will wage war against will be those who come to Christ during the seven-year Tribulation period.

Because these saints refuse to take the mark of the beast (who is the Antichrist) and will not fall in line to worship him (the Antichrist), Revelation 13:10 tells us that the Antichrist will order them to be slain "with the sword." Because Islam is renowned for using "the sword" to decapitate so-called infidels who do not surrender, some say that this is further proof the Antichrist will be an Arab leader.

In Psalm 83 we are told of a league of ten nations (or future territories) that will come together against Israel — and the verse specifically mentions Edom, the Ishmaelites, Moab, the Hagrites, Gebal, Ammon, Amalek, Philistia, Tyre, and Assyria. Today these exact territories, represented by *many* nations, are primarily Arab. As a result, some suggest this league mentioned in Psalm 83 are possibly the "ten toes" Daniel saw in his vision that is recorded in Daniel chapter 2 — and that these ten territories will form a league that will be led by the Antichrist. Others believe this league could consist of ten oligarchs or technocrats who have great authority in these territories or realms.

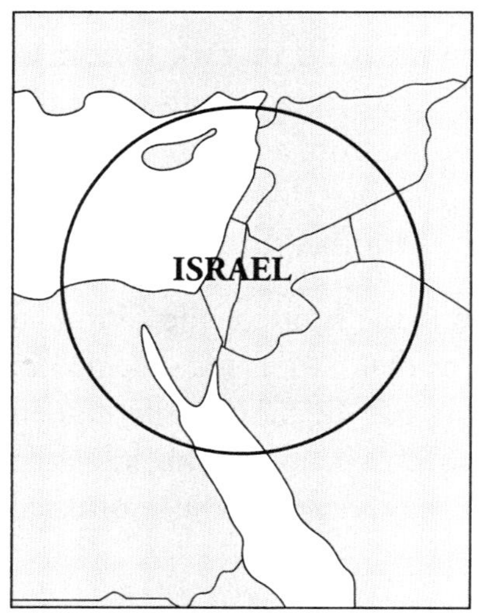

Primary Thoughts Numbers Three and Four: The Antichrist Will Be of Jewish Descent and Will Arise From Israel or From a Surrounding Arab Nation

There is yet another view that says the Antichrist will be of Jewish descent. Daniel 11:37 says the Antichrist shall not "regard the God of his fathers." Some say this phrase refers to a non-faith-keeping Jew who disregards his Jewish heritage.

It is a fact that the Jewish people do await a Jewish Messiah. But Jesus Christ is the true Messiah, so the so-called Messiah who will appear at the end of the age will be a false Messiah. But because Israel will embrace him, there are those who believe this false Messiah at the end of the age will be the Antichrist.

Some suggest that he will be Jewish by blood, but that he will arise from an Arab nation.

In summary, there are those who propose:

- The Antichrist will be a *Gentile* leader.
- The Antichrist will be an *Arab* leader.
- The Antichrist will be a *Jewish* leader.
- The Antichrist will be a *Jew who comes from an Arab nation.*

Although I have studied each of the above arguments and find valid points for each of them, I have not personally arrived at a conclusion about exactly where the Antichrist will come from. But what Scripture *does* emphatically teach is that when the Church is snatched into Heaven — *that* is precisely the moment when this evil personality will make his appearance to the world. And at that point, all the nations, peoples, and tribes of the earth — Jew and Gentile — will be so mesmerized by this person that they will, by and large, wholeheartedly follow his leadership.

Again, entire books have been written on the subject of the origins of the Antichrist, but that is not my focus. In this chapter, I have simply documented many points from Scripture that tell us about the Antichrist and his dark character and nature. When he comes on the scene, the nations of the earth will flock to him, they will be lured into his anti-god rule, and he will eventually be destroyed at the Second Coming (or Second Advent) of Christ that occurs at the end of the seven-year Tribulation period.

QUESTIONS TO PONDER

1. The Bible gives 30 different descriptions and characteristics about the Antichrist — what he will be like and what he will do. Did you realize Scripture had so much to say about this Man of Sin? After reading this chapter, what stood out to you? Were these attributes of the Antichrist new or familiar to you?

2. The Antichrist will deceive many through flatteries, signs, and "lying wonders" (*see* Daniel 11:21; 2 Thessalonians 2:9). Already, deception and lawlessness are rapidly increasing in the world today, distorting truth and leading many astray. What are some ways you see this happening? What steps can you take to strengthen your discernment and avoid being misled by false teachings or influences? (*Consider* Proverbs 2:1-5; Matthew 10:16; Romans 12:2; Philippians 1:9-10; Hebrews 4:12, 5:14; James 1:5; and 1 John 4:1.)

3. Many people will follow the Antichrist because they reject the truth (*see* 2 Thessalonians 2:10-12). In a world filled with deception, how can you train your heart and mind to recognize and hold on to truth? What daily habits can you develop to remain firmly rooted in God's Word? (*Consider* Psalm 25:5; John 8:31-32, 14:6, 16:13, 17:17; and 2 Timothy 2:15.)

4. In Chapter Three, several world leaders who served as "prototypes" of the Antichrist in the past are listed. Although the Man of Lawlessness himself will not step onto the world stage until after the Restrainer is removed, in what ways have you observed the antichrist spirit operate through individuals like that who blatantly oppose Christ? What characteristics of this antichrist spirit do you see in the world today?

5. First John 4:3 warns that the spirit of the Antichrist is already at work in the world, influencing culture and opposing Christ. How should this awareness shape your spiritual life? Would you do anything different than what you are doing now? In what ways can you be more intentional in prayer, interceding for those who are deceived or facing spiritual warfare?

6. Even in the face of evil and persecution, Daniel 7:27 reminds us that God's kingdom will ultimately prevail, and this promise is echoed in Daniel 2:44. In times

of uncertainty, oppression, or spiritual warfare, how does knowing that God's rule is eternal strengthen your faith? How can this truth shape your daily perspective, especially when faced with trials or injustice? Consider the following verses about God's eternal reign: Exodus 15:18; Psalm 9:7, 146:10; Revelation 11:15.

7. At the end of this chapter, Rick briefly described four primary thoughts about where the Antichrist may come from. What were they? Do any of these scenarios seem plausible to you?

8. What is generally believed to be the significance of the dream Daniel interpreted for King Nebuchadnezzar, as recorded in Daniel chapter 2? What are some of the differing views today about the meaning of the feet made partly of iron and partly of clay?

9. Remember, while the Antichrist will indeed be an evil individual, he will be dethroned and obliterated by a single breath from the mouth of Jesus (*see* 2 Thessalonians 2:8). Take a moment and think about the glorious entrance our Savior will make on the day the Tribulation finally ends.

Matthew 24:37-42

But as the days of Noe [Noah] were, so shall also the coming of the Son of man be. For as in the days that were before the flood they were eating and drinking, marrying and giving in marriage, until the day that Noe entered into the ark, And knew not until the flood came, and took them all away; so shall also the coming of the Son of man be. Then shall two be in the field; the one shall be taken, and the other left. Two women shall be grinding at the mill; the one shall be taken, and the other left. Watch therefore: for ye know not what hour your Lord doth come.

CHAPTER FIVE

DID JESUS EVER SPEAK ABOUT THE RAPTURE OF THE CHURCH?

Remember that the apostle Paul said the resurrection of the righteous dead and rapture of the Church was once a mystery. This event was most clearly revealed in the epistles of Paul, specifically in First Thessalonians 4:15-18, Second Thessalonians 2:1-8, and First Corinthians 15:51-53. Before it was revealed by the Holy Spirit in the pages of the New Testament, this was a *secret* that was kept under wraps until the appointed time for it to be revealed.

But you may ask, "Did Jesus ever speak about the rapture of the Church?" In this relatively short chapter, we will see that Jesus did give us glimpses about the Rapture, and we will look at those passages to see what Jesus said as He alluded to this "catching-away" event.

First, Let's Look at What Jesus Said in Matthew 24 About Events at the End of the Age

Matthew 24 is Jesus' primary teaching on end-time events. The same discourse can be found along with other important insights in Mark 13 and Luke 21. But in the passage in Matthew 24, Jesus discusses events that will precede the end of the age. He gives glimpses and insight regarding the Rapture itself; discusses events that will occur afterward, during the Tribulation; and teaches about His Second Coming (or Second Advent) at the end of the Tribulation — an event that is separate and distinct from the rapture of the Church.

These are two distinct events, and we will look at them in detail in Chapter Seven. But for the sake of simplicity, here is what you need to know. Matthew 24:4-14 deals with events preceding Christ's rapture of the Church — and verses 15 through 31 deal with events leading up to Christ's Second Coming.

It is my personal conviction that we are living in the last "moments" of this present age. Many of the signs Jesus said will be seen in the days before the very end of this age are occurring right now. You can read about these in my book *Signs You'll See Just Before Jesus Comes*. But because we are living at the very end of the present age, we have the keen ability to see and understand end-time scriptures more clearly, as we are living in their fulfillment. We are surrounded with mounting evidence of what Jesus forecast long ago, and because of where we are on the prophetic timeline, we are seeing and experiencing up-front what other generations could only see from a distance.

But in Matthew 24, Jesus addressed the rapture of the Church, which will occur as the event that triggers *the start* of the Tribulation. He also addressed His Second Coming when He will visibly return with ten thousands of His saints at *the end* of the Tribulation. When one is reading these end-time passages in Matthew 24, Mark 13, or Luke 21, it is imperative to know which event Jesus is describing in order to avoid confusion.

As we have seen, the Rapture will occur when Jesus descends into the earth's lower atmosphere to resurrect the bodies of the righteous dead and to catch away the Church. In this event, Jesus will *not* be visibly seen by the inhabitants of the earth, nor will He physically touch the earth. According to First Thessalonians 4:15-18, this is an event that will entirely transpire *in the air*.

The rapture of the Church will occur at the end of this present age and will take place entirely in the air, but it will also trigger the "day of the Lord" or what is called the Tribulation. In contrast, this Second Coming (also known as Christ's Second Advent, as we've already seen) will take place at the conclusion of the Tribulation, and in this event, Christ will visibly come with *ten thousands* of His saints. And that is when Jesus will return physically to the earth to initiate His 1,000-year Millennial Reign upon the earth.

This Gustave Doré illustration depicts the Ark floating in the background as the Flood destroys all of civilization.

Whether we are talking about the rapture of the Church or the Second Coming, Jesus stated in Matthew 24:36 that no one except the Father knows the exact moment of these events. And in Chapter Seven, we will look in detail at the difference between the rapture of the Church and the Second Coming of Christ.

Early in Matthew 24, Jesus enumerated several signs He wanted us to recognize as signs of the last of the last days. Then Jesus continues in Matthew 24:37-39, saying, "But as the days of Noe [Noah] were, so shall also the coming of the Son of man be. For as in the days that were before the flood they were eating and drinking, marrying and giving in marriage, until the day that Noe entered into the ark, and knew not until the flood came, and took them all away...."

In this passage, Jesus forecasted that the days prior to this event would be *a replication* of what was happening in the earth in the time frame prior to the Flood in the days of Noah. In my book *Fallen Angels, Giants, Monsters, and the World Before the Flood*, I explain exactly what was happening in the world before the Flood.

Since Jesus said what was happening before the Flood is going to be replicated in the time frame just prior to His coming, we need to understand what was happening then, for what was happening before the Flood will be happening again prior to the rapture of the Church and His Second Coming.

But in Matthew 24:37-39, Jesus said that Noah and His family entered the Ark, and as a result, they *escaped* the Flood that came on the world in that time. Then in Matthew 24:39-41, Jesus continued to say, "...So shall also the coming of the Son of man be. Then shall two be in the field; the one shall be taken, and the other left. Two women shall be grinding at the mill; the one shall be taken, and the other left."

EVERY WORD IS IMPORTANT, AND THE WORD 'TAKEN' IN THIS PASSAGE HOLDS A KEY TO UNDERSTANDING THE RAPTURE

The incorrect belief in *Dominion* theology or *Kingdom Now* theology is that the word "taken" pictures the removal of the *wicked* while the ones who are "left behind" will take dominion over the earth. But as you will see, this idea flies in the face of the Greek text. The Greek words alone that are used in these verses are enough to explain that Jesus is talking about the rapture of the Church not the removal of the wicked. Stay with me, and you will see that the word "taken" is from a Greek word that clearly depicts the rapture of the Church.

In Matthew 24, Jesus is giving us a glimpse into what will occur at the time of the Rapture. He said that just as Noah and his family *escaped* from destruction that came on the world at that time, at the end of the age "shall two be in the field; the one shall be *taken*, and the other left. Two women shall be grinding at the mill; the one shall be *taken*, and the other left" (vv. 40-41).

The word "taken" in verse 40 is an interpretation of the Greek word *paralambano,* which is a compound of the words *para* and *lambano*. The word *para* means *alongside*. The word *lambano* means *to receive* or *to take*. The word *para* in this context conveys *a sense of warmth as one pulls another close to his or her heart*. When these two words are compounded to form the word *paralambano*, it means *to retrieve*, *to snatch*, *to withdraw*, or *to take warmly and intimately to one's side*. It is significant that the word *paralambano* was regularly used in New Testament times to picture a moment when one came *to retrieve, take, or withdraw his inheritance*.

In Ephesians 1:18, Paul wrote that the Church *is* Christ's inheritance. Every true believer who is sealed by the Holy Spirit is included in that inheritance. If one correlates that to Jesus' words in Matthew 24:39-41, it informs us that a moment will come when Jesus will *retrieve, snatch, take, and withdraw* His inheritance — *the Church*. And the passage in Matthew 24 portrays this as a sudden and surprising moment. It is the moment when Christ will descend from Heaven *to retrieve, snatch, take, and withdraw* those who belong to Him. *That* is what the word "taken" — *paralambano* — means in the context of this verse.

In that moment, whoever is an authentic Christian — Christ's inheritance — will be supernaturally taken by Christ in the Rapture. Paul also taught in First Thessalonians 4:17 that those who are spiritually living, spiritually robust, spiritually thriving, spiritually vibrant, and spiritually vigorous — the remaining remnant of spiritually alive believers who have endured at the time of the coming of the Lord — will be *caught up* — *raptured* — to meet the Lord in the air.

We have seen that Paul told us in First Corinthians 15:52 that this event will take place in "the twinkling of an eye," which refers to a nearly indivisible moment of time, as fast as *the twinkling, twitch, or blink of an eye*. Just that fast, those who belong to Christ — that is, those who are His inheritance and therefore a part of the Church — will be snatched and taken away.

In Matthew 24:40 and 41, Jesus portrays the suddenness of this event very graphically. He said, "Then shall two be in the field; the one shall be taken, and the other left. Two women shall be grinding at the mill; the one shall be taken, and the other left."

Here, we see two people who are working side by side, when, suddenly, one of them — that is, the one belonging to Christ as an authentic part of the Church — simply disappears. But the other who does not belong to Christ is tragically "left behind." The words "left behind" are interpreted from a form of the Greek word *aphiemi*, which is a word that in this context simply pictures the one who is *left*, or *left behind*.

Christ began this portion of Scripture with the example of Noah, and it is important to remember that in addition to building the Ark for 100 years, Noah was a preacher of righteousness (*see* 2 Peter 2:5). With every pounding of Noah's tools upon the Ark as it was

Noah warned people that judgment was coming, but in spite of the fact that people were warned and were actually living in the very shadow of the Ark that could save them, they carried on indifferently.

being built, the sounds reverberated to all those who heard it, warning them that the Flood was coming. The sound was a summons for people to repent.

But in spite of the fact that people were warned and were living in the very shadow of the Ark that could save them, they carried on indifferently. Although Matthew 24:39 says people "knew not until the flood came," the truth is that if they didn't know judgment was coming, it was because they weren't listening — for Noah, a preacher of righteousness, continually declared what was coming. If Noah's words to the population of the earth and his actions in building the Ark in obedience to God were not warning enough, the Ark itself was a physical declaration that judgment was on its way.

Keeping this in mind, this also means those who are "left behind" will likely be, like those in Noah's day, those who were warned, but did not take the warning seriously. As a fellow worker at their side suddenly disappears and they are *left behind*, they will be overwhelmed with sorrow realizing that what they had been told was coming *actually happened*. Because they did not take it seriously, when the event they were warned about finally occurred, they will be sorrowfully *left behind*.

To double the impact of what He was teaching, Jesus repeated the scenario again in verse 41. But this time, He used the example of two women who were working side by side and going about their daily routines — when suddenly one of them is *caught*, *taken*, or *snatched away*, while the other one is painfully left behind with deep regret and sorrow.

Jesus said in Matthew 24:40 that two will be working in the field when one will be taken and the other will be left.

Because Jesus repeats the word "taken" twice in these verses, I want to also repeat that in the Greek text, the word "taken" is interpreted from the word *paralambano*. As explained previously, this word is a compound of the words *para* and *lambano*. The word *para* means *alongside*. And the word *lambano* means *to receive* or *to take*. Again, in this context, the word *para* conveys *a sense of warmth as one pulls another close to his or her heart*. When these two words are compounded to form the word *paralambano*, it means *to retrieve*, *to snatch*,

In Matthew 24:41, Jesus said two women will be grinding at the mill, and one will be taken and the other will be left.

to withdraw, or *to take warmly and intimately to one's side*. It is also significant and worth repeating that the word *paralambano* was regularly used in New Testament times to picture a moment when one came *to retrieve, take, or withdraw his inheritance.*

Thus, in Matthew 24:39-41, Jesus states twice that a day is coming when He will come *to retrieve, snatch, take, and withdraw* those who belong to Him. For those who are taken, it will be a glorious moment, but for those who are left behind, it will be a tragically sorrowful moment of deep regret. But in these verses, the word *paralambano* refers to the future time when God's people will be *caught away, retrieved, snatched, taken, and withdrawn.*

This is one text in which Jesus gave a glimpse into the rapture of the Church, but are there more?

Did Jesus Say Anything Else About the Rapture of the Church?

Just before Jesus faced the events of His Passion, He met with His disciples to speak the final words He wanted to leave with them. Imagine how difficult it must have been for the disciples to hear that Jesus would be leaving them, especially after they'd walked with Him for more than three years and witnessed Him perform miracle after miracle. It would have been normal for them to feel sorrowful as Jesus announced He would soon be returning to Heaven.

But in John 14:1-3, we read that Jesus told them, "Let not your heart be troubled: ye believe in God, believe also in me. In my Father's house are many mansions: if it were not so, I would have told you. I go to prepare a place for you. And if I go and prepare a place for you, I will come again and receive you unto myself; that where I am, there ye may be also."

Before Jesus went through His Passion, He let His disciples (and us) know that He was going away to prepare a place for them, and that He would eventually return to take them to the Father's house.

Timeless Words From the Master for All the Ages

In these three verses, Jesus gives the disciples — *and us* — very important points that we must never forget.

First, notice that in John 14:1 Jesus told them, "Let not your *heart* be *troubled*."

The word "not" in Greek is a negative particle, and it is intended be taken as *a prohibition*. Thus, Jesus was commanding them *to stop* being troubled. This lets us know that the disciples were so deeply troubled at hearing about Jesus' departure that He had to instruct them *to stop* letting their hearts be troubled.

Let's look at the words "heart" and "troubled" in that verse. The word "heart" is a plural of the Greek word *kardia*, which is a word used in New Testament times to picture *the heart* or *human emotions*. The word "troubled" is interpreted from a form of the word *tarasso*, a Greek word that pictures one who is *deeply disturbed, dismayed, distressed, inwardly shaken, in a state of inner turmoil, troubled,* or *is being tossed back and forth emotionally*. By using *kardia* for the *heart*, and *tarasso* for *troubled*, it lets us know that the disciples were *deeply emotionally disturbed* as they heard the news that Jesus would be leaving them.

Second, notice that in John 14:2 Jesus told them, "In my Father's *house* are *many mansions.*"

The word "house" is a translation of the Greek word *oikia,* a word that portrays *houses* or *residences,* but in this case, it pictures *an extremely large compound or grounds for an entire community.* This Greek word additionally speaks of a location that offers newcomers a warm welcome and that extends hospitality to members of one's family. Such environments were also *places of instruction and social interaction* for those who lived there.

By using this Greek word, Jesus describes Heaven as large grounds for His family — a place where all saints will be warmly welcomed, where many homes and places of residence exist, and where hospitality is extended to every member of the family who arrives there. But because the Greek word in this text also denotes *a place of instruction and social interaction,* it informs us that there will be a lot of *social interaction with others* in Heaven and that it will be a place for *continuing education and instruction.* This means that in Heaven, we will be ever learning!

But notice how many houses and places of residence Jesus said are in Heaven. He said that in His Father's sphere there are "many mansions." The word "many" is interpreted from the Greek word *pollai,* which simply means *many,* and it pictures *what exists in abundance* or *a vast multitude.* This means there will be a vast abundance of homes and places of residence in Heaven.

The word "mansions" is translated from the Greek word *mone,* which is from a verb meaning *to remain.* It denotes *a dwelling place, a habitation, a room,* or simply *a mansion.* Furthermore, it denotes *a permanent place of residence,* as opposed to a temporary residence.

Also in early New Testament times, this word particularly denoted *a safe place from which one would never be evicted* and *a place of belonging, safety, security, and stability.* Especially for early believers — and for Christians throughout history who have suffered persecution and various types of loss for their faith — the promise of *a permanent dwelling place* in the Father's compound is a sharp contrast to the loss of belonging, safety, security, and stability they experienced on Earth.

By using this Greek word *mone,* the message is given that once God's people have been warmly welcomed into Heaven and take up residence there, they will never be evicted. For Blood-washed believers, Heaven — and their places of residence there — is a place of belonging, safety, security, stability, and permanence.

Third, notice that in John 14:3, Jesus told the disciples, "And if I go and *prepare* a place for you, I will *come again*, and *receive* you unto myself; that where I am, there ye may be also."

Jesus told the disciples that He was going to "prepare" a place for them in Heaven. The word "prepare" is translated from a form of *hetoimadzo*, which means *to make ready*, and it gives the meaning of *making advance preparations*. It also carries a sense of *anticipation* for what one is eagerly awaiting to come to pass. The use of this word *hetoimadzo* tells us that Jesus is putting all His energies into making ready and preparing places — homes and residences — where His people will live in Heaven. He was also letting us know that He is *eagerly anticipating* the moment when believers will be gathered to live with Him in the Father's community, or sphere.

Heaven is a real, physical location, with the throne of God at its heart.

Heaven Is a Real Location

But notice Jesus also said He was going to prepare a "place" for them. The word "place" is interpreted from the Greek word *topos*, which speaks of *a real physical location.* It does *not* describe a figurative place, but *a real geographical location.* This means that when Jesus promised to prepare a "place" for us, He was speaking of *a real physical location, a real physical residence*, or *a real physical mansion* situated in the Father's grounds. Therefore, we know that these promises are not allegorical or figurative, but Jesus is presently preparing our residences, readying them for our arrival, and He is excitedly awaiting the moment when believers will occupy those dwelling places.

The words "come again" are interpreted from the Greek words *palin erchomai.* The word *palin* means *again*, and the word *erchomai* means *I am coming*. As a phrase, it means, *Again, I am coming!* Or, *I am coming again!* These are Jesus' own words — He said He is coming again to "receive you unto Myself" (John 14:3).

The word "receive" in John 14:3 is translated from *paralambano* — the same exact word that we saw previously in Matthew 24:40 and 41, where it is translated "taken" and is used to picture the moment when one will be *taken* and another will be *left behind*. Once again, it is a compound of the words *para* and *lambano*. The word *para* means *alongside*, and in this context, it is intended to give *a sense of warmth as one pulls another close to his or her heart* — while the word *lambano* means *to receive* or *to take*. We have seen already that, as a compound, *paralambano* means *to retrieve, to snatch, to withdraw*, or *to take warmly and intimately to one's side*.

We have shown previously in this chapter that the word *paralambano*, here translated "receive," was importantly used in the First Century to picture *one who came to take his inheritance or what belonged to him or her*. This means when Jesus comes again, He will come to "take" His inheritance, which is *the Church*. This means Jesus is only coming for those He knows belong to Him!

In Second Timothy 2:19, Paul wrote, "The Lord knoweth them that are his." When Christ descends from Heaven into the lower atmosphere to resurrect the bodies of the righteous dead and to snatch the Church into Heaven, there will be no mistakes, for He knows those who belong to Him and, therefore, who are a part of His inheritance in the Church. Thus, when Jesus said, "I will come again, and receive you unto myself," He was declaring to His disciples — and to every believer throughout history — that a moment will come when He will come again to retrieve the Church as His inheritance.

Again, Second Timothy 2:19 says, "...The Lord knoweth them that are his...." Does this scripture bring comfort to you or make you ill-at-ease? If you have embraced Jesus as Lord and are spending time in His Word and in prayer, you can rest assured you're His and you will not miss any part of His good plan for His people — including His plan to rapture His own from this earth at just the right time.

The rest of this passage talks about the lifestyle of those who are preparing to finally meet the Lord face to face. If we believe He is coming again for His Church, there will be notable characteristics in our life because we're making ready for that glorious day.

Indeed, Jesus addressed the rapture of the Church! Jesus stated that in a future moment, He will come again *to take us to Himself*. Jesus really is coming again to retrieve His people and transport them to their heavenly residence, where they will be eternally warmly welcomed to abide!

QUESTIONS TO PONDER

1. Read Matthew 24:40 and 41. The word translated as "taken" in these verses was regularly used in New Testament times to picture a moment when one came *to receive, take, or withdraw his inheritance*. Ephesians 1:18 says that the Church is Christ's inheritance, and when He comes to retrieve us, He will come for those believers who are spiritually living, spiritually robust, spiritually thriving, spiritually vibrant, and spiritually vigorous. What changes can you make to your daily life that will cultivate the spiritually thriving life Jesus is looking for?

2. When the disciples heard Jesus would be leaving them, they were sorrowful. Take a moment to imagine what the disciples might have been thinking, considering they'd just spent more than three years walking with Him and forming deep bonds with Him. How might you have responded if you were in their position?

3. Read John 14:1. Jesus told the disciples not to let their hearts be troubled over His soon-coming departure. Jesus is speaking the same thing to you right now. If you have had a troubled heart, remember Jesus gave you His Holy Spirit to comfort you (*see* John 14 and 16). Pray and ask Him to help you exercise the authority you have over your own heart and *let not* your heart be troubled!

4. Have you ever been displaced spiritually, socially, or even physically? According to John 14:3, in Christ there is a permanent and safe place for you, and it is precisely where you belong. Now that you know this truth, think of someone in your life who needs to hear it and share this Good News with him or her.

5. Jesus will come *to retrieve, snatch, take, and withdraw* those who belong to Him. For those who are taken, it will be a glorious moment, but for those who are left behind, it will be a tragically sorrowful moment of deep regret. Those who are "left behind" will likely be, like those in Noah's day, those who were warned but did not take the warning seriously. Who in your life is not heeding the very serious warnings found in Scripture? Take a moment to pray Ephesians 1:17-18 (*AMPC*) over those people.

   Father, I pray that you would grant [loved one's name] *a spirit of wisdom and revelation [of insight into mysteries and secrets] in the [deep and intimate] knowledge of God. I pray the eyes of* [his/her] *heart would be flooded with light so that* [he/she] *can know and understand the hope to which You have called* [him/her] *and how rich is Your glorious inheritance in the saints (Your set-apart ones). In Jesus' name. Amen.*

6. Second Timothy 4:8 (*AMPC*) says, "…There is laid up for me the [victor's] crown of righteousness [for being right with God and doing right], which the Lord, the righteous Judge, will award to me and recompense me on that [great] day — and not to me only, but also to all those who have loved and yearned for and welcomed His appearing (His return)." Is your heart right with God? Do you spend time in His Word and fellowship with Him daily? Do you love, yearn for, and welcome Jesus' return? If your answer to any of these questions is no, what can you do to start prioritizing your relationship with Jesus above everything else?

7. In John 14:2, Jesus says, "In my Father's *house* are many mansions." The word "house" is a translation of the Greek word *oikia*, which pictures a compound or grounds large enough for an entire community. Jesus used this word to tell us His Father's house is a place where a lot of social interaction with others and continued education and instruction will take place. How does this differ, if at all, from your mindset of what Heaven will be like? Does it make you more excited to be there? Why or why not?

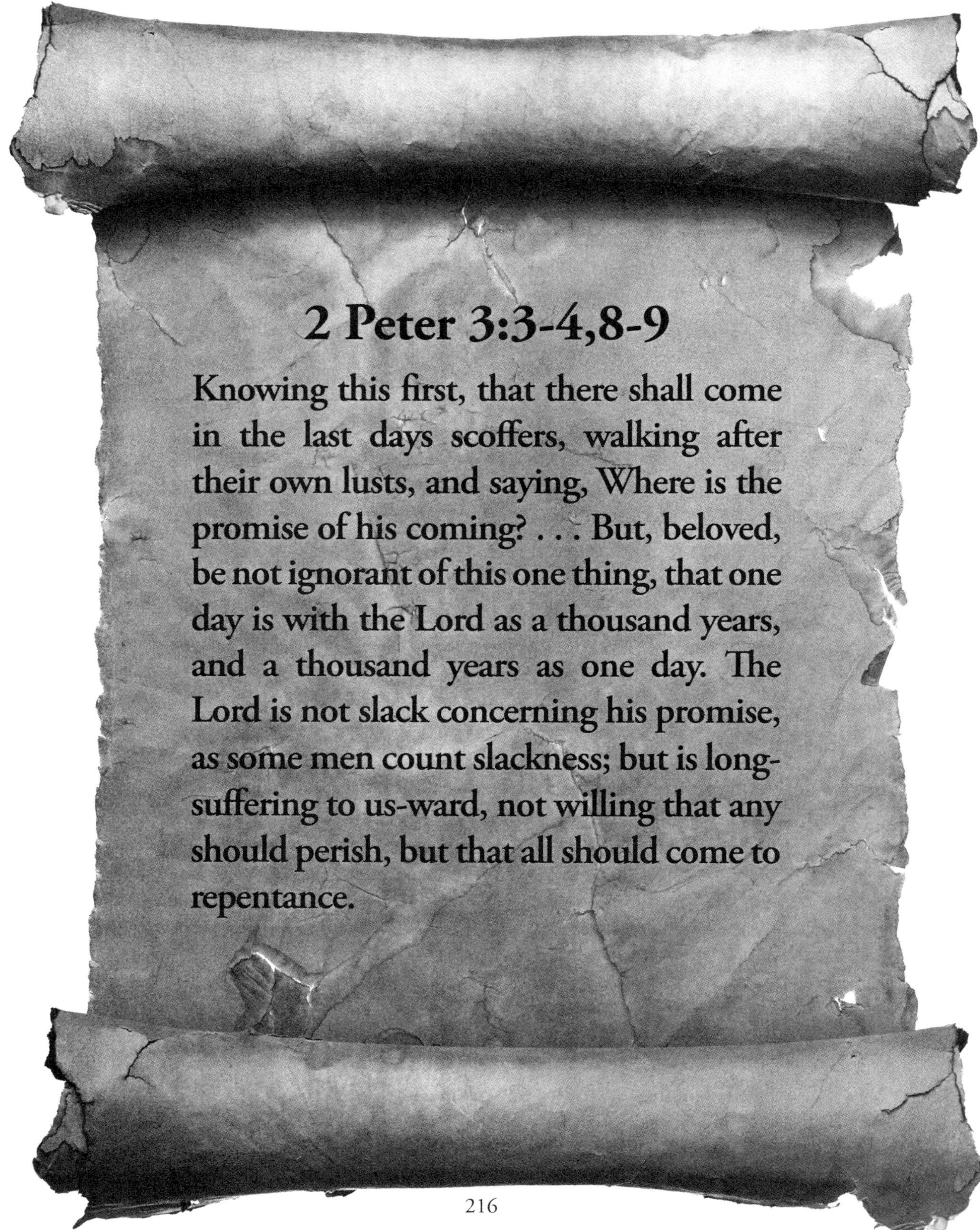

2 Peter 3:3-4,8-9

Knowing this first, that there shall come in the last days scoffers, walking after their own lusts, and saying, Where is the promise of his coming? . . . But, beloved, be not ignorant of this one thing, that one day is with the Lord as a thousand years, and a thousand years as one day. The Lord is not slack concerning his promise, as some men count slackness; but is long-suffering to us-ward, not willing that any should perish, but that all should come to repentance.

CHAPTER SIX

MOCKERS IN THE LAST DAYS

In Second Peter, the apostle Peter wrote about aspects of what will be experienced in the very last of the last days. In Second Peter 3:3 and 4, Peter wrote, "Knowing this first, that there shall come in the last days scoffers, walking after their own lusts, and saying, Where is the promise of his coming? for since the fathers fell asleep, all things continue as they were from the beginning of the creation."

Peter began by saying, "Knowing this first...."

The word "knowing" in this verse is translated from *ginoskontes* (a form of *ginosko*), which means *I know*. However, the form used in this verse describes what *must be known, always known and remembered, and never forgotten*. It has been prophetically declared long ago by the apostles and prophets, including Jesus the Chief Apostle and Chief Prophet, that scoffers would come in the last days. Peter was simply reminding his readers to know, always remember, and never forget — and not to be shocked or taken off guard by — the developments that would occur at the end of the age.

Peter said, "Knowing this first...." The word "first" is a translation of the Greek word *proton*, which means *first, foremost,* or *above all else*. As a phrase, it conveys the meaning, "Knowing, always knowing, always remembering, and never forgetting *first, foremost,* and *above all else*...."

Peter prophesied that scoffers and mockers would arise in the very last of the last days who would ridicule end-time warnings as being completely groundless.

The fact that Peter began this passage in this way alerts us that he, like a commander in the Church, was raising his voice to draw attention to something so important that those who read his message would soberly and deliberately pay heed to it and never forget it. The purpose was not to stir fear, but to prepare God's people for something inevitable that would unfortunately occur within the Church in the very end of the age — that there would arise scoffers and mockers who would ridicule end-time warnings as dramatic and completely groundless. The Holy Spirit who inspired Peter's writings lives outside the realm of time and knows the end from the beginning — and He accurately foretold through Peter what we should *know and never forget* concerning the very end of the age.

Pictured here is a Roman ship that has sailed to the last port. Such a last port was known as *eschatos*, which was a seafaring word used to describe the last port of call for a ship, and arriving at an *eschatos* port meant that it was the end of the road and the journey was finished.

After his words, "Knowing this first...," Peter said next, "That there shall come in the last days...." Even the word "that" is important, translated from the Greek word *hoti*, to specifically point to the next very important point. Peter used *hoti* deliberately to point to the fact that "...there shall come in the last days *scoffers*...."

But first, the words "the last days" in this verse are translated from the Greek words *eschaton ton hemeron*, which means *the*

NO POSTAGE
NECESSARY
IF MAILED
IN THE
UNITED STATES

BUSINESS REPLY MAIL

FIRST-CLASS MAIL PERMIT NO. 15 BROKEN ARROW OK

POSTAGE WILL BE PAID BY ADDRESSEE

RENNER MINISTRIES
1814 W TACOMA ST
BROKEN ARROW OK 74012-9950

last of days. The word "last" is from a form of *eschatos*, a word that depicts something that is *final*. It is where we derive the word *eschatology*, which is the theological study of *end times* or the study of *last things*. This Greek word *eschatos* points to the *very last* or the *ultimate end* of a thing. It was used by ancient Greeks to describe the point that was *furthest away*.

The ancient world also regularly used the word *eschatos* as a seafaring word to describe *the last port of call for a ship*. Although a ship in transit stops at many ports en route to its final destination, the word *eschatos* was used to depict *the very last port*. This last stopping-off point was called *eschatos*, and the use of this word signified that it was *the end of the road and the journey was finished*. Ancient writers also used the word *eschatos* to refer to *the final boundary of a territory* or *the farthest edge of a domain*.

Pictured here is Herod Antipas and his bodyguards who "mocked" Jesus. The same Greek word for "mock" is used by Peter to describe how scoffers will "mock" those who believe in Christ's return for the Church.

Peter's use of the word *eschatos* means he was pointing to the very end of the age. But to that word, he added the words *ton hemeron*, which mean *days*. As a phrase, it pictures *the very last days* of this present age — the Church Age. It could be interpreted as "the last of days — that is, when time has sailed to its last port and not much more time is left for the end-time journey...."

But what specifically was Peter warning us about concerning the very last of days? He wrote, "Knowing this first, that there shall come in the last days *scoffers*...." But the Greek actually says *empaigmone empaiktai*. These two words are a strange double use of the Greek word *empaidzo*. This single word *empaidzo* depicts *those who make fun of something through mockery*. It was often used to describe *playing a game with children* or to describe *amusing a crowd by impersonating someone in a silly and exaggerated way*. It might be used in *a game of charades* in which someone *comically portrays or even makes fun of someone*.

The same word is used in Luke 23:11 to describe how Herod Antipas' men "mocked" Jesus when He stood before them, which means his bodyguards *played charades* in front of Jesus, perhaps falling as if touched by His power or acting as if their blind eyes or deaf ears had been suddenly opened. It was pure mockery. There the Savior of the world stood before them — but instead of receiving from His goodness and power, they distanced themselves from Him through their mocking, scoffing pride. Salvation stared them in the face — and was theirs for the humble asking — but instead of reaching out with faith, they mocked the Son of God.

The Bible states that in the last days scoffers will come mocking those who believe we are living in the last days. Thus, one way to know that we've come to the end of this age is the presence of scoffers who arise to disdain and mock those who believe in Christ's soon return.

Scoffers Scoffing in the Last Days

Now Peter used this word — *twice* — to give it a double punch, as he foretold that at the end of days, when time has sailed to its last port and not much more time remains on the journey, scoffing scoffers and mocking mockers will rise and begin to ridicule and mock those who believe in Christ's return for the Church. The fact that the Greek phrase is *empaigmone empaiktai* — better translated *scoffing scoffers* — means this particular group of scoffers will not only occasionally mock those who believe in Christ's return for the Church, but they will give themselves wholeheartedly to it.

But Peter wasn't done giving prophetic insight into the characteristics of this mocking last-days generation that will arise to *jeer* at the precious Body of Christ that Jesus longs to draw close to His heart in the Rapture. Peter added that these scoffers will be those who are "...walking after their own lusts" (*see* 2 Peter 3:3). The word "after" is a translation of the preposition *kata*, which carries the sense of *a dominating force*. The word "lusts" is an interpretation of the word *epithumia*, a compound of the preposition *epi* and the word *thumos*. The preposition *epi* means *after* and is used here as *an intensifier* — and the word *thumos* depicts *desire* and *passion* and, often, the *uncontrolled release of desire and passion*. As a compound, it speaks of those who *are dominated by the pursuit of passionate desire or of base instincts*.

Because this is how Peter begins this passage about events at the very end of the age, it is vital to understand all the nuances in these Greek words as they are used together. The *Renner Interpretive Version* (*RIV*) of Second Peter 3:3 says:

> **Know, always know, and never forget that first, foremost, and above all else, there shall come in the last of days — that is, when time has sailed to its last port and not much more time is left in the end-time journey — mocking scoffers. I'm talking about those who sneer and jeer and make fun of those who believe in Christ's coming. These are people who are dominated and ruled by their own base instincts and who are doggedly and determinedly following after them.**

What Are Last-Days Scoffers Mocking in Particular? (A Word-by-Word Exposition of Second Peter 3:4)

Pay close attention to the following paragraphs in which I expound, word by word, on Second Peter 3:4 — and you can determine for yourself whether we're already witnessing this last-days "phenomena" of *scoffers scoffing*. Every word we'll cover is important to understanding this end-time mocking attitude that the Holy Spirit insists we *really know* and *never forget*.

'Saying'

Peter went on in verse 4 to communicate that these scoffing scoffers will be saying, "Where is the promise of his coming?" The word "saying" pictures one who *says, says, and says* or it depicts *talk that is continuous*. It could be correctly interpreted, "They go on and on, alleging, and saying...." Then Peter added that they will be mockingly alleging, "Where is the promise of his coming?"

The word "where" is a translation of the Greek word *pou*, which means *where, exactly where*, or *in what place* and is used to question whatever is being discussed. The word "promise" is an interpretation of *he epangelia*, which is the definite article *he* with *epangelia*.

The word *epangelia* is the Greek word for *an announcement, declaration*, or *guaranteed promise*, and this word was used to describe *what has been legally promised and is expected to come to pass*. Peter used the definite article *he* to state that the promise of Christ's return is a very specific promise that God has *announced, declared, guaranteed, and promised* to come to pass.

The word "coming" is from a Greek word that denotes the royal visit of a king or emperor who has come with all the power, might, and authority to deal with a situation and put everything in order. Peter used this word to refer to the long-promised rapture of the Church — and that is precisely what last-days scoffers will ridicule and mock: Christ's catching away of His Church.

'His *Coming*'

Peter said mockers will scoffingly ask, "Where is the promise of Christ's coming?" The word "coming" is from a form of *parousia*, a word we saw on page 98 that is a technical word to denote *the royal visit of a king or emperor who has come with all the power, might, and authority to deal with a situation and put everything in order*.

As we have seen, in Paul's writings, this word is used *interchangeably* to describe both the rapture of the Church and the Second Coming (or Second Advent) of Christ. To know how the word *parousia* is being used depends on the context of the surrounding verses. Here, Peter used this word to refer to the long-promised rapture of the Church — and *that* is precisely what last-days scoffers will increasingly ridicule and mock: *Christ's catching away of His Church*.

'Since'

Peter stated further that these last-days scoffers will allege and argue thusly, saying: "...For *since* the fathers fell asleep, all things continue as they were from the beginning of the creation" (2 Peter 3:4). According to the Holy Spirit, they'll say (and most of us have already heard it):

- "All this time has passed, and He hasn't returned yet."
- "Nothing has changed since people first began proclaiming it."
- "What makes you think this is ever going to happen?"

The word "since" in this verse is interpreted from the Greek word *apo*, which means *from,* and points *backward* to a time in the past.

The words "the fathers" could refer to the earliest fathers of the Christian faith, who firmly believed in and declared the promise of Christ's return for the Church at the end of the age — or it could refer to even earlier fathers of the faith, such as *Enoch*, who from the very beginning of time saw the end of the age and prophesied the eventual return of Christ (*see* Jude 14-15).

'Fell Asleep'

The next part of Second Peter 3:4 says, "...For since the fathers *fell asleep*, all things continue as they were from the beginning of the creation."

The words "fell asleep" are interpreted from a form of *koimao*, a word that means *to sleep*, but it is used metaphorically in the New Testament to picture *the dead* in Christ. This word does *not* substantiate the error some espouse that believers experience *soul sleep* in death, as this error is contrary to Paul's clear teaching that "to be absent from the body is to be present with the Lord" (*see* 2 Corinthians 5:8).

But although the context here is talking about forefathers who have died, the use of this word in the New Testament to describe the dead bodies of believers is interesting and significant, because it plainly means that Christ's ability to raise a believer's body from the dead is no more difficult for Him than someone's ability to arouse a sleeping person from a nap.

'All Things Continue'

According to the Holy Spirit's forecast in Second Peter 3:4, mockers will continue, "...Since the fathers fell asleep, *all things* continue as they were from the beginning of the creation." The words "all things" are a translation of *panta*, a word that is all-inclusive and leaves nothing out. The word "continue" is from a form of *diameno*, a compound of *dia* and *meno*. The word *dia* carries the idea of something that is *thorough*, and the word *meno* means *to abide* or *to remain*. As a compound, the word means *to thoroughly remain completely the same and unchanged.*

'As They Were'

Last-days mockers will allege that all things have continued "as they were" from the beginning of the creation. The words "as they were" are interpreted from the word *houtos*, which means *in keeping with*, *in like manner*, *in the same manner*, *exactly the same*, and, therefore, *consistent and unchanged.*

'From the Beginning of Creation'

The argument of scoffers and mockers in the very last days will be that people have been making last-days claims for *eons*, yet they can't see that anything has ever changed "from the beginning of the creation." The word "from" is interpreted from *apo*, which means *from*, but here it points *backward* to the very beginning of the creation of the world.

The word "beginning" is from a form of *arche*, picturing that which is *earliest*, but here it describes *the beginning* of creation. The word "creation" is interpreted from a form of *ktisis*, which denotes *creation* and points to the glorious event in time past when God miraculously created the world, as is recorded in Genesis 1 and 2.

All the nuances of the Greek words in this verse are important, so let's see the full flavor of them as this verse is interpreted in the *Renner Interpretive Version* (*RIV*).

RIV of Second Peter 3:4

They go on and on, alleging and saying, 'So where is the reality of the guaranteed promise of His glorious coming?' In fact, these mockers will allege,

'Come on! From the time the fathers of old died, everything continues perpetually the same, is unchanged, and is in keeping with how things have been from the very beginning of creation.'

To put the argument of scoffers in perspective, as we'll see later in this chapter, Peter prophesied by the Spirit on the Day of Pentecost that the "last days" had officially commenced (*see* Acts 2:17-21; Joel 2:28-31). That was nearly 2,000 years ago. But remember, a thousand years is as a day to the Lord (*see* 2 Peter 3:8). Therefore, on God's timeline, Peter's prophetic utterance was made "just a couple of days ago"— and we who are alive on the earth today have never been closer to the end of the age than we are right now.

So when people scoffingly ask, "Just where *is* this promise of His coming? You've been saying for *centuries* that Jesus is coming again," they don't know what they're actually saying because just as sure as Jesus is raised from the dead and seated on the Throne as King of kings and Lord of lords — and just as sure as there is day and night and seedtime and harvest on the earth — Jesus *is* coming again. His Word assures us, and we have never been closer to that great event than we are today!

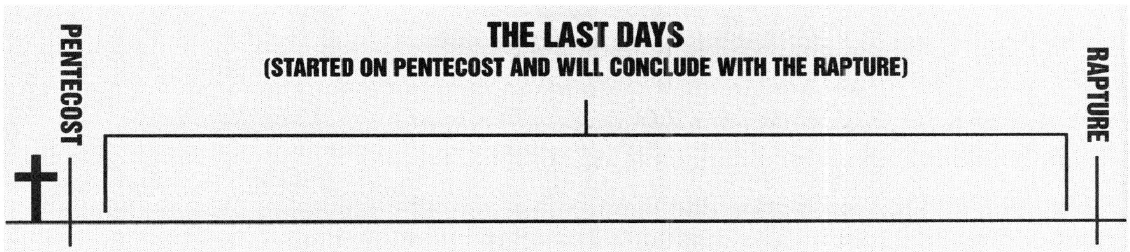

What Exactly Are the *'Last Days'*?

But these "dissenters" will argue that Christ's return is fictitious and has no basis in reality. One of their main arguments is that people have been talking about the last days and the Rapture for about 2,000 years. Since it's always important to define terms when such discussions arise, we must ask the question, *What ARE the last days?*

Ironically, these mockers are exactly right when they say people have been talking about the last days for approximately 2,000 years. But what most don't understand is that the last days actually began on the Day of Pentecost when the Holy Spirit was poured out (*see* Acts 2:16-20). Therefore, the past 2,000-year period is what is theologically called "the last days."

In Acts 2:17, Peter responded to the outpouring of the Spirit by quoting Joel 2:28 in which the prophet Joel prophesied about the supernatural happenings in the last days. Peter said, "...This is that which was spoken by the prophet Joel" (Acts 2:16). Then Peter quoted Joel nearly verbatim, saying, "And it shall come to pass in *the last days*, saith God, I will pour out of my Spirit upon all flesh..." (v. 17). When the Holy Spirit was poured out in Peter's day on the Day of Pentecost, it triggered an age that is called "the last days" — and we've been living in that age for the last 2,000 years.

But even without that Old Testament witness concerning where we are on the prophetic timeline, I remind you that when Peter wrote about the "last days" in Second Peter 3:3, he used the word *eschatos* — a word that by definition points to *the very end* of that prophetic season and, I believe, to the days you and I are living in right now. Again, by employing the use of the word *eschatos*, the Holy Spirit is literally saying, "...In the very end of days — when time has sailed to its last port and not much more time remains in the journey...."

Hence, when scoffers say, "If Christ was going to come, surely He would have come by now...people have been saying it is the 'last days' for 2,000 years," they are not only correct about the timetable of the last-days season, but they are also prophetically telling us by their scoffing arguments that we are *there* — in the very last days — on God's amazing timeline.

In his second epistle, Peter was not describing the entire 2,000-year time frame — rather, he was pointing to the final moments of that age and stating that one of the screaming signs we have sailed to the very end of this age is that scoffers will arise to mock those of us who believe the rapture of the Church is near.

Friend, no matter what you believe "near" means — whether it's five months, five years, or *fifty* years — nothing remains to be fulfilled for Christ's coming to occur. He could come *today* for a remnant that is busy about the Father's business reaping the precious fruit of the earth — *men's souls* — that He longs to gather into His Kingdom and family (*see* James 5:7).

A Day of Judgment Is Coming

In Second Peter 3:7, Peter continued, "But the heavens and the earth, which are now, by the same word are kept in store, reserved unto fire against the day of judgment and perdition of ungodly men."

The word "heavens" in Greek is the plural form of *ouranos*, which describes *all the heavens above* that God created. The word "earth" is, again, a translation of *ge*, a word that pictures *the physical planet Earth*. Peter wrote that both the heavens and the earth are being "kept in store." The words "kept in store" are from a Greek word that means *to set aside*. Peter let us know that the heavens and earth are set aside and "reserved" unto fire.

Is the Earth Really 'Reserved Unto Fire'?

The word "reserved" is from *tereo*, a Greek word that historically depicted *the uninterrupted vigilance of soldiers who were positioned to protect something of great importance*. It was also the word used to describe *the uninterrupted vigilance of shepherds who were charged to watch over sheep assigned to their watch*. Thus, soldiers charged to stand guard knew they were to be faithful and remain committed to their post regardless of assaults or the number of attackers they might encounter. Likewise, shepherds were to maintain vigilant watch over their sheep even in the face of danger or hardship. Peter used this word to depict God as the One who stands attentively on guard over the heavens and the physical earth and over all the affairs within these spheres.

Peter argued that although scoffers may be ignorant of it, God and His Word are standing guard over the heavens and the earth and all the affairs within them unto "fire against the day of judgment and perdition of ungodly men."

The word "fire" is from *pur*, a word that depicts *flames swirling, whirling, flickering, twisting, turning, and arching upward toward the sky*. It portrays *a consuming or engulfing fire*. The word "judgment" is from a form of the word *krisis*, which speaks of *a damning verdict of the court that is carried out* against the ungodly. This damning moment is so consequential that the word *krisis* is where we derive the English word "crisis." And indeed, when this event occurs, it will be *an unimaginable crisis* for those who have lived ungodly lives without repentance and who will indisputably suffer the verdict of Heaven's court.

Peter also spoke of the "perdition" of ungodly men. The word "perdition" is from a form of the Greek word *apoleia*, a word that means *rottenness*. The words "ungodly men" are from the Greek word *asebes*, which is derived from *sebas*. The word *sebas* by itself portrays whatever is *reverent, pious, respectful*, or *God-fearing*. When the prefix *a* is attached to the front of the word, it has a *canceling* or *reversing* effect, which causes it to mean *unholy* or *irreverent* and depicts those who have *no fear of God*. Here, it describes *those whose behavior demonstrates they possess no reverence for that which is holy*.

The passage is so important that I want you to see all these nuances as they are carried into the *Renner Interpretive Version* (*RIV*).

RIV of Second Peter 3:7

But amazingly, at this current, exact, present moment — even right now — the heavens above and the physical earth are being 'set aside and stored up.' That is, they are being guarded, kept, preserved, and protected by the Word [of God] until the big day of judgment, an unimaginable crisis, that will occur when an all-consuming and engulfing fire will utterly destroy the rotten and godless behaviors of ungodly men.

My Own Answer to Scoffers Who Mock the Rapture of the Church

We have seen that Peter warned at the end of the age, some scoffers will allege the Rapture is a *fantasy*. However, there have *already* been multiple raptures, and there are other additional rapture-type experiences described in Scripture. Those who know the Scriptures are well aware that the idea of a rapture-type event is not a new idea. From the book of Genesis to the book of Revelation, the Bible speaks of individuals who were supernaturally *caught away*, and we will look at those in the following paragraphs.

As we've seen, the apostle Peter prophesied that in the very last days, there would arise scoffers who mock the idea of a literal rapture as well as those who believe in it. As a confirmation of Peter's prediction of these last-days scoffers, there really is a growing number of people today who scoff at those who believe in the rapture of the Church.

Unfortunately, there is a category of people — including some Christians — who have rejected the belief in the Rapture and who mock those who believe in the *rapture* or *catching away* of the Church. But if one considers the entire record of Scripture from Genesis to Revelation, it becomes clear that the Bible speaks of *nine* rapture-type experiences.

In the pages to follow, you will see there have been multiple people who have already experienced *a catching away* of some kind, and there are others who the Bible says will experience *a catching away* or *a rapture* in the future.

As a matter of fact — *get ready* — the Church is next in line to be *supernaturally snatched* into Heaven! Friend, there really will come a time very soon when those who live for Jesus will be *supernaturally, physically caught away*, or *snatched*, in the "twinkling of an eye" as we have seen in First Corinthians 15:51-52.

But let's look at the following instances to see who in the Bible has already experienced a rapture, who has experienced a rapture-type experience, and who the Bible says will experience *a catching away* or *rapture* in the future.

ENOCH

Enoch Experienced a Rapture

First, we find that *Enoch* was supernaturally and physically *caught up* into the presence of the Lord. He lived from approximately 3384 to 3019 BC, and he was the "seventh from Adam" (*see* Genesis 5:9-19; Jude 14). He was the son of Jared and the father of Methuselah (*see* Genesis 5:22), who was the longest-living person recorded in biblical history.

As one of the first prophets in the Old Testament, Enoch played a significant role and walked so closely with God that "God took him" (*see* Genesis 5:24; Hebrews 11:5), and he did not experience natural death. *This is the first recorded rapture in Scripture!*

Although Old Testament references about Enoch are minimal, he was so respected as a prophetic voice that his writings were quoted by Jude, and some say referenced by Jesus, Paul, Peter, James, and John as well. In addition to what we know of Enoch from Genesis 5:18-24 and Hebrews 11:5, scholars generally believe Enoch penned the oldest parts of the non-canonical Book of Enoch. He was so accurate in his prophetic abilities that in the very beginning of time, he even saw a vision of the Second Coming (or Second Advent) of Christ (*see* Jude 14-15).

Jude referred to that prophecy that is also quoted from the most ancient sections of the non-canonical Book of Enoch. Jude 14 and 15 says, "And Enoch also, the seventh from Adam, prophesied of these, saying, Behold, the Lord cometh with ten thousands of his saints, to execute judgment upon all, and to convince all that are ungodly among them of all their ungodly deeds which they have ungodly committed, and of all their hard speeches which ungodly sinners have spoken against him."

Enoch's son Methuselah famously lived for 969 years and is noted for being the oldest man to ever live and die on Earth. But Enoch is actually physically older because he was raptured and transported directly into God's presence without tasting death. That means he is still living in his physical human form in Heaven today. Hence, Enoch holds the record for the longest life lived, which we can estimate to be at least 5,000 years!

The Bible tells us Enoch lived on the earth for 365 years and had many sons and daughters (*see* Genesis 5:22), but most importantly, Genesis 5:24 says, "And Enoch walked with God: and he was not; for God took him." One day, as Enoch was living in close relationship with God, he was supernaturally snatched out of this world and taken to Heaven, never tasting death.

Hebrews 11:5 says, "By faith Enoch was translated that he should not see death; and was not *found*, because God had translated him: for before his translation he had this testimony, that he pleased God." Interestingly, the word "found" is translated from a form of the Greek word ***heurisko***, which means *to search for, to seek for, and to thoroughly investigate*, which means people were really looking for Enoch, but they couldn't find him.

Where did he go? Genesis 5:24 says, "...God took him." God translated Enoch — taking him from the realm of the physical to the supernatural dimension of the spirit. This is the first record of a rapture in Scripture. God literally raptured Enoch into Heaven.

ELIJAH

Elijah Experienced a Rapture

Second, we find that *Elijah* was the second person in the Old Testament to be physically *caught up* into the presence of the Lord. Elijah lived in approximately the Ninth Century BC. According to the books of First and Second Kings, he was a miracle-working prophet who lived in the Northern Kingdom of Israel during the reign of the wicked King Ahab.

To demonstrate whose power was greatest, Elijah famously suggested a confrontation between God's power and Baal's power at Mount Carmel (*see* 1 Kings 18:19). At Elijah's prodding, Ahab accepted the challenge and summoned 450 prophets of Baal and 400 prophets of Asherah to Mount Carmel for a confrontation of divine powers. At the conclusion of that event, fire fell from Heaven to consume the sacrifice along with the earth and the water in the trench around the altar. And Elijah ordered the slaughter of the prophets of Baal (*see* 1 Kings 18:38-40).

Many pages are needed to cover the miracle-working ministry of the prophet Elijah. He is remembered for many miracles that include resurrections from the dead and even, as we saw above, calling fire down from Heaven.

But finally...a chariot of fire appeared, and Elijah was physically taken up into Heaven. He was supernaturally transported by a whirlwind of God's power and was finally lifted up into Heaven.

The account of Elijah being physically *caught up* into Heaven is found in Second Kings 2:11, "And it came to pass, as they still went on, and talked, that, behold, there appeared a chariot of fire, and horses of fire, and parted them both asunder; and Elijah went up by a whirlwind into heaven."

In that moment, the prophet Elijah was physically *caught up* into Heaven by the Spirit of God. He was translated from the natural realm into the dimension of the spirit via a flaming chariot of fire. Rather than taste death, Elijah was raptured from the earth into the very presence of God.

JESUS

Jesus Experienced a Rapture

Third, we find that *Jesus* was physically *caught up* into the clouds as the disciples watched Him supernaturally ascend into Heaven.

We read about this amazing event in Acts 1:9-11: "And when he had spoken these things, while they beheld, he was taken up; and a cloud received him out of their sight. And while they [the disciples] looked steadfastly toward heaven as he went up, behold, two men stood by them in white apparel; which also said, Ye men of Galilee, why stand ye gazing up into heaven? this same Jesus, which is taken up from you into heaven, shall so come in like manner as ye have seen him go into heaven."

This passage reveals Jesus Himself was raptured — or that He was "taken up" — into the clouds. While Jesus was blessing His closest, most devoted followers, they watched as He was physically caught up into Heaven and was translated from the earth to Heaven by the power of God.

Philip Experienced a Rapture-Type Event

Fourth, we find that *Philip* the evangelist experienced a rapture-type event. We're told in Acts 8:39 that after sharing the Gospel with a high-ranking official of Ethiopia and baptizing him in water, "...The Spirit of the Lord *caught away* Philip, that the eunuch saw him no more: and he went on his way rejoicing."

PHILIP

The words "caught away" are translated from the Greek word *harpadzo* — the identical word in First Thessalonians 4:17 that Paul used to describe the *catching away* or *rapture* of the Church. As fast as the twinkling of an eye, Philip was snatched by the Spirit of the Lord and he disappeared before the eyes of the Ethiopian leader, who saw him no more because Philip was physically *caught away* by the Spirit of the Lord. Acts 8:40 tells us, however, that immediately afterward, "...Philip was found at Azotus: and passing through he preached in all the cities, till he came to Caesarea." Philip was not *caught up* into Heaven — rather, he was supernaturally transported from one location to another at lightning speed by the Spirit of God.

PAUL

Like a scene out of a modern-day sci-fi movie, Philip simply disappeared from his physical location with the eunuch and was supernaturally transported, reappearing on the road going from Jerusalem to the town of Azotus, which was approximately 20 miles north of where he had been baptizing the Ethiopian leader!

Paul Experienced a Rapture-Type Event

Fifth, we find that *Paul* experienced a rapture-type event. Speaking to the believers at Corinth, Paul said, "I knew a man in Christ above fourteen years ago, (whether in the body, I cannot tell; or whether out of the body, I cannot tell: God knoweth;) such an one caught up to the third heaven. And I knew such a man, (whether in the body, or out of the body, I cannot tell: God knoweth;) how that he was caught up into paradise, and heard unspeakable words, which it is not lawful for a man to utter" (2 Corinthians 12:2-4).

Twice in these verses, Paul said that he was *caught up*. In both instances, he used the Greek word *harpadzo* — the same word Paul also used to describe the *catching away* or *rapture* of the Church in First Thessalonians 4:17. Note that this is the same word used to describe Philip's supernatural *catching away* in Acts 8:39.

Paul used this word to state that he himself had personally experienced a rapture-type event in which the Spirit of God *snatched* and *caught him up* into the third heaven, where he heard indescribable words of truth and revelation from the Lord.

Similar to the experiences of Enoch, Elijah, Jesus, and Philip, Paul was *caught away* and *raptured* into the realm of the spirit.

JOHN

John Experienced a Rapture-Type Event

Sixth, we find that *John* also experienced a rapture-type event. This event is described in Revelation 4:1 and 2, where John wrote, "After this I looked, and, behold, a door was opened in heaven: and the first voice which I heard was as it were of a trumpet talking with me; which said, Come up hither, and I will shew thee things which must be hereafter. And immediately I was in the spirit...."

John heard a command to "come up hither." In Revelation 4:1, these words in the original text are *anaba hode*. The word *anaba* means *up* and describes *upward movement*. The Greek word *hode* means *here*. As a phrase, it means, *Come up here* or *Move upward — here*.

Revelation 4:2 says, "And immediately I was in the spirit...." The word "immediately" is from the Greek word *eutheos*, and it means *instantly*. The words "in spirit" are a translation of *en pneumati*. This phrase "in spirit" is a term used to describe *another realm*, *another dimension*, or *a spiritual realm* far different from the natural world that surrounded John.

These words tell us that John had somehow passed from the natural realm into the realm of the spirit and was now "in spirit," or in a totally different realm.

Immediately, John was "in spirit" — he was translated from the realm of the natural into the realm of the supernatural — in a fashion similar to the experiences of Enoch, Elijah, Jesus, Philip, and Paul. Indeed, John was *caught away* and *raptured* into the realm of the spirit.

THE CHURCH

Believers at the Rapture of the Church

Seventh, the *Church* is next to experience *a catching away* or *rapture* in the near future. Yes, the next rapture that is quickly approaching is the one that involves all authentic believers.

This grand event is described in First Thessalonians 4:17, which says, "Then we which are alive and remain shall be *caught up* together with them in the clouds, to meet the Lord in the air: and so shall we ever be with the Lord."

Imagine...one day in the very near future, believers who are faithfully serving God will vanish and be supernaturally *caught up* or *raptured* into the very presence of the Lord Jesus. As we have already seen, the words "caught up" are translated from the word *harpadzo*, which means *to catch*, *to seize*, *to snatch*, or *to take away*.

In a similar way Enoch, Elijah, Jesus, Philip, Paul, and John were *caught away* and *raptured*, a moment is coming when the Church will be supernaturally *caught away* and *snatched* to meet the Lord in the air.

TRIBULATION SAINTS

Tribulation Saints

Eighth, we find that *Tribulation saints* will be physically *caught away* and *raptured* into the presence of the Lord. During the seven years of Tribulation on Earth, there will be people who will miraculously come to the saving knowledge of Christ. At a specific moment, they will be *caught away* or *raptured* into Heaven. Revelation 7:9-11 tells us that a great multitude of those who will be saved during the Tribulation will appear in the presence of the Lord.

TWO END-TIME PROPHETS

Two End-Time Prophets

Ninth, we find there are *two end-time prophets* who will be supernaturally *caught away* or *raptured* into Heaven in the future. Revelation 11:7-9 tells us that these two witnesses will prophesy on God's behalf during the first three and a half years of the Tribulation. The Bible says the Antichrist will kill them and display their dead bodies in the streets of Jerusalem for all the world to see.

But these two witnesses won't stay dead, for Revelation 11:11-12 says, "And after three days and an half the spirit of life from God entered into them, and they stood upon their feet; and great fear fell upon them which saw them. And they heard a great voice from heaven saying unto them, Come up hither. And they ascended up to heaven in a cloud; and their enemies beheld them."

The words "come up hither" in Greek are translated from *anabate hode*. The word *anabate* is a direct form of speech, which means *come up* and refers to *upward movement*.

The word *hode* means *here*. It is nearly identical to the command John heard in Revelation 4:1. As a phrase, it means, *Come up here* or *Move upward — here*.

And verse 12 says they "ascended up" to Heaven in a cloud. The words "ascended up" are interpreted from a form of *anabaino*, which means to move upward. These two end-time witnesses will visibly be *caught away* or *raptured* into the clouds in front of their enemies.

So nearly just as Enoch, Elijah, Jesus, Philip, Paul, and John were *caught away* and *raptured*, these two prophets of God will ascend into Heaven into the very presence of God, giving us yet another example of what being raptured might look like.

These nine supernatural *catching away* or *rapture-type events* all describe a sudden catching away — a snatching away — of individuals or groups that are taken from the earth into Heaven or from one location to another location, as in the case of Philip. As I told you, the idea of a catching away or a rapture is found from Genesis to Revelation.

Six of these have already taken place, and three are still to come. But the next supernatural *catching away* or *rapture* will be the rapture of the Church. At any moment, Christ will descend into the lower atmosphere and supernaturally snatch believers into the air to be with Him, and for eternity we will be with the Lord!

After reviewing this record, I simply do not know how anyone can argue against the belief in the rapture of the Church, for the idea of a *supernatural, physical, catching away* is clearly taught from the book of Genesis to the book of Revelation.

Why Is It Taking So Long for Jesus To Come for the Church?

For those who are waiting for the rapture of the Church and have experienced the ridicule of nonbelievers — and perhaps even believers — who scoff at you for believing in it, I want to encourage you to "in your patience possess ye your souls" (*see* Luke 21:19).

Second Peter 3:8 says, "But, beloved, be not ignorant of this one thing, that one day is with the Lord as a thousand years, and a thousand years as one day." What did the apostle Peter mean when he said, "...Be not ignorant of this one thing..."?

The words "be not" are a translation of *me*, a particle that means *no* or *not*, and here it is intended to be taken as *a prohibition*. The word "ignorant" is a translation of a form of the

Greek word *lanthano*, which means *to forget, to deliberately ignore*, or *to purposefully disregard*. As a phrase, it means, "You absolutely must not be forgetful of this one fact...."

Then Peter told us what we prohibitively must not forget: "One day is with the Lord as a thousand years." The words "one day" are a translation of the Greek words *mia hemera* — a combination of the word *mia*, which is the numeric *number one*, and the word *hemera*, which denotes *a twenty-four hour span of time*. As a phrase, it means *one twenty-four-hour day.*

Peter then stated that "one day is with the Lord as a thousand years, and a thousand years as one day." The word "with" in Greek is interpreted from the preposition *para*, which means *alongside of, close to, right next to*, or *directly before* the Lord. As such, He is, thus, able to see all of time in a single glance. The words "thousand years" are interpreted from the Greek words *chilia ete*, which come from the word *chilioi* — the numerical equivalent of *exactly one thousand*. The word "as" is a translation of the adverb *hos*, which means *just as, exactly as*, or *exactly like*.

To put this phrase in perspective, you may think that living 100 years is living a long time. But if God looks at 1,000 years as one day, our 100-year lifespans are about two and a half hours long! And think about this: If God promised you something years ago that hasn't come to pass yet, you simply need to hold on — it could come in just a "minute"!

God knew His plan for you before you were born, and when He tells you He's going to do something in your life, He's looking for you to trust Him for it. If you do, it is guaranteed to come, so don't let the weeks, months, or even years on the calendar upset you. Stay expectant and be ever faithful, for He who promised you is faithful to do it! He already sees in a glance how He's going to do it!

Let's see how *The Renner Interpretive Version* (*RIV*) interprets this verse.

RIV OF SECOND PETER 3:8

But it is vital that you never forget or allow yourself to lose sight of this one very important thing. Beloved — those whom I deeply love and cherish — one twenty-four-hour day before the Lord is just like one thousand years. And a thousand years is precisely like a single twenty-four-hour day.

If one uses this standard to measure time according to Scripture, it would mean the time between Creation and the birth of Christ is about 4,000 years, and from the time of Christ until now, another 2,000 years have passed.

This means that each 1,000 years signifies a "day" on God's prophetic calendar. Since indeed *one day* symbolizes 1,000 years, then from the time of Creation until now, humanity has experienced six "days" — four "days" *before* Christ's birth and two "days" *after* His birth. Thus, the two "days" (2,000 years) since His resurrection are the "last days" of the six total days. Taking into account that the Jewish calendar, which is God's calendar, is a little different, it means we are now somewhere at the end of the sixth day and about to enter the seventh day on God's timetable!

God Waits Because He is Loving and Patient

Then Peter went on to tell us *why* Christ is taking so long to return when he wrote, "...But [God] is longsuffering to us-ward, not willing that any should perish, but that all should come to repentance."

The word "longsuffering" is translated from a form of *makrothumeo*, which is a compound of *makros* and *thumos*. The first part of this compound is the word *makros*, and it depicts what is *long* or *of long duration*, similar to *a long span of time*.

The second part of the word is *thumos*, which means *anger* and depicts *a strong and growing passion*. When these words are compounded, it pictures *the patient restraint of anger* and denotes *longsuffering*.

The word "longsuffering" is a picture of something like a candle that has a very long wick and is prepared to burn a long time. It depicts one with the ability to *forbear* and to *patiently wait* until someone finally comes around, makes progress, changes, or hears what you are trying to communicate or teach him or her.

Thus, we find God is not late in fulfilling His promise — rather, He is holding out, patiently waiting, and demonstrating longsuffering toward those who are unsaved. In fact, He is waiting for the salvation of *one last person* who will repent. Make no mistake: God is not delayed, late, slow, or tardy in fulfilling His promise; He is simply holding out for the last soul to be saved.

Peter said God is "not willing that any should perish, but that all should come to repentance." The word "not" is a translation of *me*, a particle that means *no* or *not*. Although not everyone will repent and come to faith in Christ, Peter stated that it is not the heartfelt wish of God for any person to perish — therefore God is patiently waiting until the last person who will repent has done so.

The word "willing" is interpreted from a form of *boulomai*, which means *to advise, counsel, desire, intend,* or *wish*, and pictures the concepts of *careful thought, intentionality,* and *emotions*. Putting all these aspects of *boulomai* together shows the characteristics of *vigilant thought, intense emotions,* and *profound intent*. Simply put, God does not desire for *anyone* to perish!

The word "perish" is an interpretation of *apollumi*, a compound of the preposition *apo*, which means *from* or *down* and the word *olethros*, which pictures *death, destruction, doom,* and *complete ruin*. As a compound, it depicts what is *destroyed, devastated, ruined, trashed,* or *wasted*, and it portrays *complete perishing or total ruin*. It can be used to denote *a temporal state of ruin* or *eternal punishment*, both of which are true of every unbeliever who undergoes both the temporal effects and eternal tragedy of being lost.

The Holy Spirit is telling us very clearly that God is not slow regarding the promises He has made. He made them, and He will fulfill them — but He is "longsuffering" for the sake of those who still need to come to repentance. The end will occur the instant the last person who is going to be saved is brought into the Kingdom — and then we will be miraculously transformed and translated to meet the Lord in the air.

God is exceedingly patient with those who are unsaved, and He is willing to wait for the redemption of that one last person who will repent. That is the longsuffering of God — and the reason why He has waited, waited, and waited to end this period or age. God is not tardy, delayed, or slow in fulfilling His promise. He is simply holding out for the last soul to be saved.

That is why Peter wrote the words "...but [God longs] that all should come to repentance." The word "but" is a translation of the Greek word *alla*, a conjunction meant to draw readers to an important conclusion: that God longs "that all should come to repentance."

The word "all" is a translation of the Greek word *pantas*, which means *all* and is an *all-inclusive* term. Although not all will respond in repentance to God's offer of salvation through faith in Christ, God intensely desires that all come to repentance.

The word "come" is an interpretation of a form of the Greek word *choreo*, which in its simplest form means *to accommodate* or *to make space*. But it is interestingly the ancient Greek word used to describe *a dramatic performance on a stage*, and it is where we derive the first part of the word *choreography*. Here, we find that God — in His longing for all to be saved — orchestrates events to help bring a person to faith. If a person is unwilling to respond to His gracious dealings, God will do His part to bring a person to a place of "repentance."

What Is Repentance?

The word "repentance" is translated from a form of *metanoia*, a compound of the preposition *meta* and *noeo*. The preposition *meta* denotes *a change* or *a turn*, and the word *noeo* means *to think* and is derived from *nous*, which is the Greek word for *the mind*. When these two words are compounded, the new word describes in its most basic sense *a change of mind* or *a complete conversion*.

The word *metanoia* speaks of *a turn*, *a change of direction*, *a new course*, and *a completely altered behavior and view of life*. In the New Testament, this Greek word is used to denote *a complete, radical, total change*. It means *a decision to completely change one's thoughts, behavior, and actions* or *to entirely turn around in the way one is thinking, believing, or living*. Thus, the word "repent" in the New Testament gives the image of *a person changing from top to bottom — a total transformation wholly affecting every part of a person's life*.

Repentance is not the mere acceptance of a new philosophy or new idea, but it is *a conversion to truth so deep that it results in a total life change*. The idea of an across-the-board transformation is intrinsic in the word "repent." In fact, if there is no transformation, change of behavior, or change of desire in a person who claims to have repented and come to Christ in the new birth, it is doubtful that true repentance ever occurred, no matter what the person claims.

Real repentance begins with a decision to make an about-face and to change, but its *proof* can be witnessed as a person's outward conduct consistently aligns with that decision. This means the decision to repent lies in the *mind*, not in the *emotions*.

The act of repentance involves a solid, intellectual decision *to turn about-face, take a new direction, and revise the pattern of one's life*. While emotions may accompany repentance, they are not required for genuine repentance to occur. True repentance is *a mental choice to leave what is displeasing to God and to turn toward Him with all of one's heart and mind in order to obey Him*.

Although it's true that not all will be saved, God is waiting for the Gospel to reach the ends of the earth and for that last person who will respond to His call. He is not tardy, delayed, or slow in fulfilling His promise. He is simply holding out for the last soul to be saved. How great is the love and longsuffering of God! Remember, He lives outside of time and sees all of time as we know it in a *glance*. And He is willing to wait the duration of 2,000 years just for one person to finally come to repentance.

You see, God knows what hell is — it is an inescapable place of torture, torment, and suffering — and He doesn't want anyone to go there. That is why we must be serious and committed about taking the saving message of Jesus to the world, especially in this end-of-the-age hour. We must win as many souls as possible because that door is still open for the lost to be saved — to be brought into glorious reconciliation and fellowship with God, to avoid hell, and to make Heaven their eternal home.

The *Renner Interpretive Version* (*RIV*) of Second Peter 3:9 attempts to bring all these powerful word meanings into the text.

RIV OF SECOND PETER 3:9

The Supreme Lord and Master — the One with authority in every known and unknown realm — emphatically and unequivocally does not delay, slow down, or show Himself to be tardy in any way concerning the promise [that He will return], just as some have concluded to be a delay, lateness, slowness, or tardiness [in keeping His promise]; but on the other hand and all the way to the other end of the spectrum, God has chosen to hold out, to patiently wait, and to be longsuffering toward us. He is not wishing for anyone to perish, but on the contrary, He intensely desires that all would come to a place of repentance.

Because this entire text is so important, I would like for you to see its entirety in the *Renner Interpretive Version.*

RIV OF SECOND PETER 3:3-9

3 Know, always know, and never forget that first, foremost, and above all else, there shall come in the last of days — that is, when time has sailed to its last port and not much more time is left in the end-time journey — mocking scoffers. I'm talking about those who sneer and jeer and make fun of those who believe in Christ's coming. These are people who are dominated and ruled by their own base instincts and who are doggedly and determinedly following after them.

4 They go on and on, alleging and saying, 'So where is the reality of the guaranteed promise of His glorious coming?' In fact, these mockers will allege, 'Come on! From the time the fathers of old died, everything continues perpetually the same, is unchanged, and is in keeping with how things have been from the very beginning of creation.'

5 For it's just a fact that these mockers have purposefully chosen to discount, disregard, forget, ignore, snub, and pay no attention to the explicit fact that the heavens above existed since the oldest times long ago — and the earth came forth from water — and all of this came to pass by the word of God.

6 Back in those days, the civilization that existed was overwhelmed with a cataclysmic flood so immense that it was completely deluged with water, and it was so completely wiped out that not a trace of that world remains.

7 But amazingly, at this current, exact, present moment — even right now — the heavens above and the physical earth are being 'set aside and stored up.' That is, they are being guarded, kept, preserved, and protected by the Word [of God] until the big day of judgment, an unimaginable crisis, that will occur when an all-consuming and engulfing fire will utterly destroy the rotten and godless behaviors of ungodly men.

8 But it is vital that you never forget or allow yourself to lose sight of this one very important thing. Beloved — those whom I deeply love and cherish — one twenty-four-hour day before the Lord is just like one thousand years. And a thousand years is precisely like a single twenty-four-hour day.

9 The Supreme Lord and Master — the One with authority in every known and unknown realm — emphatically and unequivocally does not delay, slow down, or show Himself to be tardy in any way concerning the promise [that He will return], just as some have concluded to be a delay, lateness, slowness, or tardiness [in keeping His promise]; but on the other hand and all the way to the other end of the spectrum, God has *chosen* to hold out, to patiently wait, and to be longsuffering toward us. He is not wishing for anyone to perish, but on the contrary, He intensely desires that all would come to a place of repentance.

Friend, despite the mocking, scoffing, irreverent attitude of many in the world today, God in His great love awaits the harvest of the precious fruit of the earth — *souls*. His plan has not changed; it is simply His will that people come to a place of repentance through Christ and thereby escape the destruction of hell (*see* James 5:7; 2 Peter 3:9).

QUESTIONS TO PONDER

1. There were multiple people in Scripture who experienced a *catching away* of some kind. Before reading this chapter, did you know about all six raptures and rapture-like events that have already taken place? How does this information impact your thoughts on the three raptures that have yet to occur?

2. God knew His plan for you before you were born. Second Peter 3:8 says, "But, beloved, be not ignorant of this one thing, that one day is with the Lord as a thousand years, and a thousand years as one day." If God looks at 1,000 years as one day, our 100-year lifespans are about two and a half hours long according to Him! Has God spoken something to you about your future, your marriage, your family, your business, or your ministry that has not yet come to pass? Take some time to write down three scriptures that bolster your faith concerning the word He spoke to you. Don't give up! Hold on — the manifestation of God's promise to you could come in just a "minute"!

3. Although it's true that not all people will be saved, God is exceedingly patient with those who are unsaved, and He is willing to wait for the redemption of that one last person who will repent. Hell is a real place, and God is fully aware of the inescapable torture that awaits those who refuse His merciful gift of salvation. Second Peter 3:9 says that God is "…not willing that any should perish," so we must be serious about taking the Gospel to people everywhere. Who in your life needs to hear the Good News? Take a moment to ask the Lord for the words to say and the opportunity to speak those words to that person.

4. Many people associate repentance with an emotional experience, but Scripture presents it as something far deeper: a deliberate, life-altering decision to turn away from what is displeasing to God and walk in alignment with His truth. Looking honestly at your own life, are there sins you've allowed to remain unchecked? When you repent, do you simply express regret — or do you renew your mind, realign your heart with God's, and commit to real transformation in how you live?

5. Second Peter 3:3-4 (*AMPC*) says that "…scoffers (mockers) will come in the last days with scoffing, [people who] walk after their own fleshly desires and say, Where is the promise of His coming? For since the forefathers fell asleep, all things have continued exactly as they did from the beginning of creation." Have you ever been mocked or ridiculed for your beliefs? More specifically, have you ever been mocked or ridiculed for your beliefs about the Rapture?

RIV of First Thessalonians 4:17

Then at that exact synchronized moment, those who are spiritually living, spiritually robust, spiritually thriving, spiritually vibrant, and spiritually vigorous — I'm talking about the remaining remnant of spiritually alive believers who have endured and will still be left around at the time of the coming of the Lord — will be suddenly and supernaturally snatched away out of imminent danger, just in the nick of time, as the Lord initiates a divine rescue operation to transport them into the clouds to join those who have been resurrected. There in the air's lower atmosphere where the Lord has descended to meet them, those who were raised from the dead and the remnant who were supernaturally snatched out of danger will encounter the Lord. And at that encounter, the Lord will roll out the red carpet to give the new arrivals a royal reception to match the VIP status He knows they deserve! After that, we will always — at all times and forevermore — be with the Lord.

CHAPTER SEVEN

FIVE DIFFERENCES BETWEEN THE RAPTURE AND THE SECOND COMING OF CHRIST

In this book, I have referred to both the rapture of the Church and the Second Coming (or Second Advent) of Christ, which I want you to understand are *two different events*. Some people confuse the rapture of the Church and the Second Coming of Christ, but in this chapter, we will see five key differences between these two separate and distinct events.

Up until now, I have included the words "Second Advent" as a parenthetical reference with the phrase "Second Coming" because they are both names for *the exact same event*. And, again, this event of the Second Coming is unique and separate from the event of Christ's rapture of the Church, as we will discover in the pages to come.

But in the remainder of this chapter, I will simply use "Second Coming" to describe the event that occurs *after* the Rapture and *after* the Tribulation in which Christ returns with His saints and plants His feet on the earth to establish His Millennial Reign.

In the pages that follow, you will learn five major differences to help you understand these two holy events — the Rapture and the Second Coming — that have each been pre-planned by God on His own timetable. What you learn will help you and those around you, in your proximity or sphere, never to be confused about this topic again. *So let's begin!*

As previously noted, the rapture of the Church and the Second Coming of Christ are two separate events. When the Rapture occurs at the end of the Church Age — which is our present age — the Church will be caught up in the air to meet Christ and will be removed from the earth for a time, and the time frame that follows is a period the Bible calls the Tribulation, also known as the Great Tribulation and the Day of the Lord. The Tribulation will begin at that moment and will last for seven years. At the end of the seven-year Tribulation period, Christ will return visibly to the earth with His saints, and that event is called the Second Coming of Christ.

In a book like this, certain points are repeated because the nature of the subject requires it. But to help you grasp the difference between these two unprecedented events, the following are five key distinctions for you to understand.

DIFFERENCE NUMBER ONE:
IN THE RAPTURE OF THE CHURCH, JESUS WILL RETURN *FOR* HIS SAINTS — AT THE SECOND COMING, JESUS WILL RETURN *WITH* HIS SAINTS

In Chapter One, we saw how Paul expounded on the Rapture in First Thessalonians 4:17. In that verse, he wrote, "Then we which are alive and remain shall be caught up together with them in the clouds, to meet the Lord in the air: and so shall we ever be with the Lord."

Although this was covered in Chapter One, for review, let's take into account the meanings of the Greek words in this verse.

***RIV* OF FIRST THESSALONIANS 4:17**

Then at that exact synchronized moment, those who are spiritually living, spiritually robust, spiritually thriving, spiritually vibrant, and spiritually vigorous — I'm talking about the remaining remnant of spiritually alive believers who have endured and will still be left around at the time of the coming of the

Lord — will be suddenly and supernaturally snatched away out of imminent danger, just in the nick of time, as the Lord initiates a divine rescue operation to transport them into the clouds to join those who have been resurrected. There in the air's lower atmosphere where the Lord has descended to meet them, those who were raised from the dead and the remnant who were supernaturally snatched out of danger will encounter the Lord. And at that encounter, the Lord will roll out the red carpet to give the new arrivals a royal reception to match the VIP status He knows they deserve! After that, we will always — at all times and forevermore — be with the Lord.

Here we see that when the rapture of the Church occurs, Jesus will come *for* His people to retrieve and snatch them from the earth before the seven-year Tribulation period begins. That seven-year Tribulation period in Scripture is also called the "Day of the Lord," as we've seen, and this phrase refers to the unique period during which God will pour wrath upon the earth.

A Brief Overview of the Event of the Great Tribulation

In First Thessalonians 1:10, Paul wrote of our deliverance from the wrath that is to come. He wrote that we are waiting "...for his Son from heaven, whom he raised from the dead, *even* Jesus, which delivered us from the wrath to come." The word "wrath" is an interpretation of the Greek word *orge*, a word that depicts *divine tribulation against the ungodly*. The Greek word *orge* pictures long-building and swelling emotions that literally erupt into *wrath* or *vengeance*. It is not a sudden outburst, but something that is released after being held back for a prolonged period of time.

> The "wrath to come" speaks of a future time when *divine indignation* will come upon the guilty. God has been patient with the ungodly and with a world gone astray, and He is presently holding back judgment — but the Greek word *orge*, translated as "wrath," tells us that a specific moment is coming when God will no longer hold it back. God has patiently held it back, but when it comes, it will appear as though the wrath and vengeance of God has erupted *fiercely*, *suddenly*, and *violently* on the world scene. That specific moment will occur when the rapture of the Church has occurred and authentic believers have been taken out of the way and "delivered" from the pouring out of wrath that will subsequently take place.

Some argue, "The Church has experienced hardship and persecution, at times, to violent and deadly degrees, over the course of its 2,000-year history. Why would God deliver His Church from the wrath of the Tribulation? Aren't there believers experiencing hardship and persecution — 'wrathful' conditions — in places in the world right now?"

When God's wrath begins to be released as a fierce eruption during the seven-year period called the Tribulation, it will be unlike anything humankind has ever experienced.

Indeed, God's people have experienced hardship and suffering at the hands of the wicked ever since the Church emerged in a hostile world devoid of God and godliness many centuries ago. And more dedicated Christians are being persecuted today than at any other time in history.[1] To learn more on the current status of worldwide persecution, I encourage you to read my book *Signs You'll See Just Before Jesus Comes*. I have lived in the territory of the former Soviet Union for many decades, and my family and I live there now. I personally know scores of believers who suffered terribly for their faith. Many were unjustly treated or imprisoned — and during the years of socialistic-communistic Soviet power, a large number actually died for their faith.

So I am very familiar with the fact that believers have suffered and will continue to suffer. But experiencing hardship and persecution — even some of the worst we've seen or heard about — does not come near to the "wrath" Paul wrote about in First Thessalonians 1:10. If you read the book of Revelation (which is not the focus of this book), you can easily come to the realization that when God's wrath begins to be released as a fierce *eruption* during the seven-year period called the Tribulation, it will be unlike anything humankind has ever experienced. And this wrath will be initiated by God Himself and will not be directed at His people. Rather, it will be His holy and righteous judgment directed against unrepentant ungodliness and evil.

In fact, in Matthew 24:21, Jesus referred to the severity of that wrath when He said, "For then shall be great tribulation, such as was not since the beginning of the world to this time, no, nor ever shall be."

The word "then" in Matthew 24:21 is the Greek word *tote*, and it means *then*, or *at that time*. Jesus uses this word to refer to a certain time when there will be "great tribulation" upon the earth. The word "great" in Greek is *megale*, a word used to describe something that is *enormous*, *giant*, or *massive in size*, and it also refers to an *intensity* that is far-reaching and wide-impacting because of its sheer *enormity*.

The word "tribulation" is an interpretation of the Greek word *thlipsis*, which is a word that pictures *extreme tribulation*. It means *pressure so great that it is crushing*. It pictures non-stop pressure that is *suffocating* to those under its weight. It conveys the idea of being *crushed*, *pressured*, *squeezed*, or *stressed beyond one's wildest imagination*.

No one on Earth at that time will be able to escape the intensity of this time period...and this dreadful event will begin the moment the Church is raptured and taken out of the way.

The use of these words "great tribulation" warns that those who are living on the earth during the seven-year period called the Tribulation will experience something so intense that no one in human history has ever experienced it. Remember, Jesus said it would be "...great tribulation, such as was not since the beginning of the world to this time, no, nor ever shall be" (Matthew 24:21). Jesus makes it clear that no one on Earth at that time will be able to escape the intensity of this time period. Indeed, no one at any time in past history has ever experienced the bowls of wrath that will be poured upon the ungodly after the Church is vacated. And this dreadful event will begin the moment the Church is raptured and taken out of the way.

While I appreciate every person who has, or is, going through difficult times or persecution, this does not come near in scope or severity to the *wrath of God* that will be unleashed on earth during the seven-year Tribulation.

Jesus Had More To Say About the Intensity of the Tribulation

We've seen that in Matthew 24:21, Jesus said the Tribulation will be "such as was not since the beginning of the world to this time, no, nor ever shall be." This shows us the intensity that will be felt during this seven-year period, but to really understand this verse better, let's look at it piece by piece.

Jesus was making a unique comparison when He described the severity of the Tribulation in light of all other events in human history — or "since the beginning of the world" until "this time." The words "such as" at the beginning of this verse are a translation of the Greek word *hoios*, a word that means *of what sort* or *of what kind*, and here it describes just that — a time that is *of the sort or kind* that causes other periods of disaster to pale in comparison.

In fact, this word *hoios*, translated as "such as," points to the Tribulation as an event and time period that stands in a category by itself. That means no other time frame in the past, present, or any other time will be comparable to what will occur during the seven-year Tribulation.

The words "was not" are a translation of *ou gegonen*. The word *ou* is a negative particle that means *emphatically not*, and *gegonen* is a form of *ginomai*, which here pictures *whatever occurs or comes to pass*. As a phrase, it means *such a time has emphatically not ever occurred*.

But Jesus then adds that no time comparable to the seven-year Tribulation period has occurred "since the beginning of the world." The word "since" is a translation of *ap'* — a contracted form of *apo* — and it would be better translated *from*. The word "beginning" is translated from *arches*, which describes something *archaic* and points to *the very beginning*. The word "world" is interpreted from a form of the Greek word *kosmos*, which not only describes *the planet Earth*, but *the entire kosmos* or *universe*. As a phrase, it means *from the most archaic beginning of the world and universe*.

Jesus goes on to say, "...to this time, no, nor ever shall be." The words "to this time" are a translation of the Greek phrase *heos tou nun*. The Greek word *heos* means *until*, and the word *nun* means *right now in this very present moment*.

The words "nor ever shall be" are a translation of the Greek words *oud' ou me genetai*. The words *oud' ou me* are a triple negative. The word *oud'* is a contracted form of the Greek word *oude*, which means *neither*, and the word *ou* means emphatically *no*. The Greek particle *me* is a canceller and the third negative particle in this phrase. The words "ever shall be" are a translation of *genetai*, which is a form of *ginomai* that, again, pictures *whatever occurs or comes to pass*.

As a phrase, Matthew 24:21 could be interpreted, "That time [referring to the Great Tribulation] will be of a sort that stands uniquely in a category by itself. For such a time has emphatically not ever occurred from the very beginning of the world, until this present moment and neither will it ever happen again. No, not ever, before or again, will such a time ever occur."

Past and Modern Cataclysmic Events

There have been many cataclysmic events and times in human history, so let's consider a few of them. The following is not intended to be an exhaustive world history lesson, but it's a reminder of just a few events that most biblically minded people will recall as events that were cataclysmic in nature.

This illustration depicts the Ark in the background, floating on waters of destruction after the Great Deluge flooded the entire world in the days of Noah.

- **The Flood** at the time of Noah was an event so cataclysmic that Peter wrote, "And spared not the old world, but saved Noah the eighth person, a preacher of righteousness, bringing in the flood upon the world of the ungodly" (2 Peter 2:5).

  The word "spared" is interpreted from a form of the Greek word *pheidomai*, which indeed means *to spare*, but it also means *to treat something leniently*. Because God "spared *not*" the old world, this word emphatically means that just as God was *not lenient* and did *not* ultimately overlook the wretched moral condition of the world that existed at the time of the Great Flood, He also will not overlook or be lenient with the moral condition of our world today. The word "not" is a translation of the Greek word *ouk*, which is the most emphatic form of *no* or *not*.

  The word "old" is a translation of *archaios*, and it is where we get the word "archaic." This word denotes what is *original*, *ancient*, or *old* in terms of time and age. The word "world" is a translation of *kosmos*, which describes *the ordered world*, *a civilization*, *culture*, or *society*. The Greek depicts *an ancient civilization* that no longer exists due to the Great Deluge at the time of Noah that engulfed the ancient world, completely tore it to pieces, and destroyed it. By using this word, Peter clearly stated that an entire civilization previously existed and was utterly wiped out by a cataclysmic flood. God's justice is so steadfast that when the world of Noah's day persisted in their egregious sinful behavior and refused to repent, God eventually judged that entire ancient civilization. In fact, He judged it so steadfastly and deliberately that He wiped it out — leaving only a handful of Noah's family as survivors.

The words "bringing in" are interpreted from a form of *epago*, which denotes *the loosing of wild and vicious dogs to literally rip a victim to pieces, limb from limb.* Using this word, Peter was telling us that the Flood was fiercely destructive, like ferociously wild dogs that literally tore the old world to pieces until nothing remained of that ancient civilization. This cataclysmic event and its effects explain why it is so hard to find pieces of it in archeological digs.

The word "flood" is a translation of the Greek word *kataklusmos*, which is a compound of the preposition *kata* and the word *kludon*. The preposition *kata* means *down*, and the word *kludon* means *to wash*, as a wave washes over land. Compounded, as Peter used it in this verse, this word depicts *a complete deluge of water coming down and over the face of the entire earth.*

This word pictures waves so mighty that they covered the entire face of the earth until it was completely washed over. By the time the waters of the Flood receded, that previous civilization was non-existent — thus revealing the reason only fragments of information are known of that earlier time in human history. Interestingly, the word *kataklusmos* is where we derive the English word "cataclysm."

RIV **of Second Peter 2:5**

But wait…I want you to remember another event. I'm talking about the days in which God also did not leniently go easy on and spare the ancient civilization, except for Noah, one of eight [who survived the flood]. Noah was a herald and preacher of righteousness, and He was guarded, preserved, protected, and saved [along with seven others in his family] when his preaching released a cataclysmic flood that tore the godless, wicked civilization of that age to pieces.

There was never in human history an event to compare to the deluge that tore the ancient world to pieces during the days of Noah. It would be difficult, and, in fact, hard to imagine that *any* event could exceed a cataclysm of this proportion. This was a world-changing event.

When the human race was divided by language at the Tower of Babel, it was a world-changing event that would be difficult to overstate in terms of impact and enormity.

- **The Tower of Babel** signified a moment that is also unique in human history. Genesis 11 tells of this potentially shattering event that occurred when the whole of mankind, led by Nimrod, had set their hearts against God to do evil things in His sight.

  Genesis 11:6-9 says, "And the Lord said, Behold, the people is one, and they have all one language; and this they begin to do: and now nothing will be restrained from them, which they have imagined to do. Go to, let us go down, and there confound their language, that they may not understand one another's speech.

  "So the Lord scattered them abroad from thence upon the face of all the earth: and they left off to build the city. Therefore is the name of it called Babel; because the Lord did there confound the language of all the earth: and from thence did the Lord scatter them abroad upon the face of all the earth."

  When Nimrod's empire was destroyed at the Tower of Babel, and the human race was divided by language and then scattered across the face of the earth, it was an event that would be difficult to overstate in terms of impact and enormity. It became a world-changing event in human history as Nimrod's stronghold of evil was dismantled by this act of God's wisdom and power.

When Pharaoh's army was destroyed, and the children of Israel were delivered, it was a cataclysmic event for Egypt, and one that would be difficult to exaggerate in terms of impact and enormity.

- **The Ten Plagues of Egypt** were among the most cataclysmic events in human history, and that occurred when God delivered Israel from Egypt and showed Himself to be the God above all gods.

When one travels the Nile River in Egypt today, it is possible to see many of the sites and structures that Moses and the children of Israel saw in their day. These include the legendary Sphinx of Giza, the ancient pyramids, the temple cities of Karnak and Luxor, the Valley of the Kings, and a unique temple at Kom Ombo, dedicated to Sobek, the crocodile god. This was a majestic and powerful empire at one time, considered in its heyday to be the greatest empire of the ancient age.

But this powerful empire was oppressive toward the people of God, and when the cries of the Hebrew nation reached His ears, God raised up Moses to deliver His people from the Egyptian taskmasters and the tyrannical rule of Pharaoh. God's weapons of mass destruction were manifested in the form of ten powerful plagues — each one uniquely designed to humiliate the so-called gods of Egypt and utterly destroy the land's famed riches and resources of which they were so proud.

By the time the tenth plague ended with the death of Pharaoh's firstborn, in the midst of great despair, the wicked ruler of Egypt called for Moses. The Bible says Pharaoh "...called for Moses and Aaron by night, and said, Rise up, and get you forth from among my people, both ye and the children of Israel; and go, serve the Lord, as ye have said" (Exodus 12:31). In effect, Pharaoh cried, "Get up and get out — you and your whole clan!"

Eventually Pharaoh hardened his heart, changed his mind, and pursued the children of Israel with his army. But God opened the Red Sea and exposed a road in it that the children of Israel walked upon to the other side (*see* Exodus 14:21-22; Psalm 66:6). When Pharaoh's army tried to take the same road through the Red

Sea, God caused a wind to blow, and the raging walls of the Red Sea that were held back for the children of Israel collapsed upon Pharaoh's army and they were destroyed.

The ten plagues that led to the destruction of Pharaoh's army and the deliverance of the children of Israel were yet another cataclysmic event for Egypt and one that we still stand in awe of today. It would be difficult to exaggerate the impact and enormity of that historical event, which was certainly dramatic and world-changing.

When God's people were carried into Babylonian captivity, it must have felt as if the end of the world had come upon them.

- **The Babylonian Captivity** was an event in which the Babylonians sieged Jerusalem and a large number of Jewish people were forcibly relocated to Babylon. The first siege took place in 605 BC. After the sacking of Jerusalem and the destruction of Solomon's Temple in 587 BC, thousands more were enslaved and taken to Babylon and to other parts of Mesopotamia. The second Babylonian campaign against Jewish land occurred in 589-587 BC.

Before this Babylonian destruction took place, the population of Jerusalem was approximately 75,000 people, but by the time all the sieges ended, approximately 20,000 people were taken as slaves to Babylon and other places. One scholar suggests that, taking into account the vast number of those who died in these events — plus those who were taken into exile — the population of Judah may have been reduced to as little as ten percent of what it had been before these devastating attacks occurred. And being accused of retaining their national loyalty, the exiles were often beaten, imprisoned, and reduced to peasants in the lands to which they were exiled. This horrific ordeal lasted for 70 long years.

How could anyone exaggerate the significance and intensity of such an event? At the time, this hardship and pressure would have been overwhelming and overpowering, and surely the people of God wondered at times whether they would survive. To those who suffered this experience, it must have felt as if the end of the world had come upon them.

It is so mind-boggling to imagine the devastation of Jerusalem that it would be impossible to overstate the enormity and intensity of this event. As with the Babylonian captivity, those who experienced this catastrophic event must have felt as if the end of the world had come upon them.

- **The Destruction of Jerusalem** in 70 AD was a decisive event of the first Jewish-Roman War (66-74 AD). In that horrific and painful event in which Emperor Vespasian sent the Roman army to besiege the city of Jerusalem, as part of the siege led by the future emperor Titus, Roman troops destroyed the city and set fire to the Temple completely destroying it.

The historian Josephus wrote that more than 1,000,000 people in Jerusalem were killed during the siege. He further stated that another 97,000 were enslaved.[2] The destruction of Jerusalem was so devastating that when the siege ended, only 40,000 people had survived the rampage, and of that number, more than 10,000 Jewish men were sent to Rome to serve as slaves.

About one year after the fall of Jerusalem, a triumphal parade was held in Rome to celebrate the Roman victory over the Jews — this triumphal parade was unique in Roman history because it was the only one ever dedicated to subjugating an existing population. The event drew a crowd of spectators numbering 300,000 or more.

Emperor Vespasian, with his son Titus, wore a laurel crown and was adorned in lavish purple robes, and the parade showcased an elaborate array of artwork that included purple tapestries, rugs, gems, statues, and decorated animals, along with multi-story scaffolds displaying golden frames, ivory work, and tapestries that illustrated scenes from the war. But most importantly, these displays exhibited sacred items that were seized from the Temple in Jerusalem. These items included the golden Menorah, the golden Table of Showbread, many sacred religious texts, and 700 Jewish captives who were humiliatingly paraded as symbols of conquest.

The Second Temple in Jerusalem was so magnificent that before the Roman emperor Titus laid siege to Jerusalem in 70 AD and destroyed it, he first entered it to plunder its treasures and carry them back to Rome. Today at the Arch of Titus in the Roman Forum (*Forum Romanum*), there is a carved relief on the interior of the arch that pictures the golden Menorah from the Temple being carried into Rome in a triumphal procession, along with other treasures taken from the Temple in Jerusalem.

Most people do not realize the incalculable value of what Titus plundered from the Temple. It is so immense that once it was converted into cash, the sales of the Temple treasures were eventually sufficient to use as capital for the construction of Rome's enormous Colosseum. And the workforce that constructed the Colosseum was the group of 10,000 Jewish men who were sent to Rome as slaves.

When one thinks of the total devastation that came to the people of God at that time, it is mind-boggling. In fact, it would be impossible to overstate the enormity and intensity of that horrific historical event. As with the Babylonian captivity, those who were experiencing this catastrophic event must have felt as if the end of the world had come upon them.

Since the turn of the Twentieth Century, approximately 150,000,000 lives have been lost across the globe as casualties of war.

- **Wars, World Wars, Political Turmoil, Population Displacement, and Disease** have marked the ages. In terms of war, one scholar has stated that there have been approximately 8,700 or more wars in human history. Because of the increase in weapons, technology, and ease of transportation, the number of wars rose substantially higher in the 1800s and 1900s.

In the Twentieth Century alone there were at least 970 wars (not including smaller regional conflicts). And in recent years, at the time of this writing, we have seen the highest recorded number of state-based conflicts since 1946.[3] To make matters worse, the most violent years since the end of the Cold War have occurred in the last few years with a record number of 59 major conflicts recorded.[4]

Wars, political turmoil, population displacement, and disease are realities that we are all aware of in our age. In my book *Signs You'll See Just Before Jesus Comes*, I wrote:[5]

> **Since the turn of the Twentieth Century, approximately 150,000,000 lives have been lost across the globe as casualties of war. That horrific statistic includes world wars, regional conflicts, and continual skirmishes in parts of the world renowned for political unrest. We've experienced wars, the threat of wars, and violent disturbances in our cities.**
>
> **Our society has been disrupted by rival governments, fringe militia, factions, and groups and individuals whose hatred drives them to commit unimaginable crimes. These disturbances are no longer lurking in the distance. They have made their way to our own backyard, it seems. Reminiscent of the 'duck and cover' air-raid drills conducted in classrooms in the 1950s, now people are receiving instructions on what to do if they find themselves in the vicinity of an active shooter....**
>
> **In recent decades, the world has seen a variety of similar uprisings sweep across entire geographical areas. In each place where these revolutions have occurred, it has resulted in disturbances, upheavals, political instability, and the spawning of more insurgencies and revolts....**
>
> **It's difficult to keep an accurate count of how many revolutions have occurred in recent years. There seems to be an unleashing of demonic forces into the earth with a fury that refuses to be pacified. If there has ever been a time when it felt like all restraints have been thrown off, it is now. To one observing the news, it appears as if the lid has been taken off *Pandora's box* — and we seem to be coexisting in a warring, terroristic environment that is unprecedented in scope....**

As generations reflect on the past, true history will have recorded our own time as a moment when mayhem rocked many parts of the planet, perhaps on a wider scale than ever before. From natural appearances, it looks like an array of nations, races, religions, political parties, and ideologies is locked into a collision course against one another. As never before, it seems that nations are rising against nations and kingdoms against kingdoms....

Has there ever been a time when there was more ethnic conflict than we've seen in contemporary history? In the more recent past, such conflicts were notably localized — but today, ethnic conflict is spreading like a disease across the planet. Increasing ethnic tensions and turmoil can be found on the streets of America, Europe, Africa, the Middle East, and in every part of the world.

One might think such conflicts, especially involving race, would decrease as time moves forward. Multitudes of people have suffered bigotry, injustice, and hardships for many years to see laws changed to bring equal rights to all races. Yet racial conflicts still seem to be escalating. In fact, tensions have risen on many fronts to a boiling point....

Those who work in international affairs are well aware that these conflicts are getting worse — whether it's racial tensions in the United States, conflicting tribes in Africa, Muslim factions in the Middle East, antagonism between nations in Europe, or ethnic issues in other parts of the world. Furthermore, these conflicts are more difficult to resolve than in years past. It seems to all be leading to a less controlled, less predictable world. As power becomes more diffused and antagonism among regional powers intensifies — rendering resolutions to these conflicts becomes even more complex.

If a list of ethnic conflicts that are occurring right now were compiled, it could fill several pages. This is simply a time when conflicts among ethnic groups have erupted across vast regions of the earth. This eruption is spilling over into other regions like a plague, and it is causing national and international threats to previously peaceful parts of the world....

According to a report from *2016 World Hunger and Poverty Facts and Statistics*, more than 250,000 people die every year around the world from hunger and hunger-related causes. Another shocking report is that between 250,000 to 500,000 children become blind each year due to vitamin deficiency caused by extreme undernourishment — and half of those die within a year of their blindness.

Besides the people who actually starve to death, millions more languish in undernourished conditions. Instead of living with vibrancy and hope for the future, their lives have halted to a standstill as they focus solely on where to obtain food for themselves and their loved ones so they can continue to subsist....

The facts about poverty are alarming and disheartening. A study of this information makes it very clear why God hates poverty. These statistics expose poverty's true nature as a thief that steals time, focus, energy, talent, and even life itself. Simply stated, poverty leads to hunger — *and hunger leads to more poverty.* Without intervention to stop this sequence of events, the cycle will be unending. What poverty produces is simply devastating — a truth that cannot be exaggerated....

A world at war produces one worldwide calamity after another, one of which is famine and shortages of food. Many factors contribute to food shortfalls in different parts of the world, but the impact of wars and ethnic, political, and religious conflicts is huge on this heartbreaking issue of famine and hunger.

Exacerbating the hunger issue is the growing number of displaced people who live in countries rife with continued conflicts and fighting. As political and religious ideologies collide on an increasing level, the number of refugees is increasing commensurately, and the problem of impoverishment and hunger is growing right along with it.

Right now there are more than 1,000,000,000 people on the earth who earn less than $1.25 a day. These meager earnings make it almost impossible for them to purchase even small "doses" of food to sustain their

lives. World hunger is being felt all over the planet — and it is a sign that Jesus said we would witness just before the end of the age....

The planet is already being hard-hit with multiple diseases that are decimating populations all over the world. Even if cures exist, medicines and supplies to deal with the avalanche of disease spreading throughout the human race are often in short supply.

In addition to normal strains of disease that medical science regularly combats, today science is struggling to fight the onslaught of *newly emerging infectious diseases*. These are often actually old diseases that have had life breathed into them again. Such reemerging diseases have the potential to affect massive populations across the earth. Cures for these are frequently more difficult to find as new strains of the diseases become more powerful, and as a result, larger numbers of people are put at risk....

The U.N.'s *World Health Organization* (WHO) states that many potential epidemic and pandemic pestilences already exist in latent states. This means many life-threatening diseases are lying dormant and could be awakened at any moment to swiftly invade the human race. If even one or two of these epidemics became activated and found a way into the world's population, what could happen in a very brief period of time is unthinkable. The mere thought of this possibility has scientists and the medical world in a constant state of urgency.

The *World Health Organization* defines an 'emerging disease' as one that appears in a population for the first time — *or* one that may have existed previously, but is rapidly increasing in incidence or geographic range. The website of WHO reports:

> 'In this stage of history, professionals predict that directly before us will be the emergence of new infectious diseases and that the reemergence of "old" diseases will have a significant impact on health. A number of factors will influence this development: travel and trade, microbiological resistance, human behavior, breakdowns in health systems, and increased pressure on the environment. Social, political, and economic factors that cause the movement of people will

increase contact between people and microbes, and environmental changes caused by human activity all will contribute to the spread of disease. The overuse of antibiotics and insecticides, combined with inadequate or deteriorating public health infrastructures, will hamper or delay responses to increasing disease threats.'

The reason I share all this information is, I want you to see that past and modern, contemporary history has been filled with cataclysmic events, and we are currently living in seemingly nonstop cataclysmic events. But these catastrophes have become such a regular part of life in this present age that people have grown numb to what is happening.

However, if you take into account all the past world-shaking and traumatic events that have occurred in history — or all the unimaginable events that are occurring around the globe and society at this very time — all of them together do not even *begin* to compare to the intensity of the "great tribulation" that will take place on the earth during the seven-year period (*see* Matthew 24:21) when the inescapable wrath of God will be poured out like great "bowls" of judgment upon the world (*see* Revelation 16:1-21).

No mind can fathom what that period will be like, for it truly will be intensity on a level such as the world has never experienced at any point in history. If you compile all the pains, pressures, stresses, trials, and tribulations of world history and pile it into one seven-year time frame, it still would not come close to the Tribulation that will be experienced at that time.

This is precisely why Jesus said in Matthew 24:21, "For then shall be great tribulation, such as was not since the beginning of the world to this time, no, nor ever shall be." But as we have seen, this verse could be interpreted, "That time [referring to the Great Tribulation] will be of a sort that stands uniquely in a category by itself. For such a time has emphatically not ever occurred from the very beginning of the world until this present moment, and neither will it ever happen again. No, not ever, before or again, will such a time ever occur."

We Are Delivered From the Wrath To Come

In First Thessalonians 1:10, Paul said that those who are authentic believers will be "delivered" from the wrath of God that is to come in the near future. The word "delivered" is a form of the Greek word *rhuomai*, which means *to deliver or rescue from a dangerous situation.* It is often used in Scripture to depict God delivering and rescuing His people from peril. Paul, again, who was a linguist, knew full well the meaning of this word and used it in First Thessalonians 1:10 to declare that God will deliver and rescue His people before His wrath is poured out upon the earth. The word *rhuomai* is in many respects similar to the word *harpadzo* in that it pictures a rescue operation.

But in the New Testament, there are 18 examples of the word *rhuomai*, meaning *to deliver or rescue from a dangerous situation.* To understand the important nuances of this word, we will look at each of them. As we proceed, you will see that the word *rhuomai* was a favorite word for Paul to use when he described moments when he and his companions were miraculously delivered and rescued from dangerous situations.

Uses of the Word 'Delivered' (*Rhuomai*) in the New Testament

- In **Matthew 6:13**, the word *rhuomai* — meaning *to deliver*, *to rescue*, or *to remove from a dangerous situation* — was used by Jesus when He taught His disciples to pray. In that famous prayer called the Lord's Prayer, Jesus said they (and we) are to pray: "And lead us not into temptation, but *deliver* us from evil...." By using this word, Jesus taught that we should pray to be *delivered, rescued, and removed* from temptation, perils, and dangerous situations in life.
- In **Matthew 27:43**, the word *rhuomai* — meaning *to deliver*, *to rescue*, or *to remove from a dangerous situation* — was used by one of the thieves who was crucified alongside Jesus and infamously said, "He trusted in God; let him *deliver* him now...." The word "deliver" is translated from a form of *rhuomai*, which in this verse carries the idea of being *delivered* and *rescued* and, thus, *removed* from what Jesus was facing on the Cross.
- In **Luke 1:74**, the word *rhuomai* — meaning *to deliver*, *to rescue*, or *to remove from a dangerous situation* — is found in Zechariah's prayer where he said, "That he would grant unto us, that we being *delivered* out of the hand of our enemies might serve him without fear...." The word "delivered" is interpreted from a form of *rhuomai*, which again carries the idea of being *delivered*, *rescued*, and *removed* from the dangerous and oppressive grip of Israel's enemies.

- In **Luke 11:4**, the word *rhuomai* — meaning *to deliver, to rescue*, or *to remove from a dangerous situation* — is also used by Luke to tell us about the prayer Jesus taught His disciples to pray, which is called the Lord's Prayer. In that prayer, Jesus said we are to pray, "And forgive us our sins; for we also forgive every one that is indebted to us. And lead us not into temptation; but *deliver* us from evil." By using this particular Greek word, Luke affirmed that Jesus taught we should pray to be *delivered, rescued*, and *removed* from the evil one and from all that is malevolent in this world.

- In **Romans 7:24**, the word *rhuomai* — meaning *to deliver, to rescue*, or *to remove from a dangerous situation* — was used by Paul as he wrote, "O wretched man that I am! who shall *deliver* me from the body of this death?" In verse 25, He went on to say, "I thank God through Jesus Christ our Lord...." The word "delivered" is a translation of *rhuomai*, which once again carries the idea of being *delivered, rescued*, and *removed* from whatever is dangerous or evil. In this case, Paul rejoiced that He had been fully *delivered, rescued*, and *removed* from the body of death by the victory of Jesus at the Cross and over death.

- In **Romans 11:26**, the word *rhuomai* — meaning *to deliver, to rescue*, or *to remove from a dangerous situation* — was used by Paul when he wrote about a future time when Israel will be saved. He said, "And so all Israel shall be saved: as it is written, There shall come out of Sion the *Deliverer*, and shall turn away ungodliness from Jacob." The word "deliverer" is an interpretation of the Greek word *rhuomai*, and here it pictures Jesus as the Messiah who will one day *deliver, rescue*, and *remove* His people, Israel, from all ungodliness in the future as they call upon Him.

- In **Romans 15:31**, the word *rhuomai* — meaning *to deliver, to rescue*, or *to remove from a dangerous situation* — was again used by Paul when he asked the believers in Rome to pray that he "may be *delivered* from them that do not believe in Judaea...." Paul was in a difficult and dangerous predicament, and he was requesting prayer that he would be *delivered, rescued*, or *removed* from the clutches of evil men who intended to do him harm.

- In **Second Corinthians 1:10**, the word *rhuomai* — meaning *to deliver, to rescue*, or *to remove from a dangerous situation* — was again used by Paul to describe a past moment when God's power literally delivered him. He wrote, "Who *delivered* us from so great a death, and doth *deliver*: in whom we trust that he will yet *deliver us....*" In both instances where the words "delivered" and "deliver" are used in this verse, they are interpreted from a form of the Greek word *rhuomai*, and this unmistakably means that while the odds were stacked against Paul and his team, he and his companions were *delivered* and *rescued* and miraculously *removed* from a trial so intense that they felt as if death surrounded them.

- In **Colossians 1:13**, the word *rhuomai* — meaning *to deliver*, *to rescue*, or *to remove from a dangerous situation* — was used by Paul to describe the power of Jesus' blood to deliver and rescue each of us from the kingdom of darkness. Paul wrote that Jesus "hath *delivered* us from the power of darkness, and hath translated us into the kingdom of his dear Son." The word "delivered" is a translation of *rhuomai*, which was used by Paul to triumphantly declare that Christ's blood *delivered*, *rescued*, and *removed* each of God's children from the power of darkness. This is not an allegorical statement; we have literally been *delivered*, *rescued*, and *removed* from Satan's hold and all its evil effects by means of the Cross and the Resurrection.

- In **First Thessalonians 1:10**, the word *rhuomai* — meaning *to deliver*, *to rescue*, or *to remove from a dangerous situation* — as we have seen, was used by Paul when he wrote that we "wait for his Son from heaven, whom he raised from the dead, even Jesus, which *delivered* us from the wrath to come." Because of the payment of Christ's blood on the Cross and resurrection from the dead and our acceptance of that divine forgiveness, the Church will be *delivered*, *rescued*, and *removed* from the earth before God's wrath is eventually poured out upon the world after the rapture of the Church.

- In **Second Timothy 3:11**, the word *rhuomai* — meaning *to deliver*, *to rescue*, or *to remove from a dangerous situation* — was used by Paul to picture God's intervening power to deliver him from "persecutions, afflictions, which came unto me at Antioch, at Iconium, at Lystra; what persecutions I endured: but out of them all the Lord *delivered* me." The word "delivered" is interpreted from a form of *rhuomai*, which Paul used in this verse to depict him being *delivered* and *rescued* and *removed* from afflictions and persecutions that he experienced over the course of his ministry.

- In **Second Timothy 4:17**, the word *rhuomai* — meaning *to deliver*, *to rescue*, or *to remove from a dangerous situation* — was used by Paul to picture a moment when he stood trial before the Roman government, and possibly before Nero himself. Paul wrote that in that moment "the Lord stood with me, and strengthened me; that by me the preaching might be fully known, and that all the Gentiles might hear: and I was *delivered* out of the mouth of the lion." Once again, we find that the word "delivered" is interpreted from a form of *rhuomai*, and Paul used it to declare that he was miraculously *delivered* and *rescued* and supernaturally *removed* from powers that were determined to destroy him.

- In **Second Timothy 4:18**, the word *rhuomai* — meaning *to deliver*, *to rescue*, or *to remove from a dangerous situation* — was used immediately again by Paul when he wrote, "And the Lord shall *deliver* me from every evil work, and will preserve me unto his heavenly kingdom: to whom be glory for ever and ever. Amen." The word "deliver" is again an interpretation of the word *rhuomai*, which Paul used to state that not only had God's power *delivered*, *rescued*, and *removed* him from danger in the past, but he was also expecting God to *deliver*, *rescue*, and miraculously *remove* him from danger in the future as well.

- In **Second Peter 2:7**, the word *rhuomai* — meaning *to deliver*, *to rescue*, or *to remove from a dangerous situation* — was used by Peter to picture the moment when God snatched Lot out of the inferno that would have consumed him along with Sodom and Gomorrah. Peter wrote that God "*delivered* just Lot...." This word "delivered" that Peter used is a translation of a form of the Greek word *rhuomai*, and Peter used it to paint a dramatic picture of what occurred when God sent an angel to literally *deliver*, *rescue*, and *remove* Lot and his family from the city of Sodom just before divine judgment was poured out on them. They were rescued and snatched from danger just in the nick of time, and because Peter used this word, we know that God reached into the sewage of Sodom and "snatched" Lot and his family out *before* judgment fell on the wicked cities of the plain. This word pictures *a rescue operation* that intended *to snatch* a person out of physical or spiritual peril. It denotes the idea of *intervention*.

- In **Second Peter 2:9**, the word *rhuomai* — meaning *to deliver, to rescue,* or *to remove from a dangerous situation* — was used again by Peter to say, "The Lord knoweth how to deliver the godly out of temptations...." In both verses 7 and 9, the words "delivered" and "deliver" are again interpreted from a form of the Greek word *rhuomai*, and it unmistakably means that God knows how to *deliver* and *rescue* and miraculously *remove* His people from tests, trials, and temptations in life. Just as Lot was *snatched* out of the raging fires of destruction by the two angels God sent to investigate the sinfulness of Sodom and Gomorrah and to release judgment against those cities, God precisely knows how to deliver, rescue, and remove all His children from destructive environments.

After reviewing the use of the word *rhuomai* as it is consistently used in the New Testament, we see that this word always depicts *a rescue operation* that is intended to *deliver, rescue,* and *remove* God's people from impending danger. Because Paul used this word in First Thessalonians 1:10 to say that God has "delivered us from the wrath to come," we can soundly proclaim that God will not allow His people to suffer alongside the unrighteous. When the rapture of the Church occurs, it will be an event in which Christ will come *for* His people. It will be *a divine rescue operation to deliver, rescue, and remove* His people before divine retribution is released upon the world of the ungodly on the earth.

The Rapture describes the moment when Christ will come *for* His Church, but then at the end of the seven-year Tribulation period, Christ will return to the earth *with* His people, and this event is called the Second Coming of Christ.

Jude 14-15 speaks about the Second Coming of Christ. It says, "And Enoch also, the seventh from Adam, prophesied of these, saying, Behold, the Lord cometh with ten thousands of his saints, to execute judgment upon all, and to convince all that are ungodly among them of all their ungodly deeds which they have ungodly committed, and of all their hard speeches which ungodly sinners have spoken against him."

Here, we amazingly discover that in the beginning of time when Enoch was alive, He was so attuned to the Spirit of God that he was able to see all the way to the end of the Church Age and to see the future moment when Christ would come *with* His people. These verses are simply packed with meaning. The *Renner Interpretive Version* (*RIV*) adds flavor to these verses through the meanings and nuances of the original Greek text.

RIV OF JUDE 14 AND 15

It is amazing that even Enoch, the seventh from Adam, prophesied, foretelling in advance, about these and other events that would occur in the future, saying, 'Behold, the Lord, and when He comes, He will arrive in the midst of ten thousands — innumerable numbers — of His holy people, who will be with Him.' When the Lord comes, He will carry out the irreversible charge of guilt that Heaven's court has issued inescapably against all so-charged. In the same way a lawyer brings forth indisputable and undeniable evidence in a court of law, Heaven's court will present irrefutable and incontestable evidence to prove a charge of guilt against the godless and all the irreverent actions — beliefs, words, and deeds — that irreverent sinners have committed and have spoken so abrasively and insolently against the Lord.

Notice that in this verse, Jesus is not coming *for* His people, but instead, He is coming *with* His saints. You see, the Rapture will have occurred seven years earlier. During those subsequent seven years, as wrath is poured out on the earth, God's people in Heaven are going to be participating in the Judgment Seat of Christ (explained in Chapter Nine) and the Marriage Supper of the Lamb. But when those seven years end, Christ will descend with them at the very end of the Tribulation period to set up His Millennial Kingdom. And that coming of Christ with His saints at the end of the Tribulation is what is called the Second Coming of Christ.

Once we understand the difference between the Rapture of the Church and Christ's Second Coming to the earth, it should bring clarity to our minds and hope to our hearts that when we leave this earth — whether in death or in the Rapture — we will truly "ever be with the Lord" (*see* 1 Thessalonians 4:17).

Once again, I want you to see that at the time of the Rapture, Jesus will come *for* believers before the Tribulation begins, but at the Second Coming, He will come *with* His saints at the conclusion of the seven-year Tribulation period. The first event, called the Rapture, is what initiates the "Day of the Lord" or this seven-year period. The second event, called the Second Coming of Christ, is what occurs at the consummation of the Tribulation, and it initiates the Millennial Reign of Christ, which we will explore in Chapter Nine.

Difference Number Two: In the Rapture, Jesus Will Return *in the Air* — at the Second Coming, Jesus Will Return *to the Earth*

Paul wrote in First Thessalonians 4:17 that at the time of the rapture of the Church, Jesus will never touch the earth. Instead, Christ will descend downward from Heaven into the earth's lower atmosphere to retrieve the Church and take them to Heaven with Him.

This means that when the Rapture occurs, *Jesus will never touch the earth.* This is clearly stated in First Thessalonians 4:17, "Then we which are alive and remain shall be caught up together with them in the clouds, to meet the Lord in the air: and so shall we ever be with the Lord."

Please forgive the redundancy, but it is essential to call to remembrance the original Greek words in this verse that are so important to this point. So we'll look at the *Renner Interpretive Version* (*RIV*) of First Thessalonians 4:17, which interprets these important words.

RIV of First Thessalonians 4:17

Then at that exact synchronized moment, those who are spiritually living, spiritually robust, spiritually thriving, spiritually vibrant, and spiritually vigorous — I'm talking about the remaining remnant of spiritually alive believers who have endured and will still be left around at the time of the coming of the Lord — will be suddenly and supernaturally snatched away out of imminent danger, just in the nick of time, as the Lord initiates a divine rescue operation to transport them into the clouds to join those who have been resurrected. There in the air's lower atmosphere where the Lord has descended to meet them, those who were raised from the dead and the remnant who were supernaturally snatched out of danger will encounter the Lord. And at that encounter, the Lord will roll out the red carpet to give the new arrivals a royal reception to match the VIP status He knows they deserve! After that, we will always — at all times and forevermore — be with the Lord.

Again, when the Rapture occurs, Jesus will descend into the lower atmosphere to deliver, rescue, remove, and snatch us into the air to meet Him in the clouds. After that, we will immediately be transported to Heaven for the seven-year span of time during which our works will be carefully examined by Christ Himself at the Judgment Seat of Christ and we will be rewarded accordingly (*see* 1 Corinthians 3:13-15; 2 Corinthians 5:10). And, of course, all believers will participate in the Marriage Supper of the Lamb (*see* Revelation 19:9).

When these events are completed in Heaven at the end of seven years — and when all God's wrath has been poured out on the earth during this same time frame — that is when Jesus will return to the earth in His Second Coming with *ten thousands* of His saints, and set His feet upon the Mount of Olives. This is the Second Coming of Christ.

Just before Jesus ascended into the heavens, we are told in Acts 1:9-12, "And when he had spoken these things, while they beheld, he was taken up; and a cloud received him out of their sight.

"And while they looked stedfastly toward heaven as he went up, behold, two men stood by them in white apparel; which also said, Ye men of Galilee, why stand ye gazing up into heaven? this same Jesus, which is taken up from you into heaven, shall so come in like manner as ye have seen him go into heaven. Then returned they unto Jerusalem from the mount called Olivet...."

Thus, these angels declared to the disciples that at the Second Coming at the end of the seven-year Tribulation period, Christ will return visibly — exactly as He left them — and He will set His feet on Earth, upon the Mount of Olives. The Rapture will occur in the air, and Jesus will never touch the earth at that time. But at the Second Coming of Christ, Jesus will literally, physically return to the earth and set His foot upon the Mount of Olives in Jerusalem.

Difference Number Three: The Rapture of the Church Is a Clandestine Operation — the Second Coming of Christ Will Be Visible Worldwide

Another major difference between the rapture of the Church and the Second Coming of Christ is that the Rapture will be a clandestine operation that occurs exclusively for believers, but the Second Coming that will occur at the end of the seven-year Tribulation will be visibly witnessed by the entire world.

First, let's look at the clandestine nature of the Rapture. In Matthew 24:36-41, Jesus said:

But of that day and hour knoweth no man, no, not the angels of heaven, but my Father only. But as the days of Noe [Noah] **were, so shall also the coming of the Son of man be.**

For as in the days that were before the flood they were eating and drinking, marrying and giving in marriage, until the day that Noe [Noah] **entered into the ark, and knew not until the flood came, and took them all away; so shall also the coming of the Son of man be. Then shall two be in the field; the one shall be taken, and the other left. Two women shall be grinding at the mill; the one shall be taken, and the other left.**

In the preceding chapter, we saw that the word "taken" in verses 40 and 41 are both a form of the Greek word *paralambano*, which is a compound of the words *para* and *lambano*. The word *para* means *alongside* and conveys *a sense of warmth as one pulls another close to his or her heart*. The word *lambano* means *to receive* or *to take*. When these two words are compounded to form the word *paralambano*, it means *to retrieve, snatch, withdraw, or to take warmly and intimately to one's side.* It is significant that the word *paralambano* was regularly used in New Testament times to picture a moment when *one came to retrieve, take, or withdraw his inheritance*. This word is used in both verses 40 and 41 to picture the moment of the Rapture when Jesus will come *to retrieve*, *snatch*, *take*, and *withdraw* those who are authentic Christians and are His inheritance as the true Church.

The word "left" in both verses is also significant. We have seen that those who do not belong to Christ are tragically "left behind." The word "left" is interpreted from a form of the Greek word *aphiemi*, which is a word that here pictures the one who is *left behind*. For those who are left on the earth after the Rapture, it will be a very desperate moment. Jesus used this word to picture those who are working side-by-side and going about their daily routines, when suddenly one of them is *caught*, *taken*, or *snatched away*, while the other is painfully *left behind* with deep regret and sorrow.

These words *paralambano* and *aphiemi* clearly picture a clandestine operation that will occur when Christ supernaturally gathers His people to meet Him in the air. It will take place in an unexpected moment that will take those who are left completely off guard. Christ will not touch the earth, but will only descend into the lower atmosphere at this time. And as the Lord shouts, the voice of the archangel is heard, and the war trumpet is blasted, the righteous whose bodies are buried, and those who are spiritually living, spiritually robust, spiritually thriving, spiritually vibrant, and spiritually vigorous will be suddenly *taken*. It will be a clandestine, covert, stealth operation.

But the Second Coming of Christ that occurs seven years later, at the very end of the Tribulation period, will be an event that is *visible* and *witnessed* by the entire population of the world. There will be nothing clandestine, covert, or stealth about it.

The word "tribulation" pictures pressure so great that it is crushing — or nonstop pressure that is suffocating to those who are under its weight. It conveys the idea of being crushed, pressured, squeezed, or stressed beyond one's wildest imagination, and it is used to depict the Tribulation period during which the population of the world will suffer the adverse effects of the wrath of God that will be inescapably poured out upon the earth.

In Matthew 24:29 and 30, Jesus said, "Immediately after the tribulation of those days shall the sun be darkened, and the moon shall not give her light, and the stars shall fall from heaven, and the powers of the heavens shall be shaken: and then shall appear the sign of the Son of man in heaven: and then shall all the tribes of the earth mourn, and they shall see the Son of man coming in the clouds of heaven with power and great glory."

The word "immediately" is an interpretation of the Greek word *eutheos*, which means *at once*, *immediately*, or *straightaway*, and it pictures what happens *immediately*. Jesus said that at once, immediately, or straightaway after the Tribulation, the whole world will see Him coming in the clouds of Heaven with power and glory. The word "tribulation" in verse 29 is the same word we saw in Matthew 24:21 in which Jesus described the "great tribulation" that will come on the earth after the rapture of the Church.

But here in Matthew 24:29, the word "tribulation" is, again, a form of the Greek word *thlipsis*, a word that pictures *pressure so great that it is crushing — or nonstop pressure* that is *suffocating* to those who are under its weight. It conveys the idea of being *crushed*, *pressured*, *squeezed*, or *stressed beyond one's wildest imagination*, and it is used to depict the Tribulation period during which the population of the world will suffer the adverse effects of the wrath of God that will be inescapably poured out upon the earth.

The words "of those days" in verse 29 are *ton hemeron ekeinon* in Greek, and they refer to "those days," making it clear that the days of the Tribulation will be days *unlike* any other days that have ever preceded them. These words in Matthew 24:29 make it clear that the time period of the Tribulation will be extraordinarily unparalleled, unprecedented, and unrivaled in human history.

Jesus said that at the end of the Tribulation period, "the sun [shall] be darkened, and the moon shall not give her light, and the stars shall fall from heaven, and the powers of the heavens shall be shaken." Notice Jesus said the sun will be "darkened." The word "darkened" is interpreted from a form of *skotidzo*, a Greek word that describes *obscurity* or *utter darkness*. By using this word, Jesus states that at the very last moment of the Tribulation period, the light of the sun will literally be *put out* and there will be *utter darkness*. He continues to say that "the moon shall not give her light." Since the moon is a reflector of the sun, it is obvious that if the sun turns to utter darkness, the moon will no longer be able to reflect or to give light.

By using the word "darkness," Jesus states that at the very last moment of the Tribulation period, the light of the sun will literally be put out and there will be utter darkness. He continues to say that "the moon shall not give her light." Since the moon is a reflector of the sun, it is obvious that if the sun turns to utter darkness, the moon will no longer be able to reflect or to give light, and the earth will experience utter darkness.

Jesus then states in that moment, "the stars shall fall from heaven." The word "star" is *asteres*, which is the Greek word for *stars*, but Jesus also said they will "fall" from Heaven. The word "fall" is interpreted from a form of the Greek word *pipto*, which not only means *to fall*, but *to fall hard* or *to plunge downward*.

Jesus then adds that "the powers of the heavens shall be shaken." The word "powers" is interpreted from a form of *dunamis*, and it pictures the *strength* resident in the "heavens." The word "heavens" is a translation of a form of *ouranos*, a word that speaks of *the highest heaven*. The word "shaken" is a translation of the Greek word *saleuo*, and it means *to shake, to waver, to totter*, or *to be moved*. As a phrase, it literally means the very powers and strength of the highest heavens will be shaken to the point that they will waver, totter, and be moved.

In Matthew 24:30, Jesus says, "...Then shall appear the sign of the Son of man in heaven." The word "then" is a translation of the Greek word *tote*, and it means *then*, or *at that time*. In other words, when all the natural lights have been put out and mankind is in a state of utter darkness, at that very moment "shall appear the sign of the Son of man in heaven." The word "appear" is translated from a form of the Greek word *phaino*, which means *to visibly appear*.

The word "sign" in Greek is *semeion*, which denotes *a visibly clear sign* or something that is *clearly visible*. When all the lights go out, suddenly Christ will appear in the heavens in such a way that the whole world will visibly see this event. In fact, Matthew 24:30 says, "...And then shall all the tribes of the earth mourn...." In this grand event, the whole world will see Christ as He descends with ten thousands of His saints, and there will be those on the earth who will "mourn" when they see Him. The word "mourn" is from a form of the Greek word *kopto*, and here it refers to *one so grievously stricken that he rents his clothes*.

At that moment, the whole world will visibly see and witness the Second Coming of Christ. That is why Jesus goes on to say, "...And they shall see the Son of man coming in the clouds of heaven with power and great glory." The word "see" is interpreted from a form of the Greek word *horao*, a word that means *to behold, to perceive, to see*, or *to fully view*. Thus, we know there will be nothing clandestine about this event, for all the people of the world at that moment will behold this dazzling moment.

Just as the main lights are put out in a theater and the main character appears on stage in a beam of light for the audience to see, God will put on the greatest theatrical performance in human history as all lights go out to make ready the appearance of Christ as He comes. And when this event occurs, Jesus will come with "power and great glory" (v. 30).

The word "power" is from the Greek word *dunamis*, which denotes *strength*, and the word "glory" is from a form of the Greek word *doxa*, which speaks of that which is *utterly resplendent*. Thus, when Christ appears at the end of the seven-year Tribulation period, He will appear in all of His strength and utter resplendent glory!

At His Second Coming, Jesus Will Annihilate the Antichrist

On that day, the Lord will open his mouth, blow with His breath, and speak — and when He does, so much power will be released that it will instantly consume and remove the Antichrist from the world scene.

Paul stated in Second Thessalonians 2:8 that when Christ returns in His Second Coming, He will "consume [the Antichrist] with the spirit of his mouth, and shall destroy with the brightness of his coming."

The word "consume" is from a form of the Greek word *anaireo*, which is a word that means *to abolish*, *to do away with*, *to kill*, *to murder*, *to slay*, or *to slaughter*. The meaning here is that when the Lord comes, He will *completely obliterate* the Antichrist.

Paul then said Christ will do away with the Antichrist "with the spirit of his mouth, and shall destroy [the Antichrist] with the brightness of his coming."

The word "spirit" is a translation of the Greek word *pneuma*, which is usually translated *spirit*, but here it pictures *the breath* of the Lord's mouth. Hence, Paul was telling us that although Satan will energize the Antichrist and hold the lost world in his mesmerizing grasp, he will not even have strength to withstand *one puff* from the mouth of the Lord. The word "mouth" is translated from a form of the Greek word *stoma*, which describes the *mouth*. Thus, it means that on that day the Lord will open his mouth, blow with His breath, and speak — and when He does, so much power will be released that it will instantly consume and remove the Antichrist from the world scene.

Paul also said that Christ will "destroy" the Antichrist "with the brightness of his coming." The word "destroy" is a rendering of a form of the Greek word *katargeo*, which means *to bring to nothing*, *to reduce to waste*, *to render inactive*, *to abolish*, or *to put out of commission*.

This abolishing of the Antichrist will be accomplished also "with the brightness of his coming." The word "brightness" is a translation of the Greek word *epiphaneia*, which is a word used to depict *an astonishing, astounding, staggering, surprising, sudden, and overwhelming appearance* of a divine figure.

Depending on how it is used, the word "coming" — which is interpreted from a form of the Greek word *parousia* — can describe either the rapture of the Church or the Second Coming of Christ. This Greek word pictures *the advent or arrival of a king who alone has power to set things in order and to make every wrong right.*

Thus, when Jesus comes in His Second Coming at the end of the seven-year Tribulation period, He will arrive with all the power needed to obliterate the short-term rule of the Antichrist and to begin setting everything in order that has been out of order, making every wrong thing right as He initiates His Millennial Reign upon the earth.

All these words in Second Thessalonians 2:8 are very important. As precious as the *King James Version* Bible translation is, it does not convey all the nuances contained in the original Greek text — so let's look at this verse in the *RIV.*

RIV of Second Thessalonians 2:8

...When the Lord will come with His saints, His coming will be so grand, so glorious, so overwhelming that He will totally obliterate the Lawless One by the mere breath of His mouth. Just one "puff" from the Lord, and this evil person will be incinerated! The very presence of the Lord will cripple and immobilize him, permanently putting him out of commission.

What I want you to see from these passages in Matthew and Second Thessalonians is that the Rapture is a clandestine event, but Christ's Second Coming will be visible and witnessed by the entire world. In Revelation 1:7, the apostle John wrote about the Second Coming when he said, "Behold, he cometh with clouds; and every eye shall see him...." Hence, nothing is hidden or secret about the Second Coming of Christ. While Jesus will come to clandestinely rapture the Church, the Second Coming of Christ at the end of the seven-year Tribulation will be witnessed by the whole world.

Difference Number Four: In the Rapture, Jesus Will Not Touch the Earth — at the Second Coming, Jesus Will Put His Feet on the Mount of Olives

This section is similar to "Difference Number Two" that we looked at previously, in which we saw that Jesus in the Rapture catches away His Church in the air (not on the earth) — but at the Second Coming, He actually does put His feet on the earth, along with ten thousands of His saints.

We have already seen numerous times that when Christ comes to resurrect the dead bodies of the righteous and to rapture those who are spiritually living, spiritually robust, spiritually thriving, spiritually vibrant, and spiritually vigorous, He will only descend into the lower atmosphere above the earth — His feet will never touch the earth during that event. In First Thessalonians 4:16 and 17, Paul wrote, "For the Lord himself shall descend from heaven with a shout, with the voice of the archangel, and with the trump of God: and the dead in Christ shall rise first: then we which are alive and remain shall be caught up together with them in the clouds, to meet the Lord in the air: and so shall we ever be with the Lord."

Again the words "caught up" are translated from a form of the Greek word *harpadzo*, which means *to catch, to seize, to take away,* or *to snatch suddenly*. It pictures *snatching someone out of danger just in the nick of time*. It will be *a divine rescue operation to transport* the Church into Christ's glorious presence just before God's wrath is emptied upon the earth in the seven-year Tribulation period.

But this verse also says we will "meet the Lord in the air." As we briefly saw in Chapter One, the word "meet" is interpreted from the Greek word *apantesis*, which pictures *a grand encounter* or *a royal or VIP reception*. It is a word that specially describes *the reception of a newly arrived official or newly arrived royalty*. When such individuals arrived, the red carpet was rolled out and they were given a VIP reception. Paul knew the usage of this word, and he used it here to tell us that when we meet Jesus in the air, Christ is going to roll out the red carpet to give us a grand and glorious VIP reception!

The word "air" used in this verse is interpreted from a form of the Greek word *aer*, which describes *the lower air* or *the lower atmosphere*. It is where we get the English word *air*. The Greeks used this word to describe *the air that surrounds the earth*, or as already stated, *the lower atmosphere*.

By putting together all the original Greek meanings of these words, the *Renner Interpretive Version* (*RIV*) of First Thessalonians 4:17 expands Paul's words to help us grasp the enormity of this glorious event we call *the Rapture*.

RIV OF FIRST THESSALONIANS 4:17

Then at that exact synchronized moment, those who are spiritually living, spiritually robust, spiritually thriving, spiritually vibrant, and spiritually vigorous — I'm talking about the remaining remnant of spiritually alive believers who have endured and will still be left around at the time of the coming of the Lord — will be suddenly and supernaturally snatched away out of imminent danger, just in the nick of time, as the Lord initiates a divine rescue operation to transport them into the clouds to join those who have been resurrected. There in the air's lower atmosphere where the Lord has descended to meet them, those who were raised from the dead and the remnant who were supernaturally snatched out of danger will encounter the Lord. And at that encounter, the Lord will roll out the red carpet to give the new arrivals a royal reception to match the VIP status He knows they deserve! After that, we will always — at all times and forevermore — be with the Lord.

It's easy to see that the rapture of the Church is an event that will occur in the air, above the earth, and in this event Christ's feet will never touch the earth — rather, He will gather us to Himself in the air.

But at the Second Coming of Christ, which occurs at the end of the seven-year Tribulation, Jesus will visibly return with innumerable numbers of His saints to deal with evil and set everything in order — and He will set His feet upon the Mount of Olives. The prophet Zechariah spoke of Christ's Second Coming when he wrote, "Behold, the day of the Lord cometh.... And his feet shall stand in that day upon the mount of Olives, which is before Jerusalem on the east..." (Zechariah 14:1-4).

In Acts 1:9-11, Luke wrote, "And when he [Jesus] had spoken these things, while they beheld, he was taken up; and a cloud received him out of their sight. And while they looked stedfastly toward heaven as he went up, behold, two men stood by them in white apparel; which also said, Ye men of Galilee, why stand ye gazing up into heaven? this same Jesus, which is taken up from you into heaven, shall so come in like manner as ye have seen him go into heaven."

The place where Jesus ascended into Heaven was the Mount of Olives (*see* Acts 1:12), and what the angels mentioned in Acts 1:10 and 11, confirms the prophet Zechariah's prophecy that when the Lord returns to the earth in His Second Coming, He will physically return to the very same mountain from which He ascended into Heaven. And He will annihilate the Antichrist and establish His Kingdom headquarters in the city of Jerusalem.

Difference Number Five: In the Rapture, Jesus Will Come To *Deliver* the Saints — at the Second Coming, the Saints Will Come To *Rule* With Him

In First Thessalonians 5:9, Paul said, "For God hath not appointed us to wrath, but to obtain *salvation* [deliverance] by our Lord Jesus Christ." *God has not appointed us to wrath!* I covered this from First Thessalonians 1:10 and 4:17 in the first section entitled, "Difference Number One," so if you skipped the first part of this chapter or didn't deeply read it, please return to that section and read that text.

By the Power of the Blood of Jesus, We Are Saved From the Wrath of God

But in Romans 5:8 and 9 (*NASB*), Paul furthermore said, "But God demonstrates His own love toward us, in that while we were still sinners, Christ died for us. Much more then, having now been justified by His blood, we shall be *saved* from the wrath of God through Him."

The word "saved" in Romans 5:9 is translated from a form of the Greek word *sodzo*, and a significant part of this word means *deliverance*. The word "from" is a translation of the word *apo*, which here implies *space* or *separation* between two objects. Thus, the verse could be interpreted: "...We shall be *delivered* and *separated from* the wrath of God through him." Once again, a principle that Paul regularly stated is that God will *deliver* His people and not leave them to experience His wrath that will be poured out during the seven-year Tribulation.

Please remember that we will be "caught up together" with Jesus in the air (*see* 1 Thessalonians 4:17). Again, those words "caught up together" are an interpretation of the Greek word *harpadzo*, which means *to be seized* or *snatched out of danger in the nick of time*. Just in time — before the wrath of God begins to be poured out on the earth — Christ will snatch and receive the Church to Himself so that where He is we will be also (*see* John 14:3).

Besides the deliverance from the wrath of God to come that authentic Christians will experience in the Rapture, another deliverance these remnant believers will experience at that time is *deliverance from death*. We saw this previously in First Corinthians 15:51 and 52, where the apostle Paul wrote, "Behold, I shew you a mystery; we shall not all sleep, but we shall all be changed. In a moment, in the twinkling of an eye, at the last trump: for the trumpet shall sound, and the dead shall be raised incorruptible, and we shall be changed."

RIV OF FIRST CORINTHIANS 15:51-52

51 What I am about to tell you is so amazing that it nearly leaves me speechless, and I'm sure it will totally flabbergast you. Listen carefully, for I am going to tell you something that was previously an unknown mystery, but it has been revealed to us. Here it is: All of us will not die, but in this particular moment, all of us, both the dead and the living — those who are spiritually living, spiritually robust, spiritually thriving, spiritually vibrant, and spiritually vigorous — will be altered or changed, miraculously modified, and supernaturally transformed.

52 In a moment — a split-second, indivisible atom of time, as fast as the twitch of an eye — the last trump, a war trumpet, will loudly sound to signal the closure of the age. It will also signal that the final battle, ultimate victory, and vanquishing of all God's enemies are finally about to happen. That blast will be God's way of letting everyone know that His enemies have been judged by Heaven's court of law; that they have lost their footing and longstanding battle with Him; that judgment is about to be executed; and that He will reign victorious and supreme in total victory. And in that flash of a moment, the dead will be resurrected and will stand upright on their feet. At that exact moment, they will miraculously receive new bodies that are incapable of decay and that will never again show the effects of wear, tear, and age — timeless, immortal, indestructible bodies. And we who are still alive when all this happens will be supernaturally transformed as our old bodies are exchanged for new ones that also are incapable of decay and that will never again show the effects of wear,

tear, and age. Our bodies will literally be altered, changed, miraculously modified, and transformed into timeless, immortal, indestructible bodies.

At the moment of the trumpet sound that will signal the impending rapture of the Church, the bodies of the dead in Christ will first be raised and transformed into incorruptible, indestructible bodies. Immediately after they are raised, the authentic believers who are alive on the earth will be caught up in the air to meet the Lord, and they also will be changed and given glorified bodies that are incorruptible and indestructible. There really is a group of believers who will never taste death, but they will instead be miraculously and supernaturally transformed.

And as we have seen, immediately after the rapture of the Church, a time will begin that is called the "Day of the Lord," or the Tribulation — a time of judgment that will last for seven years. This period is also scripturally known as "Daniel's Seventieth Week" (*see* Daniel 9:20-27) and "The Time of Jacob's Trouble" (*see* Jeremiah 30:7). The moment the Church is vacated from planet Earth, the "Day of the Lord" will begin, and for seven years God will deal with the nations and with the ungodly people of the earth who rejected Him. At that time, the world will experience a time of great tribulation such as never before.

The *Rapture* will trigger that seven-year event. But the *Second Coming* of Christ will occur at the end of the Tribulation. After the Church has spent seven years in Heaven with Jesus, enjoying the Marriage Supper of the Lamb and being rewarded for what we did in obedience to Jesus on the earth, the saints will return *with* Him to the earth to reign and rule. This will be the fulfillment of First Thessalonians 3:13, Jude 14 and 15, and Revelation 1:7. Among many other prophecies, these verses state that at the Second Coming of Christ, Jesus will return *with* His saints to reign and to rule. First Thessalonians 3:13 and Jude 14 are especially important, so let's look at each of these verses.

In **First Thessalonians 3:13**, Paul wrote, "To the end he may stablish your hearts unblameable in holiness before God, even our Father, at the coming of our Lord Jesus Christ *with* all his saints."

Here, Paul referred to the moment when Christ will come with all His saints at the end of the seven-year Tribulation period, which will, indeed, be a moment of great rejoicing when Christ sets up His Millennial Reign and rules with His people.

In **Jude 14**, Jude wrote, "And Enoch also, the seventh from Adam, prophesied of these, saying, Behold, the Lord cometh *with* ten thousands of his saints...."

With these words, Jude directly quoted from the Book of Enoch, which is not a canonical book of the Bible, but in early New Testament times, it was regarded as an authentic work that contained serious Old Testament commentary. Enoch was a patriarch in biblical history, the son of Jared, and the father of Methuselah, and one of the earliest prophetic voices of the Old Testament.

The word "prophesied" is from a form of the Greek word *propheteuo*, which is a compound of the words *pro* and *phemi*. The word *pro* is a preposition that carries the idea of something *in advance of an event*, and *phemi* means *to say*, *to speak*, or *to communicate*. Compounded, this Greek word lets us know that a prophet is *a speaking* or *saying* gift, or *one who is designed to communicate a message from God*. This tells us that Enoch was divinely inspired by God to speak or communicate about an event in advance.

Enoch said, "Behold," and it is interpreted from the Greek word *idou*, which is intended to carry the idea of *bewilderment*, *shock*, *amazement*, and *wonder*. Keith Trump, an American Bible Society scholar who is a contributor to the *RIV*, has noted that the word *idou* has an Old Testament grammatical-device counterpart — a Hebrew word that is designed for prophets to use to dramatically grab the attention of their hearers. He writes that the word *idou*, furthermore, was most often used when a prophet received direct revelation from the Lord. It was a way of saying, "Look over here and pay attention! I'm seeing into the spirit realm and want to relay what I'm seeing." Hence, in this verse, Enoch was relaying what he had supernaturally been allowed to see in the far-off future.

The word "Lord" in Jude 14 is translated from the Greek word *Kurios*, a word that means *Lord*; *Supreme Master*; or *One with complete authority over every known, unknown, visible, or invisible realm*. It pictures Jesus in His Second Coming as the Lord, Supreme Master, and One with complete authority over every known, unknown, visible, or invisible realm.

Enoch stated that Christ will return "with ten thousands of his saints." The word "with" is translated from the preposition *en*, which means *in the midst* and tells us Christ will literally come *in the midst* of His people, referring to saints of the past who will descend with Him into the earth's atmosphere and to the face of the earth at the time of His Second Coming. According to this verse, He will come in the midst of "ten thousands of his saints." The words "ten thousands" are interpreted from a form of the Greek word *murias*, which here means *ten thousands* and pictures *an innumerable multitude*. The word "saints" is an interpretation of *hagiais*, the plural form of *hagios*, which pictures God's people who, once they are redeemed, are consecrated, separated unto God, and made holy.

These words are so powerful that I would like you to see the *Renner Interpretive Version* (*RIV*) of Jude 14.

RIV of Jude 14

It is amazing that even Enoch, the seventh from Adam, prophesied, foretelling in advance about these and other events that would occur in the future, saying, 'Behold, the Lord, and when He comes, He will arrive in the midst of ten thousands — innumerable numbers — of His holy people, who will be with Him.'

So once again, we see that at the Second Coming of Christ, which will occur at the end of the seven-year Tribulation, the Lord will visibly return to the earth *with* ten thousands of His saints to reign and rule upon the earth.

In Summary

We have seen that there are *five key differences* between the rapture of the Church and the Second Coming of Christ. The rapture of the Church is the next prophetic event to occur in the sequence of events at the end of the age, and although we don't know the exact day or the hour, we know we're nearing that event on God's timetable, and it could occur at any moment.

In my book *Signs You'll See Just Before Jesus Comes*, I state that "as we advance toward the golden moment of His return, Jesus said that we would see signs on the prophetic road to let us know where we are in time. But He also warned us that no one but the Father would know the exact moment when He would return (*see* Matthew 24:36). Those who have tried to fix dates on Christ's coming have embarrassingly learned that no one is able to pinpoint the exact day or hour of the Lord's return."[6]

When Jesus warned us of signs that would occur at the end of the age, He communicated them in such a way that those times would be easily recognizable, not obscured or difficult to understand. Jesus gave us concrete markers to let us know where we are on our journey, approximately how close we are to our destination, and what we need to know so we can remain safe and effective on the path.

It is my personal conviction that we are living in the last moments of this present age. We have the keen ability to see and understand end-time scriptures more clearly because we are living in their fulfillment, and we are surrounded with mounting evidence of what Jesus forecasted so long ago. Because of where we are on the prophetic timeline, we are seeing and experiencing up-front what other generations could only see from a distance.

If you have not read *Signs You'll See Just Before Jesus Comes*, I urge you to read it because Jesus gave specific predictors in Matthew, Mark, and Luke to let us know that we are leading up to the closure of this era. By reading these three gospels and comparing what Christ said in each of them concerning these events, we can assemble a list of things He said we would see as we approach the territory of the very last of the last days. In these gospels, Jesus even forecast that these particular signs would escalate in intensity as we approached the very end of the age.

But in addition to what Jesus said in the gospels, Paul reminded the Thessalonians, "But of the times and the seasons, brethren, ye have no need that I write unto you. For yourselves know perfectly that the day of the Lord so cometh as a thief in the night" (1 Thessalonians 5:1-2). In this context (and context is key to understanding *any* text), we find that the words "day of the Lord" refer here to the clandestine operation in which Christ will come surprisingly to take the Church, and this is why Paul likened it to a thief in the night.

But in this verse, Paul used very important words, and we will particularly examine the words "of," "times," and "seasons." The word "of" in Greek is actually the word *peri*, which would be better translated *concerning*. The word "times" is interpreted from a form of the Greek word *chronos*, a word that speaks of *time* in terms of *chronology*. The word "seasons" is the plural form of the Greek word *kairos*, which speaks of *a specific season or time*. A better interpretation of this verse would be, "My brothers, concerning the chronology and specific times and seasons, you have no need that I write to you."

The reason Paul did not feel the need to elaborate more was because during his short stay with the Thessalonians, he had taught them about end-time events (*see* 2 Thessalonians 2:5). Paul said he had no need to write to them about the chronology of these events or about the specific seasons and times that would mark them because he had already very thoroughly taught them these things. So although we do not know the exact day when the Rapture will take place, we can know the *chronology* of when all these events will take place very well, and we can possess an awareness of when we have entered into the *season* of the Lord's return.

In this chapter, we have seen that the rapture of the Church and the Second Coming of Christ are two separate events. We have seen that the Rapture will occur at the end of the Church Age, or our current age, and that once the Church is removed, the seven-year Tribulation period will begin. At the end of the Tribulation is when Christ will return visibly *with* His saints — and that second event is what is referred to as the Second Coming of Christ.

At Christ's Second Coming, He will destroy the Antichrist with the breath of His mouth and with the brightness of His coming (*see* 2 Thessalonians 2:8). Scripture also says Satan will be bound for 1,000 years (*see* Revelation 20:2-3), and Christ will reign in Jerusalem with His saints in His Millennial Kingdom! We will revisit these events in a later chapter.

QUESTIONS TO PONDER

1. After reading about the many past and present cataclysmic events that either have or are plaguing our world, what stands out to you? The Tribulation will be more catastrophic than all these events put together. Can you imagine living in a time in which events like these occur with even greater intensity? How does this reality shape your view of the time you have to share the Gospel with those around you so they can be rescued along with the rest of the Church?

2. While the rapture of the Church will be a clandestine operation, the Second Coming of Christ will be so obvious that the whole world will see it. What insights do Matthew 24:30 and Second Thessalonians 2:8 tell us about Jesus' glorious entrance at the time of His Second Coming?

3. In this chapter, we have seen five key differences that clearly define the Rapture and the Second Coming of Christ as two separate events. How is this the same or different than what you have been taught? How has your perspective changed after reading this chapter?

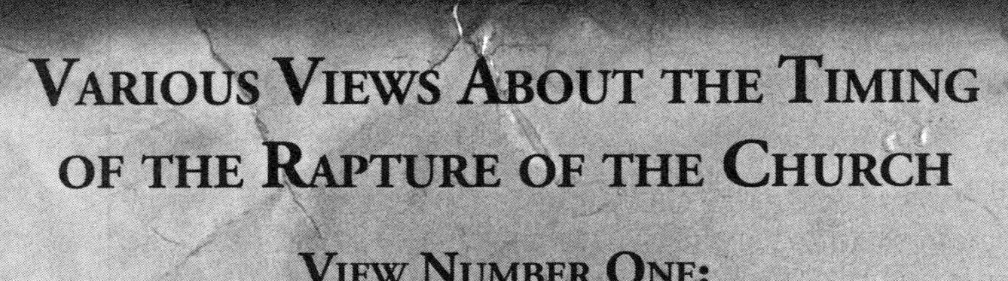

Various Views About the Timing of the Rapture of the Church

View Number One:
Pre-Tribulation Rapture

View Number Two:
Partial Rapture

View Number Three:
Mid-Tribulation Rapture

View Number Four:
Pre-Wrath Rapture

View Number Five:
Post-Tribulation Rapture

View Number Six:
Post-Millennialists

View Number Seven:
Amillennialists

View Number Eight:
Pan-Tribulationists

CHAPTER EIGHT

EIGHT VARIOUS VIEWS ABOUT THE TIMING OF THE RAPTURE OF THE CHURCH

Some argue that for the first 200 years of the Church, there was only one primary, prevailing view about the timing of the rapture of the Church. However, one must remember that when Early Church fathers were writing the earliest recorded theological documents, they were living at a time when many theological issues were being worked out. A deeper look at much of the writings of Early Church fathers reveals that they held differing views about the timing of the rapture of the Church even back then — there was no prevailing, widely agreed-upon and adhered-to view concerning the timing of the Rapture.

Others suggest that the belief in a pre-Tribulation rapture was only formed in the 1800s and that it was spread due to the writings of John Nelson Darby, a noted Bible scholar, who lived from 1800-1882 and was a leader among the Plymouth Brethren. Many consider him to be the father of Modern Dispensationalism. However, I am personally convinced that a pre-Tribulation rapture was *not* simply invented by Darby or by any man, but that it is solidly taught by the New Testament and was believed and adhered to by significantly known Early Church fathers.

But today there are quite a wide variety of views about the timing of the rapture of the Church. In this short chapter, you will see a brief summary of the *eight* primary views that are espoused by different groups today about the timing of the rapture of the Church. I will give you the basic premise of every view so you can understand each perspective and come to your own conclusion. As you proceed, please understand the following are generalized statements concerning each view, as there are additional nuances that I do not have space to discuss in detail in this book.

View Number One: Pre-Tribulation Rapture

First, we begin with the view that there will be a *Pre-Tribulation* rapture of the Church. This is my own view, as I believe this position is clearly presented in the pages of the New Testament, and it is the one that I generally feel most resembles what was espoused by some of the earliest Church fathers.

Those who hold to a pre-Tribulation rapture believe that the Church will be *caught away* or *raptured* before the Tribulation and that the Second Coming of Christ will take place at the end of the seven-year Tribulation period. This position is commonly held by dispensationalists, but there are scholars and theologians beyond the dispensationalist view who also hold firmly to this position.

The pre-Tribulation rapture of the Church view teaches:

- At the end of the Church Age, Christ will descend into the lower atmosphere above the earth to resurrect the bodies of the righteous dead and *to catch away* or *to rapture* the Church.
- Those who are *caught up* and *raptured* will be supernaturally transported to Heaven and will remain there for seven years (the same time frame as the Tribulation period that will be taking place on the earth).
- During the seven years the righteous are in Heaven, they will stand before the Judgment Seat of Christ, and each will give an account of his or her service to Christ and will be rewarded accordingly.
- Also during the seven years in Heaven, those who were transported to Heaven will joyfully participate in the Marriage Supper of the Lamb.

- At the conclusion of those seven years, Christ will visibly return to the earth with ten thousands of His saints to destroy the Antichrist, to bind the devil, and to establish His Millennial Reign upon the earth.

By what you've read so far in this book, it should be obvious that I wholeheartedly believe in a pre-Tribulation rapture of the Church. Some have asked, "Rick, what if you're wrong?" I answer that question in the final chapter of this book.

But this "pre-Trib" view espouses that at the exact moment the Church is *caught away* or *raptured*, the "Day of the Lord" — or the seven-year Tribulation period — will be triggered, and that is when bowls of judgment will be poured out upon the earth. Jesus referred to this period in Matthew 24:21 and said that it would be a time of "great tribulation" such as the world has never experienced.

As already stated, the idea of a pre-Tribulation rapture was embraced by some of the earliest Church fathers. A Second Century document called the *Shepherd of Hermas* refers to the "tribulation that is to come" — and regarding the Church, it additionally states, "You have escaped from great tribulation...."[1]

IRENAEUS
CIRCA 130 – 203 AD

Irenaeus

Irenaeus, a renowned bishop of Lyons in Gaul, who lived from approximately 130-203 AD, and wrote many important historical details about the Early Church and theological documents, wrote in his work *Against Heresies* that Enoch was an example of the rapture of the Church, and he inferred that the Rapture will occur *before* the Tribulation.

Irenaeus wrote: "For Enoch, when he pleased God, was translated in the same body in which he did please Him, *thus pointing out by anticipation the translation of the just*." Irenaeus additionally stated: "And therefore, when in the end *the Church shall be suddenly caught up* from this...*and then there shall be tribulation such as has not been since the beginning, neither shall be*."[2]

Notice that Irenaeus said, "...The Church shall be *suddenly caught up*...and then shall be *tribulation* such as has not been since the beginning, neither shall be." Some who believe in a pre-Tribulation rapture see this as confirmation that Irenaeus believed the Church would be caught away and that only after that happened would the Tribulation begin.

EPHRAIM
306 – 373 AD

Ephraim the Syrian

Ephraim the Syrian lived from approximately 306-373 AD and was renowned as a prominent scholar and theologian. Today he is remembered as one of the most notable hymnographers of Eastern Christianity and is credited as the founder of the School of Nisibis, which later became the center of learning for the Eastern Church. He is also known for his sermons and exegesis.

In Ephraim's work *On the Last Times, the Antichrist, and the End of the World*, which was written in about 373 AD, he wrote: "Why therefore do we not reject every care of earthly actions and prepare ourselves for the meeting of the Lord Christ, so that he may draw us from the confusion, which overwhelms all the world…? *For all the saints and elect of God are gathered prior to the tribulation that is to come, and are taken to the Lord lest they see the confusion that is to overwhelm the world....*"[3]

Notice Ephraim wrote of the saints being "taken to the Lord lest they see the confusion that is to overwhelm the world." Those who believe in a pre-Tribulation rapture see this as an early statement that the Church will be removed before the world is overwhelmed with the mass confusion that will mark the seven-year period of the Tribulation.

Victorinus

Victorinus was an early Christian writer whose ministry flourished in about 270 AD and who was martyred for his faith in approximately 303-304 AD under the horrific rule of Emperor Diocletian. His written works are mainly exegetical commentaries on various books of the Bible. These include commentaries on Genesis, Exodus, Leviticus, Isaiah,

VICTORINUS
3RD CENTURY AD

Ezekiel, Habakkuk, Ecclesiastes, Song of Solomon, Matthew, and the apocalypse of John. Additionally, Victorinus wrote theological works against heretical sects of the Church that were beginning to emerge in Christianity. The only works of his that have survived are his *Commentary on the Apocalypse* and a shorter work called *On the Construction of the World* (*De fabrica mundi*).

In his *Commentary on the Apocalypse*, Victorinus wrote regarding the rapture of the Church. In verse 1 of the fifteenth chapter of his *Commentary on the Apocalypse*, he wrote: "...The wrath of God always strikes the obstinate people...and these shall be in the last time, *when the Church shall have gone out of the midst.*"[4]

Those who adhere to a pre-Tribulation view see Victorinus' statement as affirming that the indignations that will be released upon the earth during the Tribulation will occur only *when the Church shall have gone out of the midst.*

Although there are some who debate these particular Church fathers' quotes, there are others who believe they at least *allude* to a pre-Tribulation rapture of the Church. I have made it clear that a pre-Tribulation rapture is my personal position, and in this book, I have provided multiple reasons for why I believe it.

But I want you to see that there are seven more views that people hold regarding the timing of the Rapture. Even if you don't agree with these perspectives, I think it is healthy for you to understand these other views about the timing of this important event so you can better understand what it is you believe and why.

VIEW NUMBER TWO: PARTIAL RAPTURE

Those who believe in a *Partial Rapture* think that only a certain category of faithful Christians will be *caught away* or *raptured* at the end of the Church Age. This view basically holds that only those who are "watching and waiting" will be *caught away* or *raptured* before the seven-year Tribulation period begins.

This concept is derived from several New Testament passages that specifically state Christ is coming for those who are watching and waiting. Among these passages are the parable of the ten virgins in Matthew 25:1-13; Paul's final words in Second Timothy 4:8; and Hebrews 9:28. Those who adhere to this view teach that Christians who are not "watching and waiting" will be left behind at the time of the Rapture. And because the passages I just mentioned are important to this conversation, we will deal with them in Chapter Ten.

If this partial-Rapture position is correct, it would categorically mean that only a certain part of what we call the Church would be raptured, and Christians who are not actively "watching and waiting" would be left behind to live through the seven years of the Tribulation. But what do these passages in Matthew 25:1-13, Second Timothy 4:8, and Hebrews 9:28 really teach? Again, we will return to these in Chapter Ten to see what we can glean from these texts that some use as a pretext for a partial-Rapture view of the rapture of the Church.

Those who hold to this position encourage the Church to be spiritually awake and ever looking for the rapture of the Church to occur. Certainly, this is the attitude we should all have, especially in light of what Paul said in First Thessalonians 4:16-17 — that Christ is coming for those who are spiritually living, spiritually robust, spiritually thriving, spiritually vibrant, and spiritually vigorous. It is easy to see how some might take this to mean only a partial-Rapture will take place at that time.

Indeed, this does make one want to perk up spiritually as Paul encouraged in his deliberate wording in First Thessalonians 4:16 and 17 and for good reason. Unfortunately, there are those who teach that regardless of how one lives, if a person once simply said "the sinner's prayer," that person will be caught up in the Rapture regardless of how he is presently living his life. This careless view has caused people to think that they are "in" regardless of how they are living. And in contrast, those who adhere to a partial-Rapture view, in essence, say there are no guarantees in Scripture that this will happen and that we must actively "work" to prove our sincerity and readiness to God. This, however, tends to reduce one's salvation to works rather than faith, which is contrary to the teaching of the New Testament.

There are several challenges with a partial-Rapture position. One of the biggest issues is that rather than the Rapture being the blessed hope of every true Christian, it becomes a "maybe-so" kind of hope that will only be experienced by those who have met the criteria of "watching and waiting." However, the Bible doesn't give criteria on what "watching and waiting" entails, so no one would ever know if he is meeting the requirement or not.

Another challenge is that a partial-Rapture position would also mean that Christians who have never been taught about the Rapture and know nothing about it would be eliminated from the Rapture and left behind simply for being uninformed.

> I have very dear friends who hold a partial-Rapture position. Although my own conclusion is different from theirs, I still respect their view and have learned much by listening to their point. But again, we will return to the passages of Matthew 25:1-13, Second Timothy 4:8, and Hebrews 9:28 in Chapter Ten to see what we can learn from these important texts.

View Number Three: Mid-Tribulation Rapture

Those who hold to a *Mid-Tribulation Rapture* view believe that the Rapture will take place at the mid-point of the seven-year Tribulation (or the three-and-a-half-year mark of the Tribulation), and this view holds that only the last three and a half years of the Tribulation will contain what is called the "great tribulation" (*see* Matthew 24:21). This view fails to answer the fact that the Bible shows God's wrath will be poured out during the entire Tribulation period and not just for the latter three and a half years — although the last half of the Tribulation will be the worst of the judgments experienced on the earth. Today there are those who rightfully say that Christians will endure many hardships before the rapture of the Church, but as I stated previously, *hardships* are not the equivalent of *wrath*.

One of my friends notes that this view would also only allow three and a half years for each person to stand before the Judgment Seat of Christ, to attend the Marriage Supper of the Lamb, and to return with Christ in His Second Coming. He states that those who adhere to a mid-Tribulation rapture see that event as a halftime exit right before the Antichrist goes into full-throttle mode. According to this view, the Church will go through some tough times but will not be on the earth for the worst of it.

> While I have friends in the ministry who take this position, my own conclusions are rooted in a pre-Tribulation rapture of the Church. However, I have learned a lot by listening to the views of others and do not see disagreements about the timing of the rapture of the Church to be a point of division or separation between me and others whom I know and love.

View Number Four: Pre-Wrath Rapture

Those who hold to a *Pre-Wrath Rapture* believe the Church will not be raptured before the Tribulation, but that the rapture of the Church will take place about three quarters of the way through the Tribulation. According to this view, the Church will be delivered — or *caught away* or *raptured* — at the third-quarter mark in the Tribulation and just before the intense wrath of God is poured out upon the earth.

This view creates numerous and significant linguistic, exegetical, and theological problems. A *pre-Wrath* rapture of the Church is difficult to back up with the chronology of events that we find in the book of Revelation. However, I have precious friends who take this position, and as I stated earlier, I respect their view and have learned much from listening to their vantage point.

View Number Five: Post-Tribulation Rapture

Those who hold to a *Post-Tribulation Rapture* essentially believe that the Church will go through the *entirety* of the seven years of the Tribulation, and that they will experience every seal, every trumpet, and every bowl of judgment right along with the condemned, lost world.

Those who believe in a post-Tribulation rapture believe that Christ will come in His Second Coming at the end of the seven years of the Tribulation — which is true in that Christ will come to the earth and set foot on the Mount of Olives at the conclusion of the Tribulation period. But those who adhere to this position of a post-Tribulation rapture believe that at nearly the exact moment of Christ's Second Coming, believers will be supernaturally snatched up into the heavens to meet the Lord. However, it will really be a U-turn event, for with a post-Tribulation rapture, those who were snatched up will then immediately descend with Christ as He places His feet upon the Mount of Olives. It would be a quick going up and an immediate going down — leaving no space for the Judgment Seat of Christ and Marriage Supper of the Lamb in Heaven.

But again, a post-Tribulation rapture of the Church basically holds that the Church will make a U-turn as it goes up to meet Christ in the air and then immediately turns around to come back down to the earth. But this raises all kinds of unanswerable questions, including why a rapture would be necessary at all in this case? And again, it leaves no time for each saint to appear before the Judgment Seat of Christ or to participate in the Marriage Supper of the Lamb.

As in the other previous cases, I have dear friends who take this position. I, of course, don't adhere to this position — but it does not separate us at all as fellow believers and ministers from fellowship with one another, and I have learned that there is much to be gleaned from the perspective of others.

But there are also Post-Millennialist and Amillennialist views that we need to consider — as well as an additional view that you may not be familiar with.

View Number Six: Post-Millennialists

A friend of mine has astutely articulated that *Post-Millennialists* are the eternal optimists of the eschatological world. They believe that the world will gradually get better through the influence of the Church until we enter a golden age of Christian rule, and that is when Jesus will return to the earth to receive unto Himself a ready-made kingdom. Until then, Jesus waits in Heaven for the world to get better and better, ready for His return. This view is not about Jesus rescuing us *from* chaos, but about us establishing His Kingdom on Earth *before* He comes back.

There are post-Millennialists who believe the Millennium will last a literal 1,000 years, but others see those 1,000 years as a figurative term for *a long period of time*. And rather than believe Christ will bind Satan in a single feat (*see* Revelation 20:1-6), they believe that the forces of Satan will be gradually defeated by the Church over a long period of time — perhaps even 1,000 years — as the Church becomes stronger and stronger over eons of time. Then, finally, when all evil is defeated and the Church reigns supreme in the earth, that is when Christ will return physically in His Second Coming. And, actually, according to this view, we are currently already living in the Millennium.

Those who are *post-Millennialists* believe that Christ is establishing His Kingdom on Earth through the Church as it fulfills the Great Commission (*see* Matthew 28:19). They expect that the vast majority of people on Earth will eventually be saved and that this will produce a time in which God will prevail in the affairs of men and nations. Post-Millennialists believe the forces of Satan will gradually be defeated as the Church preaches and becomes more powerful — and that eventually the Church will become so mighty, *and the world so reformed*, that Christ will return to a world where evil is already defeated. In other words, they believe that after an extensive era of such Church-dominating conditions on Earth, Jesus will return visibly and gloriously to end history with the general resurrection and the final judgment. This view is also similar to what has in recent years been called *Dominion* theology or *Kingdom Now*.

I emphatically do not agree with this view, but I have dear friends who take this position. I have learned to celebrate the fact that they want to see the world become progressively better and better through the influence of the Church. Although my conclusions are radically different — in fact, this position is the furthest from my own position — I respect those who hold this view, and I honor their convictions about transforming the face of the world through the authority of Christ.

As I already mentioned, where sin abounds, the grace of God will much more abound (*see* Romans 5:20). And the Church really is going to "arise and shine" by the grace and glory of God amidst an ever-darkening world (*see* Isaiah 60:1). Christ's Body is going to do supernatural exploits in the face of growing evil — and it is going to do it for the purpose of eternally rescuing those who are perishing, not just to revolutionize a twisted world system.

View Number Seven: Amillennialists

Those who hold the position of *Amillennialism* believe there will never be a literal Millenial Reign of Christ. Pure amillennialists believe when the book of Revelation speaks of "a thousand years" it is simply symbolic language that means *a long period of time*. True amillenialists believe this eternal state has already started and that we are living in it right now. In essence, amillennialists reject the idea of a future Millennial Reign in which Christ will reign on Earth.

The following is a simplistic view of what amillennialists believe:

- That Jesus is currently reigning from Heaven at the right hand of God the Father, which is, of course, true.
- That the Millennium began with the resurrection of Jesus, Jesus' ascension to Heaven, or on the Day of Pentecost, which I emphatically don't believe.

- That the task of the Church is to spread the message that Christ's Kingdom is here and is already here with nothing more to be established in a Millennial Reign of Christ.

If this view were true, it would mean that we are living in a world that is growing brighter and brighter as the ages pass.

But, indeed, we are living in a world that is becoming darker as time passes. And according to Bible prophecy, the world will become even darker — "as in the days of Noah" (*see* Matthew 24:37) — as we speed toward the end of the age. In my opinion, the perspective of amillenialists actually flies in the face of Scripture. We have clearly seen in the pages of this book that the world will eventually become a lawless place that will give rise to an Antichrist who will rule defiantly against God.

I have friends whom I value who are amilleniallists, but I see prophetic events differently from them. However, as in other cases, I can at times learn something from their view, and the fact that my view is different does not affect my appreciation for them.

View Number Eight: Pan-Tribulationists

The term *Pan-Tribulationist* is not a real theological term, but one that has been coined to describe those who say, "Well, it all sounds so confusing to me. I have no idea when the Rapture is going to take place. But I'm sure that in the end, it will all '*pan*' out. So I'm a Pan-Tribulationist!"

Many people frustratingly throw their hands into the air and say, "I don't have a clue when the Rapture will take place, but I am sure it will all work out in the end." In a sense, this position is always correct, for in the end it really will all work out. But God does not want us to live in uncertainty about the future, and that is why He provides prophetic answers to us in His Word. When the Bible is clearly understood, it brings clarity out of confusion — and clarity always contributes to peace.

An example would be if someone doesn't understand that the appearance of the Antichrist and the mark of the beast are events that will come to pass *after* the rapture. If he doesn't know that — and worries all the time about who the Antichrist is or what the mark of the beast is — he may be unduly fraught with worry and anxiety. But clearly knowing from Scripture that the identity and appearance of the Antichrist and the mark of the beast are events that will only occur after the Rapture eliminates the need for unnecessary speculation. The fact is that no one can know the identity of the Antichrist until after the rapture of the Restrainer, the Church — and since he will be the one to demand that the whole world take his mark, all this cannot occur until after his identity is revealed. And as noted, that will take place *after* the rapture of the Church.

It's important to note that God has initiated His end-time plan, and only He knows the day and the hour of these events (*see* Matthew 24:36). Therefore, any debating of "when" on our part has no effect on the unmalleable will and plan of God. In other words, our faith and what we believe or don't believe about this subject won't change the events that will occur according to God's own purposes. They will happen completely independent of what you or I think about it. But God has made clear in His Word what we need to know to cooperate intelligently with Him to fulfill His purposes and to be prepared for the events that will unfold before us.

Are We 'Escapists' If We Believe in a Pre-Tribulation Rapture — or Do We Simply Believe Scripture on This Subject?

Often those who do not favor a pre-Tribulation rapture accuse those who do of being *escapists*. Let's take a moment to explore what it means to be an *escapist* and determine if those who believe in a pre-Tribulation rapture really fit into this description.

Escapism, by definition, is a diversion of the mind often to purely imaginative activity, such as a diversion from reality. It is a method that people intentionally or unintentionally take to escape the realities of life or issues that they do not wish to confront and deal with. Often it manifests in the form of fantasy in which a person dreams of a different life or a different set of circumstances than he or she is currently experiencing.

The term *escapism* usually refers to activities, physical or mental, that are used to remove a person's thoughts from his focus on the real world around him. Very often, escapism is used to avoid discomfort or pain and as a survival mechanism to cope with difficulties. Thus, an escapist is a person who seeks distractions as a relief from unpleasant realities.

On the other hand, a *realist* is one who sees a situation as it is and is prepared to deal with it realistically. Rather than hide from the realities around him, he proceeds to deal with things straight-on. For example, a genuine faith-filled, Word-based Christian is one who sees the facts, but because he knows God's promises, he uses his faith to overcome, believing for a better outcome.

I believe in a pre-Tribulation rapture of the Church, but I am as far from an escapist as one can possibly be. Instead, I am brutally realistic about the season in which we live and about my God-given role to do my part in these times. Rather than sit idly by and merely daydream of better times, I am using my faith in the promises and power of God to see the lost world around us and many dark circumstances be changed and overcome. In addition to using my faith, I am working hard and giving every ounce of my life to staying busy until the very last moment that is available. Or, let's say, I am firmly convinced that we are to "occupy" until the very last moment when Jesus comes!

In Luke 19:11-13, Jesus taught a parable about a nobleman traveling to a far country, who first called his servants to give them a command. Those verses read, "And as they heard these things, he added and spake a parable, because he was nigh to Jerusalem, and because they thought that the kingdom of God should immediately appear. He said therefore, A certain nobleman went into a far country to receive for himself a kingdom, and to return. And he called his ten servants, and delivered them ten pounds, and said unto them, *Occupy* till I come."

The word "occupy" in verse 13 is from a form of the Greek word *pragmateuomai*, which means *to do business*, *to trade*, or *to transact*, as in *business*. This word was chiefly used as a business term that denoted one's active engagement in business affairs with the goal of making money. The use of this word meant the nobleman intended that his servants keep working, keep making money, and keep engaging in activities with the goal of being successful and prosperous in business until he returned.

This parable is often used to convey what Christians are to do until Jesus returns. As our great Nobleman, Jesus has likewise gone away for a period of time, but one day He really will come again. And until He comes, He expects each of us to keep working, keep making money, and keep engaging in activities to be successful *until* He returns. In other words, we are to continue as *realists*, not to hide and wait with fantastical *escapist* views that are ungrounded in the Truth.

Although we may discern we are living in the final moments of the age, Matthew 24:36 says that no man knows precisely when Jesus will come. So rather than sit idly by and just wait, Christ *expects* us to keep living our lives — that is, keep getting married, keep having children, keep working at our professions, keep purchasing homes, keep going to church, keep giving our tithes and offerings, keep sharing the Gospel message with others, and so on. In other words, we are to *occupy* until Jesus comes (*see* Luke 19:13)!

Over the centuries, there have been groups who have embarrassingly set predicted dates for the rapture of the Church. Because they wrongly thought they knew the exact day Jesus was coming, they sold their possessions and just "waited" for the Rapture. Then on the other hand, there have been people who loaded up their credit cards with debt because they wrongly thought Jesus was returning so soon that they would never be required to repay the debt they incurred. This kind of behavior is one reason why those who do not favor a pre-Tribulation rapture have accused those who do of being *escapists*.

But because I know Jesus is coming soon, and "the hour is coming when no man can work" (*see* John 9:4) — and because I know that God is not wishing that any should perish — the knowledge of Jesus' soon return motivates me to swing the Gospel sickle into the harvest fields. I determine to work with all my heart and strength to rescue the perishing and to care for the dying. My wife and I, our sons, and our entire ministry team are giving every ounce of our lives to fulfill the Great Commission *because* we are coming closer to the end of the age. I know that Jesus is coming, and this puts fire in my heart to do as much as I can before He returns to make sure as many as possible join us on the great day when He returns to catch away the Church.

Fruit That Remains Requires the Resources of Our Time, Money, Effort, and Energy

Our own ministry philosophy is based on John 15:16, where Jesus said, "Ye have not chosen me, but I have chosen you, and ordained you, that ye should go and bring forth fruit, and *that* your fruit should remain."

Jesus clearly taught the Father is glorified when we bring forth much fruit — and fruit that remains. Until the moment Christ descends — when the shout is heard and the trumpet is blasted — it is my assignment and heartfelt commitment to do all I can with God's Spirit helping me to reach as many people as possible with the saving and life-transforming message of Jesus!

In this verse, Jesus clearly taught the Father is *glorified* when we bring forth *much fruit* — and fruit *that remains*. He is not glorified by our idly sitting by and doing nothing. For this reason, John 15:16 is the goal that I have kept before my own eyes over the years. And *until* the moment Christ descends — when the shout is heard and the trumpet is blasted — it is my assignment and heartfelt commitment to do all I can with God's Spirit helping me to reach as many people as possible with the saving and life-transforming message of Jesus!

But in Titus 2:13, the Rapture is called "the blessed hope." We hope for it because it lies in our future. It's good and right to hope in the promises that God has given —and it is right for us to long for that moment when we will meet Jesus in the air. In fact, Paul said that we are to "comfort" one another with these words. That's not escapism — it is our blessed hope and confident expectation that every word of God proves true.

Furthermore, in First John 3:3, we read that if a person has this "hope" in himself, it purifies him. Remember, it was Jesus Himself who promised in John 14:3 that if He went away, He would come again to receive us unto Himself. He is the One who gave us this hope! It is not a fantasy; it is a blessed hope with the inherent ability to empower us and help us purify our hearts as we await His return!

So *are* we escapists if we believe in a pre-Tribulation rapture? Or do we simply believe in the promises of God?

No, we are not escapists, who deny reality and seek diversion in order to avoid the discomforts and realities around us. Instead, we use our faith to overcome the world around us and to reach as many people as possible before the clock stops ticking. But we do believe in the blessed hope that's been given to us and intend to "escape" the wrath to come upon the world when Christ comes to snatch His Church out of danger *just in the nick of time.* So in that sense, yes, we are escapists!

What if Everyone Is Wrong?

Someone may ask, "What if everyone is wrong about the timing of the rapture of the Church?" Well, if indeed *everyone* is wrong, we are only wrong by a small space of a few years. Some (including me) believe in a pre-Tribulation rapture, while others believe in a mid-Tribulation rapture (which is only three and a half years later), and others believe in a pre-Wrath rapture (which is about four years later). Still others believe in a post-Tribulation rapture (which is seven years later).

I am rock-solid convinced that the rapture of the Church will be a pre-Tribulation event and that God will deliver His people from the seven-year Tribulation period in which fierce, inescapable wrath will be poured out upon the earth.

So if everyone has somehow miscalculated what they believe about this important event, we have all only missed it by a few years. And it does not change the fact that the rapture of the Church is a promise of Scripture — and that the Second Coming will occur at the end of the seven-year Tribulation.

So, in a sense, it is true that it will all "pan out" in the end! But as I have stated, I am rock-solid convinced that the rapture of the Church will be a pre-Tribulation event and that God will deliver His people from the seven-year Tribulation period in which fierce, inescapable wrath will be poured out upon the earth.

When Abraham interceded for Lot in the city of Sodom, he asked, "...Wilt thou also destroy the righteous with the wicked?" (Genesis 18:23). Abraham knew full well that it was not the character of God to destroy the righteous with the wicked. That is why we read in Genesis 19:29 that when God "destroyed the cities of the plain, that God remembered Abraham, and sent Lot out of the midst of the overthrow...."

Just as God delivered Lot and his family from the divine wrath that fell on Sodom and Gomorrah and the other evil cities of the plain, I am personally convinced that God will also deliver His people out of the world before great bowls of wrath are poured upon it during the seven-year Tribulation period. Jesus is the same yesterday, today, and forever (*see* Hebrews 13:8), so if He delivered His people from wrath in the past, we can be certain that He will do it again in the future.

Again, you may ask, "What if you're wrong?" That is a good question to ask, and I will answer it in the final chapter of this book.

However, concerning the timing of the Rapture, among those who believe in the rapture of the Church are dear friends who take a view that is different from my own. This is not a point of division for me, for I have learned to glean from many views in life that are different from my own. I respect and value the convictions of others, just as I would expect them to respect and value mine. We will all eventually be with the Lord, regardless of when that moment occurs, so I refuse to let a view different than my own separate me from those I love and need in my life. Likewise, I urge you to not allow this to be a dividing point to keep you from others who are committed to Christ, to His Church, and to fulfilling the Great Commission!

QUESTIONS TO PONDER

1. Did you know there are eight primary views held by different groups about when the Rapture will occur? After reading this chapter, what did you learn about these various perspectives that you did not know before?

2. Among these groups, there is one that holds a view that is least similar to Rick's. Which view is this? Like Rick, what can you appreciate about one of these eschatological perspectives that differs from your own?

3. Often people criticize those who believe a pre-Tribulation rapture, calling them "escapists." Why is this term inaccurate, and what does the Bible tell us to do until the rapture of the Church occurs? (*See* Luke 19:13.)

4. At the end of this chapter, Rick poses the question: *What if everyone is wrong?* What comfort can we hold on to regardless of whether our view of the timing of the Rapture is correct or incorrect?

Joel 2:23-24, 28-29

...For he hath given you the former rain moderately, and he will cause to come down for you the rain, the former rain, and the latter rain in the first month. And the floors shall be full of wheat, and the fats [vats] shall overflow with wine and oil.... And it shall come to pass afterward [or in the last days], that I will pour out my spirit upon all flesh; and your sons and your daughters shall prophesy, your old men shall dream dreams, your young men shall see visions: and also upon the servants and upon the handmaids in those days will I pour out my spirit.

CHAPTER NINE

AN OVERVIEW OF THE PAST, A SURVEY OF THE PRESENT, AND A FORECAST OF THE FUTURE

In this chapter, I would like to provide a biblical overview of past, present, and future history. It is important to recall where we've been, consider where we are, and understand what the Bible says lies in our future.

People often ask me, "Where are we chronologically in terms of the last days?" I can help answer that question for you from Scripture. But we must begin by considering what the words "last days" really mean — and look at, as we've already briefly seen, when this period called the "last days" officially started and when it will reach its conclusion.

We saw in Chapter Six that the time frame called "the last days" started about 2,000 years ago on the Day of Pentecost when the Holy Spirit was poured out. In Acts 2:17, Peter responded to eyewitness reactions of the outpouring of the Spirit by quoting Joel 2:28, in which the prophet Joel prophesied about supernatural happenings in the last days. In that verse, Peter said, "And it shall come to pass in the *last days*, saith God, I will pour out of my Spirit upon all flesh...."

This verse is pivotal, for it tells us that when the Holy Spirit was poured out on the Day of Pentecost, it was the event that triggered what the Bible calls the "last days." Hence, from the Day of Pentecost to the present — or for the last approximately 2,000 years — we have been living in the last days.

On the Day of Pentecost, the Holy Spirit was poured out and mighty power came upon the Church of Jesus Christ. Mighty outpourings of the Holy Spirit were evidenced with signs, wonders, miracles, and mighty deeds, as the Gospel advanced into the ends of the earth.

At Pentecost, the Church of Jesus Christ experienced outpourings of the Holy Spirit with signs, wonders, miracles, and mighty deeds, as the Gospel advanced into the ends of the earth. In Acts 1:8, Jesus promised that the Spirit would come upon believers with "power." The word "power" is an interpretation of the Greek word *dunamis*, which was the very word used in the Roman world to depict *the full might of an advancing army.*

Indeed, once the Spirit came upon the Early Church, those believers were divinely empowered as a mighty spiritual army to cover vast swaths of the earth with the message of the Cross and the Resurrection. In spite of resistance, opposition, hardships, persecution, and difficulties associated with travel, early believers journeyed across the world of their time in obedience to Jesus' command in Acts 1:8 to take the Gospel first to Jerusalem, then to Judea and Samaria, and finally to "the uttermost parts of the earth."

Joel Forecasted a Mighty Move of the Spirit and a Prolific End-Time Harvest

But when the Spirit was poured out on the Day of Pentecost, Peter quoted Joel 2:28 and 29, which says, "And it shall come to pass afterward [or in the last days], that I will pour out my spirit upon all flesh; and your sons and your daughters shall prophesy, your old men shall dream dreams, your young men shall see visions: and also upon the servants and upon the handmaids in those days will I pour out my spirit."

But just a few verses prior to that, Joel also foretold, "...For He hath given you the former rain moderately, and he will cause to come down for you the rain, the former rain, and the latter rain in the first month. And the floors shall be full of wheat, and the fats [vats] shall overflow with wine and oil" (vv. 23-24).

Notice the prophet Joel said God "...*hath* given you the former rain moderately...." Joel was prophesying that an early rain of the Spirit would be "moderate" compared to the latter rain that would eventually come in the very last of days. In fact, Joel prophetically foretold that when the latter outpouring, or latter rain, of the Spirit occurs, the floors of God's house will be full of wheat, which is symbolic of the Word of God, and the vats will overflow with wine and oil, which is symbolic of the Holy Spirit.

Joel prophesied the early rain of the Spirit would be "moderate" compared to the latter rain that would eventually come in the very last of days.

The Difference Between the Early and Latter Rain

To fully comprehend the early and latter rains of the Holy Spirit that God promised His people, it is important to understand the difference between the natural early and latter rains that occur each year in Israel.

Israel's climate exhibits the unique characteristic of very distinct dry and rainy seasons during each year of planting and harvesting. Equally distinct in the rainy seasons are the "early and latter rains" — the "early" rains in the fall and the "latter" rains in the following spring. This was no doubt the picture in the prophet Joel's mind as he wrote metaphorically in Joel chapter 2 of the early and latter rains of the Spirit.

As I said, the early rains in Israel start in the fall of the year — the beginning of the rainy season, as the name "early rains" indicates. When those rains arrive, farmers rejoice, for it means the end of a long dry summer season. Those predictable early rains in the fall of the year moisten the ground and make it easier for the hard ground to be broken up and prepared for planting season and a future season of harvest. Without those early rains, it is nearly impossible to work the soil and plant seed for an eventual harvest.

Then in the spring of the following calendar year, the latter rains finally come, and these rains are much heavier. If these heavier rains had fallen first, it would have resulted in flooding, as the hardened ground of the hot months would not have been prepared to receive such an abundance of water. But the early rains prepare the soil so that when the latter rains finally come, the soil is no longer hardened, and the water can penetrate the soil and aid in bringing forth a harvest in the spring of the year.

The purpose of the early rain is to nourish and prepare the soil for the reception of seed, and the purpose of the latter rain is to give the harvest one last mighty dose of nourishment so it can reach its full, maximum potential and fruitfulness come harvest time.[1]

God will send another outpouring, the latter rain of the Spirit, and that last-days downpour of the Spirit will be mightier than any other outpouring in Church history.

Do You See the Connection Naturally and Spiritually?

Similarly, when the Spirit was first poured out on the Day of Pentecost, it was the early rain that God sent to moisten the soil so that the first Gospel preachers could preach God's Word, planting the seed of the Word in a pagan environment.

That early outpouring — or the early rain of the Spirit — came with signs, wonders, and mighty deeds. But Joel 2:23 and 24 promises that in the very last of the last days — when time has sailed to the very end of the age and not much more time remains on the journey — God will send another outpouring, the *latter rain* of the Spirit. And that last-days downpour of the Spirit will be mightier than any other outpouring in Church history.

Think of it! The early New Testament Church was not a different Church than the Church today. Those early believers comprised the Early Church of the New Covenant — and we as believers today comprise the latter New Testament Church. We are all — past, present, and future — one Church and members of one Body of our Lord Jesus Christ! And because the early rain of the Spirit, or the outpouring of the Spirit that was initiated on the Day of Pentecost, was marked by such signs and wonders, just imagine the signs, wonders, miracles, and marvels that will occur at the time of *the deluge* of the Spirit and the latter rain!

Now we can see that when Joel prophesied, "And it shall come to pass afterward [or in the last days], that I will pour out my spirit upon all flesh..." (Joel 2:28), he was actually referring to dual outpourings of the Spirit — one that would occur at the first of the last days and another that would occur at the end of the age, in the last of the last days — thus, an *early* and a *latter* rain of the Spirit. That verse doesn't insinuate there would be only two moves of the Spirit of God on the earth — recorded history, including contemporary history, confirms that there have been several big moves of God throughout time. This verse simply means that one move would mark the *beginning of the last days*, and the other move would mark *the very end of the last days.*

From the Upper Room to the Pentecostal/Charismatic Community Today

Since the earliest days of Pentecost some 2,000 years ago, the outpouring of the Spirit has continued, and today the Pentecostal/Charismatic community is the largest segment of the Body of Christ outside of the Catholic Church. In fact, consider the following statistics concerning the Christian faith worldwide.[2]

- There are approximately 1.1 billion Catholics.
- There are approximately 800 million Protestants.
- There are about 260 million Orthodox believers.
- That brings the total number in the Christian faith to more than 2 billion (2,160,000,000).
- This figure is almost one fourth of the world's population.
- Of that total number of more than 2 billion, nearly 700 million claim to have had a personal Pentecostal/Charismatic experience.
- That figure tells us approximately 1 out of every 4 Christians has had a personal Pentecostal/Charismatic experience, which is an amazing statistic considering *this started with a group of 120 believers in the Upper Room in Jerusalem!*

When the first outpouring of the Spirit occurred on the Day of Pentecost, "the soil of the earth was moistened," and the Gospel advanced. But a mightier deluge of God's Spirit will fall, at least upon a remnant of the Church, that will accelerate, enhance, and *advance* the end-time harvest at the very last of this end-times age.

James referred to this final outpouring in James 5:7, "Be patient therefore, brethren, unto the coming of the Lord. Behold, the husbandman waiteth for the precious fruit of the earth, and hath long patience for it, until he receive the early and latter rain." The final latter rain of the Spirit in this age is essential for the Lord, who is the Husbandman, to receive the precious fruit of souls for which He has patiently waited for 2,000 years.

And just as the early rain of the Spirit in the first centuries of the Church was evidenced with signs, wonders, and mighty deeds, we can expect the latter rain — or the very last outpouring of the Spirit before the Rapture takes place — to come with *mightier* power for the sake of bringing in a great harvest of souls. The vibrant remnant Christ will retrieve in the great *catching away* will not be weak and powerless, but radiant and glorious. As Paul said in First Thessalonians 4:15 and 17, that remnant will be spiritually living, spiritually robust, spiritually thriving, spiritually vibrant, and spiritually vigorous.

But as we've also seen, according to Scripture, we can accurately define the "last days" as having begun on the Day of Pentecost, which means we have been living in the "last days" since the first outpouring — or since the first early rain of the Spirit — that took place on that day. For approximately 2,000 years, the Church has been in the midst of a last-days time frame that will continue until the rapture of the Church, which is the event that closes this age and triggers the onset of the Tribulation.

Another Look at the Greek Word *Eschatos*, Which Means *Something Last* or *Final*

Although we have already studied the word *eschatos* in Chapter Six, let's look a little deeper at the word "last" as it appears in the New Testament when used in connection with the "last days." That word "last" is nearly always translated from the Greek word *eschatos*, which is a word that depicts something that is *final*. It is the Greek word from which we derive the word "eschatology," the theological study of *end times*, or it could simply refer to the study of *last things*.

Illustrated here is an ancient port that would have been similar to ones used in the time of the New Testament. A ship in transit stops at many ports en route to its final destination, but the word *eschatos* depicted the very last port on the journey.

As noted on page 226, this Greek word *eschatos* points to the *very last* or the *ultimate end* of a thing, and it was used by ancient Greeks to describe *the point that was farthest away*. In fact, the ancient world used the word *eschatos* as a seafaring word to describe *the last port of call for a ship*. Although a ship in transit stops at many ports en route to its final destination, the word *eschatos* was used to depict *the very last port* on the journey. This last stopping-off point signified that it was the "end of the road" and the journey was finished. Thus, using the word *eschatos* was like saying, "This is the end, and you can go no farther."

An example of the word *eschatos* can also be seen from the life of Alexander the Great. In his lifetime, Alexander the Great and his troops conquered vast swaths of geographical territory, and he was known to frequently found cities in those new regions that he named in commemoration of himself. According to the historian Plutarch, Alexander named 70 such cities after himself.[3]

The famous city of Alexandria in Egypt, a city on the northern shores of Egypt, was a city that Alexander the Great named after himself.

A well-known example is the famed city of *Alexandria* in Egypt, a city on the northern shores of Egypt that Alexander the Great named after himself. Another *Alexandria* was established on the shores

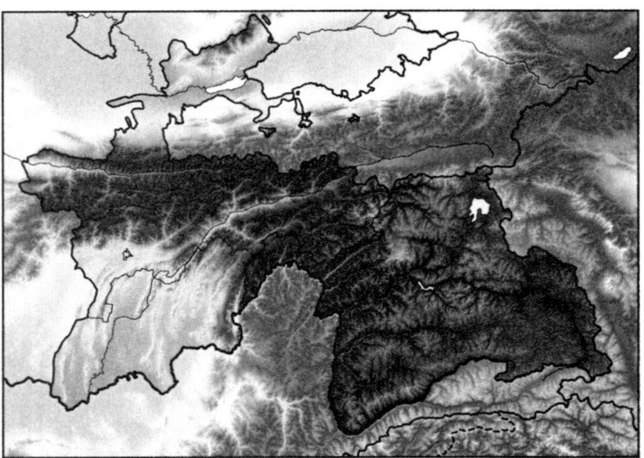

Because it seemed to be the ends of the earth, Alexander the Great founded a city there called Alexandria Eschate — a fitting name for a city believed to be at the farthest end of Alexander's vast empire.

of present-day Turkiye on the very spot where Alexander and his troops defeated King Darius.[4]

But when Alexander the Great and his troops marched far east in 329 BC into what today is called Tajikistan, that region became the northerly outpost of his empire in Central Asia. Because it seemed to be the ends of the earth, the city that Alexander the Great founded there was named *Alexandria Eschate.*

The name of this city was a mixture of the name *Alexander* and the Greek word *eschatos*. This name itself literally meant that it was *the city of Alexander at the farthest ends* of the world — a fitting name for a city believed to be *at the farthest end* of Alexander's vast empire.

But let me provide you another example to demonstrate the concept of *finality* that is associated with the word *eschatos*. This word *eschatos* could have also been used historically to describe *the very last month* of a 12-month calendar or the *very last week* in a month or the *final day* in a week. In other words, the word *eschatos* always pointed to *the very ultimate end* of a journey, a destination, or whatever was being discussed.

Again, it is important to understand the meaning of *eschatos* because although we've been prophetically living in a time frame known as the "last days" for the past 2,000 years, we have now come to *the furthest end* of this period — or to the time in which we have sailed to the very last port and there is nowhere else to go. Indeed, we have come to the *ultimate end* of this period and are now living in *the last* of *the last days.*

Once again, the entire period called the "last days" started on the Day of Pentecost nearly 2,000 years ago, and it will last until Christ descends to resurrect the dead bodies of the righteous and to rapture the authentic Church. When the resurrection of the dead in Christ and the rapture of the Church occurs, this epoch will be abruptly closed, and the next season, called the Tribulation, will begin.

THE *CHURCH AGE*, THE *AGE OF GRACE*, AND THE *LAST DAYS* — ALL TERMS FOR THE SAME PERIOD OF TIME

Some refer to this present period as the *Church Age* because it is the age in which the Church has been God's dominant vehicle in the earth. Others refer to this present age as the *Age of Grace* because it is an entire epoch in which God's grace has dominated the lives of believers.

But if we want to be biblically correct, the designation for these 2,000 years is the *Last Days*. But now, we have sailed to *the very end* of this epoch and are living in the very cusp of its finality. And we actively, prayerfully await a final outpouring — the latter rain of the Spirit — to help bring in the long-awaited precious fruit of the earth for which God has been patiently waiting for 2,000 years.

Jesus paid for this harvest of men's and women's souls with His precious blood — *and the harvest belongs to Him!* But we as the Church have been commissioned to reap it for Him. Our promise, though, for these last days is that we can expect the latter rain of His Spirit to accelerate the work and cause it to be accomplished before He comes again for His saints — both those who have died in faith and those who will be *caught up* to meet Him in the air.

Harvesting lost souls and making disciples — "teaching all nations" — is our Great Commission (*see* Mark 16:15-16; Matthew 28:19-20). And Christ as the Chief Shepherd and supreme Head of the Church has given us the wherewithal by His Spirit to do it!

Looking ahead, it is logical to ask, "If we are really living in the very last of the last days, what can we expect to happen next on the prophetic schedule?" I will answer that question, but before we look at the future of the Church, let's first take a moment to study the past history and present landscape of the Church and the winds of opposition that have beset it because they will beset God's people again.

We can expect the latter rain of God's Spirit to accelerate the work of believers and to bring forth the greatest harvest of the ages to be reaped before He comes again for His saints.

In the first three centuries of Christianity when the Holy Spirit empowered the Early Church to march into the world with the message of the Cross and the Resurrection, the Christian community was hit with a hurricane-tempest force that was unpredictable and at times very violent.

THE PAST:
A Spiritual Hurricane Hit the Church in Its Earliest Years

Especially during the first three centuries of Christianity when the Holy Spirit empowered the Early Church to march into the world with the message of the Cross and the Resurrection, a moment eventually came when the Christian community was hit with a hurricane-tempest force that was unpredictable and at times very violent. Satan sent his strongest winds to try to knock the Early Church off its feet and deluge its members with havoc and heartache. The enemy sent his strongest winds to beat down the Early Church, and if anything could have stopped the Church, it would have been the storm that raged against them in those early years.

But Jesus promised that "the gates of hell shall not prevail against it [the Church]" (*see* Matthew 16:18). Although brutal waves of assault came against the Church especially in the first 300 years — and many other times over the past 2,000 years — every turbulent episode has proven that truly *the gates of hell shall not prevail against the Church!*

As we consider what the Church has experienced over the past 2,000 years, let's continue using the analogy of a hurricane-tempest force to describe the assaults that began striking the Church in the earlier centuries.

As a hurricane approaches, its presence can be felt by a torrent of pounding rain and rising sea tides that precede it. These torrential rains and tides are sufficiently deadly by themselves — but they are merely *symptoms* of the real storm that is still gathering strength and preparing to hit land. As the massive storm gathers strength, momentum, and acceleration and forces its way toward land, the sea is pushed forward, and the swell of the waves grows higher — usually hitting the land *before* the fierce, often devastating winds of the actual hurricane. When these rising tides hit, everything in their path is ravaged with catastrophic consequences.

Hurricanes consist of belts of wind that pound the land in sequence, one after another. Individuals who do not understand how a hurricane behaves may wrongly assume the storm is calming down after each punishing "lash" of that belt of wind. But, in fact, more belts of wind are on the way to pelt and whip everything in their path. These storms have multiple bands of wind that strike relentlessly, again and again, with only a brief pause between each strike. This is precisely what happened in the earliest centuries of the Church.

I said all this to explain that, like a hurricane, there were belts of persecution that came against the Church, with occasional reprieves in between, which Christians frequently mistook to mean that the raging storm against them was finally over. But soon, another pagan leader who was antagonistic to the Gospel would rise to power, and once again, the horrific winds of opposition would begin to strike relentlessly again, again, and again, with only brief pauses between each wave of inflicted hardship and harsh persecution.

In fact, history informs us that there were multiple belts of persecutions by Roman emperors against the Church in its formative years. To gain more understanding about the episodic persecutions that came against the Church in those earliest centuries, I recommend you read, "Ten Periods of Roman Persecution" in my book *A Light in Darkness, Volume One*. Much insight can be gained by the study of this material regarding the ten episodic periods of intense persecution that raged against believers throughout the Roman Empire.

Persecution continued routinely until restrictions on Christian worship were formally rescinded during the rule of Emperor Constantine (circa 306-337 AD). In the year 313 AD, the *Edict of Milan* — or what is known as the *Edict of Toleration* — was issued by Emperor Constantine which gave Christianity legal status, and for the first time in nearly 300 years, those of the Christian faith no longer suffered governmental persecution under Roman rule.[5]

Those 300 years were brutal, but eventually, the frontside of that horrific spiritual hurricane seemed to come to an end. Many demonically inspired kings and rulers had put forth their best effort to extinguish the light of the Gospel and obliterate the Church — but no one was ever able, *or ever will be able*, to resist Jesus Christ and His Church.

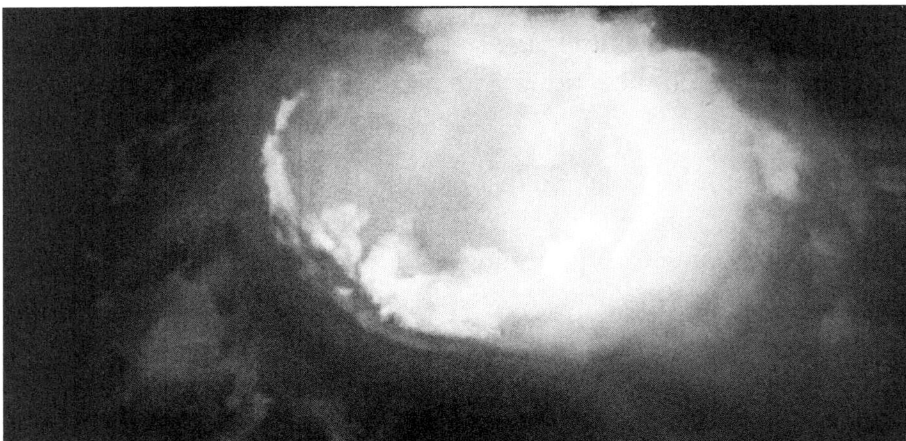

In the eye of a hurricane, some wrongly assume the storm is over. Due to the reprieve felt by the Church once the front side of that early storm of 300 years had passed, many believers made the same mistake. The pressure let up, the skies overhead became clear, and for approximately 1,700 years, the Church has, in general, freely immersed itself in missionary activity, church growth, and church planting.

The Misunderstood Eye of the Storm

One prominent feature of a hurricane is *the eye of the storm*. When the front side of a storm passes and the eye of the storm arrives, the sky overhead appears blue and clear and gives the *illusion* that the storm has completely passed. If the eye of the hurricane passes over at night, one would be able to look up and see the stars in a crystal-clear sky. But it's true that when one is in the eye of the storm, the skies overhead appear so clear that he or she might wrongly think the storm is over, not realizing that the backside of the storm is yet to come. The temperature would likely be mild, and birds might fly overhead while various animals emerge from hiding with a sense of relief. Because the pressure in the eye of the storm is the least felt, one may wrongly assume all is calm and well, but the backside of the storm is still coming with potentially devastating consequences.

Uninformed people who mistakenly think the storm has passed often emerge from their places of safety, not realizing they are placing themselves in harm's way. Deaths related to hurricanes are sometimes attributed to people who take the peaceful eye of the storm to mean the storm has passed because they misread the signs and regretfully lose their lives when they are hit by the backside of the storm, exposed and unprepared. They could be carried out to sea by the currents or hit inland by deadly flying debris. If they'd understood that they were merely in the eye of the storm, they could have remained in a place of safety and the backside of the storm would have had less effect on them. But because they failed to properly read the weather, they regrettably suffered loss.

What does this have to do with the history of the Church and the winds of persecution believers suffered in the early years?

The Early Church survived nearly 300 years of many hard-hitting winds and waves of persecution. Finally, it *appeared* that the storm ended when the Emperor Constantine issued the *Edict of Toleration* in the year 313 AD. But just as those in a hurricane may find themselves in the eye of the storm and wrongly assume as the skies clear that the storm is over, that pause was not actually the end of the storm of persecution for the Church. Instead, the Church merely found itself in the eye of the storm after the front side of the spiritual hurricane in those early years passed.

A physical eye of a hurricane can last from 10 or 15 minutes up to an hour or more.[6] Due to the reprieve from persecution felt by His Church (especially in the Western world), once the front side of that early storm of 300 years passed, it has seemed to most that the hard-hitting governmental assault experienced by our early brothers and sisters in Christ — like the deceitful appearance of the eye of a hurricane — forever ended.

After those devastating years of persecution, the Early Church finally felt the pressure let up, and the skies overhead became clear. And for the most part, for approximately 1,700 years the Church has freely immersed itself in missionary activity, church growth, and church planting. In fact, the message of Christianity became so entrenched that Western European civilization was built on the principles of Christianity, and its influence for many centuries has affected the arts, architecture, literature, science, philosophy, and technology — every sphere of Western society.

But Jesus declared that difficult times would arise again for the Church in the very last of the last days. So although the Church has lived in general peace for nearly 1,700 years — not that long ago in the mind of God — the backside of the storm has been and is still approaching. Even now, it is garnering strength to make "landfall" with fierce impact that will be felt again by authentic Christians in the very last days of the age.

Although the Church has lived in relative peace for 1,700 years, the climate is changing and believers are waking up to the fact that we are living in the very last days. They are beginning to experience the fierce backside of the storm as the lawless spirit of the age increases in brazen protest of established moral codes and becomes aggressively opposed to the Church and to the Word of God.

THE PRESENT:
The Backside of the Storm Is Approaching

While the Church has lived in relative peace for 1,700 years, the climate is changing, and people are waking up to the fact that we are living on the cusp of the finality of the very last days. We are also beginning to experience the fierce backside of this storm as the lawless spirit of the age increases in brazen protest of established moral codes and becomes aggressively opposed to the Church and to the Word of God. Just as the Early Church found themselves living amidst a hostile world, Christians today are finding themselves living in an increasingly antagonistic world, including antagonism from governmental powers that use lawfare to *accuse*, *attack*, *strike down*, and *cancel* those who oppose their lawless agenda.

Christians who tenaciously stick to their convictions and refuse to bend to the spirit of the age are frequently cast aside as narrow-minded, anti-societal bigots. As morality declines and the line between right and wrong becomes blurred, those who remain steadfast in their commitment to Christ — unmovable in their biblical convictions and sense of right and wrong — will be cast out as obstinate, unbending, and intolerant people.

While I do not want to sound negative in my appraisal of the current landscape, as a leader, I feel the need to prophetically warn that the world will try to push the Church — who once formed the "moral center" of society — out of the center so that progressive, Bible-rejecting, free thinkers can move center stage. One need not be a prophet to see these developments are moving forward at an escalating pace.

As a society, we may experience occasional reprieves from time to time, but whether we like it or not, Scripture clearly teaches that the spirit of lawlessness will increase, not diminish, at the very end of the last days. In such times when lawlessness brazenly gains a greater foothold, society will continue to view Bible-believers with disdain, ridiculing them and charging them with being judgmental. All of this results in discrimination as believers are increasingly put under pressure to conform through cleverly phrased arguments, intimidation, and manipulation. Although it may be hard to believe this could happen, the Holy Spirit foretells in Scripture that the backside of the storm, with winds of fierce opposition, will hit again at the end of the last days as the world morphs into its final phases of modification to receive the Man of Lawlessness, *the Antichrist*.

Until we are caught away in the rapture of the Church, we must be mentally and spiritually equipped and ready, as we may experience the backside of the same storm that hit the Church in its early days. The backside of the storm may be different from the frontside of the storm that assaulted the Church in its first 300 years. Aggravated periods of assault in our day and in the days to come may be shorter in duration and intensity. Nevertheless, it is absolutely vital that the Church be mentally and spiritually prepared for it.

I have noted multiple times in this book that the Greek word *harpadzo* — the word that describes the rapture of the Church in First Thessalonians 4:17 — means, for one, *to snatch out of danger just in the nick of time*. This suggests the divine rescue operation that we refer to as the Rapture will take place in a dark moment when the Church is facing difficulty and hardship. Then, all of a sudden, Christ will descend into the lower atmosphere with a shout and the blast of a trumpet to resurrect the bodies of the righteous dead and to rapture and rescue the authentic Church from peril just in the nick of time.

But the glorious remnant that Christ is coming to retrieve will not be a weak and puny people. Instead, they will have been divinely empowered to steward their call and commission on the earth as God gloriously reveals His power through them in the midst of a sea of gross darkness in the very last of the last days.

The Holy Spirit prophesied that exactly as there was a confrontation between Moses and Jannes and Jambres in the past, there will be a similar confrontation in the very last of the last days in which God's divine power will flow mightily through a glorious remnant in the last-days Church.

A Final Showdown at the End of the Age — Remember Jannes and Jambres

We have seen that a very last days outpouring is prophesied in Joel 2:23-24,28-29. But in Second Timothy 3:8-9, Paul additionally wrote about a last-days confrontation of powers that will occur before the age consummates. He wrote, "Now as Jannes and Jambres withstood Moses, so do these also resist the truth: men of corrupt minds, reprobate concerning the faith. But they shall proceed no further: for their folly shall be manifest unto all men, as theirs also was."

In these verses, Paul declared a final confrontation would occur between the powers of darkness and the power of God before the age consummates. Exactly as there was a confrontation of powers that occurred between Moses and Pharaoh's sorcerers Jannes and Jambres in the past, there will be a similar confrontation in the very last of the last days. To prepare ourselves for victory in the face of this end-times conflict, we must first answer the question, "Who were Jannes and Jambres?"

The identities of Jannes and Jambres were well documented by Jewish intellectuals who lived in the ancient city of Alexandria, Egypt. According to these Jewish historians, Jannes and Jambres were the two leading sorcerers in the book of Exodus who attempted to "withstand" Moses. As residents of Alexandria, these Jewish historians and intellectuals had access to Egypt's historical records, and by studying ancient archives, they authoritatively identified Jannes and Jambres as the two primary sorcerers who opposed Moses in the land of Egypt (*see* Exodus 7:11,22; 8:6-7).

As a matter of fact, these two sorcerers were so well known in the ancient world that Pliny the Elder, the historian Eusebius, and the noted theologian Origen each wrote about these two men.[7] In addition to these respected sources, the names Jannes and Jambres appeared *frequently* in other Jewish, Christian, and pagan sources in Arabic, Aramaic, Greek, Hebrew, Latin, Old and Middle English, and Syriac.[8]

In the days of Moses, Jannes and Jambres took a stand against Moses and the power of God. But Paul told us that in like manner, at the end of the age, there will be a contest of emerging evil powers — religious and apostate, occultic, social, and political — that will oppose the Gospel and present an alternative message. It will be a part of the end-time, worldwide mutiny that Paul prophesied about in Second Thessalonians 2:3 (*see* pages 108-110).

Paul declared that just as Pharaoh's sorcerers were unable to compete with the power of God, so, too, these end-time contenders will be unable to compete with God's mighty power that will manifest among at least a remnant of the Church. Herein, in Paul's words in Second Timothy 3:9, we find a prophecy of a final showdown at the end of the age — one in which the power of God will prove to be unbeatable in the face of evil as evil shall be met with God's mighty power and "…their folly shall be manifest unto all men…."

In Second Timothy 3:8 and 9, Paul prophesied that just as the power of God worked through Moses to confront the powers of evil in his day, God's divine power will once again flow mightily through a remnant in the last-days Church. As the Holy Spirit moves mightily in the last of the last days, this divine power will confront the folly of warped ideologies.

And just as Moses' rod "swallowed" the rods of Jannes and Jambres (*see* Exodus 7:12) there will be a demonstration of God's power in a remnant that will reveal the uncontestable power of God in a glorious Church.

In Moses' confrontation with Jannes and Jambres, for a short period of time, these sorcerers' perverted powers went head-to-head with the power of God operating through Moses, matching miracle for miracle the supernatural demonstrations of God through His chosen representative. Moses had thrown down his rod, which miraculously turned into a snake by the power of God. Jannes and Jambres, as magicians in Pharaohs' court, did likewise, also manifesting a snake in place of a rod.

But the final moment of truth came when everyone present witnessed the magicians' snake being swallowed up, completely engulfed, by Moses' snake (*see* Exodus 7:10-12). This was further emphasized for Pharaoh and his army when the ten plagues ended with the death of all of Egypt's firstborn. Pharaoh *continued* to harden his heart, chasing the children of Israel into the Red Sea, where the same mighty waters that stood congealed to allow God's people to escape *completely engulfed* the Egyptians who tried to cross behind them in pursuit.

And, friend, God will *always* have the last word against the enemy on behalf of His people. Even the grave could not hold Jesus when the enemy surely, for a brief moment, thought he had won a final victory against the Messiah. Christ's decisive resurrection proved otherwise — and, likewise, we will see the power of God in the last days *continue* to prove that Satan's power is no match for Almighty God. For this reason, we should *expect* a mighty end-times outpouring of the Holy Spirit to come with signs, wonders, and mighty deeds as we near the conclusion of the last-days time frame in which we live!

And as time marches on — during a moment when it seems the world has lost its moral mind, and darkness seems to abound on every side as the backside of this storm rises to assault the Church with sporadic and ever-increasing belts of opposition — Christ will descend to rapture, or snatch, His people out of harm's way. Those who are spiritually living, spiritually robust, spiritually thriving, spiritually vibrant, and spiritually vigorous will escape just before the trigger is pulled and the time of troubles (the Tribulation) begins on planet Earth. In this last-days showdown, Christ will indeed gather His saints to Himself in the resurrection of the righteous dead and the catching away of those vibrant remaining ones who were carriers of His glory during the mighty latter rain of His Spirit on the earth.

When Jesus steps into the lower atmosphere with a shout and a blast of the mighty trumpet of God, we will escape just before divine wrath is poured out on the planet during the seven-year Tribulation period. If this powerful series of events is what you call *escapism* on the part of the Church, then the answer is *yes* — we plan to escape the wrath that is soon coming on the earth!

But people also want to know, "What will happen *after* the rapture of the Church?" So let's turn our attention now to the future — to a time after Christ has removed the Church from the earth.

Immediately after the Restrainer, or the Church, is suddenly removed, it will trigger the moment when the curtain that has concealed the Antichrist's identity will be pulled back, and once the Church is gone, this global leader will step forward onto the world stage and into the spotlight to reveal himself.

THE FUTURE:
WHAT HAPPENS NEXT, AFTER THE RAPTURE OF THE CHURCH?

When the Restrainer, or the Church, is suddenly removed, it will trigger the moment when the curtain that has concealed the Antichrist's identity will be pulled back. Once the Church is gone, the Antichrist will step forward onto the world stage and into the spotlight to reveal himself.

We saw in Chapter Three that Paul clearly taught this in Second Thessalonians 2:6. As a reminder, that verse says, "And now ye know what withholdeth that he might be revealed in his time."

RIV OF SECOND THESSALONIANS 2:6

Now in light of everything I've told you before, you ought to be well aware by now that there is a supernatural force at work, preventing the materialization of this person and the disclosure of his identity. This restraining force I'm referring to is so strong that it is currently putting on the brakes and holding back the unveiling of this wicked person, stalling and postponing his manifestation. But

when the right moment comes, this evil one will no longer be withheld, and he will emerge on the world scene. The screen that has been hiding his true identity and guarding him from world view will suddenly be pulled back and will evaporate — and he will step out on center stage to let everyone know who he is.

In this verse, we again see that the Antichrist can only be revealed in his time. And we know it is because of the Restrainer that the Antichrist has not yet been revealed. This truth about the Antichrist's unveiling on God's timetable is so very important that if you do not recall what I wrote about it, please return to pages 111-116 to review that material.

Paul added in verse 8 that once the Restrainer, or the Church, is removed, "...*then* shall that Wicked be revealed...." The word "then" means simply *then* or *at that precise moment*, and it describes what will *immediately take place* once the Restrainer has disappeared from the earth's scene. Paul was therefore stating that the Antichrist will appear *after* the Restrainer has been removed.

Did you realize before reading this that *you* as a member of the Body of Christ worldwide are a part of a supernatural, Holy Spirit-indwelt restraining force? God has chosen to operate through us — through you and me — to hold back a vicious tide of evil that is continually attempting to unleash itself upon God's creation.

This means God is using the Church as a mighty Restrainer to hold back evil and to postpone the manifestation of the Antichrist and the onslaught of evil that will accompany his appearance at the end of the age. Paul referred to the removal of the Restrainer in Second Thessalonians 2:7, where he wrote, "...He who now letteth [the Restrainer] will let [will restrain], until he be taken out of the way." The *Renner Interpretive Version* (*RIV*) elaborates on this text as follows:

RIV of Second Thessalonians 2:7

These secretive, surreptitious dark events have been covertly in the making for a long time, yet the world at large doesn't realize that a secret plan is being executed right under their own noses. The only thing that has kept this plan from being already consummated is the restraining force that has been holding it all back until now. But one day this force will be removed from the picture — and when that happens, these iniquitous events will quickly transpire. The removal of this restraining force will signal the moment when the Lawless One will finally make his grand appearance to the world.

Similar to how slaves in ancient times received a brand or mark in their flesh that identified to whom they belonged, "both small and great, rich and poor, free and bond" will receive a mark, or brand, to denote allegiance to the Antichrist from people who live in every part of the sophisticated world.

The Mark of the Beast

A moment will finally come during the rule of the Antichrist when he will mandate the whole world (in the time of the Tribulation) to receive the "mark of the beast" that is referred to in Revelation 13:16 and 17, which says, "And he [the Antichrist] causeth all, both small and great, rich and poor, free and bond, to receive a mark in their right hand, or in their foreheads: and that no man might buy or sell, save he that had the mark, or the name of the beast, or the number of his name."

The word "mark" in this verse is interpreted from the Greek word *charagma*, a word that means *an engraving, stamp*, or *tattoo.* In the ancient world, a rancher might "brand" a cow to prove it belonged to him — it was a brand-type mark used to identify the owner of an animal, or even a person in some cases. In fact, it was a common practice to mark slaves or soldiers with a *brand* or *tattoo* to indicate their allegiance and ownership. Such a *charagma* mark provided an *irrefutable connection* between a master and slave, or between a beast and its owner.

And similar to how slaves in ancient times received a brand or mark in their flesh that identified to whom they belonged, the Antichrist will require "both small and great, rich and poor, free and bond, to receive a mark," or brand, to denote their allegiance to him and his ownership of them. These words in this verse imply universality and show that the Antichrist will have jurisdiction over every part of the sophisticated world.

But according to Revelation 13:17, this "mark" will have "the name of the beast, or the number of his name." This means every person who receives this mark will have the name of the Antichrist, or the numeric equation of his name, *branded, engraved, stamped,* or *tattooed,* into his or her flesh.

Some suggest that because the word *charagma* also means to *engrave*, this word *could* indicate the cutting of flesh to accommodate some kind of chip implantation. On page 357 of my book *Fallen Angels, Giants, Monsters, and the World Before the Flood,* I write about the goal of transhumanists to transform human beings by connecting their minds and bodies permanently to computers. It says:

> **The foundational belief of transhumanism is that human beings are weak and poor, both physically and morally. Therefore, to improve the human experience — which includes overcoming aging, disability, disease, and mental limitations — there must be a convergence between humans and technology to create transhumans that will be stronger and have greater abilities.**
>
> **The drive of transhumanists to see humans and technology merged has already been achieved in some respects. For example, after interfacing with computers and other forms of technology, some disabled people have regained certain physical features and functions that were once lost, which is a positive development. But that is not the endgame; it is only the beginning.**

On page 358 of the same book, I continued to explain:

> **Some transhumanists are looking so far into the future (which may not be as far as we think), and they envision a time when mankind as we know it will enter into a *posthuman* period. I know this sounds like the stuff of science fiction, but the fact is there are well-known companies that have already developed computer chips to be implanted into the brain or under the skin to merge humans with AI. This sounds very similar to what John jotted down in the book of Revelation about what will take place during the Tribulation (*see* Revelation 13:16; 14:9; 20:4). Hence, we're living in a time where one can not only be transgender, but he or she can also become transhuman.**

What is the long-term goal of transhumanists? The answer is singularity — the moment when humanity and technology merge and become one and transcend humanity. The dream is to so intertwine humans with technology that eventually a full convergence of bodies, minds, and emotions takes place. Ideally, transhumanists want to escape death and live forever — either through uploading one's mind to computers, cloning, or by other means of technology.[9]

I am not suggesting that computer chips are the mark of the beast; although, I do believe the goal of transhumanists is quite alarming, as the implanting of chips will at the least infringe on one's privacy and potentially affect his or her day-to-day living. But whatever the *mark* is, or however it will appear, its presence on a person's flesh or inside his flesh will be considered as proof that the person's absolute allegiance is to the Antichrist and that he or she is fully owned by him.

We are living in a time when tattoos have become fashionable. In the past, tattoos were usually signs that one had been a prisoner, had been involved in criminal activity, or had perhaps served as a sailor or soldier. It was certainly not generally viewed as a fashion statement.

But today people tattoo all kinds of images into their flesh — including names and images of those they love, song lyrics, Bible verses, symbols of the faith they embrace, numbers that have special meaning to them, and patriotic emblems.

I am not implying the mark of the beast will be a tattoo, but the current trend to *brand*, *engrave*, *mark*, *stamp*, or *tattoo* one's flesh has normalized these actions and numbed society to the idea of altering one's flesh. So when the Antichrist finally requires a "mark" of some sort to be given to the world, it will not carry the stigma that it once carried. In fact, whatever the mark is, it may actually be considered *fashionable*.

Remember, we covered in a previous chapter that an ever-increasingly lawless society is actually being groomed right now to receive the Antichrist at the time of his unveiling after the Church has been evacuated from the earth. The more those who reject God cast off moral restraints in favor of embracing a societal mentality of "anything goes," the more ready they will be to embrace the rulership of the Antichrist.

In fact, this Man of Lawlessness, or Man of Sin, will be highly esteemed by the population of the earth for the so-called "peace" he will broker — but we know that about halfway through the Tribulation, and therefore halfway through his reign, he will begin to show his true colors. All bets will be off in terms of bringing peace to a volatile world landscape — his reign of terror will unfurl like the mighty whipping, beating tail of a dragon as all those upon the earth become victims of his fierce cruelty.

Revelation 13:18 goes on to say, "Here is wisdom. Let him that hath understanding count the number of the beast: for it is the number of a man; and his number is six hundred threescore and six." It's not just the stuff of fairy tales and urban legends — the Bible actually states that the mathematical equivalent of the Antichrist's name will be *666*.

There's Still Much We Don't Know

In past decades, there has been a lot of speculation about what the "mark of the beast" is and what the number 666 means. Some have speculated that the Social Security card, other identity cards, credit cards, computer chips, and even vaccines were the mark of the beast.

Such speculation has put believers into unneeded fear about these things. The reason I say "unneeded fear" is, the mark of the beast will not be implemented until *after* the rapture of the Church. There may be precursory types or "forerunners" of the mark of the beast — in fact, some of the aforementioned items could indeed be prototypes.

But just as the identity of the Antichrist will only be revealed after the rapture of the Church, the name of the beast and his mark — that is, the Antichrist' name and the meaning of the numeric equation 666 — will not be understood completely until the Antichrist appears. Those who fixate on questions on this topic waste their time playing a guessing game.

If one genuinely receives Christ as Lord and Savior, he is sealed with the Holy Spirit and will be raptured when the Church is removed. This is the reason why there is no need for an authentic Christian who's walking with God to fear the mark of the beast. The Church will be long gone when the Antichrist issues the mandate that every person living in the sophisticated world receive this damning mark.

The Holy Spirit will be mightily active during the seven-year Tribulation period when there will be a great harvest of souls as a result of 144,000 Jewish preachers from all 12 tribes of Israel who will be sealed and anointed by God to preach the Gospel of the Kingdom.

The Role of the Holy Spirit During the Tribulation — Will He Be Present on the Earth During That Time?

The Holy Spirit will be mightily active during the seven-year Tribulation period when there will be a great harvest of souls as a result of 144,000 Jewish preachers from all 12 tribes of Israel who will be sealed and anointed by God to preach the Gospel of the Kingdom (*see* Revelation 7:4-8). The fact that these Jews will be "sealed" means they will belong to God, they will have His special protection, and they will be divinely empowered to preach during the Tribulation.

We read in Romans 11:26 and 27 that a day is coming when Israel will be saved, and these 144,000 Jewish preachers will call Israel to repentance — and as Revelation 7:9 (*NIV*) says, "a great multitude that no man could number of all nations, and tribes, and kindreds, and people, and tongues" will come to faith in Christ as a result of their preaching.

Both anointed preaching and genuine conversion require the work of the Holy Spirit. First, the work of the Holy Spirit is required for a sinner to see that he is a sinner in need of salvation. Before that happens, it is amazing how long that same sinner can live without conviction or sorrow for his behavior and lifestyle, almost numb to any sense of the wrongness concerning his actions or his life.

The Bible says that sin makes people hardhearted, spiritually blind, and past feeling (*see* Ephesians 4:18-19). Add this to the fact that they are spiritually dead and therefore unable to respond to God, and you will better understand why lost people can do what they do over and over again, often with no sense of conviction.

But all these factors change instantaneously when the Holy Spirit touches the human soul and exposes its sinful condition. A sinner feels exposed, naked, embarrassed, and confronted when the Holy Spirit wakes him up to his real spiritual condition. This is why the preaching of the Cross is so invaluable — without it, men and women will remain "unawakened" to their condition, doomed to a sinner's hell.

And this is, likewise, why repentance is such a gift. What a divine privilege it is to be alerted by the Holy Spirit that a course of action and lifestyle is wrong and will ultimately lead to a reckoning that no one in his or her right mind would want to experience! And it's no wonder that the enemy has caused some believers to feel nearly apologetic about speaking the truth in love to those who are lost that hell, like Heaven, is a real place.

In John 16:8, Jesus spoke of this precious exposing work of the Holy Spirit. He told the disciples, "And when he [the Holy Spirit] is come, he will reprove the world of sin...."

Notice Jesus said the Holy Spirit would reprove the world of sin. The word "reprove" is the Greek word *elegcho*, which means *to expose*, *to convict*, or *to cross-examine for the purpose of conviction*, as when convicting a lawbreaker in a court of law. In this case, it is the image of a lawyer who brings forth evidence that is indisputable and undeniable. The accused person's actions are irrefutably brought to light and, as a result, the offender is exposed and convicted as the law demands.

This tells us that by the time the Holy Spirit is finished dealing with a lost, sinful soul, the unsaved person will feel exposed and convicted. As the Holy Spirit enables him to hear the Word of God for the first time, that Word is so razor sharp that it penetrates his soul until he feels as if he has been cross-examined on a witness stand. Finally, the court is adjourned, the verdict is announced, and he is declared guilty. But amazingly and miraculously, once this convicting call has been issued and the sinner renders the correct response, that same Holy Spirit power woos that person toward the love of Christ, who alone has the power to remit the guilt of the person's sin and judgment and, by the power of His own blood, to exact a new verdict of "NOT GUILTY"!

John 16:8 in the Greek expresses this idea about the "convicting" work of the Holy Spirit: "But when He [the Holy Spirit] is come, He will present such convincing evidence about the world's sin that, once convinced by the Spirit's work, the entire world will stand guilty and convicted — so exposed that they will feel they have nowhere to hide from the facts...."

A major part of the work of the Holy Spirit is to convict sinners of their lost condition — that is the first step in drawing someone to the saving knowledge of Jesus Christ. The whole world stands guilty before God (*see* Romans 3:19), but until the Holy Spirit does His convicting work, the world doesn't realize it is guilty. That is why this special "convicting" work of the Spirit is so essential. Without it, mankind would remain comfortable in its sin and eternally lost — but as the Holy Spirit convicts, man becomes aware of his sinful condition and his need for God.

Jesus taught, "No man can come to me, except the Father which hath sent me draw him..." (John 6:44). No one argues that God draws us to Him through the work of the Holy Spirit. Jesus reminded us of this when He said, "And when he is come, he will reprove the world of sin..." (John 16:8). It is just a fact that without the work of the Holy Spirit to expose our sinful condition, we would still be in darkness today, eternally lost and without God.

The Bible says that the lost person is "dead in trespasses and sins" (Ephesians 2:1). How can you make a dead man see or feel? How can you convince a dead man that he needs to change?

It is impossible for a dead man to respond because, naturally speaking, dead people don't feel anything. They especially don't feel the conviction of sin. It requires a special, supernatural work of the Holy Spirit to rouse the human consciousness to its sinful condition. It is the Holy Spirit's call that touches the soul and awakens the person to his sinfulness. Once brought to this place of undeniable conviction where one recognizes that he is a sinner, the Holy Spirit then beckons him to come to repentance. In that divine moment, the human soul hears Him say, "...Awake thou that sleepest, and arise from the dead, and Christ shall give thee light" (Ephesians 5:14).

Without the supernatural work of the Holy Spirit, no sinner is able to see the truth. But when the Holy Spirit's convicting work begins, the sinner's eyes begin to be opened to his true spiritual condition and there is no escape from the facts of his or her lost state. Because people will be saved during the Tribulation as a result of the preaching of the 144,000 sealed Jewish preachers, we know the Holy Spirit most definitely *must* and will be present in the earth during that time frame.

There will be two end-time prophetic witnesses that God will speak through during the Great Tribulation. For these two witnesses to carry out their supernatural prophetic ministry, it will require the work of the Holy Spirit — another evidence that the Holy Spirit will continue His work on Earth during the time of the Tribulation.

THE TWO WITNESSES

In Revelation chapter 11, we additionally read of two end-time prophetic witnesses whom God will speak through during the Great Tribulation. These prophets will be endued with such supernatural powers that the Bible says no one will be able to stand against them until a time comes when "the beast" (*see* Revelation 11:7) will kill them, after which their bodies will lay in the streets visible to the entire viewing world. On the third day, they will be raised from the dead (*see* Revelation 11:11), and they will ascend into Heaven (*see* v. 12).

The Bible never tells us explicitly who these two end-time prophets are, but scholars have alleged them either to be Moses and Elijah or Enoch and Elijah — *or* that God will raise up two previously unknown end-time believers to be His prophetic voices during the time of the Great Tribulation.

Some speculate these witnesses to be Moses and Elijah because of the nature of the miracles they will perform, which will be so similar to the miracles that accompanied their prophetic ministries in the Old Testament. Others speculate this will be Enoch and Elijah because neither of them ever tasted physical death, as they were miraculously taken into Heaven. Those who speculate the two witnesses are Enoch and Elijah say that God will perhaps dispatch them to the earth to continue their work during the time of the Great Tribulation.

But for these two prophets to accomplish such supernatural prophetic ministry will require the work of the Holy Spirit, and this is another evidence that the person, power, and work of the Holy Spirit will continue during the time of the Tribulation.

This masterpiece of biblical art shows the Antichrist waging war against anyone who refuses to fall in line to take his mark or to worship him. He will especially target the saints who are saved as a result of the preaching of the 144,000 Jewish preachers. But as hard as he tries to destroy them, he will not be able to destroy or take their faith.

The Antichrist Will Wage War Against the Tribulation Saints

Revelation 13:7 tells us that the Antichrist will wage war against the Tribulation saints. The Antichrist, whom the Bible calls the "beast," will literally wage war against anyone who refuses to fall in line to take his mark or to worship him — but he will especially target the saints who are saved as a result of the preaching of the 144,000 Jewish preachers. But as hard as he tries to destroy *them*, he will not be able to destroy or take *their faith*.

In Revelation 7:13-15, John told us that he saw those who were arrayed in white robes, and inquired as to who they were. It says, "And one of the elders answered, saying unto me, What are these which are arrayed in white robes? and whence came they? And I said unto him, Sir, thou knowest. And he said to me, These are they which came out of great tribulation, and have washed their robes, and made them white in the blood of the Lamb. Therefore are they before the throne of God, and serve him day and night in his temple: and he that sitteth on the throne shall dwell among them."

The verse informs us that many of them who will be saved during the Tribulation will lay down their lives for their faith. In Revelation 20:4, we find that multitudes of these

Tribulation saints will be *beheaded* for their faith. That verse says, "I saw the souls of them that were beheaded for the witness of Jesus, and for the word of God, and which had not worshipped the beast, neither his image, neither had received his mark upon their foreheads, or in their hands; and they lived and reigned with Christ a thousand years."

This illustration from Edward Jakob von Steinle,1860, shows the four horsemen of the Apocalypse who are a part of the Seven Seals of Judgment that will be released upon the earth. As these seals are broken, they will set off an escalating chain of catastrophic events, intensifying God's judgment and ultimately culminating in the devastating Bowl Judgments.

The Four Horsemen and the Great Tribulation

In Revelation 6:1-17, we discover that "four horses" will be released to gallop across the earth during the Tribulation. One will be a *white horse* that will bring *deception* to the nations and could possibly represent the Antichrist himself. Another will be a *red horse* that will bring *war* to the nations, and another is a *black horse* that will bring famine to the world. Last, there will be a *pale green horse* that will bring *sickness* and *death* to the world.

These Four Horsemen are part of the Seven Seals of Judgment that will be released by Jesus Himself. As these seals are broken, they will set off an escalating chain of catastrophic events, intensifying God's judgment and ultimately culminating in the devastating Bowl Judgments.

In Revelation 16:1-21, we read that Seven Bowls of Judgments will be poured out on the earth during the last portion of the Tribulation. When these are released, it will result in the most severe judgment and "wrath" that planet Earth has experienced in its entire history.

Just as the ten plagues of Egypt were intended to give Pharaoh and Egypt an opportunity to repent, which they rejected, these judgments will be performed as God's last wake-up call for the people of the earth to turn and to repent, which they also largely will not do.

- Revelation 16:2 says the *first bowl* will be poured out on the land, and a "noisome and grievous sore" will break out on those who received the mark of the beast and who worshipped his image. This will be a specific judgment that is targeted against those who have pledged their allegiance to the Antichrist. Knowing they are under judgment, people at large will nevertheless refuse to repent.
- Revelation 16:3 says the *second bowl* will be poured out on the sea and will turn all the water to "the blood of a dead man" and every living thing will die in the sea. Knowing they are under judgment, people will nevertheless refuse to repent.
- Revelation 16:4 and 5 says that when the *third bowl* is poured out, the rivers and freshwater springs and lakes will also be turned to blood. Knowing they are under judgment, people will nevertheless refuse to repent.
- Revelation 16:8 and 9 says the *fourth bowl* will be poured out to allow the sun to scorch people on the earth with fire. Knowing they are under judgment, people will nevertheless refuse to repent.
- Revelation 16:10 and 11 says when the *fifth bowl* will be poured out, it will cause the world to be hurled into utter darkness along with pain and suffering so intense that people will gnaw their tongues in agony. Knowing they are under judgment, people will nevertheless refuse to repent.
- Revelation 16:12 says the *sixth bowl* will be poured out upon the Euphrates River, at which time, it will dry up to make way for the kings of the East to march with their armies to their own destruction. When the river dries up, spirits will be released that are likened to frogs, and they will perform demonic signs and wonders to receive the leaders of the world and to lure them into the final battle at Armageddon.
- Revelation 16:17 says when the *seventh bowl* is poured out into the atmosphere, it will result in flashes of lightning and an earthquake larger than any earthquake that has ever taken place. This earthquake will be so huge that Jerusalem will be divided into three parts, the cities of the world will fall, islands will be flooded, mountains will disappear, and giant hailstones weighing more than 100 pounds each will fall on people.

Those washed in the blood of Jesus will gather around God's table to celebrate the Marriage Feast of the Lamb — an event that will last the entire seven years that the Tribulation is taking place on the earth.

WHAT HAPPENS IN HEAVEN DURING THE TRIBULATION ON EARTH?

While the four horses of the Apocalypse are galloping unhindered and unfettered across the earth and the seven seals, trumpets, and bowls of judgment are being poured out on the earth, wonderful events will be taking place in Heaven with the redeemed who are gathered there with Christ.

Revelation 19:6 says that the apostle John "heard as it were the voice of a great multitude, and as the voice of many waters, and as the voice of mighty thunderings, saying, Alleluia: for the Lord God omnipotent reigneth." Then John heard them say, "Let us be glad and rejoice, and give honour to him: for the marriage of the Lamb is come, and his wife hath made herself ready. And to her was granted that she should be arrayed in fine linen, clean and white: for the fine linen is the righteousness of saints. And he saith unto me, Write, Blessed *are* they which are called unto the marriage supper of the Lamb..." (vv. 7-9).

The word "supper" in verse 9 is translated from a form of the Greek word *deipnon*, which pictures *a banquet*, *a dinner*, *an evening meal*, or even *a festival* that was prepared for members of the community. Here, we see God's people, Jew and Gentile, who were washed in the blood of Jesus gathered around God's table to celebrate, and this feast will last the entire seven years that the Tribulation is taking place on the earth. All around the table will be the Old and New Testament saints along with every redeemed person who has lived since. Hardship will be past, and it will be a glorious time of celebration.

But concurrently, while the Marriage Feast of the Lamb is taking place, the "Judgment Seat of Christ" will also be taking place as every single believer who has ever lived will be summoned from the table to individually stand, one-by-one, before Christ to give an account for his life. Christ's individual attention to each believer will be so focused that it will take seven years for the entire process of each person taking his or her place before Christ for that review.

The Judgment Seat of Christ will be a place of evaluation of our obedience. On the basis of that evaluation, rewards will be given and our position of service in the Millennial Reign of Christ will be determined.

A Common Misunderstanding of 'the Judgment Seat of Christ'

One common misconception is that "the Judgment Seat of Christ" will be a time when we will stand before Jesus to give account for the sins we committed in our lives. People who think this are perhaps thinking about a separate judgment — the Great White Throne Judgment for the unbeliever, which we will come to in just a few paragraphs. But the Judgment Seat of Christ is not about giving account for sin, as we will also see.

When my wife and I were adolescents, each growing up in our respective churches, we were often terrified by preachers who said, "When you stand before the Judgment Seat of Christ, a movie is going to be projected that shows everything you ever did in your life. And in that moment, Christ, the angels, all your friends, and all your neighbors — absolutely everyone — will see every sin you ever committed and every mistake you ever made."

I remember as a young person thinking to myself, *I do NOT want to see that movie*. I don't know about you, but I wouldn't want a movie to ever be made about every wrong thing I did in my life!

Is that what *the Bible* says will happen at the Judgment Seat of Christ? No, it isn't. In fact, that is totally contrary to the teaching of Scripture. Why would God deal with us about sins that have been placed under the blood of Jesus? Romans 8:1 assures us, "There is therefore now no condemnation to them which are in Christ Jesus...." And First John 1:9 says God cleanses us from all unrighteousness when we repent and confess our sins to Him — He restores us just as if we never sinned.

When you stand before the Judgment Seat of Christ, it will not be for the purpose of rehearsing every sin you ever committed. Furthermore, God is not going to deal with you about sins you have confessed and that have been placed under the blood of Jesus, where those sins were remitted and eradicated. He will never bring up those sins to you again, not even at the Judgment Seat of Christ. He isn't going to say, "Excuse Me, but I'm going to reach into your past and extract from under the blood of Jesus every sin that has already been forgiven, and I'm going to deal with you about all those sins, anyway, in front of everyone."

Once your sin is placed under the blood of Jesus, it is under the blood of Jesus *forever*. If your sin has been confessed, repented of, and placed under the blood of Jesus, it means God has removed it as far as the east is from the west (*see* Psalm 103:12). Since east will always be east, and west will always be west — therefore the two, *east and west*, can never technically meet in an infinite space — you can be sure when God says Christ's blood removes confessed sin, *that sin is removed!* And He will never deal with you about it in eternity because that sin has become non-existent in the mind of God.

Then what is the Judgment Seat of Christ actually about?

The Judgment Seat of Christ is where Christ will deal with each of us personally about how we obeyed what Jesus asked us to do. It will be a place of *evaluation*, and on the basis of that evaluation, rewards will be given and our position of service in the Millennial Reign of Christ will be determined. At this very moment *in this life*, you are in a *qualification period* for the next age, and your present obedience is qualifying you for a very long period of service in His Kingdom during the Millennial Reign — and right on into eternity! (*See* 1 Corinthians 3:13-14; 2 Corinthians 5:10.)

But let's further explore what the Bible explicitly tells us about the Judgment Seat of Christ. The apostle Paul specifically referred to this future event twice in Scripture. The first instance is found in Romans 14:10,12 (*NKJV*), where he wrote, "…For we shall all stand before the judgment seat of God...so then each of us shall give account of himself to God."

Notice that Paul said, "We shall all *stand*...." The word "stand" comes from a Greek word which means *to stand*, not crawl or grovel. Thus, when we *stand* before the Judgment Seat of Christ, we will not grovel or be shamed for our past sin, for the Judgment Seat of Christ is not a place of shame, nor is it a place of embarrassment. We're going to "stand" upright on our feet before Christ at that moment, as those who are washed in His blood and robed in His righteousness.

This illustration shows a *bema* seat of judgment. This concept is taken from the Isthmian Games which were carried out in the ancient city of Isthmia in Greece. At these events, athletes competed for a reward under the careful scrutiny of judges who watched to make sure every rule of the contest was obeyed. After the games concluded, the victors came before a platform that was called the *bema* where the judge stood to place laurel crowns on the heads of those who had competed well and according to the rules.

WHAT IS THE '*BEMA*' OF GOD?

It is interesting to note that in the original Greek text, the word "judgment" does not appear in the text at all. Instead, the Greek text uses the word *bema*. If you were going to translate the sentence correctly, it would say, "We are going to stand before the *bema* of God." This word *bema* is so very important that you must understand what it means.

The word *bema* is taken from the *Isthmian Games* — athletic games that were carried out in the ancient city of Isthmia located on the Isthmus of Corinth in Greece. This event was held every other year, alternating with the *Olympic Games*, in which athletes competed for a reward under the careful scrutiny of judges who watched to make sure every rule of the contest was obeyed. The Isthmian Games were particularly famous for foot races.

After the games concluded, the victors came before a platform that was called the *bema*. This was the place where the judge stood to place laurel crowns on the heads of those who had competed well and according to the rules. Thus, the *bema* historically was a place of *evaluation* and *designation*, not a place where the losers were whipped or condemned.

By using the word *bema*, Paul, in essence, was saying that we are like competitors who are running a spiritual race. But unlike the Isthmian Games or other similar events, our race on Earth is not a competition with other runners. As Paul wrote in First Corinthians 9:24-25, we are running in obedience to the will of God for our own individual lives in order to obtain a heavenly prize. And just as victorious athletes of the Isthmian Games appeared before the *bema* to receive a physical reward, one day we will be brought before Jesus Christ's *bema* — the platform where He will be standing — and there Christ will evaluate our various levels of obedience and will designate what kind of reward we will receive.

Just as the ancient Greeks' *bema* was not a seat of punishment for those who lost the contests, the *bema* of Christ is also not a place of punishment for us as believers. When we stand before Jesus, He is not going to whip us or castigate us for our failures. Instead, it will be a place of evaluation where Christ will weigh and assess our works, our efforts, and our faith. It will also be a place of designation where He will determine the kind of reward that should be given to us for what we did in obedience to His plan.

One by one, when it comes our turn to stand before Christ, we will be summoned from the Marriage Feast of the Lamb. And once we have finished standing before Him to receive our *evaluation* and *designation*, we will joyously return to the table to continue the Marriage Supper celebration, having been acknowledged and rewarded for our level of obedience and adherence to God's plan on the earth.

The Bible says we will each give account of ourselves to God (*see* Romans 14:12), and the words "give account" are derived from a Greek word that means *to give a factual report*. This means when we stand before the Lord, He will require us to personally give a factual report of what we did and did not do in response to what He specifically called and asked each of us to do. Did we do what He asked us to do? Did we complete our role in the "games of the Kingdom" during our time on the earth? A factual report is in my future — and it is in your future as well.

In Second Corinthians 5:10, Paul wrote that *every single believer* will be summoned to stand before Christ for this event. Paul said, "For we must all appear before the *judgment seat* of Christ; that *every one* may *receive* the things done in his body, according to that he hath done, whether it be good or bad."

The phrase translated "judgment seat" in Second Corinthians 5:10 is again translated from the Greek word *bema*, and it once again refers to the future event when Jesus will evaluate the redeemed and designate the kind of reward that each of us is to receive. The words "every one" is a translation of the Greek word *hekastos*, which is *an all-inclusive word* that embraces *every single believer*.

This means every single believer is going to appear before the Judgment Seat of Christ to receive what is due to him according to what he has done — specifically, in obedience to Christ — in his walk on the earth.

Paul stated that every believer will "receive" according to what he has done in life. The word "receive" is a translation of the Greek word *komidzo*, which means *to receive what a person has coming to him*. If a believer has worked hard and done his best to carefully obey God's plan for his life, he will have a great reward coming to him. If he was careless where the will of God was concerned and *didn't* work very hard to obey God and do what He had called him to do, he may not have much reward coming to him, even though he is still saved and still seated around the table at the Marriage Feast of the Lamb.

At the Judgment Seat of Christ, each one of us — *all* of us — will individually stand before the righteous Judge, who will rightly determine whether we did on the earth what He called and instructed us to do, as well as judge us based on our motives and attitude with which we performed those tasks and assignments (*see* 2 Corinthians 5:10; 1 Corinthians 3:8-17).

But these two events — the Marriage Feast of the Lamb and the Judgment Seat of Christ — will occur concurrently in Heaven while the four horsemen of the Apocalypse gallop across the earth and seven seals, trumpets, and bowls of judgment are being emptied upon the planet. While wrath is being experienced on the earth, Heaven will experience a celebration as the redeemed gather around the table and rejoice about the rewards they have received and future assignments they've been designated to fulfill for the next phase that lies before them in the Millennial Reign of Christ.

Just as all the lights are turned off in a theatre before a theatrical performance is about to begin, God will cause all the universe to go dark to prepare for the glorious appearing of Jesus as He returns with ten thousands of His saints, who will accompany Him to rule and reign on the earth for 1,000 years. Jesus' coming will be so glorious that the Antichrist will be consumed by the glorious splendor of His coming.

Finally, Christ Will Come To Destroy the Antichrist and Set Up His Millennial Kingdom

When the seven-year Tribulation period ends and the Marriage Feast of the Lamb and the Judgment Seat of Christ concludes, it will signal that the time has come for Christ's Second Coming with "ten thousands" of His saints who will accompany Him to the earth (*see* Jude 14).

Matthew 24:29-31 says, "Immediately after the tribulation of those days shall the sun be darkened, and the moon shall not give her light, and the stars shall fall from heaven, and the powers of the heavens shall be shaken: and then shall appear the sign of the Son of man in heaven: and then shall all the tribes of the earth mourn, and they shall see the Son of man coming in the clouds of heaven with power and great glory."

Jesus declared that at the very conclusion of the seven-year Tribulation period, "the sun [shall] be darkened, and the moon shall not give her light, and the stars shall fall from heaven." Jesus was forecasting the conditions under which He will touch down upon the earth again in His Second Coming, along with His saints. Suddenly, all the lights will go out, and darkness will encompass the heavens and the earth. Then "shall appear the sign of the Son of man in heaven: and then shall all the tribes of the earth mourn, and they shall see the Son of man coming in the clouds of heaven with power and great glory"(vv. 30-31).

Just as all the lights are turned off in a theater before a theatrical performance is about to begin, God will cause all the universe to go dark to prepare for the glorious appearing of Jesus as He returns with ten thousands of His saints, who will accompany Him to rule and reign on the earth for 1,000 years.

Jude 14 and 15 refers to this event: "And Enoch also, the seventh from Adam, prophesied of these, saying, Behold, the Lord cometh with ten thousands of his saints, to execute judgment upon all, and to convince all that are ungodly among them of all their ungodly deeds which they have ungodly committed, and of all their hard *speeches* which ungodly sinners have spoken against him."

We saw in Chapter Three that in Second Thessalonians 2:8, Paul stated that when the Lord returns in His Second Coming, He "shall consume [the Antichrist] with the spirit of his mouth, and shall destroy with the brightness of his coming."

Thus, the subsequent event that will occur at the end of the seven-year Tribulation period will be Christ coming in His Second Advent to obliterate the Antichrist. In that moment, the Lord will open his mouth and speak — and when He does, so much power will be released that it will permanently remove the Antichrist from the world scene.

Although Satan will energize the Antichrist with demonic powers, this evil person won't have enough strength to withstand one puff from the mouth of the Lord. Paul additionally said that the Antichrist will be "destroyed with the brightness of his coming." Thus, Jesus' coming will be so glorious that it will take the Antichrist by surprise, and this evil world leader will be consumed by the splendor and glory of His coming.

Although we don't know the exact sequence of all the events that will ensue as this Tribulation period is wrapped up by Christ's Second Coming, I do know biblically that Jesus will finally place His feet upon the Mount of Olives exactly as the angels prophesied to the apostles in Acts 1:11. Watching Jesus ascend into Heaven from the Mount of Olives after He arose from the dead, the apostles were addressed by two angels, who appeared and said to them, "...Ye men of Galilee, why stand ye gazing up into heaven? this same Jesus, which is taken up from you into heaven, shall so come in like manner as ye have seen him go into heaven."

The prophet Zechariah also spoke of Christ's Second Coming when he wrote, "Behold, the day of the Lord cometh.... And his feet shall stand in that day upon the mount of Olives, which is before Jerusalem on the east..." (Zechariah 14:1,4).

Jesus will set up His Millennial Kingdom and will rule from Jerusalem for 1,000 years. Revelation 20:1-3 says, "And I saw an angel come down from heaven, having the key of the bottomless pit and a great chain in his hand. And he laid hold on the dragon, that old serpent, which is the Devil, and Satan, and bound him a thousand years, and cast him into the bottomless pit, and shut him up, and set a seal upon him, that he should deceive the nations no more, till the thousand years should be fulfilled: and after that he must be loosed a little season."

Revelation 20:9-10 says, "And they went up on the breadth of the earth, and compassed the camp of the saints about, and the beloved city: and fire came down from God out of heaven, and devoured them. And the devil that deceived them was cast into the lake of fire and brimstone, where the beast and the false prophet are, and shall be tormented day and night for ever and ever."

Prior To Being Thrown Into the Lake of Fire, Satan Will Be Free One Last Time

Thus, we see that for 1,000 years, Satan will be bound — and when he is bound, everything associated with Satan will vanish from the planet — including disease, sickness, and poverty. But then at the end of the 1,000 years, Satan will be released for "a little season" to try to deceive the nations one last time. Revelation 20:7 and 8 says, "And when the thousand years are expired, Satan shall be loosed out of his prison, and shall go out to deceive the nations which are in the four quarters of the earth, Gog, and Magog, to gather them together to battle: the number of whom is as the sand of the sea."

But Revelation 20:9 and 10 says that the fire of God will fall upon those gathered, and they will be cast into the lake of fire. It says, "And they went up on the breadth of the earth, and compassed the camp of the saints about, and the beloved city: and fire came down from God out of heaven, and devoured them. And the devil that deceived them was cast into the lake of fire and brimstone, where the beast and the false prophet are, and shall be tormented day and night for ever and ever."

Revelation 20:11-12 says, "And I saw a great white throne and him that sits on it, from whose face the earth and heaven fled away; and there was no place for them. And I saw the dead, small and great, stand before God; and the books were opened: and another book was opened, which is the book of life: and the *dead* were judged out of those things which were written in the books, according to their works."

'And I [John] Saw a Great White Throne, and Him Who Sat on It, From Whose Face the Earth and the Heaven Fled Away...'

Immediately after that, all the unsaved who have ever lived will be summoned to stand before the Great White Throne of Judgment, which is only for the ungodly, not for Christ's redeemed saints. Revelation 20:11-15 states:

And I saw a great white throne, and him that sat on it, from whose face the earth and the heaven fled away; and there was found no place for them. And I saw the dead, small and great, stand before God; and the books were opened: and another book was opened, which is the book of life: and the dead were judged out of those things which were written in the books, according to their works.

And the sea gave up the dead which were in it; and death and hell delivered up the dead which were in them: and they were judged every man according to their works. And death and hell were cast into the lake of fire. This is the second death. And whosoever was not found written in the book of life was cast into the lake of fire.

Every person is going to face a future time of reckoning — for saints, it will be appearing at Christ's Judgment Seat, or *bema*. For sinners, it will be appearing before God's White Throne Judgment. Therefore, it is critical for us to know the kind of judgment we will be facing one day, according to the choices we made during our time on the earth. The question every person must ask is, *What have I done with Jesus Christ? Have I embraced Him as the only acceptable Sacrifice for Sin — the Eternal Lamb of God that takes away the sin of the world?*

And if you've made Jesus the Savior and Lord of your life, it's important to also ask yourself the following:

- *Am I doing what He is asking me to do in this life?*
- *Am I doing the general will of God by obeying His Word, the Bible — and am I doing the specific will of God by following His leading?*
- *Am I seeking His plan so that I can willingly obey it? Or am I living life unto myself — fulfilling my own plans without regard for what the Lord desires for my life?*

The truth is, this temporal life is very short compared to eternity. Our time on the earth is the only time we have to correctly prepare for our future, individual time of reckoning. Once we breathe our last breath and step over from this side of the veil into eternity, there will be no more time remaining to make these crucial choices. Our decision will have been eternally made — and we will face a reckoning at the Judgment Seat, or *bema*, as a saint or at the Great White Throne as an eternally condemned sinner.

In Heaven, there is one book called, The Book of Life, that holds the names of all those who have put their faith in Jesus Christ. If a person is saved, his or her name is written in Heaven, and those whose names are found written in The Book of Life are going to go to Heaven.

God Is a Keeper of Records — Is Your Name Written in *The Book of Life*?

Notice that in Revelation 20:12, it says, "And I saw the dead, small and great, stand before God…." That phrase "small and great" means *everyone*, regardless of his or her status — all those who died outside of faith in Christ. Verse 12 continues, "…The books were opened: and another book was opened, which is the book of life…."

Here we find that God is a keeper of records and that there are books — *plural* — in Heaven. But notice there is one book called, *The Book of Life*. It is a book that holds the names of all those who have put their faith in Jesus Christ. Remember how Jesus answered the apostles when they said, "Lord, we have authority over demons in Your name!" (*see* Luke 10:17). Jesus replied, in effect, "Don't rejoice about that; instead, rejoice that your names are written in Heaven!" (*see* Luke 10:20). If a person is saved, his or her name is written in Heaven, and those whose names are found written in The Book of Life are going to go to Heaven.

Revelation 20:12 goes on to tell us what will happen to those whose names are not found in *The Book of Life*. They will be judged according to what is written about their works on the earth in the other books. Then in verse 15, it says, "And whosoever was not found written in the book of life was cast into the lake of fire." This is the irrevocable eternal destiny of every person who dies without Christ.

As you read this passage of Scripture, you may be tempted to grieve about your loved ones who have already died without Christ. That is a true tragedy, but don't let the devil get you fixated on something that has already happened that you cannot change. What God wants you to do is focus on everyone who is still alive whom you can potentially lead into His Kingdom!

The tragic reality is that there are many people who rejected Christ and are condemned to hell today, where they will suffer torment for all eternity. It hurts the heart and mind to think about these things, but they are a reality, nevertheless. We each need to make the decision that we will do our utmost to make sure no one else goes there! That's why we must share the message of Jesus Christ at every opportunity and use the rest of our time on this earth to rescue as many people as we can so they will not stand before the Great White Throne Judgment that will most surely take place at a future time.

We've been talking about the preparation every believer will undergo as he makes ready to meet the Lord face to face at the time of the Rapture. Once again, First John 3:3 says, "…Every man [person] that hath this hope in him purifieth himself, even as he is pure." Only a person full of faith that Christ is coming again, with a vision of Heaven in his heart, will devote his life to honoring the redemption that's found only in Him and the new birth that was wrought in that individual on the day he made Jesus his Lord.

But have you ever considered the fact that while Heaven is a real place — and we will one day live there as a reality that has been birthed in our heart — hell is *also* a real place? The reality of hell must also be fostered in the heart of believers because it is a fact that every day, people are dying, leaving this earth, and going there, where they will exist in eternal torment because they failed to embrace Christ as Lord while they lived.

The more we acknowledge the reality of hell, the more stirred we should feel to rescue those who are spiritually perishing at every opportunity we get to do so. If you don't feel that stirring as you know you should, why not ask the Holy Spirit to help ignite a holy fire in your heart to boldly speak the truth in love as the occasion arises — in the hopes of sparing others from experiencing the unholy flames of the dark, inescapable prison called hell.

There will eventually be a new Heaven and a new Earth, where righteousness dwells, and that will be permanently liberated from everything associated with the influence of Satan — including evil, death, sickness, and suffering — and the planet will finally be restored to what God originally intended.

A New Heaven and a New Earth

Immediately after seeing the Great White Throne Judgment, the apostle John continued his revelation of future events, writing, "And I saw a new heaven and a new earth: for the first heaven and the first earth were passed away; and there was no more sea. And I John saw the holy city, new Jerusalem, coming down from God out of heaven..." (Revelation 21:1-2).

When this event takes place, it will herald the rule of God into the endless ages. According to Second Peter 3:13, the new Heaven and new Earth will be "where righteousness dwells." The earth will be permanently liberated from everything associated with the influence of Satan — including evil, death, sickness, and suffering — and the planet will finally be restored to what God originally intended in the Garden of Eden.

In fact, Revelation 21:4 declares that every remnant of sorrow from the previous world will have been removed. It says, "And God shall wipe away all tears from their eyes; and there shall be no more death, neither sorrow, nor crying, neither shall there be any more pain: for the former things are passed away."

- Revelation 21:1 says in the new Heaven and new Earth there will be *no more sea.*
- Revelation 21:4 says in the new Heaven and new Earth there will be *no more death.*
- Revelation 21:4 says in the new Heaven and new Earth there will be *no more mourning.*
- Revelation 21:4 says in the new Heaven and new Earth there will be *no more weeping.*
- Revelation 21:4 says in the new Heaven and new Earth there will be *no more pain.*
- Revelation 22:3 says in the new Heaven and new Earth there will be *no more curse.*
- Revelation 22:5 says in the new Heaven and new Earth there will be *no more night.*

In Summary

In this chapter, I have attempted to provide you with an overview of the past, a survey of the present landscape, and a glimpse into the biblically forecasted future. Entire volumes have been written on each of these subjects, so please understand that this is a cursory view of this immense subject. However, I felt the need to paint an overview of where we *have been*; where we currently *are* and where we're imminently going as the Church; and where we *are heading* in the ages to come — ages that will surely come into view for all the world to see and, perhaps, sooner than we think.

In the following chapter, we will see what each person needs to do to ensure that his or her spiritual status is ready for the rapture of the Church when it takes place. Remember, Jesus said, "...When the Son of man cometh, shall he find faith on the earth?" (Luke 18:8).

When Christ returns, will He find on the earth religious "players" who have faltered in the faith and become apostatized? No doubt, this will be the case for a segment of the population who professes spirituality but has abandoned allegiance to God and the knowledge of Him. Or will Christ find on the earth those who are vigilant — those who are defending the faith that saved them, holding fast to the hope of Scripture, preaching the life-saving Gospel, and keeping the fires of the Spirit burning as they await His return?

Please keep reading, for this next chapter may be the most important part of the book.

QUESTIONS TO PONDER

1. In this chapter, Rick unpacks the term "last days" and explains the difference between the early and the latter rains mentioned in Joel 2. Can you see the connection between the natural and spiritual parallels of these rains? What else did you learn from this explanation?

2. While the United States and many other countries are currently open to the Gospel, it may feel like we have been living in a relatively peaceful time. Did you find it interesting to learn that the Church is actually in an "eye of a hurricane" part of the storm? What are some signs you've observed in society that the backside of that storm is beginning to reveal itself?

3. In the last days, there will be a remnant of the Church embroiled in a showdown that will occur between the powers of evil and the power of God — just as it did between Jannes and Jambres and Moses. Are you prepared to stand in the power of God should such a conflict arrive on your doorstep? If not, ask the Lord what you can do to build your faith and confidence if such a situation arises.

4. Did it surprise you to learn that it's not just up to you to convince a sinner they need Jesus because the Holy Spirit is the One who convicts? Since He is a partner with you in bringing the lost to salvation, how does this increase your confidence about sharing Jesus with others? Does it change the way you communicate the Gospel to those who are lost?

5. In this chapter, Rick explains what really takes place at the Judgment Seat of Christ. Were you relieved to read that it will be a place of reward rather than a place of condemnation? Romans 8:1 says that there is no condemnation for those who are in Christ Jesus. Does learning about the Judgment Seat strengthen your belief that the Lord is truly not holding your past sins against you?

Matthew 25:1-13

Then shall the kingdom of heaven be likened unto ten virgins, which took their lamps, and went forth to meet the bridegroom. And five of them were wise, and five were foolish. They that were foolish took their lamps, and took no oil with them: but the wise took oil in their vessels with their lamps. While the bridegroom tarried, they all slumbered and slept. And at midnight there was a cry made, Behold, the bridegroom cometh; go ye out to meet him. Then all those virgins arose, and trimmed their lamps. And the foolish said unto the wise, Give us of your oil; for our lamps are gone out. But the wise answered, saying, Not so; lest there be not enough for us and you: but go ye rather to them that sell, and buy for yourselves. And while they went to buy, the bridegroom came; and they that were ready went in with him to the marriage: and the door was shut. Afterward came also the other virgins, saying, Lord, Lord, open to us. But he answered and said, Verily I say unto you, I know you not. Watch therefore, for ye know neither the day nor the hour wherein the Son of man cometh.

CHAPTER TEN

YOUR SPIRITUAL STATE WILL DETERMINE YOUR FUTURE

Even before you read the nine chapters of this book so far, you no doubt had become aware in recent times that the landscape of society is being altered rapidly and a season is changing.

When I was a young man, the verse in which Jesus said that "men's hearts would fail them for fear" (*see* Luke 21:26) was a distant concept. But the more I study Scripture and the events surrounding the Rapture — which will signal the end of the Church Age and the beginning of the Tribulation — the more I understand that we are right near the end.

And as one would naturally prepare himself and his household for a dangerous storm that's brewing, we as believers must not neglect the signs of the times, nor the warnings of the Holy Spirit that are eminently resounding as we catapult toward the conclusion of a long era in history. Scripture gives an admonition to continually heed throughout our lives: "...It is high time to awake out of sleep: for now is our salvation nearer than when we believed" (Romans 13:11).

A Long Era Won't Last Forever

In his fabulous book *They Lied to You About the Rapture*, my friend Alan DiDio writes:

> **The question of whether we are living in the last days has captivated a substantial segment of the U.S. population, reflecting a deep-seated curiosity both about the future and the end times. Consider these striking statistics:**
>
> - **4 in 10 adults believe humanity is living in the end times.**
> - **55 percent are convinced that Jesus will return someday.**
> - **29 percent of individuals from non-Christian religions share the belief that we are in the end times.**
> - **23 percent of non-religious adults think we are experiencing end-time conditions.**
> - **9 percent of atheists and 14 percent of agnostics also entertain the idea that we are living in the end times.**
>
> **The Pew Research Center highlights this widespread interest, underscoring a collective sense that something significant is unfolding in the world around us.**[1]

These statistics show there is an epic awareness among Christians, unbelievers, and even among atheists that we are living in the very last of the last days.

This widespread awareness reminds us of the need to make sure those we know and love are ready for what is coming, but it should also cause us to look at our own heart to see if we are really loving and longing and yearning for our Lord Jesus Christ and His coming (*see* 2 Timothy 4:8) — in other words, for the rapture of the Church.

In fact, let's look at Second Timothy 4:8, which the apostle Paul wrote at the end of his life and ministry on the earth. This verse says, "Henceforth there is laid up for me a crown of righteousness, which the Lord, the righteous judge, shall give me at that day: and not to me only, but unto all them also that love his appearing."

Earlier in Paul's ministry, as we read in First Thessalonians 4:15 and 17, he clearly wrote that Jesus is coming for those who are "alive" at the time of His coming. As we saw previously, that word "alive" is translated from the words *hoi zoontoi*, a plural form of the Greek word *zao*, and it pictures those who are *spiritually living, spiritually robust, spiritually thriving, spiritually vibrant, and spiritually vigorous*. This means Christ is coming for those who are spiritually *engaged*.

Each one of us who have called on Jesus' name must ask ourselves the question, *Do I fall into this category of a spiritually engaged one who is keeping my heart alive and burning as I eagerly await the Lord's returning?*

Christ's Coming and the Parable of the Ten Virgins

This brings to mind the passage in Matthew 25 in which Jesus describes ten virgins, five of whom had oil in their lamps and were ready for the arrival of the bridegroom — and another five who were not ready for the bridegroom's arrival. In this parable, the second set of five virgins ran out of oil in their lamps before the bridegroom arrived, and as a result, they were barred from entering the long-awaited marriage celebration.

It is difficult to form doctrine on the parable of the ten virgins or on any one scripture or passage without the corroboration of other verses. But scholars generally agree — and the passage also compares this allegory with the coming of the Son of Man — that this parable speaks of Christ's coming. And the content of the passage gives a clear warning of the need to be spiritually alive, alert, and prepared at the time of His coming for the Church.

As such, the Church is represented as the virgins — and Christ, as the bridegroom. According to the parable, five virgins are wise and five virgins are unwise. This should alert us that there are various types of people in the Church — some who will be ready for His arrival and others who will not be ready to meet the Bridegroom at His promised coming.

I don't often teach on this subject, and some ministers refuse to touch it in their pulpits for various reasons. Again, I state that it is difficult to form doctrine on the basis of the parable of the ten virgins. Nevertheless, this passage without doubt sends a *warning* of our need to be diligent and to do all that is necessary to be ready for Christ when He returns for His Church. It is imperative that we hear Christ's warning in this parable and take it deeply to our hearts.

Let's look at this parable in Matthew 25:1-13 in its entirety.

Then shall the kingdom of heaven be likened unto ten virgins, which took their lamps, and went forth to meet the bridegroom. And five of them were wise, and five were foolish.

They that were foolish took their lamps, and took no oil with them: but the wise took oil in their vessels with their lamps. While the bridegroom tarried, they all slumbered and slept. And at midnight there was a cry made, Behold, the bridegroom cometh; go ye out to meet him. Then all those virgins arose, and trimmed their lamps.

While the bridegroom tarried, they all slumbered and slept. And at midnight there was a cry made, Behold, the bridegroom cometh; go ye out to meet him. Then all those virgins arose, and trimmed their lamps.

And the foolish said unto the wise, Give us of your oil; for our lamps are gone out. But the wise answered, saying, Not so; lest there be not enough for us and you: but go ye rather to them that sell, and buy for yourselves. And while they went to buy, the bridegroom came; and they that were ready went in with him to the marriage: and the door was shut.

Afterward came also the other virgins, saying, Lord, Lord, open to us. But he answered and said, Verily I say unto you, I know you not. Watch therefore, for ye know neither the day nor the hour wherein the Son of man cometh.

The word "virgins" in Matthew 25:1 is an interpretation of the Greek word *parthenos*, and it is a word that pictures simply *a virgin*. The noted Bible scholar, Albert Barnes, states that these virgins represent the Church and are intended to picture Christ's intent to come for a Church that, like a virgin, is pure and holy.[2]

Notice in the parable all ten virgins — the wise and the unwise — had "lamps" with them. The word "lamps" is translated from the plural version of the Greek word *lampas*, which depicts *an oil-based lamp with a long wick that could burn all night if it had sufficient oil*. The fact that these virgins carried such lamps suggests the virgins were ready to wait a long time *if* necessary. Such lamps were hollowed in their construction to contain oil, and they were often carried elevated on poles so that they could provide greater light. Because in Jewish culture, the marriage event usually started at night, such lamps were needed to provide light for the bridegroom's arrival at the ceremony's venue.

In the parable of the ten virgins, both the wise and the unwise virgins had "lamps." Because in Jewish culture, the marriage event usually started at night, such lamps were needed to provide light for the bridegroom's arrival at the ceremony's venue. The ceremony occurred in phases, and the exact timing of the bridegroom's arrival was not always known, making it needful for those who were waiting to have enough oil to provide light until the bridegroom finally arr ved.

The ceremony occurred in phases, and the exact timing of the bridegroom's arrival was not always known,[3] so it was needful for those who were waiting to have enough oil to provide light *until* the bridegroom finally arrived.

Matthew 25:1 tells us that each of the ten virgins went forth to meet the bridegroom. The word "meet" is interpreted from a form of the Greek word *hupantesis*, which is a word that typically depicts *a grand encounter*. It is reminiscent of Paul's words in First Thessalonians 4:17 where he wrote, "Then we which are alive and remain shall be caught up together with them in the clouds, *to meet* the Lord in the air...."

The word "meet" in verse 17 is interpreted from a different form of the same Greek word in Matthew 25:1, which also pictures *a grand encounter* or *a royal or VIP reception*. It describes *the reception of a newly arrived official or of newly arrived royalty*. When such individuals arrived at an event, the red carpet was rolled out and they were given a VIP reception. Paul understood the usage of this word, and he used it to tell us that when we meet Jesus in the air, Christ will roll out the red carpet to give us a VIP reception!

However, notice from the passage in Matthew 25 that all ten virgins, with their lamps, went forth early to meet the bridegroom. It suggests they anticipated the bridegroom's arrival much sooner than it actually occurred. In this parable, the bridegroom, who represents Christ, came to those gathered for the festivities significantly later than was first anticipated.

The word "bridegroom" is from the Greek word *numphios*, and it means simply *a bridegroom*. In the New Testament, this word metaphorically refers to Jesus Christ as the Bridegroom of the Church. But it is interesting to note that in Jewish weddings, the bridegroom was responsible for going to prepare a place for his bride before he returned to take her to their new home. This is exactly why Jesus said in John 14:2 and 3, "In my Father's house are many mansions: if it were not so, I would have told you. I go to prepare a place for you. And if I go and prepare a place for you, I will come again, and receive you unto myself; that where I am, there ye may be also."

As the Bridegroom of the Church, Christ likewise went away to prepare a place for the Church. Since the time He ascended to Heaven nearly 2,000 years ago, He has been preparing a place, and one day soon He will come again to receive us unto Himself!

Five Were Wise and Five Were Foolish

In Matthew 25:2, we find that five virgins were "wise" and five virgins were "foolish." The word "foolish" is translated from the plural form of the Greek word *moros*, a word that depicts one who is *dense*, *dull*, or *slow*. It portrays a person who is *foolish* and therefore *a fool*. On the other hand, the word "wise" is from the plural form of the Greek word *phronimos*, a word that pictures one who is *intelligent* and therefore considered to be *wise*. These two categories are intended to represent two types of people. First, the unwise virgins represent people who are spiritually dense, dull, or slow. Second, the wise virgins represent people who are spiritually intelligent, fully engaged in their faith, and therefore wise in the way they live as they await the Lord's return.

But Matthew 25:3 tells us, "They that were foolish took their lamps, and took *no* [extra] oil with them." The word "no" is a translation of the Greek word *ouk,* which is the strongest form of no in the Greek language. Here it is meant to stress that the five foolish virgins completely failed to do what was necessary to have "oil" to last *until* the bridegroom finally arrived, and it implies they knew that only those with oil and light would be admitted to the wedding celebration.

Matthew 25:3 also tells us, "*But* the wise took oil in their vessels with their lamps." The word "but" is a translation of the Greek word *de*, which leads the reader to *contrast*. It means, "But on the other hand, the wise, or intelligent virgins, took oil in their vessels with their lamps." The word "oil" is interpreted from the word *elaion*, a word that describes *olive oil*, which typically is used in Scripture to picture *the Holy Spirit*.

However, Jesus states in this parable that in addition to taking the oil that had been poured into their lamps early on, the wise virgins knew to bring an extra supply of oil with them in case the bridegroom's arrival came later than anticipated. They were prepared with a supply large enough to last however much time was needed until the bridegroom finally appeared. On the other hand, the foolish virgins only took a short supply of oil — not enough to last until the arrival of the bridegroom.

The fact that all ten virgins slumbered, alerts us that the bridegroom "tarried" and actually came much later than any one of them initially anticipated. The word "tarried" means *to delay*, *to linger*, or *to tarry*, and it lets us know that the bridegroom took much longer to arrive than the ten virgins had originally anticipated.

The Bridegroom Tarried and the Virgins Slept

Matthew 25:5 then says, "While the bridegroom *tarried*, they all *slumbered* and slept." The fact that they *all* slumbered and they *all* slept alerts us that the bridegroom's arrival came much later than any one of them initially anticipated.

But this verse tells us that the bridegroom "tarried." The word "tarried" is from a form of the Greek word *chronidzo*, which means *to delay*, *to linger*, or *to tarry*, and it speaks of one who takes a longer time than anticipated to do something.

In Chapter Six, I wrote about Peter's words that say God is not slow concerning His promise to us that Christ will return (*see* 2 Peter 3:9). If His return is "slower," or longer in coming, than anticipated, it's because God is waiting for that last sinner to repent and come to Christ as his Savior so he can escape the eternal judgment of hell.

James alluded to this as well with his own words: "Be patient therefore, brethren, unto the coming of the Lord. Behold the husbandman waiteth for the precious fruit of the earth, and hath long patience for it, until he receive the early and latter rain [with its ensuing harvest]" (James 5:7).

Although it doesn't give a reason why, according to Matthew 25, the bridegroom *was*, in fact, delayed, and all ten of the virgins became weary and "slumbered." The word "slumbered" is translated from a form of the word *nustadzo*, which is a word that describes *drowsiness, sleepiness, tiredness*, or *weariness*. Metaphorically, "slumbered" is used to picture those who waited and waited for the Lord's soon arrival, but because it took longer than expected, they may have grown weary and fallen into a state of slumber — or indifference, or even hostility and scorn — because His coming did not occur as soon as they expected.

A Cry Is Made and the Bridegroom's Approaching Is Announced

Finally in Matthew 25:6, we read, "And at midnight there was a cry made, Behold, the bridegroom cometh; go ye out to meet him." The words "at midnight" in the original Greek text say *in the very middle of the night* and imply *the very darkest moment of the night*. This idea agrees with the Greek word *harpadzo*, which is translated "caught away" in First Thessalonians 4:17, and it is where we derive the idea of the Rapture. As we have seen, the Greek word depicts *a catching away just in the nick of time*, and it strongly suggests that the rapture of the Church will occur *in a very dark moment*.

But in our parable, the bridegroom's arrival is finally announced, and Matthew 25:6 says all ten virgins went forth to "meet" him. The word "meet" is interpreted from a form of the Greek word *apantesis*, which depicts *an encounter* or *a meeting*. This is very reminiscent of First Thessalonians 4:17, which uses another form of the same Greek word, as Paul declared, "Then we which are alive and remain shall be caught up together with them in the clouds, *to meet* the Lord in the air…."

The words "to meet" in First Thessalonians 4:17 are interpreted from a Greek word that pictures *a grand encounter* or *a royal or VIP reception*. It was a word that specially described the reception of a newly arrived official or newly arrived royalty. As noted in Chapter One, in history, when such individuals arrived, the red carpet was rolled out and they were given a VIP reception. The apostle Paul understood the usage of this word when he applied it here to tell us that when we meet Jesus in the air, He is going to roll out the red carpet to give us a grand and glorious VIP reception!

Interestingly, in Matthew 25:6, the word "meet" implies a "clamouring about" as the bridegroom's approaching is announced. Again, without formulating doctrine based on one word or verse in Scripture, I wonder if we're not already in a phase of the soon-to-come "marriage celebration" as ministers and laymen alike in the Church are excitedly waking up those who are sleeping, exuberantly announcing that the Bridegroom is soon approaching!

All ten virgins arose and inspected their lamps to see how much oil remained. When the unwise virgins realized they were depleted of oil as they awaited the bridegroom's arrival, they implored the wiser virgins to share their oil with them lest they miss the marriage celebration.

At the Midnight Hour, They Trimmed Their Lamps

In the parable we're studying in Matthew 25, at about midnight, or in the darkest moment of the night, suddenly, all ten virgins clearly understood the announcement that the time had finally come for the bridegroom to arrive. Matthew 25:7 says that in response to His approaching arrival, "all those virgins arose, and trimmed their lamps."

The word "trimmed" is interpreted from a form of the Greek word *kosmeo*, which means *to put in order*. To put their lamps in order, they had to look into their lamps to see how much oil remained. If the oil was depleted, it meant they needed to refill their lamps.

The time to meet the bridegroom had finally arrived, so all ten virgins inspected their lamps to get things in order for the bridegroom's long-awaited arrival.

But after the foolish virgins realized their lamps had run dry and they didn't have an additional supply with which to refill them, Matthew 25:8 tells us that "the foolish said unto the wise, Give us of your oil; for our lamps are gone out." The words "gone out" mean *to extinguish* and picture something *depleted* or that has *run dry*.

Thus, the foolish virgins showed such a lack of diligence and forethought that they completely ran out of oil. Although the foolish virgins *appeared* to be ready because they carried lamps, their lamps ran dry because they had not made preparations to bring sufficient oil to refill them in the event the bridegroom's arrival was delayed.

Matthew 25:9 tells us the unwise virgins pleaded with the wise virgins to share their oil with them, but the wise answered, saying, "...Not so; lest there be not enough for us and you: but go ye rather to them that sell, and buy for yourselves."

In response, the foolish virgins left their posts and went away to see if they could quickly find more oil. But Matthew 25:10 says, "And while they went to buy, the bridegroom came; and they that were ready went in with him to the marriage: and the door was shut."

Matthew 25:10 says the wise virgins — those who'd made sure they had enough oil to replenish their lamps — were "ready" and went in with the bridegroom to the marriage celebration. The word "ready" is translated from a form of the Greek word *hetoimos*, which is a word that depicts a state of *readiness* or *preparedness*. It portrays a person so *diligent* that he has exercised *forethought*, which resulted in the condition of being ready. The use of this word means the wise virgins had exercised enough forethought to ensure they had enough oil *even if* the bridegroom's coming was later than initially expected.

The Early New Testament Church as a whole lived in a state of fiery readiness and fervent expectation of Christ's return. That state of spiritual readiness empowered them to, by the power of the Holy Spirit, turn the world "upside down" in their generations. God is stirring the current New Testament Church to a similar state of readiness in preparation for a move of His Spirit that has the potential to turn this evil age on edge as many are gloriously swept into the Kingdom.

The wise virgins went with the bridegroom into the wedding, and it was a joyous event. But once they were admitted, "the door was shut," and when the other unwise virgins arrived, they were prohibited from entering the festivities.

The Wise Went With Him to the Wedding — and the Door Was Shut

Matthew 25:10 says the wise virgins "went in with him to the wedding." The word "wedding" is from a form of the word *gamos*, a word that pictures *the joyous celebration of a wedding*. But verse 10 says that once they were admitted, "the door was shut."

The word "shut" is translated from a form of the Greek word *kleio,* which means *to lock shut*. It is a fact that in Jewish wedding celebrations of ancient times, once the door was closed and locked shut, no latecomers were granted entrance.[4] For the virgins who were unprepared in this parable, the penalty was severe, but they knew full well that having oil in their lamps was a requirement to be admitted to the wedding. So while this penalty is severe, it was fully known to them that if they had no oil in their lamps when the bridegroom arrived, they would not be admitted.

Thus, the five virgins called *wise* were so named because they were diligent to make sure they carried enough oil for a longer period of waiting. The five virgins called *foolish* were so named because of a lack of diligence, resulting in their running out of oil before the bridegroom arrived. When the bridegroom finally arrived, *only* the wise virgins were ready and therefore invited to join the celebration.

Although the unwise virgins pounded on the door and pleaded to be admitted, it was too late, for the door was closed and locked shut, and no latecomers were to be granted entrance. Twice the unwise virgins cried out, "Lord, lord," but the bridegroom answered them, "I do not know you."

'I Know You Not'

Matthew 25:11 says after the door was shut and it was too late to be admitted to the wedding celebration, the other unprepared virgins cried out at the door, "...Lord, Lord, open to us."

The word "open" is a word that signifies the opening of a door to allow *access*. So even though they had failed to be ready on time, the foolish virgins somehow wrongly assumed that the bridegroom would nevertheless have mercy on them, overlook their lack of diligence, override the already stated conditions for entry, and open the door for them.

This verse says they cried out, *"Lord, lord!"* This is a translation of the Greek word *Kurie* or *kurie* and is *verbatim* the same exact word found in Matthew 7:21-23, "Not every one that saith unto me [Jesus], Lord, Lord, shall enter into the kingdom of heaven; but he that doeth the will of my Father which is in heaven. Many will say to me in that day, Lord, Lord, have we not prophesied in thy name? and in thy name have cast out devils? and in thy name done many wonderful works? And then will I profess unto them, I never knew you: depart from me, ye that work iniquity."

Likewise, in Matthew 25:12, the bridegroom answers the five foolish virgins, "...Verily I say unto you, I know you not." The word "verily" is *a firm statement of fact.* The word "not" is translated from the Greek word *ouk*, the most emphatic form of the word *no* or *not*. The word "know" is interpreted from the Greek word *oida*, and it means *to know by personal experience.*

Notice that twice the unwise virgins called the bridegroom, "Lord, lord," but in the parable, he answered that he had no personal connection with them and did not know them. Even though they "appeared" to be virgins like the others, there was something inwardly so defective about them that the bridegroom — which we know from verse 13 is a reference to Christ Himself — did not recognize them at all.

'Watch Therefore'!

Finally in Matthew 25:13, Jesus finalizes this parable by warning: "Watch therefore, for ye know neither the day nor the hour wherein the Son of man cometh."

At last, Jesus explains that the entire parable is about His coming for those who are waiting for Him with "oil in their lamps" — *prepared and ready*. And Christ's final declaration in His parable is that it is imperative that we respond to this message by determining to stay alert and to "watch therefore" for the arrival of "the Son of Man."

The word "watch" is from the Greek word *gregoreo*, and it depicts *one on high alert* or *one whose attitude is to never let up in being attentive, watchful, and wide awake*. Then Jesus states the reason we must be watchful: "...Ye know neither the day nor the hour wherein the Son of man cometh." The word "neither" is *ouk*, which we now know is the strongest form of *no* or *not*. As it is used here, it means you emphatically do not know and cannot know "the *day*" or "the *hour*" when He will finally come.

Even if we sense we are in the season of the Lord's coming, it is not possible to pinpoint the exact day or exact hour when Christ will descend into the lower atmosphere to snatch away His people to Himself.

The word "day" in this verse refers to *a specific day*, and the word "hour" refers to *an exact hour*. This means that even if we sense we are in the season of the Lord's coming, it is not possible to pinpoint the exact day or exact hour when Christ will descend into the lower atmosphere to snatch away His people to Himself.

I want you to understand from this parable that Jesus knew His coming would come later than many in the Church ever expected. Even the Early Church thought Christ would return at any time and lived their lives fervently — engaged and spiritually alive — according to that belief and blessed hope.

And according to this parable, some of those who are living on the earth at the time of His coming will be spiritually wise and diligent all the way to the very end and will joyously be caught away, at which time they will be admitted to the Marriage Feast of the Lamb. And those who have gone before them in time — *all the way back to the very first Christians* — will be resurrected first as "the righteous dead" as Jesus fulfills His promise *exactly* and gathers His own for a grand, heavenly celebration!

But this parable makes us ask if it's possible that there will be those who are found errant in their faith and will be "locked out" of the Marriage Feast of the Lamb? Second-guessing on this question is too serious, and failing to be ready is a serious misgiving and price to pay. Thus, we *must* respond to the Parable of the Ten Virgins as a divine admonition to "be holy even as He is holy" (*see* 1 Peter 1:15-16) — to walk closely with Him in a constant state of readiness for any moment that the Lord will come.

He *will* come "as a thief in the night" (*see* 1 Thessalonians 5:2; 2 Peter 3:10) — "at any moment." We must determine to continually have a full supply of oil in our lamps, maintaining the fires of the Spirit in our hearts that burned so brightly when we first believed.

Because I feel responsible to the Lord in the position He has given me, I must state again that while it is difficult to form doctrine from the Parable of the Ten Virgins, we are to take this parable as a sober admonition to be waiting, watching, and ready for the Lord's return.

Jesus Is Coming for Those Who Are Ready and Are Watching for His Return

There are many scriptures that tell us Jesus is coming for those who are ready — for those who are looking for and eagerly awaiting His return. The following are some of those verses.

- Matthew 24:42 says, "*Watch therefore*: for ye know not what hour your Lord doth come."
- Matthew 25:6,13 says, "And at midnight there was a cry made, Behold, the bridegroom cometh.... *Watch therefore*, for ye know neither the day nor the hour wherein the Son of man cometh."
- Mark 13:35-37 says, "*Watch ye therefore*: for ye know not when the Master of the house cometh, at even, or at midnight, or at the cockcrowing, or in the morning:

Lest coming suddenly He find you sleeping. And what I say unto you I say unto all, *Watch*."

- Luke 12:37 says, "Blessed are those servants, whom the lord when He cometh *shall find watching....*"
- Luke 12:40 says, "*Be ye therefore ready also*: for the Son of man cometh at an hour when ye think not."
- Luke 12:42 and 43 says, "And the Lord said, Who then is that faithful and wise steward, whom his lord shall make ruler over his household, to give them their portion of meat in due season? *Blessed is that servant, whom his lord when he cometh shall find so doing*."
- Philippians 3:20 and 21 says, "For our conversation is in heaven; from whence also *we look for the Saviour, the Lord Jesus Christ*: Who shall change our vile body, that it may be fashioned like unto His glorious body, according to the working whereby he is able even to subdue all things unto himself."
- First Thessalonians 1:9 and 10 says, "For they themselves shew of us what manner of entering in we had unto you, and how ye turned to God from idols to serve the living and true God; And *to wait for His Son from heaven*, whom He raised from the dead, even Jesus, which delivered us from the wrath to come."
- First Timothy 6:14 says, "That thou keep this commandment without spot, unrebukable, *until the appearing of our Lord Jesus Christ*."
- Titus 2:11-14 says, "For the grace of God that bringeth salvation hath appeared to all men, Teaching us that, denying ungodliness and worldly lusts, we should live soberly, righteously, and godly, in this present world; Looking for that *blessed hope*, and *the glorious appearing of the great God and our Saviour Jesus Christ*; Who gave Himself for us, that He might redeem us from all iniquity, and purify unto Himself a peculiar people, zealous of good works."

Jesus Is Coming for Those Who Love and Eagerly Hope for His Appearing

Likewise, there are scriptures that tell us Jesus is coming for those who love and eagerly hope for His coming. The following are some of those verses.

- Second Timothy 4:8 says, "Henceforth there is laid up for me a crown of righteousness, which the Lord, the righteous judge, shall give me at that day: and not to me only, but unto all them also that *love his appearing*."
- Hebrews 9:28 says, "So Christ was once offered to bear the sins of many; and unto them that *look* for him shall he appear the second time without sin unto salvation."
- First Peter 1:13 says, "Wherefore gird up the loins of your mind, be sober, and hope to the end for the grace that is to be brought unto you *at the revelation [appearing] of Jesus Christ*."
- First John 3:2-3 says, "Beloved, now are we the sons of God, and it doth not yet appear what we shall be: but we know that, when He shall *appear*, we shall be like him; for we shall see him as he is. And every man that hath this hope in Him purifieth himself, even as he is pure."

In Light of All This, We Must Examine Ourselves To Make Sure We Are Ready

To ensure we are ready for the moment Christ comes to rapture the Church, we must be willing to probe deeply into our hearts to determine if our spiritual status is what we think it is.

When Paul addressed believers in Second Corinthians 13:5, he said, "Examine yourselves, whether ye be in the faith; prove your own selves. Know ye not your own selves, how that Jesus Christ is in you, except ye be reprobates?"

The word "examine" in this verse is interpreted from a form of the Greek word *peiradzo*, a word that pictures *an intense investigation*. The use of this word informs us that Paul was not speaking of a surface investigation, but of *a deep probe* into one's own heart to see if he or she is really in the faith. As a phrase, the original Greek means, "Examine and deeply probe your lives to determine if you are really in the faith...."

Paul then added that we are also to "prove" ourselves. That word "prove" is interpreted from a form of the Greek word *dokimadzo*, a word that means *to approve after testing*. It is the very same word used in the ancient world to illustrate *a test used to determine real and*

In the ancient world there were a lot of counterfeit coins, so a process was developed to see what coins were real or fake. Paul used this concept to urge us to probe our hearts to see if our faith is real or if it is counterfeit, for there are so-called believers who act like us and talk like us, but a deeper probe reveals that they are not of us.

counterfeit coinage. Counterfeit coins looked very authentic — and there were so many counterfeit coins in circulation in ancient times that it became an accepted practice to test them to determine if they were real or counterfeit. If tested and proven as fake or counterfeit, they were rejected. Only if the coins were tested and proven authentic were they approved for public circulation and accepted as a form of payment.

Paul used this word to urge us to probe our hearts to see if our faith is real or if it is counterfeit. The fact is, there are so-called believers in the Church who act like us and talk like us, but a deeper probe reveals that they are not of us.

This is the category of people John referred to in First John 2:18 and 19 (*AMP*), which says, "Children, it is the last hour [the end of this age]; and just as you heard that the antichrist is coming [the one who will oppose Christ and attempt to replace Him], even now many antichrists (false teachers) have appeared, which confirms our belief that it is the last hour. They went out from us [seeming at first to be Christians], but they were not *really* of us [because they were not truly born again and spiritually transformed]; for if they had been of us, they would have remained with us; but *they went out* [teaching false doctrine], so that it would be clearly shown that none of them are of us."

These so-called believers did not pass the test — *dokimadzo* — of a true, saving belief in Christ.

But the word "prove" in Second Corinthians 13:5, translated from *dokimadzo,* was also a word used to picture the act of refining metal *by fire* to remove its impurities. First, the metal was placed in a fire that burned at a certain degree of heat; then it was placed in a fire burning at an even higher degree; and finally, it was placed in a *blazing* fire that burned

The word "prove" in Greek pictures the act of refining metal by fire to remove its impurities. Paul told us to "prove" ourselves to assure the genuineness of our faith and to make sure there are no hidden impurities that would cause our faith to be weak when it is needed to be strong.

at the *highest* degree of all. Three such tests were needed to remove from the metal all the unseen impurities that were hidden from the naked eye.

From the viewpoint of the human eye, the metal looked strong and ready to be used even prior to those tests. But unseen defects were resident in the metal that would have shown up later as a break, a fracture, or some kind of malfunction. To be assured the metal was free of defects and ready to be used effectively, with no breakdown, these three purifying tests at three different degrees of blazing hot fire were required. The fire was hot and the process was lengthy, but the tests were necessary in order to achieve the desired result.

This historic meaning is also carried into Paul's call for each of us to "prove" ourselves. You see, one may seem to have a genuine and strong faith, but the genuineness of one's faith is revealed by fiery tests that expose faith's true nature. The tests that come may not be sent by God, but regardless of the source, such tests expose impurities and reveal the weakness or strength of one's faith.

In ancient Athens, the word *dokimadzo* was also used to describe the process of testing the character of individuals before they were permitted to be installed in any public office. Being a public officer was so serious that to find out if an individual possessed the right inner character for such a notable position, he was thoroughly examined to see if he could pass a character test. This intense examination was carried out by a supreme council, and its purpose was to determine if a candidate was worthy to hold a public office. If a candidate was approved, he could be chosen for public leadership — but if he failed the character test, he would be eliminated from any public leadership in society.

Just as candidates in the ancient world were put through an intense test to determine if their character was sufficient to hold public office, Paul urged us to probe and test our heart to discover what is really at the core of our being.

We have seen in Chapter One that there are "spiritual mannequins" who have a form of godliness but lack the real substance within (*see* 2 Timothy 3:5). But by allowing the Holy Spirit to probe deep into our beings to test us, we will be able to determine our real spiritual status. Especially in light of the Lord's coming and the prospect of eternity, it is imperative that we deeply probe our hearts to make sure we do not fall into the category of those who say, "Lord, lord," yet He responds to them saying, "I never knew you."

The Bible says a day is coming when everything on the earth will melt with fervent heat, and the earth and all its works will be burned up — and that means everything built by man will vanish, including monuments like the Pyramids of Giza that have stood the test of time for thousands of years.

This Earth and Its Works Will Pass Away, But He Who Does the Will of God Will Live Forever

In Second Peter 3:10, Peter wrote, "But the day of the Lord will come as a thief in the night; in the which the heavens shall pass away with a great noise, and the elements shall melt with fervent heat, the earth also and the works that are therein shall be burned up."

Each time I ponder this verse, my mind goes to one day long ago when our family stood at the foot of the Great Pyramid of Giza in Egypt while we were on a trip. We had spent that entire week floating down the Nile River, touring all the sites of ancient Egypt, which were thousands of years old. We were all amazed at how well the condition of these ancient locations had been preserved.

But finally, we stood at the foot of the ancient, massive Great Pyramid of Giza. It, too, was in marvelous condition, especially considering that it had been standing there for many thousands of years. It was very evident that the Great Pyramid had been built solidly so that it would stand as an eternal remembrance to the Egyptian king who built it.

But as I stood there with my family, I told my sons, who were young at the time, "This pyramid has stood here for thousands of years, but a day is coming when it will be completely dissolved. The Bible tells us a day is coming when everything on the earth will melt with fervent heat, and the earth and all its works will be burned up. That means a day is coming when none of these monuments will exist any longer. Everything built by man will vanish, including these monuments that have stood the test of time for thousands of years. The only thing that will last is what people have done for Jesus Christ."

Of course, the scripture I referred to was Second Peter 3:10. This verse says that a day is coming when "...the heavens shall pass away with a great noise, and the elements shall melt with fervent heat, the earth also and the works that are therein shall be burned up."

According to Peter, a day is coming at the very end of the age when everything we presently see and know will be changed. Even the heavens as we currently know them will pass away. The words "pass away" in Second Peter 3:10 are from the Greek word *parerchomai*, which pictures something that is *temporary* and will soon be *passing away*.

Peter said the present heavens will pass away with a "great noise." The words "great noise" are from the Greek word *rhoidzedon*. This word describes *a sound so loud that it is nearly deafening to those who hear it*. It further carries the idea of *a tremendous rushing, hissing, sizzling, cracking sound* or *a noise so thunderous that no one can escape it*.

When these events transpire, the heavens and all "the elements" shall melt with a fervent heat. The word "elements" is the Greek word *stoicheion,* and it refers to *everything that exists* — from the heavenly bodies in the sky overhead to the mountains, the earth, the buildings constructed by man, and even the smallest atomic particles. Absolutely nothing will survive the transforming, purifying fire that will melt everything.

The word "melt" in this verse is from the Greek word *luo,* which normally means *to loose*. But in this case, it pictures *the dissolving of matter* and *the complete dissolution of the earth's elements*. This melting of the elements will occur because of a "fervent heat."

The words "fervent heat" come from the Greek word *kausoomai*, which depicts *a fire so intense that nothing escapes its fierce blaze*. It was used by medical writers to convey the idea of *a fever that consumed a victim*. This is *an intense, raging, blazing, blistering, burning fire that consumes* and, hence, *purges* everything it touches. And absolutely nothing from this physical world that has been built by man will survive when Jesus purifies the present world and creates a new Heaven and a new Earth.

But years ago on our family trip to Egypt, I reminded my sons of all this because I wanted them to know that the only thing to survive this life will be what we do for Jesus Christ. We tend to think that houses, buildings, and the things we construct in life will live forever. But the truth is, even the structures that are built to survive through the ages of time will eventually pass away.

Since only that which is done for eternity will outlast this world, we can see why Peter asked the question, "Seeing then that all these things shall be dissolved, what manner of persons ought ye to be in all holy conversation and godliness?" (2 Peter 3:11).

A day is coming when all the material possessions you own and hold dear will be "dissolved." The word "dissolved" is from the Greek word *luo*, which is the same word mentioned in Second Peter 3:10 to describe the *complete dissolution* of everything that presently exists. By using this word, Peter was alerting us to the fact that nothing we presently own will last forever. *In light of this truth, how should we view our material possessions, and how should we prioritize our lives?*

> The truth is that too often, we devote the bulk of our time to our homes, gardens, cars, businesses, or other worldly affairs. Although we must give attention to the basic things that are necessary to life, we make a huge mistake if we focus on these temporal matters while neglecting eternal matters that will actually pass from this life into the next. Only that which is done for the Lord will last. Everything else will be left behind in a world that will one day be consumed with a fervent heat. John corroborates this truth in First John 2:17, where he wrote, "...The world passeth away, and the lust thereof: but he that doeth the will of God abideth for ever."

Since everything will be dissolved and "pass away," doesn't it make sense that we invest spiritually in our present and future lives? How should this knowledge affect the way you live? Peter asked, "Seeing then that all these things shall be dissolved, what manner of persons ought ye to be...?" In other words, since the heavens and the earth and everything in them are temporary and will one day pass away, what should have your greatest attention and devotion?

Unsaved men in today's world live for the present. While they often do great philanthropic works and long for their names to be remembered in future generations by perhaps having their names on buildings or streets named after them, every building that bears a person's name will one day evaporate.

On the other hand, those who live for eternity, walk by faith, and obey what the Word of God tells them to do will make a name for themselves that will be remembered in Heaven for all of eternity. Doing what God has told them to do may include doing things that are philanthropic or building buildings, neighborhoods, and monuments. But when the physical structures they have built one day "melt" along with everything else, the "faith" they have put to work in obedience to God's command will reach into eternity — and for *that* they will be richly rewarded.

But the message I conveyed to my sons that day in front of the Egyptian pyramids is the same message I want to ask you today:

- Are you investing in eternity — in works of obedience to Jesus that will stand the test of time (*see* 1 Corinthians 3:13-14)?
- Or are you consumed only with natural things that will one day melt along with everything that exists?

What Should Be Our Response?

In Second Peter 3:11 and 12, Peter asked, "Seeing then that all these things shall be dissolved, what manner of persons ought ye to be in all holy conversation and godliness, looking for and hasting unto the coming of the day of God, wherein the heavens being on fire shall be dissolved, and the elements shall melt with fervent heat?"

Verses 13 and 14 continue, "Nevertheless we, according to his promise, look for new heavens and a new earth, wherein dwelleth righteousness. Wherefore, beloved, seeing that ye look for such things, be diligent that ye may be found of him in peace, without spot, and blameless."

The word "dissolved" in verse 11 is translated from a form of the word *luo*, which, as we've seen, means to be *loosed*, and it pictures *the coming apart of everything* that presently exists. It means, "Seeing then that everything that exists right now will eventually come to pieces, will pass away, and will cease to exist, what manner of persons should you be?"

The words "what manner" are interpreted from the Greek word *potapos*, which means *what kind, what manner, what sort*, or *what type* of people "ought ye to be in all holy conversation and godliness." The word "ought" is translated from the Greek word *dei*, a word that depicts what is *mandated* or *required*. By using this word, Peter thusly declared that God expects each of us to have *a correct response* to the knowledge that we are living in a temporary world that is passing away. Hence, he asked us, "Exactly what sort of person should this knowledge mandate or require you to be?" Peter answered the question himself in verse 11 when he stated that this knowledge should make us want to possess a "holy conversation and godliness."

The word "holy" in this phrase is from a form of the Greek word *hagios*. The first time this word appears in Scripture is in Exodus 3:5 as *hagia* in the Greek Septuagint of the Old Testament, and it is in reference to the "burning bush," from which God said to Moses, in effect, "The place where you are standing is holy." This word *hagios*, from this point forward throughout the Bible, is the word used to denote the holiness of God, the holy presence of God, or anything that God deems to be *holy*.

The spot where Moses stood in Exodus 3:5 was a place on this earth where God dwelt — and it was so holy that no worldly contamination was permitted there. In that hallowed moment, Moses crossed the threshold that separated the natural realm from the realm that God called "holy."

The real Mount Horeb in Saudi Arabia is pictured here, and it is the spot where Moses stood and where God dwelt — a place so holy that no worldly contamination was permitted there. In that hallowed moment, Moses crossed the threshold that separated the natural realm from the realm that God called "holy."

In the Old Testament Greek Septuagint and in the Greek New Testament, the Greek word for "holy" is translated from various forms of this Greek word *hagios*. It is one of the most important words anywhere in the entire Bible, so it is vital to understand exactly what the word "holy" means. It can describe something that, even though it was once common, has now become *consecrated, holy, separated, and sacred* — never again to be regarded as common or used in a common way. This means anything "holy" is in a category that is *separate* and *sacred* from other things.

The word "holy" in the name "Holy Bible" signifies that it is in a category all by itself, and every time you call that precious Book by its name, you are affirming that it is like no other book, that it is set apart into a special, consecrated, holy category, and it is different from all the other books in the world.

Here's a simple illustration to make this word "holy" understandable. The King James translators were some of the earliest to give the Bible's full name as the Holy Bible. The word "Bible" is in reality a translation of the Greek word *biblios*, which simply means *book* or *a scroll of writing*.

But as I mentioned earlier, the word "holy" — the Greek word *hagios* — means *consecrated, holy, separated, sacred*, or *never to be regarded or used in a common way*. Anything that is "holy" is in a category that is separate and sacred from other things. That means the Holy Bible is a special book that's *consecrated, separated, and set apart* from all other books.

In fact, the Holy Bible is so *different* that no other book in the world that has ever been written compares to it. If you walk into a library, you can probably find a copy of the Holy Bible on its shelves. But even though it is located in a library full of books, the word "holy" in the name "Holy Bible" signifies that it is in a category all by itself. And every time you call that precious Book by its name, you are affirming that it is like no other book, that it is *set apart* into *a special, consecrated, holy category*, and it is *different* from all the other books in the library.

But let's return to the example of Moses that day on Mount Horeb. When Moses approached the burning bush, God told him to remove his shoes because he was standing on "holy" ground. Because that word "holy" in this context is also a translation of a form of the Greek word *hagios*, it tells us that God consecrated and sanctified that particular spot on the mountain.

If you had been there at that mountain, you likely would have thought it looked no different from other mountains in the region. Although there was nothing particularly unique about that mountain in terms of its appearance compared to other mountains, God's presence had touched it, and His divine presence supernaturally *separated* it from all other mountains and *set it apart* into a *holy* category. It became so *sacred* that it became known as the *Holy Mount.* Although nestled as one mountain amidst an entire mountain range of regular mountains, the "holy," set-apart one ceased to be normal from that day onward, for when God's presence came upon it, its status changed.

When you see the word "holy," you must therefore keep in mind these ideas of *consecration, separation, sacredness,* or being placed into *a unique category.* Understanding this gives the background to how and why both Peter and Paul used the word "holy" in their epistles.

Paul used a form of *hagios* to describe Christians as saints. Before they belonged to Christ, they were normal human beings like everyone else, but the moment the blood of Jesus cleansed them and the Holy Spirit moved into their hearts, God's divine presence set them apart and made them so different that God immediately saw them in a special, holy light that is different from those who are unsaved.

For instance, Paul wrote to the Christians in Rome and began his letter in Romans 1:7, saying, "To all that be in Rome, beloved of God, called to be saints...."

When people see the word "saints," they sometimes imagine people with an ethereal glow about them and halos above their heads! But the word translated "saints" is actually a form of the Greek word *hagios* — the same word that means *holy* and describes something that has been *consecrated, sanctified, separated, and set apart* for special use.

Paul used this word to describe Christians, who, before they belonged to Christ, were normal human beings like everyone else. But the moment the blood of Jesus cleansed them and the Holy Spirit moved into their hearts, God's divine presence *set them apart* and made them so *different* that God immediately saw them in *a special, holy light* that was *different* from those who were unsaved.

So when Paul called the Christians in Rome "saints," he was saying that God had made them *holy* and had called them to be *different,* to be *sanctified,* and to be *separate* from the rest of the world. The use of *hagios* lets us know that because of the blood of Jesus and the indwelling presence of the Holy Spirit, each Christian is to be *consecrated, different,* and *separated.* Every authentic believer in Jesus Christ is now in an entirely new category that is holy. Just as the presence of God touched Mount Horeb and made it holy, the moment the blood of Jesus washed you and the Holy Spirit entered your spirit, God *consecrated* you, *separated* you, and *set you apart* for Himself. And this is the way we should walk. We might look like regular people, but in actual fact, there is nothing regular about us.

As new creations in Christ (*see* 2 Corinthians 5:17) who are separated into a higher, holy category, we are expected by God to adjust our thinking to His holy, written Word and behave accordingly. Paul confirmed this in Romans 12:1 and 2: "I beseech you therefore, brethren, by the mercies of God, that ye present your bodies a living sacrifice, holy, acceptable unto God, which is your reasonable service. And be not conformed to this world: but be ye transformed by the renewing of your mind, that ye may prove what is that good, and acceptable, and perfect, will of God."

We should no longer think and act as we once did, because we are not who we once were. We are new, different, and holy — and that means we must think differently, talk differently, and act differently. Now, as believers, we must learn to live in a way that reflects who we really are!

All this leads to the word "conversation" in Second Peter 3:11, where Peter asked, "Seeing then that all these things shall be dissolved, what manner of persons ought ye to be in all holy *conversation* and *godliness*." Peter's answer was that knowing we have been set apart should cause us to long to act *holy* in "conversation and godliness." The word "conversation" is translated from the Greek word *anastrophe*, which actually means *behavior*, *conduct*, or *lifestyle*. It pictures *the ups, downs, twists, and turns of one's life*, or his *total lifestyle*. It pictures *one's rising up, sitting down, going in, going out, everything he says and does, and all the twists and turns of one's life* — or *every aspect of one's existence*.

The word "godliness" is translated from a form of the Greek word *eusebeia*, which is a form of a compound of the preposition *eu* and *sebomai*. The preposition *eu* means *good*, *well*, or *swell*, and speaks of something that is *wonderful*. The word *sebomai* pictures what one *esteems*, *reverences*, or *worships*. Compounded as *eusebeia*, it speaks of *an individual's deep sense of devotion, godliness, piety, and reverence*, or it pictures one's *spiritual life*. Thus, Peter was also stating the knowledge that this present life is temporal and that Christ is coming soon should ignite a deep spiritual passion in each of us. This is the correct response to all that Peter revealed in these verses.

Let's look at the nuances of the Greek meaning of Peter's words in the *Renner Interpretive Version* (*RIV*) of this verse.

RIV of Second Peter 3:11

Since all things will perish in this very manner [with a heat so intense that it will absolutely melt everything that exists in the earth and in the heavens above], you need to ask: What sort of person does this require you to be? Do you not see and agree how essential it is that you live your life in a way that reflects that God has touched you, set you aside, and consecrated you for His special purposes? This should make such a difference in your whole lifestyle that it affects your rising up, sitting down, going in, going out, everything you say, everything you do, and all the twists and turns of your life. And along with that holiness, it should produce a level of godliness and piety in the way you live.

But then Peter said in verse 12 that in addition to having a lifesytle of holiness that is marked by spiritual passion, we must also be "looking for" the coming of the Lord. The words "looking for" are an interpretation of a form of *speudo*, a word that pictures one who does all in his power *to accelerate*, *to hasten*, or *to quicken* a situation. It is where we derive the English word "speed." He wrote: "Looking for and hasting unto the coming of the day of God, wherein the heavens being on fire shall be dissolved, and the elements shall melt with fervent heat."

Can Times and Seasons Be Changed?

The use of this word unmistakably means there are things the Church can do *to accelerate*, *to hasten*, or *to quicken* the coming of the Lord. This inference is that the date of this event may be accelerated by the correct response of God's people. Previously in verse 9, Peter stated that God is not slack or slow in keeping His promises, but that He is patient because He wants to give every person who will repent an opportunity to do so.

To speed up the end of all things, we must therefore do our part as the Church to reach the unsaved — for as soon as the last person who will be saved finally comes to Christ, the events leading up to the Rapture will begin. The voice of the archangel and the trump of God will sound, and the righteous dead will be resurrected. Then those who are "alive and remain" will be caught up, along with the "righteous dead," to meet the Lord in the air!

Peter reminded us that a day is coming "wherein the heavens being on fire shall be dissolved, and the elements shall melt with fervent heat." The word "heavens" is the plural form of *ouranos*, which is used by Peter to picture *all of the heavens above*. He stated that they will be "on fire," which is interpreted from a form of *puroo*, a derivative of *pur*, a word that depicts *brightly burning fire with flames swirling, whirling, flickering, twisting, turning, and arching upward toward the sky.*

The form Peter used here means *to set on a blazing and refining fire*. It denotes a thing so hot with fire that it glows from the intense heat. Thus, Peter declared that a day is coming when the heavens above will be set on fire to such a degree that they will literally glow with a blazing fire. This agrees with Malachi 4:1: "...Behold, the day cometh, that shall burn as a oven; and all the proud, yea, and all that do wickedly shall be stubble: and the day that cometh shall burn them up, saith the Lord of hosts, that it shall leave them neither root nor branch."

The word "dissolved" is once again interpreted from a form of *luo*, a word that depicts the act of *untying* or *unloosing* and pictures what is *loosed* or *unraveled*. It means *to utterly undo or unravel a thing until it falls apart or is destroyed*. This means no natural earthly element or grandiose buildings or monuments built by man will escape this moment. This word also means *to come unraveled* and *to completely pass away*. And what will pass away are the "elements" in the world.

The word "elements" is interpreted from a form of *stoicheion*, which simply means *elements* and includes *everything that exists* — from *the heavenly bodies in the sky overhead* to *the mountains, the earth, and the buildings constructed by man* and even *the smallest atomic particles*. So in this verse, this word means all the *elements*, including everything known to man.

Peter also said the elements — or everything currently known to man in the physical world — will eventually "melt." The word "melt" is interpreted from a form of *teko*, a Greek word that means *to melt*, like a fire melts metal into molten material. Thus, as a metal worker heats existing metals to the point of melting so he can refashion them, at this future moment, God will melt all presently known elements and materials into a molten form so He can refashion them into a new Heaven and new Earth. And He will do it with a "fervent heat."

The words "fervent heat" are interpreted from a form of the Greek word *kausoo*, which denotes *a fire so intense that nothing escapes its blaze*. As we saw earlier, this word was used by medical writers to convey the idea of *a fever that consumed a victim*. It is *an intense, raging, blazing, blistering, burning fire that consumes and purges everything it touches*. Thus, it pictures *an inescapable heat that consumes everything*, with nothing escaping.

The following interpretation of Second Peter 3:12 carries all these important nuances into the verse:

RIV of Second Peter 3:12

Live with a full expectation and do all you can on your part to speed up the powerful arrival of the day of God. In that day, the heavens above will ignite and glow with a blazing fire, and the heavens as we know them will literally come unraveled and completely pass away. And all the elements, including everything known to man — due to this intensively burning heat that consumes everything — will literally be melted and reduced to molten liquid.

God Promises New Heavens and a New Earth

Peter then soundly reminded us in Second Peter 3:13, "Nevertheless we, according to his promise, look for new heavens and a new earth, wherein dwelleth righteousness."

The word "nevertheless" is a translation of *de*, a conjunction intended to lead the reader to the next important point, which is that "we, according to his promise, look for new heavens and a new earth, wherein dwelleth righteousness." The word "promise" is a translation of a form of *epangelia*, which is the Greek word for *an announcement, declaration, or guaranteed promise*, and it was used as a legal term *to describe what has been legally promised and is expected to come to pass.* Peter here stated this is a very specific promise that God has *announced, declared, guaranteed*, and *promised* to come to pass. Hence, it pictures God's *guaranteed promise* to His people.

We Can Confidently Expect the Promise of God To Come To Pass

The words "look for" are interpreted from a form of *prosdokao*, which denotes *a peering forward with pregnant anticipation toward the expected delivery of what's been promised.* Peter exhorted those who are passing through this world, as pilgrims, to yearn for a new Heaven and Earth with righteousness serving as its permanent foundation.

Rather than fixate on the present life alone, we are urged by Peter to remember His promise that He is coming for us, and to look forward to the moment in the future when there will be "new heavens and a new earth, wherein dwelleth righteousness."

The word "new" is interpreted from a form of *kainos*, which does not refer to something old that has been amended, fixed, or repaired — but, rather, to something that is

The new heavens and new earth that Peter declared will eventually come will not be a remake, repair, or revision of the heavens and earth that existed before, but will be brand-spanking new heavens and a new earth that no one has ever previously seen.

brand-spanking new that has never existed before. Thus, the new heavens will not be a remake, repair, or revision of the heavens that existed before, but they will be *brand-spanking new heavens that no one has ever previously seen.*

The word "heaven" is the plural form of *ouranos*, as we've seen, which pictures all the *heavens above*, while the word "earth" is a translation of *ge*, a Greek word that refers to *the physical planet Earth*. And Peter emphatically stated that in the future the new heavens and new earth will be a place where "dwelleth righteousness."

The word "righteousness" is a translation of the Greek word *dikaiosune*, and it describes *righteousness and justice*, picturing the righteous, just standards of God. And Peter joyfully declared that the new heavens and the new earth will be a place where the righteous standards of God "dwelleth."

The word "dwelleth" is interpreted from a form of *katoikeo*, which is a compound of the preposition *kata* and the word *oikeo*. The word *kata* means *down*, and the word *oikeo* means *to dwell* and is importantly a derivative of *oikos*, which is the Greek word for *a permanent home* or *permanent place of residence*.

As the compound *katoikeo*, a form of which Peter used in this verse, it pictures one who *settles down* (*kata*) *to live in* one location (*oikeo*). It is a picture of one who has settled permanently into a house and feels completely *at home* there. Because he has chosen to settle down, this individual now experiences the sense of comfort, security, and permanence that naturally accompanies this state of being.

The *Renner Interpretive Version* (*RIV*) of Second Peter 3:13 puts all of these powerful word meanings and nuances into the text.

RIV of Second Peter 3:13

> **However, we live according to the promise He has guaranteed to us, and we are enthusiastically anticipating brand-spanking new heavens and a brand-spanking new physical earth, in which justice, righteousness, and the standards of God permanently dwell.**

But then, finally, Second Peter 3:14 says, "Wherefore, beloved, seeing that ye look for such things, be diligent that ye may be found of him in peace, without spot, and blameless."

The word "wherefore" is a translation of *dio*, a conjunction that means *wherefore*, *therefore*, or *in light of all these things*. The word "look" is from a form of *prosdokao*, a word that denotes *a peering forward with pregnant anticipation of the expected delivery of what's been promised*. The words "such things" speak of all the promises of God in the future that belong to those who are "diligent."

Diligent, in Peace, Without Spot, and Blameless

The word "diligent" is interpreted from a form of *spoudadzo*, which means *to do something with eagerness*, *to do something with diligence*, or *acting responsibly, quickly, and with attentiveness*. It pictures *one so diligent, excited, and energetic that he puts his whole heart into the principle or task before him*. It also means *to do something with excitement, enthusiasm, and haste because it is so important, serious, or urgent* or *to give one's best efforts to a project or task and to do it enthusiastically*.

The word "found" is from a form of *heurisko*, a word that denotes *an intense, scholarly research that yields a discovery*. It is where we derive the word "eureka," and in this sense carries a note of *euphoria*. This is the reason the *RIV* translates it, "...When He makes a final examination of you, He will euphorically find you to be without blemish, fault, spot, or stain...."

The word "peace" is a translation of the word *eirene*, a very full-bodied word that depicts the following:

- *the cessation of war.*
- *an end of conflict.*
- *a time of rebuilding and reconstruction after war has ceased.*
- *distractions removed.*
- *a time of prosperity.*
- *the rule of order in the place of chaos.*
- *calm, inner stability that results in the ability to conduct oneself peacefully even in the midst of circumstances that would normally be traumatic or upsetting.*

The word *eirene* is the Greek equivalent for the Hebrew word *shalom*, which expresses the idea of *wholeness, completeness, or tranquility in the soul* that is unaffected by outward circumstances or pressures.

The words "without spot" in Second Peter 3:14 are interpreted from a form of *amometos*, which is a form of the word *momaomai* with the prefix *a*. The word *momaomai* denotes *a moral or spiritual stain that spoils one's reputation*. Thus, it pictures *one who is discredited, disgraced, and dishonored* and whose reputation is now *tarnished*. But the prefix *a* has a canceling or reversing effect.

So when an *a* is affixed to the front of *momaomai*, forming the word *amometos*, a form of which is used in this verse, it pictures *one who was previously discredited, disgraced, dishonored to the point that his or her reputation is tarnished, but who has become free of a previous discredited, disgraced, dishonored, or tarnished reputation.*

Thus, when this word is applied to a believer, it gives the picture of one who, regardless of his or her past, is now *free of disgrace and tarnish*. It depicts one who is cleansed by the blood of Christ, and it likewise presents to such a recipient the goal of afterward living with *a spotless reputation*.

These verses from Second Peter 3:11-14 give us personal instruction about how we should live and what should be our aim as we await the coming of the Lord. I am including the entire passage in the *Renner Interpretive Version* (*RIV*) as follows:

RIV of Second Peter 3:11-14

11 Since all things will perish in this very manner [with a heat so intense that it will absolutely melt everything that exists in the earth and in the heavens above], you need to ask: What sort of person does this require you to be? Do you not see and agree how essential it is that you live your life in a way that reflects that God has touched you, set you aside, and consecrated you for His special purposes? This should make such a difference in your whole lifestyle that it affects your rising up, sitting down, going in, going out, everything you say, everything you do, and all the twists and turns of your life. And along with that holiness, it should produce a level of godliness and piety in the way you live.

12 Live with a full expectation and do all you can on your part to speed up the powerful arrival of the day of God. In that day, the heavens above will ignite and glow with a blazing fire, and the heavens as we know them will literally come unraveled and completely pass away. And all the elements, including everything known to man — due to this intensively burning heat that consumes everything — will literally be melted and reduced to molten liquid.

13 However, we live according to the promise He has guaranteed to us, and we are enthusiastically anticipating brand-spanking new heavens and a brand-spanking new physical earth, in which justice, righteousness, and all the standards of God permanently dwell.

14 In light of all these things, beloved, whom I deeply love and profoundly cherish, since you are fully anticipating and expecting these things to come to pass, you must do everything you can to be attentive, diligent, and responsible so that when He makes a final examination of you, He will euphorically find you to be without blemish, fault, spot, or stain of any type to the point that you have a blameless reputation and are living in a state of peace. And that peace will be so real that it brings cessation to wars in your life, closure to conflicts, removes distractions, allows a time for rebuilding and reconstruction, ushers in prosperity, fosters the rule of order in the place of chaos, and produces a calm, inner stability that results in the ability to conduct yourself peacefully even in the midst of circumstances that would normally be traumatic or upsetting.

ONE MORE IMPORTANT MESSAGE WE MUST TAKE TO HEART

We must never forget that a part of our God-given task is to take the Gospel to those who are drowning in sin and bring them the only life-saving message that will breathe the life of God into them and give them a place in His eternal family. The Great Commission that Christ gave to every believer is so important that He has asked every Christian to participate to make sure the unsaved hear the message. God is depending on you and me to be willing vessels to get this message to them. *Aren't you thankful that someone was willing to share this message with you?*

This is so important that I want you to see the sobering words that God spoke through the prophet Ezekiel concerning the task of taking the message to those who are unsaved: "When I say to the wicked, 'You shall surely die,' and you give him no warning, nor speak to warn the wicked from his wicked way, to save his life, that same wicked man shall die in his iniquity; but his blood I will require at your hand.

"Yet, if you warn the wicked, and he does not turn from his wickedness, nor from his wicked way, he shall die in his iniquity; but you have delivered your soul" (Ezekiel 3:18-19 *NKJV*).

These verses clearly state that we are responsible to warn the unsaved that they need to get their hearts right with God. If we choose not to share the Good News that can bring salvation to relatives, friends, co-workers, or acquaintances — and then they die in their sin — Ezekiel says God will hold us accountable for their souls. God is actually saying to us, "Their blood I will require at your hand."

That means if you or I could have warned those in our lives who are unsaved and we choose to ignore this responsibility, God will hold us accountable for not telling them what they needed to know. In these verses, God in essence also says, "If you do warn the wicked and tell them the truth about the consequences of sin and they don't repent, then they will die in their iniquity, but you will not be held accountable for their souls."

God respects the right of every person to say yes or no to Jesus Christ. Each person can choose how he or she will respond to His invitation, even if it is an eternally fateful choice. You and I are not accountable for people's choices in this matter.

However, we are accountable for making sure the unsaved we encounter in life understand their need to be saved. We are accountable to share the good news of Jesus' saving power with them as the Holy Spirit leads. We will not give account for their choice, but we will give account for whether or not we obeyed the Holy Spirit and shared the Gospel with them.

Famed British missionary and renowned author C. T. Studd felt such deep conviction to win the lost that he wrote, "Some wish to live within the sound of church or chapel bell; I want to run a rescue shop within a yard of hell."[5]

This profound revelation of hell drove him to reach as many as he could with the Gospel because he understood the urgency of this task. Many Christians are nonchalant about the subject of soul-winning, but God is not nonchalant about this subject. God was so serious about winning souls that He sent His own Son into the world to pay for their salvation with His own precious blood.

Remember John 3:16, which says, "For God so loved the world, that He gave His only begotten Son, that whosoever believeth in Him should not perish but have everlasting life." This is a message that must be proclaimed from the lips of every person who has placed his or her faith in Jesus Christ for the remission of sin.

God made the greatest sacrifice of all by giving His greatest Gift to procure salvation and deliverance for those who believe and to place them into His eternal family. Now not only is He asking us to do our part to share this life-saving message with others, but He also passionately desires that we hold on to our faith in Christ with all the love and zeal that burned in our hearts when we first believed. Christ is coming again for such to receive us unto Himself for all eternity.

QUESTIONS TO PONDER

1. As Rick shares in the first chapter and again in this last chapter, Jesus is coming for those who are *spiritually living, spiritually robust, spiritually thriving, spiritually vibrant, and spiritually vigorous.* After reading through this book, does it inspire you to become more spiritually engaged in your walk with the Lord?

2. What stood out to you in the Parable of the Ten Virgins? Do you feel that you have been wise or foolish in preparing for the Lord's return? In Rick's teaching on "Symbols of the Holy Spirit," he mentions that oil is inseparably linked to God's presence. What are some ways you can be sure you are making more room for the presence of God in your life during this season of waiting?

3. The Ten Virgins grew weary and tired while they were waiting for the Bridegroom. Have you ever grown weary of waiting on a promise from the Lord, only to watch it later come to pass *suddenly*? If so, what was that experience like? Read Psalm 40:1-3, Acts 1:7-8, Acts 2:1-4, Hebrews 6:12, and Hebrews 10:23 to encourage and strengthen your faith during this season of waiting.

4. Jesus said in Matthew 7 that we can identify true believers by the fruit produced by their lives. What kind of fruit is produced by your life? Do you need to submit your heart and motives to the Lord so that He can reveal any impurities that are hindering your faith? Are there some adjustments the Lord has been asking you to make so that the fruit produced by your life is good, abundant, and full of life? What is holding you back?

5. First Corinthians 7:29-31 (*MSG*) wisely states, "I do want to point out, friends, that time is of the essence. There is no time to waste, so don't complicate your lives unnecessarily. Keep it simple — in marriage, grief, joy, whatever. Even in ordinary things — your daily routines of shopping, and so on. Deal as sparingly as possible with the things the world thrusts on you. This world as you see it is fading away." Considering the message in this chapter that only what is done for eternity will last, what are some areas of your life you can simplify, or perhaps eliminate, that will allow you to make more room for eternal things?

6. The Bible says that Jesus is coming back for a Church that is "holy and without blemish" (*see* Ephesians 5:27). Did it surprise you to learn that the definition of

a "saint" is someone who is called to be different from the world and walk in holiness? Read again the *RIV* of Second Peter 3:11 found in this chapter. What are some areas of your life that you can change so you are less entangled with the world and its unholy ways?

7. As you finish reading this book, ask the Lord how you can prepare your heart in greater measure for His coming. Are there biblical truths you need to study to strengthen your faith? Are there environments or relationships in your life that are currently hindering your faith? Are there people around you that need to hear the Good News of Jesus Christ so they, too, can be free of the bondage of sin? Ask the Lord how you can make adjustments so that you are walking in holiness and in the Spirit, uncontaminated by the world's ways and shining your light as a believer in dark places.

8. Were you surprised to discover how much the Bible has to say about the Rapture, the Antichrist, and the Tribulation while reading this book? After digesting the information in these pages, do you still have questions that are unanswered? Jeremiah 33:3 says, "Call unto me, and I will answer thee, and show thee great and mighty things, which thou knowest not." Take your questions to the Lord in prayer, and ask the Holy Spirit, our Teacher, to reveal the answers to you.

1 Thessalonians 4:15-18

For this we say unto you by the word of the Lord, that we which are alive and remain unto the coming of the Lord shall not prevent them which are asleep. For the Lord himself shall descend from heaven with a shout, with the voice of the archangel, and with the trump of God: and the dead in Christ shall rise first: then we which are alive and remain shall be caught up together with them in the clouds, to meet the Lord in the air: and so shall we ever be with the Lord. Wherefore comfort one another with these words.

CHAPTER ELEVEN

WHAT IF I AM WRONG?

The passage of Scripture on the facing page is foundational to everything you have read in this book and to what I have written. It's important to note that when Jesus came the first time, all the religious leaders got it wrong. The scriptures and identifying markers about Jesus' first coming were all in Scripture, but the spiritual leaders of that time remarkably misread them, overlooked them, or altogether missed them. However, they did not have the indwelling Holy Spirit to help them, as we have living inside us as believers, and He is the Teacher of all teachers!

Some have asked, "Rick, *what if* what you've taught about a pre-Tribulation rapture is wrong and we all end up going through the Tribulation or at least through part of it? Wouldn't that mean your teaching on this subject has wrongly prepared people for what is to come?"

I will briefly answer that question.

First, I really do not believe the Church will go through the Tribulation for all the reasons that I have stated in this book. But *if* I am wrong and the Church does goes through the Tribulation, or part of it, I believe my clearly stated belief that the Rapture is going to occur *in an exceeding dark and difficult time* — and that we will be caught away *just in the nick of time* — is enough to awaken each of us to the fact that we must be mentally and spiritually prepared. As we speed to the end of the age, the world will grow darker, and we will likely find ourselves living in exceedingly difficult times in the days ahead.

Second, I firmly believe authentic Christians will escape the wrath that will be poured out during the seven years of the Tribulation. However, the very fact that the word *harpadzo* means *to snatch out of danger just in the nick of time* alerts me to the fact that things may become so dark that we may *feel* as if we are living in the Tribulation. We may wonder, *Could it possibly get any darker or more difficult in the days before the Rapture takes place?*

But then...*just in the nick of time*...Christ will descend into the earth's lower atmosphere to catch the Church out of harm's way.

Third, I noted in the Introduction to this book that I came to my own Bible-based conclusions about the Rapture as an adult, but because the subject seemed to be such a contentious question among so many people, I steered clear of it for years. I didn't want to lose the opportunity to reach someone who needed the trusted teaching of the Bible that I could bring to them. But as I grew older, I felt the Holy Spirit assigned me a responsibility to bring the trusted teaching of the Bible to people across the world. So I embraced the need to address what I am convinced the Bible says about this important subject.

Fourth, I have noted over the years that when someone like me publicly takes a position about the Rapture, critics come out of the woodwork to nitpick and even accuse those who believe in a pre-Tribulation rapture of being a false teacher. As I stated previously, it is difficult for me to understand this behavior, for although I may disagree with the conclusions of others who take a different view from my own, I have always found it beneficial to hear their views and learn from their perspectives.

As I have shown in this book, even if I do not agree with the conclusions of others, I respect their views and appreciate their convictions. But *if* what I believe about a pre-Tribulation Rapture is incorrect — or if *everyone* is incorrect in some respect — the fact is that we are only off by a matter of a few years. We can all rejoice that in the end, *Jesus WILL come!*

Fifth, I pray this book has been a blessing to you and that it has helped you better understand where we are in time — and how close we are to the moment when Jesus will descend into the lower atmosphere to beckon the Church to "break camp" and move upward and onward to join Him at the Marriage Feast of the Lamb.

I think it's clear that many years of study went into the making of this book. I have asked many to read it, including those who hold a view different from my own, because I love and respect them so much.

Sixth, as I stated in the Introduction, if you disagree with my conclusions, please continue to treat me as the brother who knows and loves the Word of God; believes in and stands on the integrity of God's Word; and is convinced that this is the greatest hour of the Church Age! Please remember that I have given and *am giving* my life on the frontlines for the life-saving message of the Gospel to be preached — to bring the trusted teaching of the Bible to those in need of spiritual life and strength around the world.

Seventh, as a final note, I echo the words of the apostle John in Revelation 22:20 and 21 that say, "He which testifieth these things saith, Surely I come quickly. Amen. *Even so, come, Lord Jesus.* The grace of our Lord Jesus Christ be with you all. Amen."

ENDNOTES

Introduction

[1] "A Thief in the Night," IMDb, 1972, https://www.imdb.com/title/tt0070795/. Accessed April 21, 2025.

Chapter One

[1] Gullög Nordquist, "The Salpinx in Greek Cult," journal.fi: Finnish scientific journals online, [Note: PDF available to download] https://journal.fi/scripta/article/view/67232. Accessed January 13, 2025.

[2] Jorge Álvarez, "Aristoxenus of Tarentum, the philosopher who authored the oldest known treatise on music, and healed by playing the flute," LBV Magazine Cultural Independiente, November 22, 2024, https://www.labrujulaverde.com/en/2024/11/aristoxenus-of-tarentum-the-philosopher-who-authored-the-oldest-known-treatise-on-music-and-healed-by-playing-the-flute/. Accessed January 14, 2025.

[3] "Jerome," Jewish Virtual Library: A Project of AICE, https://www.jewishvirtuallibrary.org/jerome-x00b0. Accessed January 14, 2025.

Chapter Two

[1] Gullög Nordquist, "The Salpinx in Greek Cult," journal.fi: Finnish scientific journals online, [Note: PDF available to download] https://journal.fi/scripta/article/view/67232. Accessed January 13, 2025.

[2] Nikolaos Xanthoulis, "Salpinx: The Ancient Greek Trumpet," The International Trumpet Guild Journal, October 2006, page 42, ACADEMIA, https://www.academia.edu/1039305/Salpinx_The_Ancient_Greek_Trumpet. Accessed March 20, 2025.

[3] Meyer's NT Commentary, "2 Thessalonians 2," Bible Hub, https://biblehub.com/commentaries/meyer/2_thessalonians/2.htm. Accessed March 20, 2025.

[4] "Bible Commentaries: 2 Thessalonians 2, The Pulpit Commentaries," StudyLight.org, https://www.studylight.org/commentaries/eng/tpc/2-thessalonians-2.html. Accessed March 20, 2025.

[5] "ἀτμίς," Transliteration "atmis," BlueLetterBible.org, https://www.blueletterbible.org/lexicon/g822/nasb20/mgnt/0-1/. Accessed March 21, 2025.

Chapter Three

[1] "Bible Foregrounds 1: The "Restrainer" in 2 Thessalonians 2:6-7," Retro Christianity: Reclaiming the Forgotten Faith, January 27, 2007, https://www.retrochristianity.org/2007/01/27/bible-foregrounds-1-the-restrainer-in-2-thessalonians-26-7/. Accessed March 18, 2025.

Chapter Four

[1] "שָׁנָה," Transliteration "*šᵊnâ*," BlueLetterBible.org, https://www.blueletterbible.org/lexicon/h8133/kjv/wlc/0-1/. Accessed April 26, 2025.

[2] "3488. yethib," Bible Hub, https://biblehub.com/hebrew/3488.htm. Accessed May 2, 2025; Keith Trump, Trump of God Ministries, Getting Greek [Note: Information in these passages provided by Rev. Keith Trump. Contact information: TrumpofGod.org, GettingGreek.org].

[3] Keith Trump, Trump of God Ministries, Getting Greek [Note: Information in these passages provided by Rev. Keith Trump. Contact information: TrumpofGod.org, GettingGreek.org].

[4] "5057. nagid," Bible Hub, https://biblehub.com/hebrew/5057.htm. Accessed May 2, 2025; Keith Trump, Trump of God Ministries, Getting Greek [Note: Information in these passages provided by Rev. Keith Trump. Contact information: TrumpofGod.org, GettingGreek.org].

[5] "6743. tsalach," Bible Hub, https://biblehub.com/hebrew/6743.htm. Accessed May 2, 2025; Keith Trump, Trump of God Ministries, Getting Greek [Note: Information in these passages provided by Rev. Keith Trump. Contact information: TrumpofGod.org, GettingGreek.org].

[6] Keith Trump, Trump of God Ministries, Getting Greek [Note: Information in these passages provided by Rev. Keith Trump. Contact information: TrumpofGod.org, GettingGreek.org].

[7] Keith Trump, Trump of God Ministries, Getting Greek [Note: Information in these passages provided by Rev. Keith Trump. Contact information: TrumpofGod.org, GettingGreek.org].

[8] Keith Trump, Trump of God Ministries, Getting Greek [Note: Information in these passages provided by Rev. Keith Trump. Contact information: TrumpofGod.org, GettingGreek.org].

Chapter Seven

[1] Doug Bandow, "Christianity Is the World's Most Persecuted Religion, Confirms New Report," CATO Institute, March 7, 2022, https://www.cato.org/commentary/christianity-worlds-most-persecuted-religion-confirms-new-report. Accessed March 18, 2025; "The 2025 World Watch List," Open Doors, https://www.opendoorsus.org/en-US/persecution/countries/. Accessed March 18, 2025.

[2] "Of the War — Book VI," Translated by William Whiston, The Genuine Works of Flavius Josephus, UChicago.edu, https://penelope.uchicago.edu/josephus/war-6.html. Accessed March 18, 2025.

[3] "New data shows record number of armed conflicts," The Peace Research Institute Oslo (PRIO), June 10, 2024, https://www.prio.org/news/3532. Accessed March 18, 2025.

[4] Ibid.

[5] Rick Renner, *Signs You'll See Just Before Jesus Comes* (Shippensburg, PA: Harrison House Publishers, 2018) pp. 51,54,63,65-66,72-73,75-76,83-85.

[6] Rick Renner, *Signs You'll See Just Before Jesus Comes* (Shippensburg, PA: Harrison House Publishers, 2018) pp. 18-19.

Chapter Eight

[1] "The Shepherd of Hermas, First Book: Visions, Fourth Vision, CHAPTER II.," Roberts-Donaldson English Translation, Early Christian Writings, https://www.earlychristianwritings.com/text/shepherd.html. Accessed March 18, 2025.

[2] "Against Heresies (Book V, Chapter 5)," Translated by Alexander Roberts and William Rambaut, NewAdvent.org, https://www.newadvent.org/fathers/0103505.htm. Accessed March 19, 2025; "Against Heresies (Book V, Chapter 29)," Translated by Alexander Roberts and William Rambaut, NewAdvent.org, https://www.newadvent.org/fathers/0103529.htm. Accessed March 19, 2025.

[3] St. Ephraim the Syrian, "ON THE LAST TIMES, THE ANTICHRIST, AND THE END OF THE WORLD," ORTHODOX CHRISTIANITY, https://orthochristian.com/101157.html. Accessed March 19, 2025.

[4] "Commentary on the Apocalypse," Translated by Robert Ernest Wallis, NewAdvent.org, https://www.newadvent.org/fathers/0712.htm. Accessed March 19, 2025.

Chapter Nine

[1] Dr Phillip Brassfield, "The Latter Rain," DESTINY LEADERS, September 20, 2022, https://destinyleaders.com/the-latter-rain/. Accessed March 19, 2025.

[2] "Christian Traditions," Pew Research Center, December 19, 2011, https://www.pewresearch.org/religion/2011/12/19/global-christianity-traditions/#6bccc38a1322c1dcf9df3c7162b1be97. Accessed March 21, 2025.

[3] "Plutarch on Alexander," Translation by M.M. Austin, Livius.org, July 15, 2020, https://www.livius.org/sources/content/plutarch/plutarchs-alexanders-fortune/an-ancient-assessment-of-alexander/. Accessed March 21, 2025.

[4] Megan Deak, "Famous Cities Founded By Alexander The Great," WorldAtlas, August 8, 2023, https://www.worldatlas.com/ancient-world/famous-cities-founded-by-alexander-the-great.html. Accessed March 21, 2025.

[5] The Editors of Encyclopaedia Britannica, "Edict of Milan," Britannica, https://www.britannica.com/topic/Edict-of-Milan. Accessed March 20, 2025; Conor McNamara, "Constantine's conversion and the Edict of Milan," Koinesúnē, April 15, 2024, https://koinesune.com/stories/constantines-conversion-and-the-edict-of-milan. Accessed March 20, 2025.

[6] "The EYE OF THE STORM," EurexShutters, https://eurexshutters.com/eye-of-storm-hurricane-eye-wall/#:~:text=eye%20wall's%20ferocity.-,How%20Long%20Does%20the%20Eye%20of%20the%20Storm%20Last?,safe%20until%20the%20storm%20ends. Accessed April 16, 2025.

[7] "Jannes and Jambres," BiblicalTraining.org, https://www.biblicaltraining.org/library/jannes-and-jambres. Accessed March 20, 2025; "Jannes and Jambres," Bible Gateway, https://www.biblegateway.com/resources/encyclopedia-of-the-bible/Jannes-Jambres. Accessed March 20, 2025.

[8] Wayne Jackson, "How Did Paul Learn about Jannes and Jambres?," Christian Courier, https://christiancourier.com/articles/how-did-paul-learn-about-jannes-and-jambres. Accessed March 20, 2025.

[9] Rick Renner, *Fallen Angels, Giants, Monsters & the World Before the Flood*, (Shippensburg, PA: Harrison House Publishers, 2024) pp. 357-359

Chapter Ten

[1] Alan DiDio, *They Lied to You About the Rapture: How to Prepare for What's Coming* (Shippensburg, PA: Destiny Image Publishers, 2025) p. 25

[2] "Bible Commentaries: Matthew 25, Barnes' Notes on the Whole Bible," StudyLight.org, https://www.studylight.org/commentaries/eng/bnb/matthew-25.html. Accessed April 17, 2025.

[3] "Ancient Jewish Wedding Customs and Yeshua's Second Coming," The Messianic Prophecy Bible Project, https://free.messianicbible.com/feature/ancient-jewish-wedding-customs-and-yeshuas-second-coming/. Accessed April 17, 2025.

[4] BIBLE PROPHECY by PAGE 0727, "THE GALILEAN WEDDING," GivingHimtheGlory.com, August 25, 2021, https://givinghimtheglory.com/2021/08/25/the-galilean-wedding/. Accessed April 18, 2025.

[5] Stephen Ross, "Charles Thomas (C.T.) Studd," Wholesome Words: Missionary Biographies, https://www.wholesomewords.org/missions/biostudd.html. Accessed May 2, 2025.

ILLUSTRATION AND PHOTO CREDIT ACKNOWLEDGMENTS

RENNER Ministries would like to thank the following picture libraries as well as individual copyright owners for permission to reproduce their images. Copyright inquiries should be directed to Rick Renner Ministries, social@renner.org.

Photo credits are listed by chapter and page.

COVER / DUST COVER:

Cover *Abstract painting background*, Adobe Stock Photo, Azahara MarcosDeLeon; Cover, *Apocalyptic Symphony Unveiling the Trumpets' Cataclysmic Descent*, Adobe Stock Photo, Techtopia Art; Cover, *Antichristo 1,* Adobe Stock, JUSTIN; *Trumpet Man*, Generated with AI, D. Lee.

FRONT MATTER:

xix *Jimmy Evans*, Courtesy of Tipping Point Ministries.

INTRODUCTION:

Private Collection — RENNER

1 *Trumpet Man*, Generated with AI, D. Lee.

CHAPTER 1:

Alamy

36 *St. Jerome Writing* by Caravaggio, Alamy Stock Photo, CBW.

37 *CATHOLIC CHURCH VULGATE BIBLE about 1592*, Alamy Stock Photo, Pictorial Press Ltd.

Creative Commons

30 *Salpinx Player*, Hoplita tocant el salpinx. Lècit de finals del segle VI o principis del V a. C., Museu arqueològic regional Antonio Salinas de Palerm, Creative Commons.

Private Collection — RENNER

7 *Trumpet Man*, Generated with AI, D. Lee.

11 *Royal Tapestry*, Generated with AI, R. Renner Rousch.

13 *Priest*, Generated with AI, D. Lee.

20 *Leaders*, Generated with AI, D. Lee.

21 *Politics*, Generated with AI, D. Lee; *Soldiers*, Generated with AI, D. Lee; *Stocks*, Generated with AI, D. Lee.

22 *Jesus*, Generated with AI, D. Lee.

24 *Horses*, Generated with AI, D. Lee.

26 *Archangel*, Generated with AI, D. Lee.

Royalty-Free

6 *Vintage blank paper scroll isolated on white background with copy space*, Adobe Stock, Rangizz.

9 *The Rapture*, Adobe Stock, Benjamin Haas; *Relentless Souls hell fire. God soul. Generate Ai*, Adobe Stock, Juliars.

15 *Magnifying Glass Focused on a Detailed World Map*, Adobe Stock, Damerfie.

18-19 *Soul leaves the body of a deceased person on a couch, ascension*, Adobe Stock, Александра Замулина.

27 *An orthodox Jewish man blowing Shofar under blue sky with white clouds outdoors, on the Jewish High Holidays in Rosh Hashanah and Yom Kippur,* Shutterstock, ChameleonsEye.

42 *Divine Resurrection Radiance: Ascending Messiah in Glorious Light*, Adobe Stock, Evgeniia Freeman.

Chapter 2:

British Museum

66-67 *Black-figured plate, attributed to the painter Psiax*, © The Trustees of the British Museum.

Getty Images

48 *Sarum Master Bible*, Finnbarr Webster/ Getty Images.

Private Collection — RENNER

47 *Trumpet Man*, Generated with AI, D. Lee.

62 *Light,* Generated with AI, D.Lee.

64 *Twinkling of an Eye*, Generated with AI, D. Lee.

74-75 *Smoke*, Generated with AI, D.Lee.

79 *Seed to Flower*, Generated with AI, D. Lee.

84 *The Walk*, Anastasia Khofmann, Illustration/ Special Commission, 2025 Renner Collection.

85 *A Meal on the Shore,* Anastasia Khofmann, Illustration/Special Commission, 2025 Renner Collection.

88 *Walking With Jesus*, Generated with AI, D. Lee.

89 *Road to Emmaus*, Generated with AI, D. Lee.

Royalty-Free

46 *Vintage blank paper scroll isolated on white background with copy space*, Adobe Stock, Rangizz.

61 *Strong Man Pushing the Wall*, Shutterstock, ADfoto.

71 *A drooping flower with wilted petals is brought to life by a vibrant drop of water glistening in warm sunlight*, Adobe Stock, Ihor.

72 *Gravestones in an American Cemetery*, iStock, MarcBruxelle.

77 *Farmer's hand planting seed in soil stock photo*, iStock, Bohdan Bevz.

81 *Dark brown background*, Adobe Stock, Kokotewan.

86 *Jesus Christ Answers Doubts of Saint Thomas*, iStock, Wynnter.

87 *Antique photo of paintings: Jesus appearance*, iStock, Ilbusca.

90 *Jesucristo resucitado-ascendiendo al cielo*, Generated with AI, FreeP!K Stock Photo.

Chapter 3:

Alamy

97 *St. Paul Writing his Epistles*, Alamy Stock Photo, Valentin de Boulogne, Art Collection 3.

104 *Ancient Roman coins approx 2000 years old*, Alamy Stock Image, Kevin Moore.

116 *Ancient roman sculpture of the emperor Hadrian,builder of Hadrian's wall*, Alamy Stock Image, Harrison Neil, Prisma by Dukas Presseagentur GmbH.

128 *Cicero's Speech Attacking Catiline in the Roman Senate*, Alamy Stock Image, Schmidt Hans W., Vidimages.

143 *Rear view of puzzled man scratching his head against concrete wall filled with question marks*, Alamy Stock Image, Christian Horz.

Creative Commons

116 *Bust of Roman Emperor Nero*, Capitoline Museum, Rome, Creative Commons; *A 1st century CE marble bust of Roman Emperor Domitian, r. 81-96 CE*, (Musée de Louvre, Paris), Photographed by Mary Harrsch, Creative Commons.

Private Collection — RENNER

95 *Trumpet Man*, Generated with AI, D. Lee;

96 *Trumpet Man*, Generated with AI, D. Lee.

99 *Jesus Coming for the Rapture*, Generated with AI, D. Lee.

101 *SMGraphic*, Created by K. Holder.

114 *Bible*, Generated with AI, D. Lee.

120 *Restraining Hand*, Generated with AI, D. Lee.

129 *ArchangelMichael*, Generated with AI, D. Lee.

134 *Worship,* Generated with AI, D. Lee.

Public Domain

104 *Silver Denarius of Roman Republic, Rome, 83 BCE. 1953.171.7*, American Numismatic Society, Public Domain.

116 *Bust of Roman Emperor Trajan*, Found in 1803 in Ostia, purchased in 1811 in Rome, Photographed by Bibi Saint-Pol, Public Domain; *Benito Mussolini 1940*, Agfacolor photo by Henri Roger-Viollet (1869–1946), Public Domain; *Henry A. Kissinger*, Public Domain; *King Charles III*, Public Domain.

Royalty-Free

94 *Vintage blank paper scroll isolated on white background with copy space*, Adobe Stock, Rangizz.

106 *Dirty Kitchen in a Commercial Restaurant*, Adobe Stock, Isz.

116 *Saint Gregory*, Shutterstock; *Napoleon Bonaparte*, iStockphoto, GeorgiosArt, W. Holl; *Adolf Hitler*, Shutterstock; *Anwar Sadat*, Shutterstock; *Mikhail Gorbachev*, Shutterstock.

118 *Religious Icons*, Shutterstock.

122 *Antichristo 1,* Adobe Stock, JUSTIN.

123 *Top Secret Folder File with Slight Grunge*, Shutterstock.

131 *Man stands on stage*, Adobe Stock, Lashkhidzetim.

133 *Holy Spirit came down like dove stock photo*, iStock, Ig0rZh.

137 *Thunder Light Striking*, Generated with AI, FreeP!K Stock AI Image.

144 *Old worn paper sheet and scroll isolated on white*, Adobe Stock, Andrey Kuzmin.

145 *Justice and law concept, Male judge in a courtroom striking the gavel*, Adobe Stock, Sebastian Duda.

CHAPTER 4:

Private Collection — RENNER

153 *Trumpet Man*, Generated with AI, D. Lee.

Royalty-Free

152 *Vintage blank paper scroll isolated on white background with copy space*, Adobe Stock, Rangizz.

193 *Old worn paper sheet and scroll isolated on white*, Adobe Stock, Andrey Kuzmin.

194 *Nebuchadnezzar Dream: Gigantic Statue - made of four metals - head of gold full body image standing over ancient Babylon*, Adobe Stock, James Middleton.

195 *Babylonian Map,* iStockphoto*; Persian Empire Map,* Shutterstock.

196 *Greek Empire,* Shutterstock*; Roman Empire,* Shutterstock.

197 *European Union,* Shutterstock*; Ottoman Empire,* Shutterstock.

198 *Israel Map,* Shutterstock.

Chapter 5:

Alamy

205 *The Rising of the Waters from John Milton's Paradise Lost.* 1667, black & white engraving, Doré, Gustave. 1832-1883 © Timewatch Images/Alamy Stock Photo/Public Domain.

209 *Two Women Shall Be Grinding at the MILL*, Alamy Stock Photo, Elmore Alfred, Artmedia.

Creative Commons

208 *Millet, les Glaneuses, cité par Auguste Rodin*, Paru dans le livre L'Art, entretiens réunis par Paul Gsell, Grasset, 1911. Creative Commons.

GoodSalt

207 *Noah and the Ark*, GoodSalt.

Private Collection — RENNER

203 *Trumpet Man*, Generated with AI, D. Lee.

Royalty-Free

202 *Vintage blank paper scroll isolated on white background with copy space*, Adobe Stock, Rangizz.

210 *Last Supper of Christ*, iStock, St. Nicholas Church, Sedmak.

212 *Majestic golden throne surrounded by luminous clouds and ethereal light, evoking a sense of divine royalty and grandeur*, Adobe Stock, Bramcrye.

Chapter 6:

Alamy

218 *The Roman Empire - ships at a port Ship. Sail. Sails. Boat. Boats. Oar. Oars. Raft. Rafts. Naval fleet. Illustration*, Alamy Stock Image, Lebrecht Music & Arts.

233 *Philip the Evangelist and the Ethiopian Eunuch*, Alamy Stock Image, Julius Schnorr von Carolsfeld, history_docu_photo; *Saint Paul of Tarsus*, Alamy Stock Image, Chronicle.

234 *Saint John the Apostle*, Alamy Stock Image, North Wind Picture Archives.

Lev Kaplan, Artist and Illustrator

219 *The Mocking of Jesus,* Renner Collection, © Lev Kaplan, Illustration/Special Commission, 2025 (https://www.kaplan-art.de/).

Private Collection — RENNER

217 *Trumpet Man*, Generated with AI, D. Lee.

218 *Scoffers*, Generated with AI, D. Lee.

220 *Scoffers Scoffing*, Generated with AI, D. Lee.

225 *The Last Days Timeline*, Renner Collection, L. Moore.

236 *Tribulation Saints*, Generated with AI, D. Lee.

236 *Two Witnesses*, Generated with AI, D. Lee.

Royalty-Free

216 *Vintage blank paper scroll isolated on white background with copy space*, Adobe Stock, Rangizz.

222 *Christ, heaven and hell stock photo*, iStock, Ig0rZh.

226-227 *Fire isolated over black background stock photo*, iStock, OlgaMiltsova.

228 *God, 18th century Bible illustration stock illustration*, iStock, Mashuk.

230 *Victorian bible illustration The translation of Elijah stock illustration*, iStock, JonnyJim.

232 *Ascensión de Cristo*, iStock, Zu_09.

235 *The Rapture*, Adobe Stock, Benjamin Hass.

239 *Antique Clock Face* © rossco/Adobe Stock.

241 *Thinking About Relationship Struggles*, Adobe Stock, SolStock.

Chapter 7:

Alamy

257 *The Flight of the Prisoners*, Alamy Stock Photo, Historic Illustrations.

GoodSalt

253 *Noah's Ark in the Flood* © Pacific Press/ GoodSalt, Inc.

Private Collection — RENNER

247 *Trumpet Man*, Generated with AI, D. Lee.

277 *Battle*, Commissioned, Illustrated by Anum Khan, RENNER Private Collection.

Public Domain

256 *The Seventh Plague*, 1823 painting by John Martin, Public Domain.

258 *La distruzione del tempio di Gerusalemme*, Francesco Hayez 1867, Public Domain.

Royalty-Free

246 *Vintage blank paper scroll isolated on white background with copy space*, Adobe Stock, Rangizz.

255 *Tower of Babel*, Generated with AI, FreeP!K Stock Image.

259 *Anti-riot police give signal to be ready. Government power concept. Police in action. Smoke on a dark background with lights. Blue red flashing sirens. Dictatorship power stock photo*, iStock, Zeferli.

Chapter 8:

Alamy

291 *SAINT IRENAEUS Greek prelate and Bishop of Lugdunum (Lyons); known for his writings against gnosticism Date: circa 130 - circa 200*, Alamy Stock Image, Chronicle.

Private Collection — RENNER

289 *Trumpet Man*, Generated with AI, D. Lee.

Public Domain

292 *Ephrem the Syrian*, 11th Century, Artist Unknown, Public Domain.

293 *Portret van Theodorus Gaza*, Adolf van der Laanschrijver, Public Domain.

Royalty-Free

288 *Vintage blank paper scroll isolated on white background with copy space*, Adobe Stock, Rangizz.

Chapter 9:

Alamy

322 *Moses and Aaron meet Pharaoh and Aaron turns his rod into a snake*, Alamy Stock Image, Robert Leinweber, Lebrecht Music & Arts.

335 *Death on a Pale Horse*, Alamy Stock Image, Benjamin West, The Picture Art Collection.

336 *The Four Horsemen of the Apocalypse*, Alamy Stock Image, Pictures Now.

341 *Antiquite romaine : "L'homme politique et general romain Titus Flaminius (228-174 avant JC) aux Jeux isthmiques a Corinthe proclame la liberte des ci*, Alamy Stock Image, SPCOLLECTION.

Archaeology Illustrated (Balage Balogh)

313 *Ur, Sumer, Southern Mesopotamia, The Great Harbor and Ziggurat,* Archaeology Illustrated, © Balogh, Balage (archaeologyillustrated .com); *Alexandria*, Archaeology Illustrated, © Balogh, Balage (archaeologyillustrated.com).

Creative Commons

314 *Tajikistan Relief Map*, NordNordWest 2020, Creative Commons.

Private Collection — RENNER

307 *Trumpet Man*, Generated with AI, D. Lee.

327 *666,* Generated with AI, D. Lee.

334 *Two Witnesses*, Commissioned, Illustrated by Anum Khan, RENNER Private Collection.

338 *Dinner*, Generated with AI, D. Lee.

339 *GreatWhiteThrone*, Generated with AI, D. Lee.

344 *Battle*, Commissioned, Illustrated by Anum Khan, RENNER Private Collection.

347 *Opening Scrolls*, Generated with AI, D. Lee.

Royalty-Free

306 *Vintage blank paper scroll isolated on white background with copy space*, Adobe Stock, Rangizz.

308 *Descent of the Spirit, a scene from the bible. Engraving from 1870. Engraving by Gustave Dore*, iStock, D. Walker.

309 *A dramatic stormy sky with dark clouds and heavy rain pouring down over a landscape*, Adobe Stock, Stock by Hemal.

310 *Wet Torrential Rain*, Adobe Stock, Vectorwin.

315 *Ripe Wheat Against a Blue Sky*, iStock, Lermannika.

316 *Hurricane Lester on Approach to Hawaii*, Shutterstock, BEST-BACKGROUNDS.

318 *Tornado eye,* iStock Image, koto_feja.

320 *Hurricane Just Ahead sign with a bad day*, Adobe Stock, Gustavofrazao.

325 *Antichristo 1,* Adobe Stock, JUSTIN.

331 *Holy Spirit came down like dove*, iStock, Ig0rZh.

346 *Relentless Souls hell fire. God soul. Generate Ai*, Adobe Stock, Juliars.

349 *Bible*, iStock, Oliver_Jungmann.

351 *Earth in the space*, iStock, almir1968.

Chapter 10:

Alamy

371 *Ancient Roman coin with portrait of emperor Licinius, old bronze money on hand close-up on vintage background. Concept of Rome, Empire, texture, colle*, Alamy Stock Image, Vyacheslav Lopatin.

Bridgeman Images

366 *The Foolish Virgins*, Illustration for The Coloured Picture Bible for Children (SPCK, c 1890). © Look and Learn / Bridgeman Images.

Creative Commons

377 *Peak of Jabal Maqla*, December 2022, Creative Commons.

GoodSalt

359 *The Ten Virgins*, GoodSalt, Inc.

Private Collection — RENNER

355, *Trumpet Man*, Generated with AI, D. Lee.

363 *10 Virgins 2,* Generated with AI, D. Lee.

365 *10 Virgins 3,* Generated with AI, D. Lee.

Public Domain

361 "*Parable of the 10 Virgins,*" by Eugene Burnand 1908 "The Parables" published by Berger-Levrault, Public Domain.

Royalty-Free

354 *Vintage blank paper scroll isolated on white background with copy space*, Adobe Stock, Rangizz.

367 *Modern hour glass gold*, Adobe Stock Image, Sevector.

372 *Hot liquid steel flows from metallurgical ladle. Molten metal being poured into container. Furnace casting in ironworks factory. Molted iron production. Sparks, smoke, industrial manufacture concept*, Adobe Stock, Vadym.

373 *Pyramids in Egypt*, iStock, Milos Tomic.

378 *Holy Bible on white background*, iStock, JackBuu.

379 *Worship Hands Raised*, iStock, SplashofPhotography.

384 *Beautiful Blue Sky Background*, Adobe Stock, Merydolla.

388 *Blank Standard Warning Sign*, Dreamstime, Getanov.

Chapter 11:

Private Collection — RENNER

393 *Trumpet Man*, Generated with AI, D. Lee.

Royalty-Free

392 *Vintage blank paper scroll isolated on white background with copy space*, Adobe Stock, Rangizz.

PRAYER OF SALVATION

When Jesus Christ comes into your life, you are immediately emancipated — totally set free from the bondage of sin! If you have never received Jesus as your personal Savior, it is time to experience this new life for yourself. The first step to freedom is simple. Just pray this prayer from your heart:

Lord, I can never adequately thank You for all You did for me on the Cross. I am so undeserving, Jesus, but You came and gave Your life for me anyway. I repent for rejecting You, and I turn away from my life of rebellion and sin right now. I turn to You and receive You as my Savior, and I ask You to wash away my sin and make me completely new in You by Your precious blood. I thank You from the depths of my heart for doing what no one else could do for me.

Thank You, Jesus, that I am now redeemed by Your blood. On the Cross, You bore my sin, my sickness, my pain, my lack of peace, and my suffering. Your blood has removed my sin, washed me whiter than snow, and given me rightstanding with the Father. I have no need to be ashamed of my past sins because I am now a new creature in You. Old things have passed away, and all things have become new because I am in Jesus Christ (2 Corinthians 5:17).

Because of You, Jesus, today I am forgiven; I am filled with peace; and I am a joint-heir with You! Satan no longer has a right to lay any claim on me. From a grateful heart, I will faithfully serve You the rest of my days!

If you prayed this prayer from your heart, something amazing has happened to you. As a result of your decision to turn your life over to Jesus Christ, your eternal home has been decided forever. Heaven will now be your permanent address for all eternity. God's Spirit has moved into your own human spirit, and you have become the "temple of God" (*see* 1 Corinthians 6:19). What a miracle! To think that God, by His Spirit, now lives inside you! And He has become your Heavenly Father. You are a child of God!

Now you have a new Lord and Master, and His name is Jesus. From this moment on, the Spirit of God will work in you and supernaturally energize you to fulfill God's will for your life. Everything will change for you as you yield to His leadership in your life — and it's all going to change for the best!

ABOUT THE AUTHOR

Rick Renner (**renner.org**) holds an earned ThD (Doctor of Theology) from a prominent Russian university and is a respected Bible teacher and leader in the international Christian community. He is the author of an extensive list of books, including bestsellers *Sparkling Gems From the Greek 1* and *2*, and his accumulated titles have sold millions of copies worldwide. Rick's understanding of the Greek language and biblical history opens up the Scriptures in a unique way that enables his audience to gain wisdom and insight while learning something brand new from the Word of God.

Today Rick is the overseer of the Good News Association of Churches, founder of the Moscow Good News Church, pastor of the Internet Good News Church, founder of Media Mir, and president of the Good News Channel — the largest Russian-speaking Christian satellite network in the world, which broadcasts the Gospel 24/7 to countless viewers in more than 83 nations. He is also the founder of TBV, a national channel that broadcasts to all of Russia.

Rick is the founder of RENNER Ministries in Broken Arrow, Oklahoma, and host to his TV program, also seen around the world in multiple languages via television, Internet, and satellite. He leads this amazing work with Denise — his wife and lifelong ministry partner — along with their sons and committed leadership team.

CONTACT RENNER MINISTRIES

For further information
about RENNER Ministries or
to reach out for prayer, please
contact the office nearest you or
visit the ministry website at:
www.renner.org

ALL USA CORRESPONDENCE:
RENNER Ministries
1814 W. Tacoma St.
Broken Arrow, OK 74012
(918) 496-3213
Or 1-800-RICK-593
Email: renner@renner.org
Website: www.renner.org

MOSCOW OFFICE:
RENNER Ministries
P. O. Box 789
101000, Moscow, Russia
+7 (495) 727-1467
Email: blagayavestonline@ignc.org
Website: www.ignc.org

OXFORD OFFICE:
RENNER Ministries
Box 7, 266 Banbury Road
Oxford OX2 7DL, United Kingdom
+44 1865 521024
Email: europe@renner.org

RIGA OFFICE:
RENNER Ministries
Unijas 99
Riga LV-1084, Latvia
+371 67802150
Email: church@goodnews.lv
Website: www.goodnews.lv

facebook.com/rickrenner • facebook.com/rennerdenise
youtube.com/rennerministries • youtube.com/deniserenner
instagram.com/rickrrenner • instagram.com/rennerministries_
instagram.com/rennerdenise

BOOKS BY RICK RENNER

Apostles and Prophets
Build Your Foundation*
Chosen by God*
Christmas — The Rest of the Story
Dream Thieves*
Dressed To Kill*
Easter — The Rest of the Story
Fallen Angels, Giants, Monsters, and the World Before the Flood
The Holy Spirit and You*
How To Keep Your Head on Straight in a World Gone Crazy*
How To Receive Answers From Heaven!*
Igniting a Powerful Prayer Life
Insights on Successful Leadership*
Last-Days Survival Guide*
A Life Ablaze*
Life in the Combat Zone*
A Light in Darkness, Volume One, *Seven Messages to the Seven Churches* series
The Love Test*
My Peace-Filled Day
My Spirit-Empowered Day
My Victory-Filled Day
No Room for Compromise, Volume Two, *Seven Messages to the Seven Churches* series
Paid in Full*
The Point of No Return*
Renner A to Z — Comments and Quotes by Rick Renner on 400 Bible Topics A to Z!
Renner Interpretive Version of James and Jude (RIV)
Repentance*
Signs You'll See Just Before Jesus Comes*
Sparkling Gems From the Greek Daily Devotional 1*
Sparkling Gems From the Greek Daily Devotional 2*
Spiritual Weapons To Defeat the Enemy*
Ten Guidelines To Help You Achieve Your Long-Awaited Promotion!*
Testing the Supernatural
365 Days of Increase
365 Days of Power
Turn Your God-Given Dreams Into Reality*
Unlikely — Our Faith-Filled Journey to the Ends of the Earth*
Why We Need the Gifts of the Holy Spirit*
The Will of God — The Key to Your Success*
You Can Get Over It*

*Digital version available for Kindle, Nook, and iBook.
Note: Books by Rick Renner are available for purchase at:
www.renner.org

SIGNS YOU'LL SEE JUST BEFORE JESUS COMES

208 pages
(Paperback)

As we advance toward the golden moment of Christ's return for His Church, there are signs on the road we're traveling to let us know where we are in time. Jesus Himself foretold the types of events that will surely take place as we watch for His return.

In his book *Signs You'll See Just Before Jesus Comes*, Rick Renner explores the signs in Matthew 24:3-12, expounding on each one from the Greek text with his unique style of teaching. Each chapter is written to *prepare* and *embolden* a last-days generation of believers — not send them running for the hills!

The signs on the road are appearing closer together. We are on the precipice of something new. Soon we'll see the final sign at the edge of our destination as we enter the territory of the last days, hours, and minutes *just before Jesus comes.*

To order, visit us online at: **www.renner.org**
Book Resellers: Contact Harrison House at 800-722-6774
or visit **www.HarrisonHouse.com** for quantity discounts.

HOW TO KEEP YOUR HEAD ON STRAIGHT IN A WORLD GONE CRAZY

DEVELOPING DISCERNMENT FOR THESE LAST DAYS

400 pages
(Paperback)

The world is changing. In fact, it's more than changing — it has *gone crazy*.

We are living in a world where faith is questioned and sin is welcomed — where people seem to have lost their minds about what is right and wrong. It seems truth has been turned *upside down*.

In Rick Renner's book *How To Keep Your Head on Straight in a World Gone Crazy*, he reveals the disastrous consequences of a society in spiritual and moral collapse. In this book, you'll discover what Christians need to do to stay out of the chaos and remain anchored to truth. You'll learn how to stay sensitive to the Holy Spirit, how to discern right and wrong teaching, how to be grounded in prayer, and how to be spiritually prepared for living in victory in these last days.

Leading ministers from around the world are calling this book essential for every believer.

To order, visit us online at: **www.renner.org**
Book Resellers: Contact Harrison House at 800-722-6774
or visit **www.HarrisonHouse.com** for quantity discounts.

LAST-DAYS SURVIVAL GUIDE

A Scriptural Handbook To Prepare You for These Perilous Times

496 pages
(Paperback)

In his book *Last-Days Survival Guide*, Rick Renner masterfully expands on Second Timothy 3 to clearly reveal the last-days signs to expect in society as one age draws to a close before another age begins.

Rick also thoroughly explains how not to just *survive* the times, but to *thrive* in the midst of them. God wants you as a believer to be equipped — *outfitted* — to withstand end-time storms, to navigate wind-tossed seas, and to sail with His grace and power to fulfill your divine destiny on earth!

If you're concerned about what you're witnessing in society today — and even in certain sectors of the Church — the answers you need in order to keep your gaze focused on Christ and maintain your victory are in this book!

To order, visit us online at: **www.renner.org**
Book Resellers: Contact Harrison House at 800-722-6774
or visit **www.HarrisonHouse.com** for quantity discounts.

BOOKS THAT CAN MAKE YOU A SPIRITUAL POWERHOUSE!

LIFE IN THE COMBAT ZONE

How To Survive, Thrive, and Overcome in the Midst of Difficult Situations

272 pages
(Paperback)

The battle lines are drawn. A collision course is set. In the coming battle, will you rush the front lines or shrink from the conflict? Although the risk is great, the rewards for engaging in the fight are sure.

In *Life in the Combat Zone,* author Rick Renner encourages you to *fight* like a Roman soldier, *train* like a Greek athlete, and *work* like a farmer — all to become that unwavering warrior who hears God's voice, surrenders to His call, and willingly enters the combat zone poised to win.

Spiritual conflicts are real and unavoidable. There are no shortcuts to victory, but there *can* be an inevitable outcome. Rick will help you discover the key qualities you'll need to withstand the heat of the battle so you can emerge triumphant and receive the victor's crown.

To order, visit us online at: **www.renner.org**

Book Resellers: Contact Harrison House at 800-722-6774
or visit **www.HarrisonHouse.com** for quantity discounts.

CHOSEN BY GOD

God Has Chosen *You* for a Divine Assignment — Will You Dare To Fulfill It?

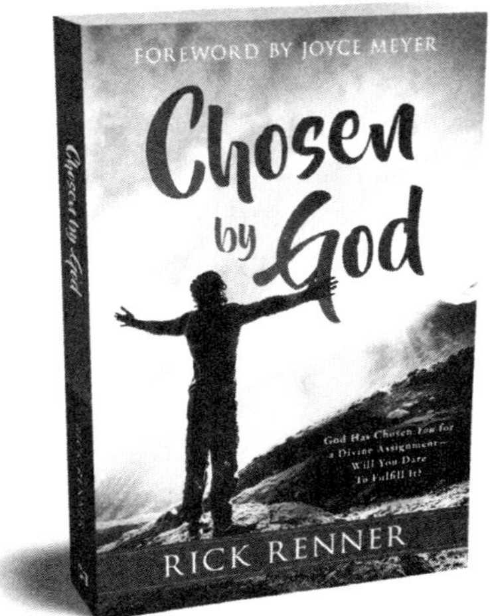

304 pages
(Paperback)

Rick Renner's book *Chosen by God* will help you overcome your limited thinking about following God's plan for your life. *Rest assured, God has a plan!* And He will thoroughly prepare you to fulfill it if you'll say yes with all your heart and stir yourself to pursue it.

God is calling you to do something significant in the earth for Him. What's holding you back? This book will *thrill* you with the possibilities that await — because you are chosen by God!

To order, visit us online at: **www.renner.org**

Book Resellers: Contact Harrison House at 800-722-6774 or visit **www.HarrisonHouse.com** for quantity discounts.

A LIFE ABLAZE

Ten Simple Keys to Living on Fire for God

448 pages
(Paperback)

Do you struggle to keep the fire of the Holy Spirit burning in your heart as it may have burned earlier in your life? Do you sometimes feel like all that's left are a few small glowing embers — and that perhaps even those embers are starting to die out and become cold?

How do you stoke the embers of the fire within you so that those flames begin to burn red-hot in your heart again? Once you have that fire burning hot and bright, how do you sustain and grow the intensity of that inner fire for the rest of your time on this earth?

In *A Life Ablaze,* Rick teaches you about the ten different kinds of fuel you need to stay spiritually ablaze for years to come. As you learn about these fuels, you will discover how to throw them into the fire in your heart so you can keep burning spiritually.

Topics include:

- What is the real condition of your spiritual fire right now?
- What to do if your spiritual embers are about to go out.
- What to do to help others whose flames are burning low.

To order, visit us online at: **www.renner.org**

Book Resellers: Contact Harrison House at 800-722-6774 or visit **www.HarrisonHouse.com** for quantity discounts.

RICK'S ALL-TIME BESTSELLERS

DRESSED TO KILL

A Biblical Approach to Spiritual Warfare and Armor

504 pages
(Paperback)

Rick Renner's book *Dressed To Kill* is considered by many to be a true classic on the subject of spiritual warfare. The original version, which sold more than 400,000 copies, is a curriculum staple in Bible schools worldwide. In this beautiful volume, you will find:

- 504 pages of reedited text in paperback
- 16 pages of full-color illustrations
- Questions at the end of each chapter to guide you into deeper study

In *Dressed To Kill*, Rick explains with exacting detail the purpose and function of each piece of Roman armor. In the process, he describes the significance of our *spiritual* armor not only to withstand the onslaughts of the enemy, but also to overturn the tendencies of the carnal mind. Furthermore, Rick delivers a clear, scriptural presentation on the biblical definition of spiritual warfare — what it is and what it is not.

When you walk with God in deliberate, continual fellowship, He will enrobe you with Himself. Armed with the knowledge of who you are in Him, you will be dressed and dangerous to the works of darkness, unflinching in the face of conflict, and fully equipped to take the offensive and gain mastery over any opposition from your spiritual foe. You don't have to accept defeat anymore once you are *dressed to kill*!

To order, visit us online at: **www.renner.org**
Book Resellers: Contact Harrison House at 800-722-6774
or visit **www.HarrisonHouse.com** for quantity discounts.

SPARKLING GEMS FROM THE GREEK 1

1,104 pages
(Hardback)

Rick Renner's *Sparkling Gems From the Greek 1* has gained widespread recognition for its unique illumination of the New Testament through more than 1,000 Greek word studies in a 365-day devotional format. *Sparkling Gems 1* remains a beloved resource that has spiritually strengthened believers worldwide. As many have testified, the wealth of truths within its pages never grows old. Year after year, *Sparkling Gems 1* continues to deepen readers' understanding of the Bible.

SPARKLING GEMS FROM THE GREEK 2

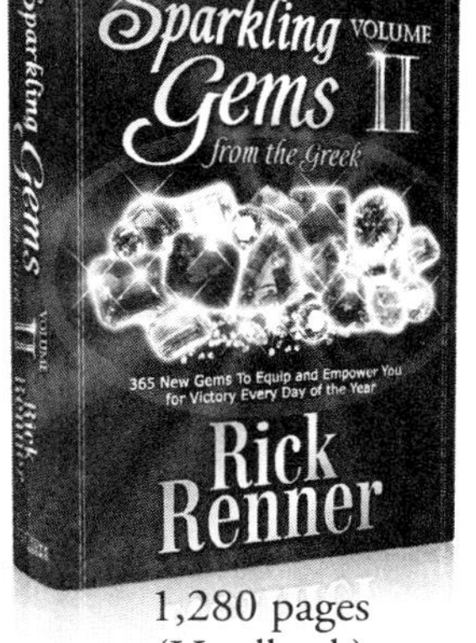

1,280 pages
(Hardback)

Rick infuses into *Sparkling Gems From the Greek 2* the added strength and richness of many more years of his own personal study and growth in God — expanding this devotional series to impact the reader's heart on a deeper level than ever before. This remarkable study tool helps unlock new hidden treasures from God's Word that will draw readers into an ever more passionate pursuit of Him.

To order, visit us online at: **www.renner.org**
Book Resellers: Contact Harrison House at 800-722-6774
or visit **www.HarrisonHouse.com** for quantity discounts.

STUDY AND JOURNAL ON ONE EXCLUSIVE TOPIC FOR 31 DAYS!

MY PEACE-FILLED DAY

A Sparkling Gems From the Greek Guided Devotional Journal

256 pages
(Paperback)

Do you feel like you're on a merry-go-round of stress and anxiety that just won't stop? Do you feel like the circumstances around you are shouting *loudly* as you search for peace and calm?

Help is here! You *can* live in peace — fearless and free!

In *My Peace-Filled Day: A Sparkling Gems From the Greek Guided Devotional Journal*, Rick Renner shares 31 teachings, expounding from his thorough knowledge of the Greek language, to help you take hold of the God-given peace that belongs to you. As you devote yourself to the scriptural truths in each devotional — and journal your answers to thought-provoking questions — the power of God will melt away the fears, anxieties, and cares of this world until His peace takes centerstage in your life.

Don't let the turmoil of this world swirl you into an emotional frenzy. As you encounter God on every page of this devotional journal, you will find yourself living the peace-filled life your loving Heavenly Father wants for you!

To order, visit us online at: **www.renner.org**
Book Resellers: Contact Harrison House at 800-722-6774
or visit **www.HarrisonHouse.com** for quantity discounts.

IGNITING A POWERFUL PRAYER LIFE

A Sparkling Gems From the Greek Guided Devotional Journal

256 pages
(Paperback)

Igniting a Powerful Prayer Life: A Sparkling Gems From the Greek Guided Devotional Journal can take you from feeling overwhelmed by the signs of the times to enjoying a serene sense of wholeness and well-being as you walk and live in God's presence.

You are not impotent against the struggles of broken families and relationships, decaying morality, rumors of wars, and unstable economies! The Father longs for you to release His power in your sphere through prayer. You only need to know how.

In *Igniting a Powerful Prayer Life*, Rick Renner uses scriptural principles and spiritual wisdom that can set ablaze in your heart a passion for potent prayer. Each lesson in this 31-day journal also includes a prayer and a confession to put the Word in your mouth and stimulate a fervent, effectual prayer life.

Don't stand by and let the enemy oppress or destroy you *or* your family. Use this guided journal to ignite your prayer life and set your world *on fire* with the power of God!

To order, visit us online at: **www.renner.org**
Book Resellers: Contact Harrison House at 800-722-6774
or visit **www.HarrisonHouse.com** for quantity discounts.

MY SPIRIT-EMPOWERED DAY

A Sparkling Gems From the Greek Guided Devotional Journal

240 pages
(Paperback)

When faced with life's difficulties, do you long for a personal coach to guide you? Do you feel inadequate, even powerless, to achieve what God has asked you to do?

You can experience the same inseparable union with the Holy Spirit that empowered Jesus during His earthly ministry! With the Holy Spirit's help, *you* can participate for yourself with His mission to be your ultimate Comforter, Advocate, Counselor, and Friend.

In *My Spirit-Empowered Day: A Sparkling Gems From the Greek Guided Devotional Journal*, Rick Renner shows you how to escape a powerless Christian life. This interactive journal includes thought-provoking questions that will engage your heart and mind to go deeper with the Holy Spirit.

Through 31 insightful devotional entries, Rick unveils from the Greek text the purpose of the Holy Spirit in a Christian's life. Rick's teaching will help you understand the workings of the Holy Spirit, discover how to receive divine guidance, and exercise spiritual power and authority.

Experience a life of close fellowship with the Holy Spirit and see your life flourish under His favor!

To order, visit us online at: **www.renner.org**
Book resellers: Contact Harrison House at 800-722-6774
or visit **www.HarrisonHouse.com** for quantity discounts.

MY VICTORY-FILLED DAY

A SPARKLING GEMS FROM THE GREEK GUIDED DEVOTIONAL JOURNAL

240 pages
(Paperback)

Are unseen forces working against you? Does fear, doubt, or defeat keep trying to gain a foothold in your life?

You don't have to put up with it! God has given you the authority to overcome every attack of the enemy. You *can* recognize and close the doors the enemy is using to gain access to your life — and fortify your heart and mind with the truth of God's Word.

In *My Victory-Filled Day: A Sparkling Gems From the Greek Guided Devotional Journal*, trusted Bible teacher Rick Renner equips you with the tools you need to face spiritual battles with confidence and lasting victory. This interactive journal includes thought-provoking questions that will engage your heart and mind to go deeper in your understanding of spiritual warfare.

Through 31 insightful devotional entries, Rick uncovers gems from the Greek New Testament that describe how to use spiritual weapons effectively to dismantle strongholds and gain ground. This journal gives you the Bible-proven tactics to rise up, fight back, and live victoriously.

Embrace God's plan for victory today and turn every conflict into a testimony of triumph!

To order, visit us online at: **www.renner.org**
Book resellers: Contact Harrison House at 800-722-6774
or visit **www.HarrisonHouse.com** for quantity discounts.

MORE RICK RENNER CLASSICS

CHRISTMAS

THE REST OF THE STORY

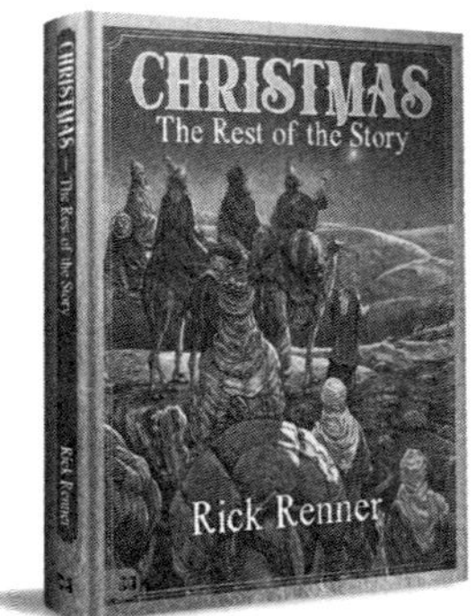

304 pages
(Hardback)

In this storybook of biblical history, Rick takes you on the "magical" journey of Christ's coming to Earth in a way you've probably never heard it before. Featuring full-color, original illustrations, *Christmas — The Rest of the Story* gives the spellbinding account of God's masterful plan to redeem mankind, and vividly portrays the wonder of the Savior's birth and His "ordinary" life marked by God's *extraordinary* plan.

If you want to be taken back in your imagination to this earth-shaking course of events that changed the history of the whole world, this book is a *must-have* not just for the Christmas season, but for all time. *Topics include:*

- Why God chose Mary and Joseph.
- The significance of the *manger* and *swaddling clothes.*
- Why angels viewed *God in the flesh* with such wonderment.
- Why King Herod was so troubled by this historical birth.
- How we can prepare for Christ's *next* coming.

Christmas — The Rest of the Story is sure to be a favorite in your family for generations to come! Jesus' birth is truly *the greatest story on earth* — perhaps never more uniquely told than in the pages of this book.

To order, visit us online at: **www.renner.org**

Book Resellers: Contact Harrison House at 800-722-6774 or visit **www.HarrisonHouse.com** for quantity discounts.

EASTER

The Rest of the Story

304 pages
(Hardback)

At the moment of Christ's death on the Cross, the day darkened and the earth shook — but what about the days and hours leading up to His crucifixion? What happened in those critical moments, and why did it happen?

In this *must-have* Easter classic, Rick Renner walks you through the pages of history, diving deep into the world's most famous story to reveal the riveting truths and harrowing details of Jesus' last moments on Earth. In this vivid storybook equipped with full-color, original illustrations, you'll learn:

- Why hundreds of soldiers — not just a few — met Jesus to arrest Him.
- The physical and mental abuse Jesus endured before the Crucifixion.
- What Jesus meant when He said, "It is finished!"
- What Jesus has been doing for the last 2,000 years.

Whether you've heard this story before or this is your first time reading it, Jesus' death and resurrection will come alive as you draw face to face with the brutality Jesus endured and the unflinching love He displayed on the Cross.

To order, visit us online at: **www.renner.org**
Book Resellers: Contact Harrison House at 800-722-6774
or visit **www.HarrisonHouse.com** for quantity discounts.

THE RENNER INTERPRETIVE VERSION (RIV) OF FIRST AND SECOND PETER

A Parallel Study Bible for People of Faith

384 pages
(Hardback)

Dive deep into the Greek New Testament with Rick Renner in this brand-new volume of the *RIV*!

In these two power-packed epistles, Peter, an apostle and disciple of Jesus, wrote to the Church imploring believers to live holy lives and endure the persecution and suffering they were facing as a result of their faith, even warning them to remain steadfast as the time for Jesus' return draws near. As Rick expounds upon the original language of the Greek in contemporary speech that is easy to understand, you will learn that Peter's encouragement and warning was not only timely for the Early Church, but offers wisdom for believers facing hardship and deception in today's world as well.

Using the comprehensive footnotes and commentary found on each page, you can study the meaning behind the powerful words Peter wrote. The *RIV* will open the Scriptures like you've never seen them before, encouraging your faith, prompting your obedience, and preparing you for the soon return of our Lord Jesus. This is a volume you do not want to miss!

To order, visit us online at: **www.renner.org**
Book resellers: Contact Harrison House at 800-722-6774
or visit **www.HarrisonHouse.com** for quantity discounts.

NOTES

NOTES

NOTES

NOTES

NOTES

NOTES

NOTES

NOTES

NOTES

Equipping Believers to Walk in the Abundant Life

John 10:10b

Connect with us for fresh content and news about forthcoming books from your favorite authors...

Facebook @ **HarrisonHousePublishers**

Instagram @ **HarrisonHousePublishing**

www.harrisonhouse.com